Condemned Property?

Dusty Earl Trimmer

Author during radio interview in summer 2014

First published by Dog Ear Publishing
4010 W. 86th Street, Ste H
Indianapolis, IN 46268
www.dogearpublishing.net

ISBN: 978-1-4575-2533-9

This book is printed on acid-free paper.

Printed in the United States of America

DEDICATION & MEMORIAM

Jack "Bud" Gainey and I fought side by side together in Vietnam from 1968–1969, and we remained close friends after the war. Vietnam was the major cause of his death thirty-seven years after he came home.

Martha "Marty" Gainey served and fought by Bud's side after his return home. She fought the VA; she fought the system tooth and nail for her beloved husband, who was in a wheelchair for most of his years after Nam. Marty died before Bud at age fifty-three … In more ways than one, Vietnam was the cause.

In November 2005, Bud and I sat on the lawn outside a nursing home in Massillon, Ohio, where he had been confined, and we reminisced. We talked about Marty. We talked about Ohio State football, and we talked about Nam. I remember the words that he uttered softy to me that afternoon:

Dusty, we always had to hurry up and wait in the Army, one line after another. Someone once said that time heals all. It's looking like I'll be jumping into another line for that—soon!

Bud Gainey died several months later at the age of fifty-eight from a multitude of health complications, some Vietnam War-related. He and Marty died without receiving a dollar of disability compensation for his damages from the Vietnam War, leaving behind a loving daughter, Jennifer, and loving son, Jack. Tragedies such as this are all too common for families of Vietnam veterans, but this one I was a witness to.

Note: During the writing of this book, at least seven members of Bravo Company of the 3rd 22nd of the 25th Infantry passed away prematurely, and several others remain in an uncertain or whereabouts-unknown status!

TABLE OF CONTENTS

And the coffins came home to every city, town, and village … but the media wouldn't allow Americans to separate this war from the innocent young warriors sent to fight it! It is okay to hate war, despise it if you must, but **NOT THE WARRIOR!**

OPENING STATEMENT

WARNING: This is not a book that you will sit down and read in one night. Reading *Condemned Property?* will be and should be a journey for its readers. It could end up on a shelf in your permanent library as a "keepsake." You may be compelled to pick it up again and again to refer to.

Condemned Property? was written to honor our fallen warriors during and after the Vietnam War. And the living warriors of that war who are still fighting their demons. When much of America shunned many of the Vietnam War's returning warriors, that in itself was one of the greatest defeats that the United States has suffered in any war. Old news? Not to us.

WE WHO WENT THERE AND MADE IT BACK WILL NEVER FORGET!

To all who purchase this book, please know that profits after expenses will be generously shared with disabled veterans, homeless veterans, and highly rated military charities such as the following:

- Army Emergency Relief
- Fisher House Foundation
- Semper Fi Fund/Injured Marines
- Intrepid Fallen Heroes Fund
- Navy-Marine Corps Relief Society
- National Military Family Association
- Cease Fire House Inc.
- Wounded Warrior Association

Please understand that the opinions and statements in *Condemned Property?* are probably not shared in kind by some Vietnam veterans. However, of the hundreds I know and personally spoke with in regards to the book—many with whom I shared early editions of the book, including most of my surviving platoon brothers who have contributed content—few of them offered any disagreement to the material they read. That war was a long, long time ago in a far-off land, and memories of many days over there have dimmed. However ... some memories are clear and vivid as though the events **JUST HAPPENED YESTERDAY!**

The events described in this book happened exactly as I remember and portrayed them or as my Nam brothers remember and portrayed

them. It reveals autobiographical, exhaustive historical facts, personal and shared experiences with Vietnam War documented facts as they really happened.

There are little-known facts in the book about the Vietnam War that few who read it are likely to have been knowledgeable about, such as:

- How/why South Vietnam's resistance to North Vietnam's attempted takeover of the south was actually spearheaded by other North Vietnamese!
- How/why the Vietnam War could have and should have ended … with a complete American victory!

Because I believe in what I have put together in *Condemned Property?* and I want to hear from the readers, I will open up that avenue by providing my mailing address. Hopefully, by opening up my availability and possible vulnerability, we can begin a friendly and productive dialogue with each other and maybe develop some new and lasting friendships. Please feel free to write to me with your thoughts, comments about *Condemned Property?* and its content.

Dusty Earl Trimmer
P.O. Box 500
Twinsburg, OH 44087
www.dustytrimmer.com

I am aware that my novice attempt at writing a book of this size may not be as fluid as most book readers are used to; however, I hope and pray that my willingness to take the time to authentically put my experiences, observations, concerns, and sentimental feelings in writing will be accepted with the authentic and sincere intentions I have put forth with this effort.

How were Vietnam's American warriors any different from America's previous war combatants? We, too, were very young and innocent when we were taken from our homes to fight a controversial war in an unfriendly, far-off land. We, too, were scared and lonely … we also needed support from homes of fellow Americans … we also dreamed of a girl we left behind … home sweet home … Mom's apple pie … and we also missed OUR MOMS!

Today, many of our moms, dads, and uncles (who may have fought in WWII) have outlived us, and we suffer terribly from our war—a war we did not start; we just went because we were told to go.

Today, we still suffer terribly when our minds wander back to that war, thinking of those youthful, smiling faces of our war brothers and then suddenly ... THEY WERE IN BODY BAGS!

On December 12, 2012, I participated in a teleconference with VA officials and veterans from several different VA locations. A very brief synopsis of what I took away from that one-hour teleconference follows:

- Over thirty veterans tuned in, mostly Vietnam War veterans. My primary takeaway from listening to their problems and complaints about VA is ... *Condemned Property?* is a necessary story. A story that nearly every American should gravitate to. I believe some readers will be mesmerized and compelled to finish this book. Most important, I believe that most who purchase *Condemned Property?* will retain it for many years to come as a valuable keepsake.

In writing this book, I am exercising my right as an American citizen under the first amendment of the United States Constitution, which protects the freedom of speech, freedom of religion, and freedom of the press, as well as the right to assemble and petition the government.

ABOUT THE AUTHOR

I am Dusty Trimmer. I was a combat infantry soldier in the Vietnam War from 1968–1969. I am *still* a soldier. I did not go to West Point. I did not teach at Army colleges or military schools. I did not graduate from college, even though I attended classes for seven and a half years at four different universities—majoring in *nothing*. I worked full-time while attending night classes for most of those years … just like an infantry grunt did in the Vietnam War, working day and night.

Unable to find or keep a job, mostly because few employers wanted to take a chance on a crazy Vietnam veteran, I created a career for myself after changing jobs almost two dozen times after returning from Vietnam in 1969 up until 1980. I was offered numerous management positions by different publishers. I chose to decline all of them. On January 1, 1987, I formed my own company to represent high-level multibillion-dollar trade publishing companies in the scientific research market.

As a marketing and sales consultant, I earned dozens of sales achievement awards along with higher distinctions from 1972–2012. Although I did not marry until my fortieth birthday in 1984 to the lovely Ginny Brancato, I am a proud stepfather to four and step-grandfather to seven grandchildren.

As a combat infantryman, more often than not, I walked at the head of the combat mission as the point man during the bloodiest year of the Vietnam War. Over 16,000 Americans came home in coffins that year.

I earned awards and decorations like most combat warriors did, if they lived long enough. I am proud of them, as any combat warrior should be and I will cherish them forever … displaying them in the privacy of my home.

This is my first book. However, I wrote an article that appeared in *Vietnam, Our Story—One on One* that was published back in 1991 by Gary Gullickson, who was a Marine Vietnam combat veteran. Gary is no longer with us.

A picture of me holding the helmet that was shot off my head during an ambush in 1968 has been prominently displayed at the National Vietnam Veterans Art Museum, has appeared on several military websites, and was most recently published on the U.S. Army Historical Society's 2012 Calendar.

This book is not many things that a reader might expect it to be, but it is different to be sure. It does not have a plot. There is no moral to the story. In fact, its end … is not the end, as it has not happened yet.

There is a comprehensive collection of factual historical data inside this book, which will never lose its value to those who have an interest in the Vietnam War and to what is happening to those who served in South Vietnam. I do jump around a lot in the book, but that is the way I have led my life, multitasking seven days a week with business and personal adventures. It is so difficult to cram enough of life into each and every day, and I always have the feeling that we will run out of time before we get everything done that we think we need to—a sign of the times, I guess.

Condemned Property? has been difficult to put together in an organized format since I wrote the first chapter. Everything kept changing as I wrote, as the memories kept coming back … good and bad. I'm not sure that the information I kept adding has caught up to where I wanted this book's ending to be. Then again … this story has not ended yet because Vietnam vets die every day.

Condemned Property? is not a sit-down read in one night or two nights. There is not a compelling conclusion that you can hardly wait to reach. You can jump around with your reading just as I wrote it. You can read parts of it whenever time permits. I hope you will consider it a valuable keepsake for years to come.

The Vietnam War continues for me and most of my Nam brothers. America's longest war lasted from 1962 to 1973 (or 1959–1973, depending on who's counting) for America, ending officially for South Vietnam in 1975. However, this war just keeps on going, and it could end up being a 100-year war … or until the last Vietnam War vet dies!

Vietnam is as relevant today as it was in the 1960s, 1970s, and 1980s; therefore, I believe my story will be important to every American who cares about this country and its future.

One of the most important reasons for publishing this book is that I am very concerned about the preservation of the Vietnam War veteran generation and our families.

PROLOGUE

Personal Message To Every Nam Vet!

So many of us have been quiet about that war for oh, so long. We who have survived are old now. We are in our mid sixties to early seventies ... those of us who are still alive. We were young when we were soldiers in that hellhole called South Vietnam. Being soldiers changed most of our lives forever. Most of us loved our country when we were young soldiers, and most of us still love our country. We did our job in a brave manner even though we were scared stiff, and even though we didn't know it. We were obligated to go to Vietnam and obey our orders once we were there ... **regardless of the consequences.**

Many of us were just eighteen or nineteen years old, and many of us were twenty to twenty-five years old as well. We bonded together when we were ripped apart in battle, and many of us never saw each other again ... we cried and we were mad—*very* mad. Those guys were our brothers, we lost them just like that, and we still wonder WHY. To this day, we cry when we think of them. **But the dying from that war—our war—has not stopped!**

I have been to the funerals of too many Vietnam veterans in the last ten years; some were from my platoon. All of them died very prematurely from poisons or stresses handed to them, compliments of our war. Over there in Nam, we were never given the opportunity to say good-bye. This is why I try to make as many Vietnam vet brothers' funerals as I can, no matter what part of the country, to say good-bye. To this day I still dread good-byes.

Those of us who have survived by fate or chance have tried to push our memories into the farthest corners of our minds and keep them locked up. For the most part, many of us succeeded in doing that ... for the most part.

The years have zoomed by, all of a sudden it seems. We are no longer young, but most of us are *still* soldiers. Something strange is happening to many of us, something we are having a difficult time understanding and dealing with. Those memories that we thought were locked up in a remote part of our brains have been breaking loose and running rampant into our daily thoughts and our nightly dreams.

Some of us want to open up, but still there are so few who will listen—just like it was when we came home from Vietnam. My memories have resurfaced, and I can't put them back into the remote corners of my brain. It has been painful to write this book, and I did quit several times. But I had to finish it. I just had to try to tell America what we went through over there ... what we are going through now, and alert people to what our brothers and sisters from the Gulf-Afghanistan-Iraq wars are going to go through.

Many of us remain bitter. Many of our brothers lost their ability to work and became part of the homeless population and are unable to take care of themselves. There are thousands of us totally disabled—from physical and mental wounds. Hundreds of thousands of Vietnam veterans have died an early death while disability claims were pending—leaving behind their families. Therefore, another reason for this book is to try to help **preserve Vietnam veterans who are still alive!**

Many of us have come to believe that the VA has been deliberately stalling our disability claims, hoping we will just grow weary and quit fighting—or just die. Thus, the cliché came about … **DENY, DELAY … TILL YOU DIE!** Maybe so. But a lot of our Vietnam vet brothers fought the VA long and hard. And because they did, things are so much better now than they were in the 1970s and 1980s.

Comrades, again I say this … **WE DID NOT QUIT OVER THERE UNDER THE WORST CONDITIONS IMAGINABLE, AND BY GOD, WE SHOULD NOT QUIT NOW!**

Personally, from what I have heard and witnessed on a firsthand basis, the VA has come a long, long way, and I think they will continue to get better. But—you know what? It just seems as though nothing ever gets changed or improved upon when it comes to the government unless there is some major **OUTRAGE to force changes!**

Vietnam vets were a tough lot over there. Those of us who have survived should be even tougher in our elderly state—BUT MANY ARE NOT! I'm afraid many of us have become passive, and in some instances, we just don't give a damn anymore.

Sometimes I get frustrated when hearing about another Nam vet who doesn't want to talk about it. I know the pain, but if more of us don't open up and talk about it, more of us will die leaving untold stories. Please, talk about it on behalf of all those who are not here today. Yes, we are fading away, my fellow Vietnam veteran brothers, as old soldiers do. I personally do not want to leave this world just yet. I do not want to leave it without attempting to tell our fellow Americans one more time what happened over there … **and what is happening to us now**.

It is true that our fellow Americans, and America itself, are much better off when the sacrifices of America's brave warriors are known by many. America needs to know. So please read the book, read it again, share it, and tell *your* story to someone.

When I told a non-Vietnam veteran who served for the U.S. Army during the DMZ Conflict in South Korea about this book, his quick response to me was this:

Dusty, you had better write and publish that book as soon as possible because I read where Vietnam veterans are actually dying at a faster rate than World War II veterans!

This is why I believe this book *must* be published ASAP. If you know a Vietnam veteran or if you are one of those Vietnam combat veterans who is still suffering and is on the verge of giving up—if you are suffering and have sought help or are suffering and have not sought help, maybe in denial of requiring help, or you are one of those who really needs a "wake-up" call or you know someone like this ... **this book is for you.**

Condemned Property? **was written for every living patriotic American who genuinely cares about the history and the future of our great country. Vietnam veterans, relatives, and friends of living or deceased Vietnam veterans—or veterans of all other wars that Americans fought in—this book is intended for all of you.**

There is no monetary reward in this world that can erase the wounds, which cannot be seen, touched, or heard. Just talk and no action put forth on the healing process is unforgiveable, and that is mostly what we Vietnam combat veterans were handed for most of our years since returning home. Talking about healing without putting that talk into action is nothing more than moving on, with the wounds getting deeper and less healable.

To many Vietnam vets, nothing that we have ever experienced in our lives has been more gratifying than serving side by side with others in the Vietnam War. Nothing will ever compare to it, and the Lord knows how I have searched for it ... from the Everglades to rattlesnake hunts to exploring the Amazon jungle. In an odd way, I personally still long for the Vietnam experience again. Sure, I couldn't wait to get out of there in 1968–1969. But the experience is an infection leaving its mark on you, actually torturing you with the longing to relive something similar.

Move on? I am having a difficult time with that. There are multiple reasons for many of us who seek and receive therapy and yes ... compensation. That war has changed most of us FOREVER, and some Nam vets are unwilling to admit to that. I believe they may be living in a closet and don't want to come out of it. They may not be able to or they just refuse to seek or accept help.

Buy This Book—For Your Grandchildren!

I cannot deliver this book's message through a video game, nor turn it into a movie. This is it. So I hope those who read it will pass it on to their grandchildren—to read of course.

Vietnam remains a touchy subject. It disturbs people, causes pain, and divides people. Our country's so-called finest academic institutions refused to discuss or teach the Vietnam War with respect for decades after the war ended in 1975. And people wonder why we who fought there almost never talked about it in the 1970s, 1980s, or 1990s. Fortunately, there were a few people who wanted to and needed to know WHY there was a Vietnam War in the first place and why it remains so taboo to discuss.

Today one can find some Vietnam War history classes at most colleges. And there are the multitude of movies ... *The Deer Hunter, Apocalypse Now, Platoon, The Green Berets, Coming Home, Born on the 4th of July, First Blood* and other Rambo flicks, *Missing in Action* and other Chuck Norris flicks, *Full Metal Jacket, We Were Soldiers, Good Morning Vietnam*, etc.

In the 1970s, a few books came out about the Vietnam War. There came many more in the 1990s and 2000s, even within the past five years. Many of them were very well done and became best sellers. However, many were also poorly written for one reason or another, but mostly because the unqualified authors were NOT "real" Vietnam combat veterans.

My book delivers a great amount of factual historical information. It also presents more current news about the Vietnam combat war veterans, where they are today, and where they may be headed in the near future. ANYONE who served and fought in any of America's wars or has been exposed to the aftermath of America's wars is an excellent candidate to read this book. Which means ... virtually EVERY AMERICAN who was born here or who came here legally and has become a patriotic American should read this book.

Those early movies of the '70s and '80s depicted Vietnam combat soldiers as warriors who were deranged, wounded mentally, disturbed ... with lost innocence and not likely to ever adjust to the world we came home to. This image was partially accurate for some, very accurate for others. However, despite the trauma we suffered, many of us made a decent life for ourselves. Oliver Stone—like him or not, he is an excellent example of a successful Vietnam combat war veteran. **Oliver Stone said that Vietnam traumatized him for the rest of his life.** Stone participated in some of the heaviest combat engagements that the 25th Infantry Division was faced with in the Vietnam War's bloodiest years ... 1967 and 1968.

Today, forty to fifty years after leaving Vietnam, many Vietnam combat veterans remain disturbed. Many are very ill from war-related problems.

Those who remain alive today are facing an uncertain future—**I hope all of them will read this book.**

Our patriotic brothers and sisters who served in the Gulf War, Iraq War, and Afghanistan War should read this book. Many of them are suffering from similar PTSD problems that Nam vets suffered from for several decades before PTSD was even recognized by the VA and the medical community.

Although I did not begin writing this book until March 2012, I have been writing it in my mind since I started to realize I could never forget Vietnam and quit trying to hide the memories. That might have been just fifteen to twenty years ago. I've always wanted to write a book, but I also wanted it to actually help others, if possible.

Since one of my goals is to reach non-Vietnam War participants, I have offered some definitions of some often-mentioned terms and events for their convenience.

Throughout *Condemned Property?* I will refer to VC or Viet Cong, NVA or North Vietnamese Army, or ARVNs, which is the Army of the Republic of Vietnam.

Viet Cong (VC) were South Vietnamese guerrilla warriors fighting for the communist cause of North Vietnam. ARVNs were South Vietnamese soldiers fighting alongside the United States and other allies against the VC and NVA.

China and the Soviet Union supported the communists' cause with a massive and continuous supply of weapons and ammunition, including artillery and armored vehicles. In some cases, China was known to participate with their own soldiers. Australia, New Zealand, South Korea, Thailand, and the Philippines were allies to South Vietnam and the United States. Each of these participated with combat personnel on a limited basis.

I will often mention the Tet Offensive of 1968. Actually, there were a series of Tet Offensives, depending on who is counting ... Tet I, Tet II, Tet III, etc. Briefly, the Tet Offensives could be described as follows—in as few words as possible as this subject will be covered in more detail later in the book. The Tet Offensive of 1968 took place in January through the fall months. Virtually every major city in South Vietnam was attacked in January and February 1968, even Saigon itself. Tet was the Vietnamese Lunar New Year holiday, and so the multiple attacks were a complete surprise to American forces and our allies. There was a truce in place at the time, which the NVA and VC broke.

The initial Tet Offensive was fought off quickly and decisively, and the VC would never fully recover. Later, a massive continuation of the Tet Offensive, which was even bloodier, was also fought in a very decisive fashion in May and June 1968 with devastating losses to the enemy.

There is a glossary of Nam terms at the end of this book for the non-Vietnam vets' convenience.

My Early Combat Trauma

Most of the early years of my childhood were spent in Cleveland, Ohio's tough eastside neighborhood known as Hough. It was so tough there that my three-wheel tricycle was stolen one night when I was barely old enough to ride it.

When I started kindergarten at Hough Elementary, some of the bigger boys (black and white) would pick on me just because I was littler and skinnier than they were. They were never fair fights—one on one—and I dealt with it as best I could. I would arrive home with a bloody nose and lots of scratches quite often. Yes, bullying is as old as sin itself. Even 8th-degree black belt Chuck Norris claimed he was bullied in his childhood years.

Both of my parents worked full-time jobs. Dad was a bus driver and Mom was a waitress at two Kenny King's restaurants, so they were not home much when I came home from school. I would clean up my wounds before they came home as best I could and never told them about the fights, unless forced to do so.

Some people might go through their entire life without ever getting into a fight. Heck, I had dozens of them already at age five, and I quit counting them after that. I did not lose them all, but most times, I was outnumbered, so the end result was unavoidable in those instances.

One could classify me as a combat-tested veteran, and I was still in the single-digit years of my life. Then one day when I was six or seven years old, a really tough, husky black kid named Butch (who never picked on me) came up and intervened when two other boys were harassing me. They were older than Butch, but he put them both on the ground in quick fashion. Man, was he tough.

Butch and I became great buddies over the next year. It turned out that his father was a professional boxer, which turned out to be an advantage for me. Butch gave me boxing lessons in the evenings, and it paid off handsomely … I didn't get into fights nearly as often anymore, and when I did, it was more often than not that my attacker ended up with the bloody nose. Butch made sure I wasn't ganged up on as he was usually nearby while I fought my own battles. Since those years, I have always been eager and willing to step up and intervene for underdogs.

My mother and father got divorced when I was in the first grade, and I had to spend some time in a boarding home, separated from my sister, Sherry. It was not a positive experience for me, as the boarding home's owner was mean to us, and I was no longer in the same neighborhood as Butch. We still went to Hough Elementary School together, and I was glad of that. Still, I had lost my best friend to hang out with, my sister, and my parents at age six. Needless to say, I was confused and scared, but I don't remember having anger back then, just a feeling of insecurity. I seemed to have enough fight in me to survive those very trying years … no doubt, my friend Butch helped me a lot.

Mom remarried and so did my father. I went back and forth, living with each one until the court awarded my mom the responsibility of raising Sherry and me. Our new stepfather, Jim Robinson, tried his best with us because our mother really loved us so much. It is difficult for a couple of kids seven and five years old to understand what is going on. There was so much upheaval and change. But we always knew that our mother was there for us, and as I said, our stepfather, Jim Robinson, did the best he could. I will always be grateful to him. It was not an easy situation for him either. Plus, he and Mom brought us a brother and two more sisters—we love them dearly.

We moved from Hough to an all-white neighborhood and that was okay, but I always missed my buddy Butch. He and I were like brothers and we both knew it—so did his mom and dad. I will never forget Butch.

The west side of Cleveland, near Halloran Park on West 117th Street, was a lot easier for me. Right off the bat, I established myself as one of the toughest kids in my age group, and most of my friends were tough kids as well. In fact, one member of our little clan of nine- to ten-year-olds became a "hit man" and a major muscle man for one of Cleveland's most famous gangsters, Danny Greene. My pal's name was Keith Ritson. They were both killed in true gangland style back in the 1960s … while I was serving with the U.S. Army in Vietnam. Keith and I fought each other once; it was a draw, and neither asked for a rematch.

Basically, I did not incur many problems as I spent my years of the second grade to the sixth grade on Cleveland's west side. My sister Sherry, half-sister Carole, and I got along well together, and I took on the role well as their older brother. I did not get into nearly as many fights anymore, as playing baseball became my primary activity.

The next move for us took place while I was in the middle of the sixth grade. When our move took us to the small country village of Twinsburg, Ohio (population 2,082), I had to take the sixth grade over.

Twinsburg was great—an excellent move for me—and I still consider it my hometown to this day with great pride. In Twinsburg, I was re-introduced with blacks, and that was just fine with me—we bonded very well. Not many problems with spending the rest of my teenage years in Twinsburg.

Twinsburg was a country town with several large farms which I worked on, and it had plenty of ponds and a creek to fish from, catch frogs, turtles, etc. It was a blast growing up from age twelve on in the little Twinsburg village.

Some of those great friends I made back then are some of my best friends today … black and white. Twinsburg seemed like a place that time forgot, but actually, it was ahead of its time in terms of integration. There were no racial problems in Twinsburg … my black brothers were truly bro's back then—**still are today.**

My two very best friends in Twinsburg were named Fred—Fred Cornell and Fred Robertson. All three of us met in the sixth grade and have kept the bond forever. We lost Fred Cornell to cancer a couple years back. Fred Robertson lost a brother in Vietnam during the same time that I was over there. I knew his brother well. Freddy R. and I hang out together constantly. We golf together. We love the Ohio State Buckeyes together. We frequent many of our alma mater's high school athletic events together—along with many other brothers who went to Twinsburg. When someone in Twinsburg sees either one of us, we are usually asked how the other one is.

Freddy R. truly understands my pain from Vietnam, and I am comfortable discussing some things that happened over there with him. Freddy R. has impacted my life in ways I am indebted to him for. He is a dedicated Christian man and a very positive influence for me and the demons that I still have from Nam.

*THEY Won't Believe This!

"They," whom I refer to here and at the end of some chapters, were the opposition to the American military efforts to win the Vietnam War. "They" could be the anti-establishment hippies of the '60s, the anti-war protesters, left-wing media, or various anti-war organizations (also left wing) such as Students for a Democratic Society (SDS). At the very end of many chapters, I have added a brief statement which pertains to the content of that chapter and which will attempt to throw a jab at left-wing anti-war beliefs during (or after) the Vietnam War. **"They won't believe this"** will be a profound statement based on *fact*, not opinion. Most readers should appreciate them.

"They" might also refer to the inept American politicians who did not know what a military strategy was, and kept our senior commanders' hands tied throughout the war. "They" could also refer to the lot of prima donna officers who were in Vietnam's combat environment just long enough to get a medal and advance their career. The late Colonel David Hackworth once referred to the breed of young officers in Vietnam as "the perfumed princes."

Chapter 1

OUR STORY ... WHY NOW?

First, here is a factual account of an incident that happened on October 17, 2012, as told by a good friend of mine who was reading an earlier edition of my book on an airplane:

I was on a plane yesterday flying back from Houston and I was reading Dusty's book. A lady sitting next to me kept glancing at it. As the plane landed and we were taxiing to the terminal, she asked if I was a publisher and I told her "no", but that a good friend of mine had served in Vietnam and was writing a book about his tour of duty there. She said her father had served three tours in Vietnam and that he died in 1999 of Agent Orange-related cancer. Tears came to her eyes and she said to tell the author (meaning Dusty), "Thank you for serving our country" and "thank you for writing the book". She said her dad never got over the war and that she has a sister who was conceived during a time between tours when he was home and that her sister has many, many health issues that she believes were because of her dad's exposure to agent orange.

- LaDonna Herrera

The Helpful Book?

I guess if I had to present a mission statement for this book, I would say briefly … it is meant to be a helpful book. I know that it has already helped some people who I shared early editions with. How? It motivated them or re-motivated them to begin or resume their battle with that 900-pound gorilla, the Veterans Administration (VA). Here is what one U.S. Navy veteran told me:

Dusty, I think that your book will be able to help a lot of veterans of any war. It has already helped me. I was admittedly thinking of giving up on my appeal to VA for a disability claim. I sent the VA "tons" of letters and documentation, but I was still turned down. It hurt! You were the motivating factor in my not giving up. This time I brought in a Veteran Services Officer and also the Disabled American Veterans (DAV) which was your suggestion. It has paid off, as I got someone's attention.

Reading *Condemned Property?* and referring back to it can help a veteran, family member, or friend in two ways. It may:

1) Make you mad enough to do something for yourself or someone else.
2) Bring your head out of the sand where you've had it for too long.

Those are two reasons I have written this book NOW. I will continue stating more reasons for our readers' convenience. When you have finished reading this book and you feel ready to take on your adversaries, just make sure you do these simple things first:

1) Make sure you are aimed in the right direction. If not, calibrate your sights immediately; this will save you precious time.
2) Make sure your weapon and ammunition are clean. We don't want any M-16 type of jams on this mission.
3) Know your purpose and stay with it.
4) Research your adversary for weaknesses so that you can coordinate your assaults.
5) Do not accept NO for an answer. Regroup and prepare for another assault.
6) Remain flexible; be ready to modify your battle plan.
7) Don't be shy about calling in for reinforcements; talk to other veterans about your battle plan.
8) Fire when ready and … FIRE AT WILL!
9) Wait no more than ninety days for a response. Reload and fire again by letter, fax, email and telephone.
10) Last, be prepared for a direct attack, a personal visit at your local DAV office … just walk in.

Okay, continuing with more reasons on WHY NOW?

<u>Because</u> Vietnam IS still a highly debatable topic.

<u>Because</u> America still has not learned from the Vietnam blunder and needs to be reminded why it still matters.

<u>Because</u> so many Vietnam vets still are unable to or just won't talk about Nam—so I am doing it here. Looking at the suicide rate of the veterans coming home from our most current wars should startle everyone.

<u>Because</u> the so-called lessons from the Vietnam War that should have been learned by our country's politicians are being ignored. VFW statistics from June 2013 show that every day twenty-two veterans commit suicide. **THAT IS TWENTY-TWO PER DAY!**

<u>Because</u> I was one of the 2.8 million or so Americans who served in the Vietnam War, more specifically, one of an estimated 450,000 who actually were classified as combat.

<u>Because</u> I was one of the few who came home seemingly in one piece ... seemingly?

<u>Because</u> ... as everyone out there who is breathing is fully aware, many Vietnam veterans never came home alive!

<u>Because</u> ... as most people are oblivious to, many Vietnam veterans chose not to come home to the coldness that would have greeted them.

<u>Because</u> many Vietnam veterans are still trying to find their way home.

<u>Because</u> many Vietnam veterans may never find their way home, not in this lifetime.

<u>Because</u> I don't want any more Vietnam veterans to prematurely end up as **CONDEMNED PROPERTY?**

<u>**Because**</u> **... preserving the Vietnam War veteran has become a LIFE-TIME COMMITMENT for some of us.**

Aside from a concussion or two, a few minor nicks, and all the other inconveniences all of my brothers endured and much more, I was indeed one of the lucky ones who was able to walk home on two sound legs.

Although the early part of this book will resemble an autobiography, this is not a "me" story. **My Nam brothers from yesteryear, today, and future years are the story.** Guys such as Bug ... Tets ... Ski ... Best ... Boo ... George of the Jungle ... Boone ... Smokey ... Slick ... Bud ... Shorty ... Babyson ... and Tex ... to name a few. These guys make the story and all those who pioneered before us—GOD, THOSE GUYS WERE SOMETHING!

Everyone who served in the Vietnam War has a worthwhile story. Some have already told theirs. Most have not and most of those are unable to tell. I understand why, but I remain hopeful that more of them will open up ... before they leave this earth. I was unable to talk about Nam until just a few years ago when Hanoi John Kerry attempted to become the President and Commander in Chief of the USA's Armed Forces. Oh geez ... what a disaster that would have been, which I will address later in this book.

It amazes me how clear many of the memories and images from 1968–1969 are to me after forty-plus years. Then again, the media keeps reminding us about things like how we lost the war ... My Lai's massacre ... and the fall of Saigon ... to this very day!

Basically, we Nam vets wrote out a blank check to our country, using our lives as collateral when we were sent to Vietnam. Our country, rather our government, over-spent that check like they do everything else. But this time it cost the lives of a few million Vietnamese people

and several hundred thousand (maybe two million) American soldiers. The few of us who remain alive are in the fight of our life to keep from dying prematurely as so many of our Nam vet brothers already have.

Too many disability claims are still not being taken care of with T.L.C. for "real" Vietnam vets. It's an old story and this country should be ashamed at how its fallen warriors and their families continue to be treated—*or not treated*.

Will the telling of my story, one Vietnam veteran survivor, impact anything? I don't know—maybe not, but maybe so. If so, it was worth the effort and the stress of writing this book to tell our story—and stressful it was.

My brothers and sisters who served in Vietnam deserved more than America has ever been willing and able to give them. Four-plus decades later, the Vietnam War still ignites passion, anger, and massive depression for many of us who served there. Many of us will die with these feelings—without resolve. My goal is to try to prevent many of these premature deaths from continuing without resolve.

Please make NO MISTAKE; this book is about trying to preserve the Vietnam War generation, the veterans who fought there, their families and anyone who was touched by that war. I am not writing Vietnam veterans off as *CONDEMNED PROPERTY?*, which is why there is a question mark in the title.

Several sources say over two million of us have died prematurely after coming home, and we will continue to die off each and every day if we don't do an **ABOUT-FACE** in our lives with our attitudes and our lifestyles. I believe we can do this because I believe **IT'S NEVER TOO LATE!**

To this day, there are oh so many silent Vietnam veterans who still have not opened up and talked about the war, even with, or especially with, their family members. I completely understand, as it has been extremely difficult for me to write this book. Doing so has reopened old wounds embedded in the depths of my memory. And it has been quite difficult to convince other Vietnam veterans to share a story or an opinion to be included in this book. I expect many of them will refuse to read it … what a shame.

Several times, I thought about stopping this project, but we never quit over there in Nam (even though our country quit on us) for our brothers, and I do not want to quit for them now. So … onward was my decision and maybe, hopefully, this story will help some veterans, whether they served in Vietnam, Afghanistan, Iraq, the Persian Gulf, Korea, or otherwise.

With the passing of three brothers of our 1st platoon of Bravo Company 3rd 22nd while I was writing this book, I became even more motivated to finish it.

My Nam vet brothers and sisters served proudly and bravely, and in our minds, we fought for the same reason that others did in WWI, WWII, and Korea: to preserve freedom … or so we thought.

Many veterans who returned from Vietnam were ridiculed for their participation in that ugly war forty to fifty years later. This lack of validation for our **service to our country** forced many of us to keep the horrors and atrocities we witnessed or experienced bottled up inside … often to the day some vets died prematurely.

MOST OF US WHO WERE SENT TO VIETNAM WERE PREPARED TO GET WOUNDED. PREPARED TO BE TAKEN PRISONER! PREPARED TO RISK OUR LIVES! WE WERE NOT PREPARED TO BE ABANDONED BY OUR COUNTRY WHEN WE CAME HOME!

Sometimes the truth is too hard to handle, especially when our media has been covering up that truth … for decades! Therefore, some of my story may be hard to swallow for some.

Another very important reason I have written this book is because I believe we should care about how our soldiers are trained, equipped, led, and welcomed home when they return from war today and in future wars. This should be a moral obligation toward those who were asked to serve and protect our freedom on our behalf.

N E W S F L A S H … America did NOT lose the war in Vietnam! The Viet Cong and North Vietnamese (and Chinese) armies were soundly defeated by our forces from 1962–1973 … **FACT!**

Vivid Memories …

These are a few memories from my experiences in the Vietnam War that remain extremely clear today—like they happened yesterday …

My "Going Away Party to Vietnam" was held on High Street at Ohio State University in Columbus, Ohio, on or about March 1, 1968, hosted by my great friend to this day, Gary Ockunzzi, of Aurora, Ohio. That evening on High Street carried over into the next morning of March 2nd. I woke up on the front lawn of Gary's frat house … and I did not make my scheduled flight to Fort Lewis—not that day. The U.S. Army was forgiving, and they had a seat available for me the next day … it was off to Fort Lewis, where I would be expedited in very quick fashion.

Cam Ranh Bay … lots of white sand!

When I landed in Vietnam at Cam Ranh Bay in March 1968, it is true that we could hear artillery far off in the distant background. So we did not sleep so well those nights as we were now … IN COUNTRY!

The next morning was a typical Army day … if you were stationed some place outside of Honolulu, Hawaii. We saw blue skies … lots of lily-white sand (lots of sand) and the very clear waters of the South China Sea. Cam Ranh Bay Air Base was one of three aerial ports where U.S. military personnel entered or departed South Vietnam for their tour of duty.

Cam Ranh Bay was a vital logistic complex for the air support of the Vietnam War. It was, however, a very secure area. In fact, it was pretty much like a resort area that one would see in the Caribbean. But we would never get the opportunity to "dig our toes" into Cam Ranh's beautiful waters—NEVER!

Cam Ranh was easy to fall in love with. There were quite a few Americans there—civilians and Vietnam veterans who chose to stay there rather than return to the USA. But my stay at Cam Ranh was short. Within two and a half days after I arrived, my orders came down. The next day I would not wake up to waves of the South China Sea. So much for my R&R in Vietnam.

While in Vietnam most of my time was spent as an infantry grunt, the last part as a base camp warrior. Hopefully, telling about my life before Nam and what I've done with it afterward can still inspire a few who have not yet been able to turn things around because ... **IT'S NEVER TOO LATE!**

What still bothers me most is that it is usually other Nam vets or one of their relatives or friends who asks us about Vietnam. Other people still don't want to hear about it and think we should just put it out of our minds. **Nam will be with those who experienced it forever.**

Getting egged and booed at Oakland when we came home in 1969 didn't bother me as much as Cleveland's so-called Coming Home parade in 1988. It was interrupted by, of all things, protesters of the Vietnam War! They were probably in kindergarten when my buddies and I were being ambushed in the Iron Triangle. **Actually, we Nam vets put this event together with very little support from corporate Cleveland.**

It made me sick when I read a newspaper article about how most of Cleveland's mega corporations did not contribute to our twenty-year reunion and parade. Surely, some of the corporate people were there, or people close to them had to be touched by Nam in some way. God, that infuriated me back then.

The 2nd and 12th 25th Infantry (formerly 4th Infantry Division) in Dau Tieng was my first combat assignment after filling sandbags in Cam Ranh Bay. The 2nd and 12th had just been hit pretty hard along the Cambodian border where the Ho Chi Minh Trail filtered into South Vietnam. Our mission was to be the blocking force to prevent the North Vietnamese from getting to Saigon. Even though Tet hit them hard, I spent only two and a half days with them ... the 3rd 22nd was hit harder, nearly wiped out for the third time since January, and they were my next stop.

I hooked up with the 1st Platoon, Bravo Company of the 3rd and 22nd, which was the same company as in the movie *Platoon*. We were to be the replacements for the guys who fought at Soui Tre, Soui Cut, and the Battle of Good Friday ... these were huge battles, but of course, the American media ignored them because they were major American victories.

We talked about our future reunion after Nam as though all of us would surely be there ten to twenty years later. Only sparingly did we suffer a death or severe casualty during April or May, until May's mini-Tet Offensive.

In 1972, I completely totaled a sports car while driving at the estimated speed of 127 miles per hour. (Since Nam I was headed for self-destruction again, it seemed. I almost accepted an offer to join the mercenaries.) Now I had a lot of hospital time, about two months, to think about my life, where I was going, and where I had been. I had too much time on my hands, watched too many soap operas, and the hospital bill just grew and grew.

Every day in that hospital, there wasn't a day that Nam didn't come into my thoughts. Why was I there? Who sent me there? Why weren't they there? Why had I given up on myself since coming home after fighting so hard? Why?! **Why did so few care?**

After more hospital time and plastic surgery from car accident number one, I quit my job of seven and a half years as a quality control and receiving inspector and gave them no reasons. I knew that I needed another challenge. So I jumped into another combat arena ... selling advertising space. Little did I know Nam had trained me for this.

The hospital and medical bills were never paid off, and the insurance company reimbursed me about $7,500 less than what I paid for the car, so I still owed that money. They told me to accept it or they would repair it rather than total it, and getting all of the parts could take up to a full year. Thanks a lot! So five years after Nam I was backed into another ambush and had to fight my way out. Again I thought seriously about the mercenaries as I desperately needed the money so badly now.

From 1973 to 1980, I worked for seventeen different companies, giving it my all each time, but the favor was not returned at any of those stops. One employer went bankrupt, another moved without notice, and one just plain cheated me out of $10,000, so my next stop was personal bankruptcy in 1980. **Once again, I had to start from the bottom.**

In 1983, I took off for a three-day Everglades warm-up to get me ready for fourteen days in the heart of the Amazon jungle. This was almost what I was looking for, and I intended to meet with some mercenary contacts during this trip.

The people down there were exactly like the poor souls in Nam, but without the oriental look. There was even a revolution going on, and the buildings in Iquitos, Peru, were in rubble from sabotage. It was like being back in Nam, and I was sort of enjoying it, even though it brought back my jungle rot and horrific memories.

In the summer of 1988, members of the platoon and their wives somehow pulled off a twenty-year reunion for us. Unbelievably, fifteen members of the platoon and their families showed up. Most had not seen each other since Vietnam in 1969 ... the emotions that were felt were simply indescribable. Our old friendships had been re-strengthened for life. And we got to say "good-bye" to each other this time, which was terribly painful.

How can you forget a man who fought beside you every day for a lifetime? A lifetime is exactly what Vietnam seemed like to us, yet it also **seems like it just happened yesterday**. It was only yesterday, wasn't it? It sure seemed like it was to me.

Then on January 1, 1988, I formed my own company, The Roland Group. The years since bankruptcy were good. Putting in fifteen-hour workdays helped! We were an independent publishers' rep organization, and I was still selling advertising, just like the first sales job I had.

Many of the techniques and strategies I use now are copied from our search-and-destroy missions near the Cambodian border in 1968. I even developed a promotion campaign that was also taken from the propaganda campaigns used against us by the North Vietnamese and Viet Cong. Funny, isn't it? It has been successful until now.

In Vietnam, it always seemed as though the enemy was everywhere. Perception was one of their weapons. At The Roland Group, we have utilized the art of perception in our sales plans by making our competitors think we are everywhere too, and that they cannot beat us.

We soften up our prospects with the artillery (propaganda), and then the infantry (salesperson) comes in to mop up and earn the order.

The Vietnam experience has been an up-and-down experience for me and my family. The memories are mostly sad, and they seem like they were only yesterday, so tears still come to my eyes as they are right now during this writing.

When I came back from Nam, people said things like "You're lucky it wasn't a big war like the other ones, so it couldn't have been too bad!" ... "You were over there? No kidding! How long? Didn't know you were gone." ... "Well, we're glad you're back. Now it's time to forget that. What's done is done." ... "That was a mistake. Too bad you had to be involved with it ... Want to go golfing tomorrow?" **Damn that war ... no one understood it!**

We used to swim in or wash ourselves in rivers that Agent Orange had run off into, not to mention where the natives dumped their refuse. We brushed our teeth—when we could brush them—in water that had little critters swimming around in it. We used to pull blood-sucking leeches from our bodies that were three to six inches long!

We were attacked by thousands of red ants that had a sting as painful as a bee sting—they could hold up or redirect an entire company of soldiers ... exposing us to other dangers! We would wake up often with things like six-inch orange centipedes ... black scorpions ... or funnel web spiders ... in our boots or *on our bodies*. We humped through smelly, boot-sucking swamps, with cobras and bamboo vipers always a threat!

One typical or "average" day could include search-and-destroy sweeps of three to five clicks through thick jungle, rice paddies, and pineapple swamps in 100° heat and 100% humidity! Often, our daily sweep would be interrupted by a combat assault. Helicopters would transport us to another "hot zone" where a sister company was under heavy attack—we would be dropped into the middle of the battle. IF it ended that day, we would then be flown back to complete our sweep if it was still daylight!

Sometimes our search-and-destroy sweep was stopped cold in its tracks when the enemy sprang an ambush on us and other troops had to be combat assaulted in to help us survive the day.

Unlike the other wars America fought in, when we took casualties, we stayed in the bush—and continued fighting—as replacements came and went. Never a rest, no grieving time … it was like we were being punished, like they (our country?) wanted us to die! **I THOUGHT WE WERE THE GOOD GUYS!**

After a major battle in a place called the Boi Loi Woods, in the morning, we were checking the enemy dead bodies—the Viet Cong almost always pulled their wounded off, but some were left, and our ARVN (South Viet soldiers) were yelling frantically—pointing at some of the body count, **"Chinese, these are Chinese soldiers!"** China never admitted to sending troops to Vietnam, nor did our own government publically acknowledge it … but they were there.

Sometimes our frustrations over there would turn into uncontrollable rage, which we turned loose on the enemy and even worse … sometimes OURSELVES!

One morning after an all-night firefight one of our killed in action (KIA) was an American second lieutenant from another company … he was shot in the back by one of his own. Not much was ever said about it again, but we knew that it was not an accidental killing.

One day when a bunch of my grunt brothers came into Cu Chi, one of my hooch-mates made some terrible degrading remarks about their IQ and what little purpose they had. After my hands were pulled from the death grip I had on his neck, he continued taunting me and so I dashed to my locker for the M-16. Before the others could get to me, I had already pulled the trigger … SAFE! It was on SAFE. "Thank God!" I said as they pulled the gun from my hands. My god, what did I almost do?

God prevented me from killing a fellow American that day because when I attempted to shoot my fellow American; the M-16 was still on S-A-F-E!

That jerk reported me, but the others refuted his story. I was moved to a bunker with a guy from 3/4 Cav, whose tank was mined while he was driving it, so he was pretty messed up. The next six weeks with him were pure fun and excitement … NOBODY BOTHERED US! The rumor was that after being released from the hospital, he crunched a Vietnamese vehicle that was in the way of his tank … allegedly there were people in it. He refused to pull aside because of the mines he hit before—he should not have even been out there after what he had been through. No wonder no one bothered us!

My two best buddies in Nam were a tough Irish kid from South Amboy, New Jersey, and an even tougher black kid from South Chicago. Their nicknames were "Smokey" and "George"—like George of the Jungle. George had been a member of the Blackstone Rangers, one of Chicago's most fearless gangs back in the 1960s. He was also a member of the Black Panthers—but in Nam, we had to fight side by side each and every day. We tried to keep the friendship together over the years after Nam, but I think we reminded each other of memories that were just too painful to reenact, so we drifted apart. *Yet I thought of them often.*

I was never afraid of the dark until Nam! When the sun went down over there, the Viet Cong were active. To this day I have hallucinations with lifelike visuals of a Viet Cong or North Vietnamese at my bedside … to this day!

I have had several therapy sessions over the last few years with my VA psychologist in Ohio. He is one of the very few people I've ever known who has shown that he's genuinely interested in hearing the stories from a Vietnam veteran. These talks help me tremendously … don't know if I would even be here this day without him! His name is Dr. Robert Marcus.

Most Nam vets I know or served with who experienced the horrors of combat have carried their burdens with them to this day—all too many have died with those burdens. WHY DIDN'T OUR COUNTRY TAKE BETTER CARE OF US? **I THOUGHT WE WERE THE GOOD GUYS!**

I was so confused during the first dozen years or so after Vietnam that I often entertained the idea of becoming a professional soldier … a mercenary?

As I watched one Vietnam veteran after another fade away over the last several years, I started to realize that I would never get over that rotten war and that I needed help in dealing with my horrors.

When we came home, people were always telling us, "You have to get over that war." Even today, some people are still telling us that. How the hell do you get over watching people die who fought by your side day and night for what seemed like an eternity? They died in Nam and they have been dying ever since we came home because **VIETNAM IS STILL KILLING US!**

Our brothers who fought in the Gulf Wars in Iraq and Afghanistan have no idea what is in store for them and their families … ten, twenty, thirty, fifty years later! Wait till someone says to them, "That war was over twenty years ago. Why can't you get over it?!"

Sometimes we would rescue Viet kids from a village that had been terrorized by Viet Cong. Some of us had thoughts of possibly adopting a Viet kid. Maybe it was from the guilt we harbored from what was being done to their families and their country by the Viet Cong, North Vietnamese, Chinese and … by Americans.

I know that God has stepped into my life many times during and after Vietnam. About one week before I was departing for my trip to South America in 1983 to "explore opportunities," I met someone who would become the love of my life, and for this reason only I chose to come back home after I was done in South America. I'm convinced that my "Higher Helper" had something to do with this!

*THEY Won't Believe This!

The veterans coming home from today's wars are the sons, daughters, nephews, and nieces of many who booed, shunned, cursed, spit on, and betrayed Vietnam War veterans when we came home. Oh my! I wonder if today's veterans know that their parents, uncles, and aunts may have done that during the Vietnam War? Then again, they could not have known the truth, as the Walter Cronkite darlings of the TV media had completely brainwashed them with lies and false information about what was really taking place in Vietnam.

Hard to believe, but Vietnam had its own Audie Murphys—as shocking as that may be to some. Therefore, I have dedicated some brief mentions throughout the book of a few of those heroes … *our* heroes of *our* war.

Chapter 2

THE BRAINWASHING

It is believed that the term **brainwashing** *first came into use in the United States in the 1950s, during the Korean War, to describe the methods applied by the Chinese communists in their attempts to produce deep and permanent behavioral changes in foreign prisoners, and to disrupt the ability of captured United Nations troops to effectively organize and resist their imprisonment. The Chinese term* xǐ nǎo *(洗脑, literally translated as "to wash the brain") was first applied to methodologies of coercive persuasion used in the "reconstruction" of the so-called feudal thought patterns of Chinese citizens raised under pre-revolutionary regimes.*

(Source: *New World Encyclopedia*)

When did it begin for future combatants of Vietnam? In my opinion, the process of brainwashing used to instill "emotional deadness" into future Vietnam veterans began when we first entered boot camp, where we were soon brainwashed into believing that the Vietnamese were not trustworthy or worthy of being viewed as human beings. They were gooks, dinks, zipper heads, slant eyes, SOB's, etc. So we were brainwashed into believing this from that point on.

Unfortunately, as I would find out later in life, this "brainwashing" was a form of mind abuse, and it would have a long-term effect on most of us who experienced intense combat situations. So when we finally arrived in the combat arena, it was easy to kill a "gook" or a "dink." Because, after all, they really weren't human beings, were they? When we came home, this dehumanization and desensitization transformed us into people who had great difficulty enjoying the same things in life that other people were able to find pleasure in. For us, showing love and compassion toward others required a numbing of our reactions to the many horrible deaths and horrors that surrounded us in Vietnam.

In basic training at Fort Knox, I didn't take the military as seriously as they would have wanted me to. That began to change as advanced infantry training in Fort Polk, Louisiana, was more of a wake-up call to us now that Vietnam was just around the corner and these would be our last moments to get ready for what Nam had in store for us.

Little did I know at the time, I was being trained to live each day as if it were going to be my last. Unfortunately, no one taught us how to wind down after the war, and many of us still look at every day as though tomorrow is "iffy." Ironically, I began to realize that many of my childhood heroes were jungle experts. For example … Tarzan comic books were my favorite. I never missed a Tarzan movie. Jungle Jim was next. There were also those John Wayne WWII movies in the jungles! There was the "Swamp Fox," Francis Marion.

American explorers and pioneers also intrigued me: Davy Crockett, Daniel Boone, Jim Bowie, Stephen Austin, and Custer. I didn't want to believe any of the negatives I heard about George Armstrong Custer.

The jungle always fascinated me. Hot, wet, green, steamy, exotic, magnificent. Sure, the jungle had its drawbacks, but finally I would experience the ultimate testing of one's self against all odds—this would be the ultimate challenge I was looking for.

So I had graduated from Boy Scouts to sleeping in tents at Fort Polk to a bona fide COMBAT INFANTRY SOLDIER! Now I slept in the elements, and they were cruel beyond my wildest imagination. It didn't take long for my attitude toward **jungle warfare—Nam style**—to become extremely negative.

Fighting an enemy in the jungle is an art. The jungle becomes a great equalizer for a technology-challenged enemy such as the Viet Cong were. The jungle is one of the only environments where U.S. forces cannot bring our vaunted technological edge upon an invisible enemy.

From the very first day I set foot on Fort Polk (Little Vietnam) for advanced combat infantry schooling, I was terrified, but I was also determined to make it. Obviously, the reason that my brave fellow soldiers and I were sent there was to try to prevent ourselves from being killed in Vietnam. Nevertheless, Polk was an eight-and-a-half-week nightmare. Many of us were willing to be shipped directly over to Vietnam rather than spend any more time enduring the horrors of Fort Polk. This place had it all: swamps, rats, gators, poisonous snakes, and a sweltering heat that drained the life out of us. That was the everyday reality of Fort Polk, and it was designed to prepare us for the next level, which was Vietnam.

In order to fight successfully in the jungle, one has to have trained or lived in it. I feel that the bayous of southern Louisiana and the climate at Fort Polk provided me with that training. Living in the jungles of Vietnam itself gave me the opportunity to live like the enemy and, therefore, learn to think like the enemy … but we had to do it very quickly. **Imagine this: Over there, one of the few things we had to look forward to was congratulating each other for KILLING ANOTHER HUMAN! I wonder how our draft-dodging buddies would have dealt with that.**

When I left Fort Polk, Louisiana, in March 1968, I was in the very best shape of my entire life at 167 pounds, with a twenty-nine-inch waist, and had run a mile with uniform and combat boots on in 4:58 minutes during Advanced Combat Infantry Training. In Vietnam, I lost forty pounds in four months, weighing in at Dau Tieng on July 3, 1968 ... at 127 pounds.

The jungle life in Vietnam was lonely and depressing. I soon felt trapped like a caged lion, and it would be an eternity before I was free—IF I made it. In our first few weeks, man, did we want to go home! The only way out was 1) in a body bag or 2) with several Purple Hearts. Either was a heavy price to pay, but it happened way too many times for many combat soldiers. Then again, after a few weeks in the jungle, I began to feel as though I belonged out there and that I had always been out there. What a strange feeling that became ... ADDICTED TO THE JUNGLE!

When your country's politicians send you to war to be killed at the tender age of twenty or younger and you survive the ordeal, you come out of it thinking that your life is meaningless to yourself and to others around you. Once your own country demonstrates that you are expendable, you begin to believe it, and it creates a bitterness that soon turns to hate.

Depression sets in, and then many Nam vets reach out for help (at least the ones who still care and haven't given up). Before that, alcohol and drugs were the solution; these substances only deaden the grief and when they fail to work anymore, suicide then becomes a viable solution. **THANK YOU, AMERICA.**

My first several years back in the USA after Nam, maybe between 1970–1979, are almost a complete blur to me today. And yet, I remember hundreds of incidents that happened in Nam in one hellacious year. How is that possible? I mean, how could that one year be so vividly recollected in my mind? For me, alcohol day after day was the answer to forgetting ... so I thought!

The first car that I totaled stands out to me because I know that on that evening I was suffering from a genuine case of **"I don't give a damn anymore so I am going to end it right here and now."** That was in 1972. Why? Because very few people knew how troubled I was about what happened in Nam, and frankly, even if it was a shallow caring, that only made me feel worse and more alone. After all, they had their own issues to deal with.

When I got back to Twinsburg, Ohio, it was in March of 1969, and I almost prayed for people to ask me what it was like in Vietnam. I'm glad that I didn't have very high expectations because no one seemed to think that my Nam experiences were very important. Sure, many would politely say to me, "Glad you're home. Now it's time to forget all of that stuff and put it behind you."

Forget that stuff over there?! What were they referring to, all of the twenty-year olds who came home in body bags? Obviously the media screen back home had worked, as the general public thought all that was going on in Nam was a little police action. While the extensive casualty rate wasn't released yet to the general public, my fellow combat soldiers in Nam and I KNEW the truth and the depth of the ordeal.

Since coming home over forty years ago, over and over, people have been telling me to forget that year of my life. I kind of did while I was drinking so heavily in the 1970s and 1980s. Today ... Nam is vividly there; it isn't going away.

At times, I think that some of us became robotic zombies. It was like we were put into a trance or hypnotized, yet we were still able to respond to what was going on around us. I don't believe the will to live ever left us; it's just that we proceeded more out of habit or being on some kind of "automatic pilot" than being in a fully awake and conscious state. Perhaps this is why some of the guys turned to drugs and also why mood-altering substances became more popular after we left Nam. Maybe the correct description of how some of us became could be called "comatose." In the medical world a person who is confused, fails to respond to normally painful stimuli, i.e., sound and lights, is described as being comatose.

The medical world also states that a person may become comatose from a variety of conditions: drug abuse, neurological injuries, and blows to the head, falls, and other such head injuries. Sad thing is, these conditions can be deliberately inflicted to save oneself from the extreme pain of brain trauma.

To us dirt-eating, mud-sucking grunts, Vietnam was an endless nightmare of bad days. Besides the never-ending fear of death, we had to endure a host of miseries: merciless humps through a sun-scorched landscape packing eighty pounds, combat assaults, brain-boiling heat, humidity, dehydration, heat exhaustion, sunburn, red dust, torrential rains, boot-sucking mud, blood-sucking leeches, steaming jungles, malaria, dysentery, razor-sharp elephant grass, bush sores, jungle rot, moaning and groaning, meals in green cans, armies of insects, red fire ants, poisonous centipedes, mosquitoes, flies, bush snakes, vipers, scorpions, spiders, rats, incoming fire, body bags, and a thousand more discomforts, including loneliness. Despite all this, we combat infantry warriors did our jobs well and then ... **CAME HOME TO WHAT?**

In *Brainwashed for War: Programmed To Kill*—**a must read for any combat veteran, Matthias Chang writes that Americans have been brainwashed for war our entire lives. From the Cold War of our childhood to the Vietnam War and now, the so-called "War Against Terror." The goal ... make us mindless supporters of killing the enemy.**

Polk's Vietnam Is Tiger Ridge

Propaganda—Perception—Reality!

Perception is reality—so it has been said, right? In World War II, the Japanese utilized a very effective propaganda war on our American troops. Tokyo Rose was the name given by American troops to many women of American-Japanese descent who would broadcast propaganda for Japan—directed toward the Americans in WWII. Tokyo Rose would be broadcast throughout the Pacific regions with a message of doom and gloom being the ending result for America. The Japanese also distributed tens of thousands of leaflets with propaganda messages on them, warning American GIs that their case was a hopeless one—that defeat by Japan was inevitable, telling them to lay down their weapons and go home to their families.

This propaganda war seemed to have an effect on our troops as the Japanese were creating a perception with Americans that Japan was winning the war; whether they were or not, that propaganda war was seemingly working.

Long before Japan used these tactics, it was being done by Genghis Khan and his Mongol "hordes." Did I say Mongol "hordes"? Fact is, Genghis Khan's armies rarely outnumbered their enemies, at least not at the beginning of his war efforts to conquer and kill anyone who breathed. It wasn't until later, as his conquests gained more momentum and more support, that the Mongol "hordes" would have an advantage in numbers over their victims.

In the earlier years, Genghis' armies utilized unique tactics—which I won't go into here as that would require a separate book, and I am not a history expert. But it is known that the tactics Genghis used succeeded more often than not in creating a perception of reality that Genghis had superior numbers, when in fact the Mongols were usually outnumbered by the enemy!

These battle tactics would often create a perception that Genghis' approaching armies could not be defeated, so the intended adversaries would simply lay down their arms without a fight and beg for mercy. Unfortunately, Genghis gave no one any mercy. He destroyed the villages, raped and pillaged its inhabitants, and forced able-bodied males into his armies. Genghis Khan was a military freak, a genius who was advanced well before his time.

Some of us Vietnam vets think we had a tough time. Here are a few obstacles Genghis was faced with and overcame on his way to conquering the known world in the 1200s:

- Genghis Khan's (Temujin) father was poisoned when Genghis was just eight. His entire family was disowned and cast out to forage and beg for food.

- Genghis remained illiterate, and yet by the time he died in 1227, his rule would include most of Asia and Eurasia, becoming the largest land conquest in history at the time.

- Intuition, tenacity, and bold psychological warfare tactics from a man who was illiterate? Go figure!

- Many tried to overthrow his rule from within. Genghis brutally punished them and rewarded loyalty. Therefore, he ruled until he died—unchallenged.

Genghis Khan's propaganda weapon—he would send spies to infiltrate a targeted village, spreading the word of the oncoming Mongol hordes. In most cases, the village would surrender and, unfortunately, the systematic slaughtering would follow the invasion.

Enter the Viet Cong …

They slaughtered the villagers. Created fear and forced loyalty. Genghis Khan was doing that 765 years before the Viet Cong were even born, but they carried out the same acts of slaughter for intimidation purposes … with ultimate victory as their goal.

The Viet Cong had no Genghis Khan to lead them, although their allegiance to Ho Chi Minh in North Vietnam was most impressive. This kept them together as a formidable fighting force, despite their massive losses to us in battle.

Just like the Mongols, the VC were extremely mobile—constantly on the move, usually initiating the first contact with their adversary with the element of surprise. The Mongols wore light armor. Their adversaries were bogged down with heavier armor. The Mongols rode smaller but swifter horses. You guessed it—the enemy rode larger and slower horses. Seldom did the Viet Cong stay in one place for more than two or three days, and of course, they were masters at camouflage. They also traveled light, but then their tunnels heading to underground camps were never far away.

The VC's lifestyle was not any better than that of the Mongols—some 750 years earlier. But the VC remained dedicated to their cause no matter how tough it became ... go figure!

One huge advantage the VC and NVA had over Americans was that they chose the time and place for a confrontation with us. I guess that was the reason for General Westmoreland's search-and-destroy tactics during the day and platoon-sized ambush attempts at night. One U.S. military study found that 88% of all engagements in the ten-year Vietnam War were initiated by communist troops. No wonder we slept very lightly—and we still do to this day.

Another propaganda type of tactic the VC used was to probe a U.S. firebase by firing mortars or .51 caliber rounds at us for a few minutes and then disappear. Then we would retaliate by calling in artillery and maybe even some tactical (expensive) air strikes after such menial provocation. Often, this resulted in damage and death to a nearby village—creating bad feelings toward us. I don't know how often this happened, but it did happen often.

There was a perception that the VC were always near, that they were watching us twenty-four/seven, and that they could attack anytime—anywhere they chose. Problem was ... we never knew if that attack, if and when it came, would be a full-scale regimental-sized human wave attack or a much smaller unit of hit-and-run snipers. We always had to be prepared for the worst ... day and night.

The North Vietnamese had their own version of Tokyo Rose. She was called "Hanoi Hannah." Hanoi Hannah's broadcasts of propaganda came on radio Hanoi. She would read the names of newly killed or captured Americans and play unpopular war songs in an attempt to affect us with negative feelings about the war.

Many of Hanoi Hannah's broadcasts would mention exact locations of specific combat units in the field. Below is an excerpt from one of her broadcasts:

Hello, GI, how are you? It seems to me that you have been poorly informed about how the war is going for you. Nothing is more confused than to be ordered into a war to die or to be disabled for life without an explanation of your presence here. GI, they may give you a medal but only after you are dead.

Hanoi Hannah's voice can be heard today in the video game *Battlefield Vietnam*.

The mind game of this war was like that of no other war before—or since. While we would seemingly win a major encounter, the VC/NVA always had the option of retreating to the safe sanctuaries in Cambodia, Laos, and North Vietnam or VC loyal villages. During most of the war we were not allowed to follow the enemy with a counterattack across those borders. What a mind game this war was! It frustrates and angers me to this day. To me, the faces of a Viet Cong or NVA soldier resembled demons, and they were terrifying. They seemed to be smiling—almost laughing. I guarantee you that laughing was not what we were doing in battle.

Once in their safe sanctuary, the VC/NVA regrouped and returned to do it all over again and again and again and again. And they would still leave leaflets behind for us to see.

How important was propaganda in the big picture? I surely don't know, but it contributed to the end result of the war. This "police action" over there was not a BB gun fight. What most people have still overlooked is this:

- Over 58,000 Americans died over *there*.
- Over 10,000 allied forces died over *there*.
- An estimated 275,000 South Vietnamese forces died *there*.
- Over two million North Vietnamese and Viet Cong died *there*.
- Millions of unknown civilians died *there*.

DO THOSE NUMBERS RESEMBLE A BB GUN FIGHT?

One of Genghis Khan's most difficult conquests was overcoming several thousand peasants and farmers in Hungary who fought a guerrilla-style war against the Mongols. This tactic was not anticipated, and it put a temporary halt on the Mongols' inevitable victory.

Guerrilla warfare dates back before Genghis Khan. Sun Tzu, in his *The Art of War* (written around 500 BC), was probably the first and was emulated by communist leaders Mao Zedong and Ho Chi Minh.

How about **our** war for independence? Guerrilla warfare and propaganda tactics were used there. In a way, our ancestors, the colonists who fought for our independence, *which we enjoy today*, were sort of like the Viet Cong against the British. (Sure, I realize different circumstances existed around both wars.)

Our media romanticized the Viet Cong as being this huge underdog, much like our early colonial patriots actually were in the Revolutionary War. Had the Vietnam War been solely between the Viet Cong and us, that war would have ended in 1968 after or during the Tet Offensives. Guerrilla warfare and a propaganda war alone could not have defeated the U.S. military.

The Viet Cong were on their way out before the Tet Offensives of 1968. The Tet counteroffensives by the USA should have sealed the Viet Cong's fate. From early or mid 1968, the guerrilla and propaganda wars were pretty much an afterthought. But the damage had been done, and **IN STEPPED THE ARMY OF NORTH VIETNAM!**

In basic training and advanced infantry combat training, there was never any mention of the North Vietnamese Army (NVA). It was always VC, Viet Cong, Victor Charley, booby traps, mines, etc. that we were brainwashed to be aware of in Vietnam. Oh, they were there when we got there all right, but after the near annihilation of the Viet Cong in 1968, it became a different war, one that I don't recall us being prepared for. The NVA took the initiative during 1968, there afterward, and clearly more Americans were killed by Soviet- and Chinese-supplied weapons than booby traps and mines. SURPRISE!

The NVA regiments were an organized and more traditional force to be reckoned with. They had tanks, artillery, and endless resources, compliments of China and the Soviet Union. To me, it seems like the Viet Cong (who were South Vietnamese people) were set up to be sacrificed by their North Vietnamese "brothers" to lay the groundwork for a North Vietnamese victory.

BUT ... backing up here, that propaganda thing had already done its job—compliments of North Vietnam's new ally ... **the American media.** They carried the torch for the defeated Viet Cong and prolonged the war—causing a non-victory for their own country.

I remember the letters from home. My girlfriend's letters used to tell me how the newspapers were saying that we were losing the war. My Nam brothers were getting letters with the same message. We would compare letters, then look around at each other and wonder if we were fighting in the same Vietnam War that our media was reporting to the American people.

History documents a multitude of unsuccessful guerrilla-type wars, which included propaganda campaigns to support them.

When I was humping in the jungles, swamps, and rice paddies of Nam, I was not yet aware of Genghis Khan's great military prowess or his art of mastering PERCEPTION in battle. **But I did learn it from the Viet Cong with on-the-job training (OJT).**

Guerilla Warfare & Sales Career

In my sales career, which has spanned from 1972 to the present (over forty years), it became obvious to me pretty darn quickly that in order to be successful, I would have to find ways to make myself unique—to stand out from the pack. I found that the guerrilla warfare experience in Vietnam could be my answer—if I could convert some of those tactics into the selling war. Make no mistake ... the art of selling in the field or on the road was every bit as challenging as Vietnam was. Both offered ultimate tests for survival in a jungle. People began to say this about me: "He's everywhere ... he's everywhere!" It wasn't very long until my guerrilla warfare tactics were successful in sales. Eventually I became extremely successful at it, forcing me to decline on a dozen or so offers to move into management. That decision was easy for me—I was a **GRUNT** and I belonged in the field, doing face-to-face battle against our adversaries, just like Nam.

Trust me, my aggressive selling style did rub a few people the wrong way. These people were usually the pompous type, in love with their stature and

power. In many cases, my roadblocks usually came from far-leftwing femi-nazi types who were not receptive to my aggressive style. Then again, many female marketers became some of my staunchest supporters. Regardless, I have prevailed for forty-plus years in representing dozens of publishing companies. One could say this about my track record ... **"HE OUTLASTED THEM!**

Briefly, here are a few of the accomplishments that I am most proud of in my selling career from 1972–2013, which my combat experience in Vietnam helped prepare me for:

Salesman of the Year Award – 1993

- Survived eight ownership changes.
- Outlasted twelve different presidents/CEOs.
- Outlasted thirty different publishers/associate publishers/sales managers.
- Offered/declined fourteen different management offers.
- Won **(earned)** nineteen Salesman of the Year awards.
- Built #1 share of market and have kept it for thirty straight years.
- Set one year sales revenue record of $3.2 million in 2001.
- Total sales revenue has surpassed $80 million.

Those years of sales success from 1980 to present were preceded by one failure after another from 1970–1979. I left or was kicked out of seventeen different jobs. I don't think I made it through two consecutive years in that time without engaging in a single car accident ... totaling four vehicles. The damages to myself, my self-worth, were massive. But I always got up and walked or crawled away from them—except the 1972 Pantera crash at 127 miles per hour. Brentwood Hospital was my residence for a long time in 1972.

In January 1980, I was flat-out BROKE when I decided to respond to a classified newspaper ad for an advertising space salesperson. Something told me that this was it—this was the turning point in my life that I needed. The day I was scheduled for my interview at the Marriott on Chagrin Boulevard in Beachwood, Ohio, it snowed and snowed. All of the freeways were closed down. It didn't matter to me. My gut feeling told me I had to make this interview, so I took the back roads and I called ahead to let the interviewer know I was coming. I made it—one hour late, but he waited for me.

John Pfuelb was my interviewer's name. Gordon Publications was the company he represented. This man and I had instant rapport. It was like I knew him from a previous life. He hired me on the spot, and the rest of the story could fill another book by itself.

John Pfuelb could tell I was struggling. He also knew I was a Vietnam veteran, which was a plus in his mind—that sure made me happy.

The ending of this story has not arrived yet. Although John Pfuelb has moved on to other career opportunities, he and I worked together for more than twenty years very successfully. I am still with what used to be Gordon Publications, lasting through several ownership changes, and John Pfuelb and I are still great friends. I remain grateful to him for giving me an opportunity, for sticking with me so that I could eventually BE ALL THAT I COULD BE!

Although I repaid John Pfuelb for his confidence in me with a track record of sales that was somewhat instrumental in helping him get promoted many times, and he has acknowledged this, I feel indebted to him to this day as I do to everyone in my life who has stood behind me. I have been blessed by many of those people, but John Pfuelb went wa-a-a-y out for me. Thank YOU, John! The Vietnam War and my experiences with fighting the Viet Cong contributed unbelievably to these sales accomplishments. The Viet Cong also showed me the real meaning of the words "tenacity" and "persistence."

I am not—never was—the best ad salesman in the company or in the arena of publications where I competed. However, no one ever out-persisted me ... **NO ONE!**

I also wish to mention that I have read all I could about the magnificent conquests of Genghis Khan. It was interesting and it was worth it ... for my business and for my personal life.

From 1965–1973 our country conscripted thousands of young men—some were boys—and forced them into a kill-or-be-killed situation ... in another country about 10,000 miles away from America's borders. **Kill or be killed ... those were our orders!**

Please don't misunderstand me here. I still believe the Vietnam War had merit, and history books would be kinder had our government not kept our hands tied. The Domino Theory was a real threat—just not as severe as we were brainwashed into believing. However, when a country's government spends billions on training half a million very young men to become killers of other humans, there should have been a program in place to defuse us when we came home. **Why wasn't it there?**

To this day, as a 68-year-old Vietnam War combat veteran, when I get angry, it can turn to **RAGE! Therefore, the VA medicates me to protect others from that potential RAGE.** I don't recall having the potential of such anger flare-ups as a child or as a teenager, nor does anyone else who knew me in my early years ... not of this dangerous magnitude.

When the Vietnam War began to wind down in the 1970s time frame, it is no secret that the troops were starting to rebel, as it was now obvious that America's politicians had no intentions of trying to win this war. In fact, I could rephrase this and say that America's politicians had cruel intentions, which were to drag the war on for as long as they could so that more money could be made by the elite few, knowing victory was not a goal!

Fragging, which did happen during the mid-1960s of the war, became more common in the seventies. Now, those young men who were brainwashed into becoming killers were taking out their rage on their own kind ... officers or noncommissioned officers. (This is common knowledge by most Vietnam veterans.)

In 1972, there were few American units in combat heavy or frontline areas. In 1973, all American units had been put as far away from harm's way as possible ... the Vietnam War was over for Americans.

Now back home, there were several hundred thousand or so Vietnam War combat veterans running around in society who had been professionally BRAINWASHED!

Minor Inconveniences of Nam ...
Other Than Combat Horror Itself!

Honestly, I have thought a lot about those other "minor irritations" that my combat infantry grunt brothers and I had to deal with when we weren't pre-occupied with those sneaky little Viet Cong rats. For instance:

- Malaria ... if not treated properly, led to a very painful death!

- Hepatitis A & E ... some victims could experience symptoms for 6-12 months!

- Typhoid Fever ... mortality rate of contacted was about 20%.

- Food or Water-borne Diseases ... acquired through eating/drinking local foods not rationed by the U.S. military.

- Dengue Fever ... delivered by our friendly mosquito population. Sometimes shock, hemorrhage led to mortality!

- Plague ... transmitted by fleas from rats. Death was possible.

- Chikungunya ... mosquito-borne viral disease similar to Dengue Fever. Lasts 3-10 days.

- Leptospirosis ... bacterial disease that affected humans and animals. Infection contracted through water, food, or soil contaminated by animal urine, which combat infantry grunts were constantly exposed to!

- Schistosomiasis ... caused by parasitic flatworms in fresh water. Bladder cancer possible.

- Lassa Fever ... viral disease carried by rodent urine.

- Aerosolized Dust or Soil Disease ... acquired through inhalation of contaminated rodent urine!

- Meningococcal Meningitis ... bacterial disease causing inflammation of the lining of the brain and spinal cord. Death occurs in 5-15% of cases within 24-48 hours of onset!

- <u>Rabies</u> ... viral disease of mammals transmitted through the bite of an infected animal. Affects central nervous system, causing brain damage. Rabid mammals were common.

- <u>Jungle Rot</u> ... tropical ulcer caused by microorganisms usually on exposed parts of the body. Possible deep tissue invasion, bone involvement, leading to amputation.

- <u>Dysentery</u> ... an intestinal inflammation, especially in the colon, that leads to severe diarrhea with mucus or blood in the feces. Abdominal pain likely.

- <u>Heat Illnesses/Heat Stroke/Heat Exhaustion</u>

- <u>Dehydration</u> ... can be caused by dysentery or from rapid fluid loss, and it can be life threatening!

Kit Carson Scout (Former Viet Cong) and Me
August 1968

- <u>Insect Bites</u> ... ant hordes, centipedes, scorpions, mosquitoes, bacteria-carrying flies, fleas. Poisonous and deadly.

- <u>Poisonous Spiders & Snakes</u> ... several species, all deadly!

- <u>Leeches & Maggots</u> ... disgusting and also disease carrying!

- <u>Shits in the Jungle</u> ... having to do it in the bush without Kleenex or toilet paper; having to use tropical leaves with parasites or animal urine on them!

- <u>Isolation & Depression</u> ... from all of the above mentioned, in between the horrors and inconveniences of combat. Depression was unavoidable for combat infantry grunts!

- <u>Bathing in Agent Orange</u> … we had to bathe in bomb craters, rivers, streams where Agent Orange had been sprayed—there was no avoiding it!

- <u>Cellulitis</u> … bacterial infection of the skin. Spreads rapidly, swells, and can sometimes be life threatening.

Jumbo Scorpion For Breakfast—Live?

It was daybreak sometime in July of 1968, and I was just beginning to wake up. We had been in a firefight outside of Trang Bang the previous day, and we were all pretty edgy, not to mention very tired from very little sleep last night. All of a sudden, I felt something move on my neck, and it woke me up instantly. It felt like needles moving on my neck! Suddenly someone screamed at me, "TRIMMER, DON'T MOVE!" So I froze, still feeling the eerie movement on my neck. I wasn't a real happy trooper right then. Then one of our Kit Carson Scouts ran over to me quickly and grabbed it. A **jumbo black scorpion** was the crawling critter that was dancing on my neck that morning. We had enough discomfort to handle without waking up to a four-inch-long **black scorpion** threatening to jab his poison into my jugular vein.

Kit Carson Scouts were former Viet Cong guerrillas who had come over to our side under the South Vietnam government's "Chieu Hoi" program. Most of them made great scouts for us. However, some could not be trusted and were believed to be spies for the Viet Cong. But hey—this Kit Carson Scout was A-OK in my book.

They knew how to live off the land, and they knew the terrain we were humping in. They were also capable of spotting booby traps better than we were, and of course, they understood the tactics of the Viet Cong quite well since they used to run with them.

Well, this particular Kit Carson Scout seemed like the real deal. He seemed to genuinely like Americans and disliked the NVA with a vengeance.

Oh, by the way … he was still holding that **black scorpion**, dangling it in front of me with this sly grin on his face. Then all of a sudden … he ate it live! He chewed it up—everything but the stinger on its tail. "Very good," he told us. Yeah, sure, as I held back from puking up right there. Okay, another day and … GOOD MORNING, VIETNAM!

I'll tell you what—I have a very vivid memory of that black scorpion … on my neck both before it was consumed and there after it was consumed alive and raw. Still I can't imagine it … I mean, this thing had two sharp claws and a very intimidating tail. Oh sure, I've heard that they can be pretty tasty if/when they are cooked/roasted properly … Oh what the heck, I might give it a try someday.

10,446 AMERICANS DIED IN VIETNAM FROM DISEASES AND/OR ACCIDENTS!

Imagine this … when we went out on ambush, we had to leave the mosquito repellent behind because the VC were like dogs—they could smell it 100 yards away. So, lying there in the bush with no protection from the mosquito air attacks ALL NIGHT, we had to deal with it. The mosquitoes were like flying piranhas—relentlessly attacking for our blood. It was almost a blessing when we had to spring an ambush because then we could go back to our unit and sleep the rest of the night WITH MOSQUITO REPELLENT ON.

C-Rations Or … Rice?

Three months into Nam, we came to a point where we'd had it with the cardboard-tasting C-rations. We entered a Vietnam town, and there was a sit-down restaurant there, even though it was not a five-star restaurant … maybe zero stars. Our mouths were watering for something other than C-rations or spider-infested bananas or rotted pineapples!

Obviously, it was critically important that we never let our guard down when passing through these seemingly friendly small towns, but sometimes the temptation was just too much to handle—an opportunity to taste something other than cardboard for a meal! Well-cooked Vietnamese, Cambodian, or Thai food can be awfully tasty. It certainly beats raw scorpion meat and stale C-rations.

So listen up; here is what one of those small Vietnamese village restaurants might have on their menu:

- **Com** – boiled rice. Not bad. Includes dishes of pork, fish, shrimp, and vegetables.
- **Banh Chung** – sticky rice cake, a Vietnamese traditional dish. Made of glutinous rice, pork meat, and green bean paste wrapped in a square of bamboo leaves and more rice.
- **Pho Noodles** – probably the most popular food EVER among the Vietnamese. Breakfast is most common for this offering, but even Vietnamese will snack at times, and pho noodles would be a prime snack. By the way, this dish is made from rice.
- **Com** (grilled) – grilled rice, a fall morsel.

- **Banh Cuon** –rice floured steamed rolls. Breakfast is the choice here for most Vietnamese. But with C-rations as one's only alternative, Banh Cuon can be eaten anytime by most American military personnel.
- **Bun** – rice vermicelli here. This is supposedly a rare and luxurious delicacy to the Vietnamese.
- **Faifo Dainty (Danang)** – not a well-known Vietnamese dish to this day. Guess what? It is made from or with something called … RICE! **Ahhhhgggh!**
- **Hue Beef Noodle Soup** – consists of shredded meat and rice noodles.
- **Com Hen (Hue Mussel Rice)** – made with hot white rice and is usually part of every meal in a Vietnamese family. Includes banana leaves, mint, star fruit, bamboo shoots, lean pork, green vegetables … and more rice.
- **Banh Cuon Trang Bang** – rice cakes; the best in Vietnam, made from local rice … what else?

If you haven't come to this conclusion yet—right to the point—I have boycotted anything edible that included rice in the makeup ever since I came home from Vietnam.

The next day we were ordered to listen up. There was a VC supportive village that we would check out the next day—unfortunately, it was not even in Vietnam. It was in Cambodia! I was completely okay with this except they waited so long for this decision, and this search-and-destroy mission would take us across several miles of RICE fields! I have yet to enter a Vietnamese or Thai restaurant since leaving Nam!

Enjoying A Warm Bath … Vietnam Style!

Imagine sharing your evening bath with these substitutes to your rubber ducky: water snakes, leeches, giant swimming bugs that bite, poisonous frogs, water rats, floating garbage, smelly scum, black, stinking muck, and Agent Orange runoff. Would that give some people PTSD for the rest of their lives or what? Well, your faithful Vietnam combat soldiers in the Army and Marines had to deal with this *and* like it—almost!

Every time we finished plodding through waist- and chest-high swamps like I just mentioned above, we wanted to take a bath somewhere, in something and soon. But the closest health spa and Jacuzzi didn't offer us much incentive. It was just another bomb crater filled with stagnant, smelly, and polluted water with critters.

Ah yes, I remember those days of luxury so vividly. Nothing like the simple pleasure of taking a warm bath in clean, fresh water as the cares of the day just faded away, along with our aches and pains of our all day-long search-

and-destroy sweeps and counter ambushes. Yeah, RIGHT! **Oh well …
"Fluff" it—don't mean nuttin!**

The Rats of Vietnam

Bamboo Rats

I swear, some of the bamboo rats that crawled over us in the swamps and rice paddies were over two feet long, including the tail—and may have weighed as much as a large cat. They were not one of our favorite native critters over there, and receiving a bite from one of them could cause some serious health issues. Still, to the Vietnamese people, even though rats were a nuisance for their crops, they were also a very popular source of protein (yeah, they ate them). NO, THANK YOU!

Rat soup, fried rat, curried rat, and grilled rat. One could find any of these on the menu at a South Vietnamese restaurant. I would rate them as one-star establishments based on cleanliness and menu selection. Service wasn't too bad, maybe a two-star rating.

Of course, there is a difference between city rats and rice paddy rats. The former munch on anything and carry many diseases. The country or rural rats feed mostly on rice. So the farmers swear by their country rats and say that **"they taste like chicken."**

River Rats

The Riverine Patrol Force was strategically important because of the extensive inland waterways in South Vietnam, especially in the southern areas where the largest segment of South Vietnam's population lived, which is where the "rice bowl" existed. Personally, I had just one experience working with what was called the Riverine Patrol. I was one of three infantrymen who rode security on these boats in the Phu Cong area of South Vietnam's War Zone C. We were working with factions of the U.S. Army's 1st Infantry Division in July 1968 and, of course, the U.S. Navy.

This was neat duty by our standards—riding in a Riverine Patrol boat with a breeze in our faces rather than humping on foot in the swamps. Don't get me wrong; it was still dangerous. It was a river search-and-destroy mission.

Patrol Boats River (PBR) had twin .50 caliber machine guns and one M-60 machine gun. Usually a grenade launcher came with the package. I remember a couple of Navy SEALs working with us. These SEALs also went out on night ambushes, hit-and-run types, and did a lot of reconnaissance patrols for intelligence purposes with very small squads of six to seven SEALs.

We took enemy fire a few times and, of course, we returned the favor, but the river patrols were mostly uneventful, at least while I rode on them.

Tunnel Rats

OH BOY, if these guys did not deserve a pay raise, then no one did. The Viet Cong's extensive tunnel complexes often led to underground base camps and/or hospitals. A "real" combat tunnel rat usually came from a combat engineer unit. They had to work with explosives such as blowing up a tunnel or dismantling a booby trap, etc. Man, what these guys went through, and all they had for protection were handguns that fired as quietly as possible to help prevent themselves from going deaf from the sound.

These guys had to deal with confrontations with poisonous snakes down there, holding a flashlight in one hand and their handgun in the other, with very little room to let the snake pass by—picture that in your mind! We had an Australian tunnel rat assigned to us for a while. He was fearless. **GOD BLESS THE TUNNEL RATS OF THE VIETNAM WAR! (More on this in Chapter 4.)**

Captured Viet Cong emerging from tunnel

TROPIC LIGHTNING NEWS

Vol 3 No. 03 TROPIC LIGHTNING NEWS January 15, 1968

MASSIVE TUNNEL FOUND

2ND BDE – U.S. Army tunnel rats aided by members of the Vietnamese Province Reconnaissance Unit (PRU) have uncovered what 25th Div intelligence officials believe to be the main Viet Cong underground infiltration route through the Iron Triangle centered 48 Kms north-northwest of Saigon.

The tunnel complex was uncovered during the land-clearing portion of Operation Atlanta. According to 1LT Thomas Seitzinger, a 4th Bn, 23rd Inf. platoon leader, his team of tunnel rats have searched some five miles of the tunneling which generally runs in a north-south direction.

The exact length of the tunnel network is not known, however the PRUs stated that it takes three days and nights to travel its length.

At several points, the main passageway is interrupted by side tunnels, which, according to the PRUs, runs to Ben Cat on the eastern boundary of the Triangle and to the Ho Bo Woods on the west.

"Every time we'd reach a point where the tunnel had collapsed from Air Force bombs, the PRUs would look around and say 'dig there' and sure enough we'd find it again," explains Seitzinger.

Seitzinger explained that the Viet Cong dug their tunnel by sinking shafts at various distances to certain depths. They then dug connecting tunnels. This was repeated over and over again. After the tunnel was completed, the shafts were filled in. The PRUs can spot the location of the shafts by the slightly different color of the ground and vegetation around the shafts.

SSG Donald Neves of Greenville, S.C., has much admiration for the PRUs as he has worked and lived with them for the past 14 months.

"They would save your life in a minute," said Neves. Recently, one PRU they call "Joe" was walking point, and spotted an anti-personnel mine about 50 meters away, he was credited with possibly saving the lives of several men, explained the two year veteran of Vietnam.

"Crawling through the tunnel has been kind of nerve wracking at times," remarked one of the tunnel rats. "We've encountered snakes, spiders, bats and ants, Viet Cong bodies and dud rounds and booby traps that we had to take our first," he continued.

(Source: http://www.25thida.org/TLN/tln3-03.htm)

Thanks Again To President Johnson

If there was one good thing that resulted from President Johnson's order to end the bombing of North Vietnam and the Ho Chi Minh Trail on October 31, 1968, it was that the B-52 bombers became available to fill their spare time on in-country strikes on the Cu Chi and Iron Triangle underground tunnel complexes … the **Viet Cong's headquarters!** These 500- to 750-pound high-explosive bombs would leave mile-long paths of complete destruction. The B-52 strikes were heard fifteen to twenty miles away as hundreds of thousands of pounds of earth, trees, bushes, and buildings (and Viet Cong bodies) were tossed into the air.

The Iron Triangle was destroyed between the years of October 1968–1972 and so was the sacred haven of the Viet Cong ... their massive tunnel complexes. Oh sure, a few diehard Viet Cong continued to hang on, but the Viet Cong guerillas were almost destroyed as a viable fighting force. This happened too late to affect the war's outcome.

The rumblings from the North had already begun—the North Vietnam Army was just beginning their fight. Their warfare tactics were far different than the Viet Cong's guerilla style. It has been estimated by several sources that more than 600,000 Viet Cong met their maker between the years of 1965–1968, and by early 1970, about 80 percent or more of the combat in the Vietnam War against us was being carried on by the North Vietnam Regulars.

This was a victory that the American media never publicized. It did not matter, as our long and hard-fought victory against the VC came way too late to change the outcome of the Vietnam War. The war's severe unpopularity back home had already taken its toll—**the Vietnam War's fate was set.**

Those unbelievable tunnels of Cu Chi are to this day a symbol of the Vietnamese communists' tenacity and endurance against an enemy with superior firepower. We were fought to a draw temporarily by an enemy that countered our superior technological advantage with an uncanny and cunning ability to wage psychological warfare.

The Viet Cong forced us to fight them at their level for most of the war—at a primitive level of horrible darkness that has embedded memories with those of us who fought at that level ... till this day of our lives.

Very few of the Viet Cong tunnel guerillas lived till the end of the Vietnam War. But America had given up long before the war's end was officially announced. In the end, the North Vietnamese Army took all of the glory. And when our American tunnel rat brothers came home from the unbelievably horrible underground war, their story was ignored by the American media. Another example of **STOLEN VALOR!**

Corrupt Rats – Robbing From Their Own Brothers

Ever wonder why quite a few contractor-mercenary companies seemed to be in the news in Iraq and Afghanistan—some of them as casualties? Oh, those poor, brave, patriotic Americans, risking their lives over there for our troops in harm's way. Oh my—pity, pity, pity those poor souls.

NOT SO FAST! Many of those poor little rich boys are or were senior noncommissioned officers (NCOs) who gained valuable experience in Vietnam ... working **the black market**! While there were many heroes in the

Vietnam War, brave men and women who risked their lives to save another comrade, the fat, beer-drinking senior NCOs who were living like kings or mafia dons back at base camp were literally robbing the combat troops out in the bush … taking the shirts off of their backs!

Not only do a lot of phony so-called veterans lie about being in the Vietnam War, many were never in Southeast Asia at any time during their lives. Plus, many Vietnam vets were part of the corruption problem, robbing us of tens of billions of dollars in clothes, food, weapons—supplies of every kind … in **the black market!**

My dear Nam vet brothers, you saw them whenever you managed to get a short one- to two-day breather back in your base camp. There was ALWAYS plenty of cold beer and soda pop back at headquarters, and the senior NCOs there always had a clean set of fatigues and fresh boots, clean, dry socks, etc. The stinking C-rations, bananas and rice from the natives, and warm beer was our routine menu! It is a FACT that only 350,000 troops ever fought in combat in Vietnam, while hundreds of thousands lived like kings in hooches with PXs, shows, R&Rs, and prostitutes at their call.

Chew on this thought … **THOUSANDS OF OUR WEAPONS AND AMMO NEVER REACHED US.** Instead they ended up in the hands of those who were trying to kill us—compliments of our own corrupt senior NCOs who ran **the black market**.

When our boots rotted off our feet, it was because the replacements had been sold for profit. This happened with medical supplies, too. Oh god, is that the lowest, most unscrupulous act ever or what? Worse than the drug trafficking?

I spent a couple weeks in Tay Ninh Hospital in the fall of 1968 for infections in my feet and leg (knee). After I was released, I made a startling discovery. There were stacks and stacks of clean jungle fatigues and clean boots everywhere in the basecamp. And beer? There were pallets of beer stacked up. I asked many questions as I remembered our eighty-eight-day mission in the boonies where we had to wear the same set of clothes and boots until they literally rotted off our bruised, scratched-up, and infected bodies.

I should have been as upset as I was elated when I was transferred from Tay Ninh to Cu Chi—upset because of the combat brothers I would be leaving and because they were probably getting rid of me due to the questions I was asking. Elated because I was going to a more secure area—still a combat zone. In fact, Cu Chi was the Viet Cong's headquarters.

I heard of these things from many during my last few months as a base camp warrior. In Cu Chi, it was going on all around us. At our level we could do nothing about it—even if we knew who the culprits were who were profiting from selling the supplies meant for combat troops.

We have so much to be proud of as Vietnam combat vets, but every war had their black eyes. **The black market** was operating for decades before the Vietnam War and continues today—bigger than ever, I am told.

Americans Were Not The French

To this day, the so-called media experts tend to refer to our enemies in the Vietnam War as "the poor little underdog" fighting against, defeating, and overwhelming the more technologically advanced American military. **Another of the many myths about this war, and it stinks!**

Yes, the Viet Cong were outnumbered and outgunned by America, but they had geography on their side. The VC were poorly armed and equipped in comparison to our military, but they also had the element of surprise on their side.

What our media has always failed to give proper credit to is the best pound-for-pound fighting force in all of Asia … the North Vietnamese Army. Remember, the North Vietnamese embarrassed a modern force by overwhelming the French forces at Dien Bien Phu in 1954. That overwhelming victory by the Viet Minh (North Vietnamese) left only 3,000 French survivors of a force of 22,000!

The military failure of the communist Tet Offensive in January-February 1968 awakened a sleeping giant. The Viet Cong were decimated by American forces during Tet, and the North Vietnamese suffered huge losses as well in their battles at places such as Hue.

North Vietnam wasn't going away despite their losses. It seemed as though two NVA would pop up in place for every one we killed—so it seemed. The NVA were clearly not anything like their barefoot guerilla counterparts who used ambushes and booby traps against us. North Vietnam's army was just as well equipped for ground combat as we were. In some ways they had several advantages such as:

- NVA infantry had modern Soviet-supplied AK-47 assault rifles, the RPD machine gun, and the RPG anti-tank weapons. These were more than a match for our M-16 rifles, M-60 machine guns, or our armored vehicles.
- NVA also outnumbered us in most battles by 3-1 odds or greater; plus they also had the element of surprise.

- NVA had another weapon … the Chinese. More than once we found Chinese Army Regulars mixed in with the body count of NVA after a battle.

Fact is, we were usually outgunned by the NVA in ground combat. Fortunately, we could usually rely on artillery or air support to turn the odds in our favor.

In Mark W. Woodruff's book, *Unheralded Victory*, he documents that while North Vietnam was able to deploy virtually its entire army to South Vietnam, some 400,000 NVA, there were never more than approximately 80,000 American combat troops available to confront them in face-to-face battles. Therefore, it is deceiving when we say America had over 500,000 troops committed during the peak of the Vietnam War in 1968–1969.

Over 80 percent of all American casualties were incurred by the few combat battalions. Historians should note that American troops were badly outnumbered on the battlefields of Vietnam. Americans who fought there and survived should be proud of this. BUT … THE MEDIA CONTINUES TO STEAL OUR VALOR!

By the time the Paris Peace Accords were signed on January 23, 1973, THE NORTH VIETNAMESE ARMY HAD BEEN DEFEATED! After years of head-to-head battles with the Americans and our allies, the drain of manpower on the NVA and the decimation of the Viet Cong … the communists WERE DEFEATED!

Unfortunately, we were wrong in assuming that the Paris Peace Accords would end the war, with America as victors, and South Vietnam would survive on its own. North Vietnam was expected to honor the border with South Vietnam, similar to the conflicts in Korea.

No one could have predicted the events that were to transpire over the next few years after the Paris Peace Accords were signed:

- The Arab-Israeli War
- The Soviet Union and America resumed/increased their cold war with each other.
- The Soviet Union and China once again poured money and military support into North Vietnam, and the NVA war machine was soon back to full strength.
- Americans were long gone from South Vietnam, and military support to South Vietnam could not ever be restored to the level that it once was.

- Without America's support, the South Vietnamese government was collapsing at an alarming rate; so was their military.

Oh, by the way, France—Vietnam's colonizer, prime instigator to bringing our military into "their" war with Vietnam, and a potential benefactor of an America/South Vietnam victory over North Vietnam— REMAINED NEUTRAL DURING OUR WAR WITH NORTH VIETNAM!

The Vietnam War ended in defeat for America, although America had destroyed the Viet Cong in 1968–1969, and furthermore, the North Vietnamese Army was running out of gas (literally) by 1972–1973 ... WE HAD WON THAT WAR! But historians will document the ending to the Vietnam War to their liking, depicting the "underdog" North Vietnamese and their Soviet and Chinese backers as the clear winners.

- Back home, Vietnam veterans in wheelchairs and veterans hospitals had to watch this distortion of history in the making because the American media did them no favors. Over 58,000 Americans died over there ... for what?
- Hundreds of thousands of Americans have died prematurely back here ... for what?
- One million+ Vietnamese civilians died over there ... for what?
- Tens of thousands of American Vietnam veterans continue to die prematurely over here ... WHY?

The total damage goes much, much deeper than the losses to date. Today still, many Vietnam veterans could become **CONDEMNED PROPERTY OF THE VIETNAM WAR and not even be aware of it!**

They Fought Like This Day Was Their Last!

THEY had an iron will—we did too. We made them cry as THEY made us cry—but their country did not quit and our country quit on us! They fought for their Uncle "Ho". We fought for ourselves.

- THEY had already overwhelmingly defeated one western power: France.
- THEY were taller and stronger than South Vietnamese soldiers.
- THEY had stamina, resilience, determination, and heart. They suffered from heat, humidity, diseases, fatigue, hunger, and maybe the worst adversary of all, loneliness, as we did.

- THEY had to endure the pounding of our bombs and artillery, which was relentless day and night. Our air strikes, our helicopter gunships, and our search-and-destroy missions on the ground—this gave them NO TIME FOR REST. How did they do it and WHY?
- THEY were not immune to the leeches and swarms of insects. And they had no place to hide from our aircraft. They were more likely to catch malaria than we were and more likely to die from it than we were.
- THEY withstood Operation Rolling Thunder from March 1965 until November 1968, where America dropped over one million tons of bombs, missiles, and rockets on North Vietnam. They kept making the ghastly trip down the Ho Chi Minh trail day after day, month after month, year after year despite the tonnage of explosives being dropped on them.
- THEY had to endure the monsoons just like we did. Flash floods blocked their paths, making them easy targets for our air power and superior artillery … **yet they marched on.**
- THEY persevered through the largest search-and-destroy mission of the Vietnam War by a multi-division force of 30,000 combat soldiers in early 1967. The Iron Triangle was a communist stronghold, specifically for the Viet Cong, and they were infiltrating into South Vietnam at a rate of 150,000 per year.

We mauled them by the tens of thousands. Those who survived escaped into Cambodia. One search-and-destroy mission called **Operation Cedar Falls** was called a major victory by our American commanders. But they reemerged in 1968 with a vengeance in the **Tet Offensive**, which included attacks against Saigon, so our "Saigon cowboys" got some excitement. We won the battles; we conquered territory (that we would relinquish). They would regroup and take the conquered territory back, often without having to fight for possession. This mind-boggling battle pattern never ended for the rest of 1968 and 1969 as well.

It is obvious today that our supreme commanders never adjusted their battle plan … or they just never understood what was happening, including General Westmoreland, our ultimate supreme commander.

- THEY were prepared to make unimaginable sacrifices in human lives to reach their long-range goal for a victory. They lost more than 500,000 of their military from 1966 on—yet the replacements kept filling the vacancies. They were prepared to go on and on, despite the massive human loss factor.

- THEY had a tradition of opposing foreign invaders from China, Japan, France, and now, we Americans. They were committed to a sacred-like salvation of their country—we were the newest invader, and they were going to fight until the end.
- THEY had an assault weapon (AK-47) that was more reliable than ours (M-16). The AK-47 often proved its reputation of being rugged and reliable; however, it was probably less accurate than the M-16. The early M-16s performed horribly in the jungles and swamps of Vietnam, and this became the target of a Congressional investigation. It wasn't until the Vietnam War was almost half over that the M-16's improvements gained a majority of acceptance with the combat warriors who had to use them. Unfortunately, many Americans had already become a casualty because of a malfunctioning M-16.

More M-16 comments … in the September 2012 issue of *VFW* magazine, in an article by John L. Plaster, a retired U.S. Army major, he is a bit kinder to "America's Black Rifle," the M-16. However, he does mention this about the M-16's performance in the pre-Tet years of 1965–1966:

*So many malfunctions were reported that the military and later, Congress, launched investigations. Experts testifying before Congress explained that the switch from a 1:14 rate-of-twist barrel to the faster 1:12 had … **REDUCED LETHALITY BY 40%!***

The 5.56mm cartridge was designed to use IMR 4198 powder, but in a cost-cutting move, the Army had substituted with surplus WCC-846 powder, which burned dirtier with a higher chamber pressure that boosted the rate-of-fire beyond specifications.

As America's first automatic rifle to blow carbon directly into the receiver, carbon buildup was a major cause of malfunctions, along with such a high rate-of-fire. Chrome-plating the chamber reduced failures to extract, while a new buffer slowed the rate-of-fire. Our platoon leaders constantly yelled at us to keep our M-16s clean, but the Viet Cong didn't always cooperate.

I can personally add to this. While the M-16 may have had some advantages over our counterpart, the AK-47, I can recall at least a dozen incidents of an M-16 malfunctioning during a battle. **This was not good.**

- THEY were expected to sacrifice ALL; **we just wanted to get out of that place.**
- THEY considered military service to be an honorable and highly esteemed way of serving their country. Some Americans did as well; most did not.

- THEY perceived an American soldier to be a vicious, heavily armed mercenary who would torture or kill them if they were captured, so fighting to the death was preferred over surrender.
- THEY who were sent to the south to fight Americans would not be expected to return or be heard from again by their family and friends.
- THEY who died in the south were never sent home to the north. Their bodies were burned or buried in large holes, sometimes by the hundreds. North Vietnam's cemeteries are filled with tombstones without bodies.
- THEY also pulled the strings on most or all Viet Cong activities. All control—military and political—came directly and ultimately from the Communist Central Committee of North Vietnam. True, the VC had a degree of freedom in the southernmost battles of South Vietnam, but it was Hanoi that issued the assignments.

THEY were the North Vietnamese Regulars, one very formidable fighting force. They were completely different from the enemies America faced in previous wars. They rarely surrendered. We either captured them or killed them. But they kept on and on. How were we ever going to win a war against this mentality? Every day, Americans continued to be killed or crippled, and every day we just wanted to go home and forget Vietnam! **WE ARE STILL TRYING TO FORGET NAM AND COME HOME!**

North Vietnamese Army
NVA: The Army of North Vietnam

Four-star General Vo Nguyen Giap led Vietnam's armies from their inception, in the 1940s, up to the moment of their triumphant entrance into Saigon in 1975.

Possessing one of the finest military minds of this century, his strategy for vanquishing superior opponents was not to simply outmaneuver them in the field but to undermine their resolve by inflicting demoralizing political defeats with his bold tactics.

This was evidenced as early as 1944, when Giap sent his minuscule force against French outposts in Indochina. The moment he chose to attack was Christmas Eve. More devastatingly, in 1954 at a place called Dien Bien Phu, Giap lured the overconfident French into a turning-point battle and won a stunning victory with brilliant deployments. Always he showed a great talent for approaching his enemy's strengths as if they were exploitable weaknesses.

Nearly a quarter of a century later, in 1968, the General launched a major surprise offensive against American and South Vietnamese forces on the eve of lunar New Year celebrations. Province capitals throughout the country were seized, garrisons simultaneously attacked, and perhaps most shockingly, in Saigon the U.S. Embassy was invaded. The cost in North Vietnamese casualties was tremendous but the gambit produced a pivotal media disaster for the White House and the presidency of Lyndon Johnson. Giap's strategy toppled the American commander in chief. It turned the tide of the war and sealed the General's fame as the dominant military genius of the 20th Century's second half.

(Source: John Colvin, Author of *Giap: Volcano Under Snow*)

Make no mistake about this statement ... the Viet Cong were also one of the most formidable infantry adversaries the United States military has ever fought against. Many of them may have been local villagers, women and men, even teenagers, but most of them were hardened warriors from very early ages. Their older relatives had fought and defeated the French, the Japanese, the French a second time, and before that, they had fought the Chinese, Cambodians, and Thais. The Viet Cong were bred and trained into warriors with on-the-job war training programs. Although the NVA did provide some guidance.

Many, though not all, did see the battle with the U.S. and the Saigon regime as a true war of independence, and they fought like it. By the time they were in their mid-teens, they had already been trained in the basic skills of guerrilla warfare.

The lady VC did not sit back at their hooches and play housewife. These guerrilla forces were not gentle misses, and they carried out ambushes on Americans side by side with their male terrorist buddies.

Viet Cong intelligence was not to be taken lightly, although our young, inexperienced, and sometimes arrogant U.S. officers often did just that. The VC scoped out our base camps with spies at every level—in our kitchens, maids in our hooches, house boys for our officers—penetrating everything from small base camps to the Embassy in Saigon. The VC had also infiltrated the South Vietnamese military from top to bottom.

In order to defeat the VC in ground combat, the U.S. infantry unit needed to be flexible, fast, and could never underestimate the VC as a fighting unit. As hardened grunts who made it past the first several months, we knew what the VC were about, and we respected their capabilities ... unlike the masses of U.S. lieutenants who came and went faster than we could count them. Too few of the junior officers knew what they were doing, and unfortunately they were never in one place long enough to learn what to do. As the war became less popular at home, fewer quality officers enlisted. **So the same costly mistakes were made day after day, week after week—and good men died because of this.**

We grunts who were lucky enough to make it through a full one-year tour of duty might see several different platoon leaders, company commanders and battalion commanders in a twelve-month period. It's a miracle that there weren't more junior officers intentionally shot (fragged) by the grunts. Then again, there may have been many more that went unreported.

The 3rd 22nd had more good sergeants than most units. Maines, Broussard, Gainey, and Daniels stand out in my mind. I've seen three of them since coming home from Nam. Gainey died a few years ago. Nam killed him and his wife in my opinion, and Daniels died in July 2013 after a long and stressful battle with Agent Orange-caused diabetes. Gainey and I became good friends back home, and he lived just an hour away. Daniels still lived where he was bred, in southeastern Texas. I have seen him several times, and we called each other very often.

The platoon sergeants respected their hard-core grunt troops—unlike many of the junior officers. Colonel David Hackworth attested to this fact in his book, *Steel My Soldiers' Hearts*:

Cadets and new leaders who show ineptitude and little leadership ability—such as that walking atrocity Lieutenant William Calley of My Lai, massacre infamy—should be immediately eliminated. More than any major enemy victory, the shame and horror of My Lai caused the American people to withdraw their support for the war effort.

Leading men into combat is one hell of a job. I could never have done it, which is why I chose to remain a grunt point man most of the time. On the battlefield, decisions have to be made in a split second, and bad ones get good men killed. I did not want that burden.

The Viet Cong knew what a junior officer usually meant. I think that is one reason why they usually had this snide grin on their faces during an attack. I didn't much care about who the junior officer was when I walked point, as I knew that my grunt brothers and the platoon sergeant would carry their load and cover my back. And they trusted me to lead them safely.

To this day, I look back and admire the job that Maines and Daniels did as our squad and platoon sergeants. We accepted their leadership. I hope that they are proud of the job they did because they earned that right, and I don't know a single platoon brother still living today who would say otherwise.

Being a successful combat leader has to be the toughest profession on earth, one with few rewards. I guess when the battle is over and we say to our platoon sergeant, "You're a damn good man," that's the reward he would appreciate the most. Colonel Hackworth also said this after his last tour of duty in Vietnam:

One important lesson to be drawn from the war in Vietnam is that a lightly equipped, poorly supplied guerrilla army cannot easily be defeated by powerful and sophisticated armies, using conventional tactics. To defeat the guerrilla, we must become guerrillas. Every insurgent tactic must be copied and employed against the insurgent. The marvels of modern technology have caused some to believe that exotic gear has replaced the man with the rifle. It is not true. Never in the history of modern warfare has the small combat unit played a more significant role … and the brunt of the fighting falls squarely on the platoon. The outcome of the war will be determined, in large part, by the skill, guts and determination of the platoon leaders.

We were extremely fortunate to have Sergeants Maines, Daniels, and later, Broussard, as our platoon leaders.

I saw very few officers in combat. I never saw a major or colonel, let alone a general, out in the bush except once, when our brigade commander, Col. Flynt, flew over us when we were being ambushed. He was dropping grenades on the VC from his little and very vulnerable bubble-looking chopper—that was pretty awesome and inspiring. I can remember several really sharp captains, and they were darn good, too. Back at the safe base camps, it seemed like officers outnumbered the regular enlisted men. **That was another form of betrayal, as many American career officers in Vietnam did not share the same risks of combat that my brothers and I did.**

When an officer wanted to stay in the field beyond three, four, or six months, he was often suspected as not being with the program or one who had just "gone bush" and was not trusted by his base camp officer colleagues. It was a catch-22 for them. Therefore, we had to count on our platoon sergeants to make sound decisions that might keep us all alive until the end of our tour.

Former five-star general of the U.S. Army and 34th President, Dwight D. Eisenhower, once said this about his soldiers: **"A SOLDIER'S BLOOD MAKES THE GENERAL GREAT!"**

Captured NVA – September 1968
Near Cambodia

Ho Chi Minh Trail – August 1968

Brainwashing IS Betrayal

If you refer to www.killology.com and then look up Lieutenant Colonel David Grossman's biography, it would be worth anyone's time. He is an internationally recognized author, speaker, scholar, and soldier who is also known as an expert in the field of human aggression and the roots of violence and violent crimes. Colonel Grossman is the author of *On Killing: The Psychological Cost of Learning to Kill in War and Society*, which was nominated for a Pulitzer Prize.

As I have stated in this book, very few of us really want to kill another human being, not as the aggressor or from a self-defense mode. Most of us have a very strong resistance to killing. It has also been observed and verified by many sources that the military has a powerful training or conditioning process, especially through advanced military combat training, that allows or forces the well-trained combat warrior to get past the inborn resistance of killing. In my opinion, this was our brainwashing training.

In the Vietnam War, there was an exceptionally high rate of aggressive firepower unleashed at will on our enemies. Today there are endless purification programs available to "un-brainwash" returning combat warriors. Yes, these programs are now available to Vietnam combat veterans as well … forty to fifty years LATE!

I know very few Vietnam combat veterans who did not experience or witness civilian casualties. I know of fewer who have been able to forget those memories ... therefore PTSD is magnified. All combat warriors have certain things they are unable to share with anyone except another combat veteran or a VA psychologist.

Homeless veterans with PTSD and suicides continue at alarming rates. Many of the PTSD victims die prematurely from that illness with heart attacks and other disorders ... prematurely. Brainwashed combat warriors are indeed victims! They need and deserve better treatment for their mental wounds just as our physical wounds get tended to. Somehow, our government (President Obama, Veterans Affairs, or Department of Defense) needs to restore, enable, improve the sense of pride, rationality, sense of judgment, etc. that we had before the brainwashing began.

People are telling us NOW that what we did in the Vietnam War had to be done, just as WWII veterans had to do what they did. But no one ever tells the Vietnam veteran that we "helped to save the world." If they really, really took the time to analyze that war and what happened in Southeast Asia after the war ended, I doubt any rational human being would disagree that the **Domino Theory** was very real. **STAY PROUD, NAM BROTHERS. We did fight to preserve FREEDOM, but our "big brother" in Washington never wanted us to win.**

There were many stories like these, but here are two excellent examples of how the "brainwashing" of our minds was never on hold.

One fairly new guy wasn't in country for more than two weeks. He was still a private first class when he "tangled" with an eight-foot KING COBRA. He was on a routine search-and-destroy mission when he saw and heard movement behind him. When he turned around, there it was—a magnificent but menacing-looking king cobra coiled for the strike ... which it did. Fortunately, one of his squad brothers ran to the ambush site and shot the cobra as it was striking repeatedly at the PFC, who had fallen down just a few feet away from the deadly snake. Before the snake died, it barely missed the soldier by inches! Five minutes later, the platoon was ambushed and the PFC was shot!

A young officer sat down under a large clump of bamboo after a long and exhausting search-and-destroy sweep outside of Duc Hoa's swamps. The officer had nearly dozed off when he heard movement in a tree directly above him. It was a five-foot DEADLY BAMBOO VIPER! The snake dropped from the tree at the same second the officer sprang out of the way. They both hurried into different directions. What a mind game Nam was, day and night.

Bottom line—military training for those destined to take their skills to the jungles of Vietnam was a "brainwashing" that would stir up more resentment and caged rage than most of us had ever felt in our lives. Then when we did finally experience combat, some of us were left with wild, violent impulses, and we needed to level them on someone or something. **Brainwashing mission completed!**

Brainwashed and Deadly ...

Forty-four years ago in 1969, the My Lai atrocities rocked America. The My Lai Massacre actually took place on March 16, 1968 when U.S. Army soldiers slaughtered hundreds of women, children, old men, and their livestock at the villages of My Lai and My Khe. It was also reported that many of the defenseless civilians were also sexually assaulted, tortured, and mutilated. The horrible event was not made public until a full one and a half years after the killings.

My mentioning of My Lai is not to freshen old wounds. I'm sure all of my war brothers are still appalled at what happened there. One report claims over seven hundred civilians died there. Other reports claim the final death toll ranged from three hundred to five hundred. Innocent babies were killed. People were shot in the back, some while they were on their knees praying for mercy. Lieutenant William Calley, who ordered the massacre, was seen by several witnesses to have murdered fifty to sixty helpless villagers who had already been captured.

Was this a true example of what brainwashed, out-of-control soldiers were about in Vietnam as the media has constantly broadcast? Of course not. In fact, it was other Americans who arrived at the scene to stop the horror that was happening, even to the point of threatening to shoot those Americans who were out of control.

WAR IS HELL! But when our government or any government attempts and succeeds in brainwashing its soldiers and then arms them with unlimited firepower ... **be prepared for anything.**

My Lai wasn't the only massacre in the Vietnam War. It was just the most highly publicized ... by the American media. Here are a few other massacres that were documented during the Vietnam War. I wonder if any of them sound familiar to the non-Vietnam vets who read this book.

Go Dai Massacre (February 26, 1966)
Also known as the Binh An Massacre, where the South Korean Army slaughtered unarmed villagers within one hour—380 KIA.

Tay Vinh Massacre (February/March 1966)
Estimated unarmed citizens killed by South Korean Army were 1,265 KIA.

Dien Nien-Phuoc Binh Massacre (October 10, 1966)
South Korean forces mercilessly killed citizens in a temple and then murdered children in a schoolyard—280 KIA.

Binh Hoa/Binh Tai Massacres (October 1966)
South Korean forces again massacred defenseless villagers—268 KIA.

Dak Son Massacre (December 5, 1967)
Two Viet Cong battalions conducted a "vengeance" attack of a Montagnard village that opposed the Viet Cong. The VC used flamethrowers—2,000 KIA.

Hue Massacre (January/February 1968)
Estimated death toll of civilians killed by Viet Cong and North Vietnamese Army was 5,000-6,000 KIA.

Phong Nhi/Phong Nhat Massacre (February 12, 1968)
South Korean Marines ran through the village, killed everyone they saw, and left them there ... 69 - 109 KIA.

Ha My Massacre (February 25, 1968)
South Korean Marines slaughtered everyone in this village, and then bulldozed their bodies into one mass grave—body count not available as EVERYONE WAS KIA.

My point here is—My Lai was a freak incident for American troops. There were countless atrocities committed by the communist forces, too many to document. In the aftermath of most of these horrible acts, it was the Americans who came in after the massacres and took care of the wounded and the homeless children. My war buddies and I contributed as well.

I read somewhere that there were an estimated 36,000 to 50,000 civilians assassinated by the VC and NVA from 1961 to 1973. Figures after that are not available and may have been even worse as the NVA overran all of South Vietnam in 1974 and 1975.

No one can justify My Lai or any of the other isolated incidents committed by American forces. **But they were isolated.** Combat infantry and related military Americans conducted "millions" of combat missions during the war. We had endless opportunities to get out of control and rampage the countryside, but **we did not do that**. On the other hand, it is a documented fact that VC and NVA war crimes were a daily—DAILY—**exercise for their operations**.

The My Lai Massacre was a horrible happening. Unfortunately, the Ameri-Cong media brainwashed many Americans into believing that My Lai was typical of what the Americans did in Vietnam … that we were "baby killers."

In 1972, near An Loc, the North Vietnamese slaughtered too many Viet civilians to accurately count. Most bodies were destroyed afterward. Estimated total: "thousands" KIA. Do you think the enemy we fought was also brainwashed? **BRAINWASHING IS DEADLY!**

*THEY Won't Believe This!

VC POWs

Throughout the Vietnam War since 1964 when the first anti-war protests began, America's media portrayed the Viet Cong as the heroes of this war—as so-called freedom fighters against a corrupt democratic government and its imperialist ally, the United States of America. After the war ended, the North Vietnamese discarded the Viet Cong like unwanted stepchildren and achieved their original goal of a united communist nation. The people of South Vietnam clearly did not want this.

Chapter 3

25th INFANTRY & VIET CONG HEADQUARTERS … CU CHI!

From 1955 to 1963, the 25th Infantry was getting prepared for guerilla/jungle warfare in Vietnam and/or in neighboring countries in Asia. The 25th was the only U.S. Army unit doing this training. The training was said to be all too frighteningly real, and many of the soldiers suffered disturbances—which were not made public at the time. This is described in great detail in *The Tunnels of Cu Chi* by Tom Mangold and John Penycate.

The Vietnam War began to heat up in 1962, so units of the 25th Infantry were sent from Hawaii to a special advanced jungle warfare training in Thailand, an ally of the United States. While this training was rough and authentic-looking, it was not even close to the reality of what the Vietnam War was like. The 25th made it official in December 1965, when the entire division deployed to become a fighting force in Vietnam. The first airlift took elements to Pleiku in the central highlands. The majority of the division arrived by sea and set up headquarters at Cu Chi, unknowingly sharing the same location (underground) with the Viet Cong's main headquarters.

Killing Viet Cong on a daily basis became a way of life that was forced onto the U.S. Army's 25th Infantry Division, and the Tropic Lightning did not let America down with their unknowing assignment. Places like this were often in the *U.S. Army Times* newspaper … Trang Bang, Hoc Mon, Bo Loi Woods, Hobo Woods, Iron Triangle, Dau Tieng, and later … Tay Ninh, Nui Ba Den, etc., as these were hot spots throughout the war.

Combat units such as The Manchus, The Wolfhounds, The 3/4 Cavalry, The Regulars, and others met the Viet Cong in their element day in and day out as well as nighttime, never giving our very capable enemy any time for rest. That was the job of the 25th Infantry Division in the Vietnam War … at all costs.

Someone else said that the Cu Chi base camp was the American way of "getting right into the faces of Victor Charley," the Viet Cong. I don't think that we who fought the VC over there had a full appreciation of what we were up against until long after we came home to the USA and read about Cu Chi's significance in the war.

Cu Chi was the main headquarters for the 25th Infantry. Cu Chi's elaborate tunnel network was also the main base camp for the Viet Cong. Therefore, it is no wonder that the 25th Infantry Division took the most casualties of any military division, and the 25th Infantry Division destroyed more Viet Cong than any other military division during the entire war.

Tunnel rats were kept very busy in the Cu Chi area and beyond. The VC tunnel network reached from Saigon to Cambodia, spanning several hundred miles. *Tunnels of Cu Chi* is an excellent read on this phenomenon.

Construction of these tunnels originated during the war with France, then were enlarged substantially for the benefit of us Americans. Because of our massive firepower from the air, thousands of VC lived underground for most of the entire war … what a life and what determination.

Having peeked into some of these dark, unbelievably hot, filthy, coffin-like holes, I cannot comprehend to this day how our enemy lived like that. Even at the entry point of one of these holes, it was already difficult to breathe. I am sure glad I was not small enough to qualify as a tunnel rat.

Cu Chi was also nicknamed "Hell's Half Acre" because of the extremely fierce battles that had taken place there. The ground war against the VC and their tunnel network would eventually prove to be a bad idea. Although we killed tens of thousands, our casualties were also high. Eventually, the areas surrounding Cu Chi were bombed and Agent Orange sprayed into a barren state. Unfortunately, millions of Americans and Vietnamese would face the aftermath of the poisons of **Agent Orange**.

In *The Tunnels of Cu Chi*, the Cu Chi area is referred to as "the most bombed, shelled, gassed, defoliated, most devastated area in the history of the Vietnam War." Another term used for the Cu Chi area was "Mole City"—and rightfully so.

I first saw Cu Chi briefly in April of 1968. It was a giant dust bowl at that time, constantly being harassed by the VC. My Nam brothers and I spent most of our time in the thick jungles well outside of Cu Chi. Those jungles were extremely thick in our early months of 1968. That would not be the case when we left in early 1969, due to **Agent Orange.**

Cu Chi's immediate area was arguably the most heavily sprayed area in Vietnam with Agent Orange. It seemed like we could taste the chemicals that were being sprayed all around us.

For the Viet Cong, life in the tunnels was extremely difficult. Air, food, and water were scarce, and the tunnels were infested with ants, poisonous centipedes, scorpions, spiders, snakes, and vermin. Most of the time the VC would spend the day in the tunnels working or resting and come out only at night to scavenge for supplies, tend their crops, or engage us in battle. Sometimes, during periods of heavy bombing or American troop movement, they would be forced to remain underground for many days at a time. Sickness was rampant among the people living in the tunnels, especially malaria, which was the second largest cause of death next to battle wounds.

Div Kills 400 Around Cu Chi

By LT Bruce Burton

In two weeks of continuous contact, elements of six 25th Inf Div battalions have killed more than 400 Viet Cong during the fighting in the Cu Chi area.

Battles raged along Highway 1 from the outskirts of Saigon to the north of the division's base camp at Cu Chi. Heavy fighting also broke out during the Tet period from the Ho Bo Woods to Duc Hoa in the northern and southern extremes of Hau Nghia Province.

Soon after the Viet Cong shattered their declared Tet truce, the 1st and 2nd Bns, 27th Inf "Wolfhounds" airlifted into the Saigon area to reinforce American units defending the capital. When it became apparent that more troops would be needed to handle the string of coordinated attacks along Hau Nghia Province's stretch of Highway 1, units were dispatched from the 3rd Bde, 25th Inf Div.

Both the 3rd Bn, 22nd Inf and the 2nd Bn, 12th Inf came in heavy contact within hours of arriving under 2nd Bde control at Cu Chi.

The 1st Bde's 4th Bn (Mech), 23rd Inf already under the operational control of the 2nd Bde on a land clearing operation in the Ho Bo Woods, also saw heavy action in the Viet Cong Tet offensive.

The 2nd Bn, 27th Inf airlifted into Tan Son Nhut Air Base where the 3rd Sqdn, 4th Cav was repulsing a massive enemy assault. The "Wolfhound" battalion set up a base nearby and began to battle enemy units poised to strike at the Tan Son Nhut military complex and at the capital.

Also on January 31, an ambush patrol from the 1st Bn, 27th Inf killed 15 Viet Cong and captured a 75mm recoilless rifle. Reinforcements from the battalion's forward base at Duc Hoa killed 22 more and captured a second 75mm recoilless rifle.

Three companies made heliborne assaults into the Saigon suburb of Hoc Mon, which the Viet Cong had overrun the night before. The American force immediately began clearing operations.

In the early stages of the fighting around Cu Chi, the 3rd Bn, 22nd Inf and the 4th Bn (Mech), 23rd Inf bore the brunt of the action.

Within days, however, the 2nd Bn, 12th Inf also became fixed in a continuous struggle to push entrenched Viet Cong from two villages to the east of the Cu Chi base camp. (Source: http://www.25thida.org/TLN/tln3-09.htm)

Viet Cong Attack Anywhere—Cu Chi Too!

The Cu Chi base camp was not completed until June or July 1966. This was clearly an "in your face" gesture to the Viet Cong, who had literally owned the Cu Chi area until then.

At Cu Chi base camp, a school was set up called The Tropic Lightning Academy, which was a miniature version of the Vietnam War. It included tunnels, mines, booby traps, and an area of heavy vegetation. This was the beginning of producing "Tunnel Rats" to go into the ground after the Viet Cong in their base camp.

While I was still there, about two weeks before I was to fly home in February 1969, Cu Chi was attacked, and serious damage was inflicted by, I believe, forty to fifty Viet Cong. This attack came from the tunnels where the attackers had been sleeping much of the daytime before the attack.

Amazingly, most of the VC attack force made it out of Cu Chi safely … they knew precisely how and where to exit just as they had entered Cu Chi, as though they were ghosts in the night. Left behind were thirteen dead VC, thirty-eight dead Americans, and many more wounded. Fourteen CH-47 Chinook helicopters were blown up by satchel charges. And this happened in a so-called "safe area"—when I had two weeks left in Nam!

Needless to say, the general attitude around Cu Chi the next day left a lot of scared and worried soldiers. This wasn't supposed to happen to one of the U.S. Army's largest and most heavily armed base camps. We were thinking … what if they attempted this with a much larger force and attacked from multiple directions? **WHAT IF?!** Fortunately for me, my twelve-month vacation in South Vietnam and Cambodia would end in two weeks.

About two weeks into Nam, even though I wrote home as much as I could, it was painful and frustrating in that I couldn't tell the family what we were doing, and it took so long before their reply would make its way back to me—IF it found me. Lots of mail got lost.

My mother was a Baptist missionary and Sunday school teacher. How could I describe my day to her and not make her worry? Here is a hypothetical letter to my lovely mom (I never sent):

Dear Mom,

Having fun, weather is beautiful, people are really friendly, food is great, I am sleeping well, we get fresh/clean clothes every day, we get eight restful hours of sleep every night, we go to a spa on Fridays—get massages. Golf on Saturdays is a blast in these swamps (not much roll), we do lots of nature hikes in the day (the scenery is so relaxing), and we even go on overnighters in the jungle … We play cards a lot—I'm the champion at Old Maid, which we play for C-rations!

We take lots of FREE helicopter rides about every other day, and we practice jumping out of them when the locals are actually shooting at us. This is better than video games—HONEST! Some days we get FREE boat rides on the Saigon River, but I don't understand why the people in the villages try to sink our boat.

Oops, sorry, Mom, really gotta run; was just told we have to perk up, stay awake all night, and be prepared for something called a HUMAN WAVE ASSAULT. Should be an interesting experience. I'll write home to you and describe all the details soon.

Love ya, Mom.
Your Soldier, Dusty

HOW THE HELL DO YOU WRITE HOME TO MOM AND TELL HER WHAT REALLY HAPPENED?

Just over two weeks in country, here is a copy of an actual letter I sent to a couple of buddies back in Twinsburg, Ohio:

4/11 – 4/13/68
Dear Rick & Frank,

I'm finally permanently stationed and I can truly say I'm not in the best spot. My original orders had me going to Saigon as a security guard, and believe me, that wasn't too hard to take. Well, that didn't last long as I was reassigned to the 2nd and 12th of the 25th. Well, the 25th had us scared 'cause we heard about their high body count and casualty rates, not to say anything about the Wolfhounds. We heard about them on the plane over here. Well, I was in the field with the 2nd & 12th 2 ½ days and was point man both times. They operate out of a fire support base, so there wasn't too much danger at night either. I pulled L.P. one night and it was my luck that we were mortared 3 times that night, but the artillery shut them up fast each time. Well, on our third day we heard about the news that three of us were getting reassigned, but we didn't know where. We just hoped it wasn't going to be the 3rd & 22nd. Their reputation is the worst in the 25th and most of Nam. The reputation was that they went wherever the action was and that their famous Bravo Co. was the worst. They tell us this company has killed more Charleys than any Army company in Nam, but to coincide with that, their casualty rate is also highest. Well, on Good Friday, Bravo (1ˢᵗ Platoon) was hit and overrun by a regimental human wave of NVAs. Only four men were left of the first PLT. And the total count for the night was 28 KIAs and 61 WIAs to 188 NVA body count, not including the ones that were dragged off and the ones we found buried Sat. (when I got there, and incidentally I was point again).

Saturday night we went in and now we have enough men (replacements) for two squads in the 1ˢᵗ PLT.

Now for the second phase of my letter. Saturday nite at 10:30 P.M. the first PLT was awakened to act as a reactionaryfForce. We weren't told anything and all thought it was just a test for us since we were mostly all new. Well, we found out later as they lined us up in two files with a squad of recons, 1 tank and 2 APCs that it was not a test. The problem was that some Arvonnes turned VC in the Arvonne Compound outside of Dau Tieng (where I'm stationed) and they held a couple bunkers. They were supposed to have made an attempt to assassinate the No. 1 South Vietnamese advisor and failed but had injured several Arvonnes before taking over the cement bunkers. We moved in, surrounded them, and after an interpreter tried to talk them into surrendering they opened fire on us, hitting one American in the side of the head and ear. He fell right on me; man, I never saw so much blood. I got him back to a jeep and we took him back. I guess he was all right but the Arvonnes had about a dozen casualties. We couldn't open up with any big stuff 'cause of the women and children scattered around. So we stayed there all night and at day break all hell broke loose for 20 minutes or more, 50's, tanks, 79's, M-16's, 60's and 90's. Well, they were all dead, 8 of them. So that's a description of my first experience in action. I looked like I got hit a dozen times from all the blood that guy poured on me, I can still taste it and smell it, but the smell wasn't as bad as those NVA bodies we dug up earlier in the day.

Well, it's Sunday and right now we're pulling Road Security for your boys, the Combat Engineers. Tonight we have Ambush Patrol, then back out to the field Monday to the same spot where the 3ʳᵈ & 22ⁿᵈ fought their 4 hour battle on Good Friday. When I'm going to sleep I don't know—-but when I get home (and I am coming, but I'm not so sure about being in one piece?) I'm going to blast anyone who was a base camp warrior over here andsays how easy it was and how much fun we had over here. Also—anyone who says the Marines do everything and catch all the hell is in trouble too. Really—Rick, I haven't seen anything yet, but the Infantry is really hell.

Well, on the good side of things, we have the monsoons coming and Charlie doesn't fight much then.

Well, I've seen the paddies, canals, plantations and the thing we have most of at Dau Tieng is jungle (triple canopy) and you can have it all. Oh yes! The heat is beautiful—118degrees in the shade and these are the winter months.

Guess I've babbled enough, I know you've seen enough here and you probably don't want to be reminded of it. So when you or Frank get a chance, let me know how the world is, be seeing ya in 11 months.

Yours Truly,
Dusty

During the time I wrote this letter, I lost track of where I was, what unit I was with, and when. So the dates got confused … and this was only my first month in combat.

The 3rd Brigade was the first 25th Division element alerted for Vietnam service. The 1st Battalion, 14th Infantry was transferred to the 3rd Brigade as its third battalion and the 2nd Battalion, 9th Artillery was attached as the direct support artillery battalion as well as Troop C, 3/4th Cavalry as the brigade's reconnaissance element. On 28 December 1965, the 3rd Brigade began arriving at Pleiku in the Central Highlands of Vietnam. Called Operation Blue Light, it was the largest airlift of U.S. ground forces ever undertaken up to that time. The 1st Battalion, 69th Armor in May 1966, joined the 3rd Brigade. The brigade engaged North Vietnam regulars along the Cambodian border and then Viet Cong mainline forces in Quang Ngai province for which it received a Valorous Unit Award.

The rest of the 25th Division began arriving at Cu Chi northwest of Saigon in January 1966. Last to arrive was the 1st Brigade on 29 April 1966. Before leaving Hawaii, the brigade received two battalions from Alaska, the 4th Battalions of the 9th and 23rd Infantry to bring it up to strength. During the period from the summer of 1966 to the spring of 1967, the 25th Division was the largest division in Vietnam with four brigades under its command, the division's 1st and 2nd Brigades as well as the 3rd Brigade, 4th Division and the 196th Light Infantry Brigade. From September through November 1966, these units participated in Operation Attleboro in War Zone C east of Tay Ninh City. It was up to that time, the largest major unit operation of the war and after intense fighting in November resulted in the defeat of the 9th Viet Cong Division. Lessons learned were successfully applied by the Tropic Lightning in Operations Cedar Falls and Junction City conducted in War Zone C in early 1967. For an additional description of Operation Attleboro see the Introduction of the official U.S. Army historical study of operations Cedar Falls-Junction City.

In April 1967, the 196th was transferred to Chu Lai in I Corps, thus reducing the division to three brigades. On 1 August 1967 Headquarters and Headquarters Company, 3rd Brigade less personnel and equipment rejoined the 25th Division. Its battalions remained in the central highlands and were reassigned to the 4th Division. Based at Dau Tieng, the 3rd Brigade, 25th Division assumed command of the former 3rd Brigade, 4th Division units, the 2/12th Infantry, 2/22nd Infantry (Mechanized) and 3/22nd Infantry. The 2nd Battalion, 77th Artillery was assigned to the 25th Division Artillery. In exchange the 4th Division at Pleiku assumed control of the units formally with the 25th Division's 3rd Brigade except for Troop C, 3/4 Cavalry and several other company-level support elements which rejoined the division at Cu Chi less personnel and equipment.

From 1966 to 1970, the Division fought the North Vietnamese Army and the Viet Cong north and west of Saigon. During the 1968 Tet Offensive the 25th stopped the Viet Cong attempts to seize Tan Son Nhut airfield and participated in the defense of Saigon. The Tropic Lightning consistently defeated the Communist forces wherever they found them in the Iron Triangle, Boi Loi Woods, HoBo Woods, Hoc Mon, Tay Ninh, War Zone C and Cambodia.

The Vietnamization of the war and the withdrawals of U.S. forces began in 1969. On 8 December 1970, the 25th Infantry Division departed Vietnam at color guard strength for Schofield Barracks less its 2nd Brigade, which became a separate brigade under II Field Forces control. The 2nd Brigade operated in the Long Binh and Xuan Loc areas east of Saigon until its departure at color guard strength for Schofield Barracks on 30 April 1971. The 25th Infantry Division served gallantly for 1,716 days in Vietnam, received participation credit for twelve Vietnam campaigns and being twice awarded the Vietnamese Cross of Gallantry with Palm, Eight Tropic Lightning units were awarded Presidential Unit Citations and eleven received Valorous Unit Awards. 21 Tropic Lightning soldiers were awarded the Medal of Honor.

(Source: 25th Infantry Division website)

25th Infantry Division Vietnam War
21 Medal of Honor Recipients

Name	Rank	Unit	Place	Date
Daniel Fernandez	Specialist Fourth Class	Co. C, 1st Battalion (Mech), 5th Infantry	Cu Chi, Hau Nghia Province	Feb 18, 1966
Ronald Eric Ray	Captain (then 1st Lt.)	Co. A, 2d Battalion, 35th Infantry	la Drang Valley	Jun 19, 1966
John F. Baker, Jr.	Sergeant (then Pfc.)	Co. A, 2d Battalion, 27th Infantry	Republic of Vietnam	Nov 5, 1966
Robert F. Foley	Captain	Co. A, 2d Battalion, 27th Infantry	Near Quan Dau Tieng	Nov 5, 1966
Joseph Xavier Grant	Captain (then 1st Lt.)	Co. A, 1st Battalion, 14th Infantry	Republic of Vietnam	Nov 13, 1966
Ted Belcher	Sergeant	Co. C, 1st Battalion, 14th Infantry	Plei Djerang	Nov 19, 1966
Maximo Yabes	First Sergeant	Co. A, 4th Battalion, 9th Infantry	Near Phu Hoa Dong	Feb 26, 1967
Stephen Edward Karopczyc	First Lieutenant	Co. A, 2d Battalion, 35th Infantry	Kontum Province	Mar 12, 1967
Ruppert L. Sargent	First Lieutenant	Co. B, 4th Battalion, 9th Infantry	Hau Nghia Province	Mar 15, 1967
Kenneth E. Stumpf	Staff Sergeant (then Sp4c.)	Co. C, 1st Battalion, 35th Infantry	Near Duc Pho	Apr 25, 1967
Riley L. Pitts	Captain	Co. C, 2d Battalion, 27th Infantry	Ap Dong	Oct 31, 1967
Nicholas J. Cutinha	Specialist Fourth Class	Co. C, 4th Battalion, 9th Infantry	Near Gia Dinh	Mar 2, 1968
Paul Ronald Lambers	Staff Sergeant	Co. A, 2d Battalion, 27th Infantry	Tay Ninh Province	Aug 20, 1968
Robert W. Hartsock	Staff Sergeant	44th Infantry Platoon (Scout Dog)	Hau Nghia Province	Feb 23, 1969
Marvin R. Young	Staff Sergeant	Co. C, 1st Battalion (Mech), 5th Infantry	Near Ben Cui	Aug 21, 1968
John E. Warren, Jr.	First Lieutenant	Co. C, 2d Battalion (Mech), 22d Infantry	Tay Ninh Province	Jan 14, 1969
Stephen Holden Doane	First Lieutenant	Co. B, 1st Battalion (Mech), 5th Infantry	Hau Nghia Province	Mar 25, 1969
Charles Clinton Fleek	Sergeant	Co. C, 1st Battalion, 27th Infantry	Binh Duong Province	May 27, 1969
Hammett L. Bowen, Jr.	Staff Sergeant	Co. C, 2d Battalion, 14th Infantry	Binh Duong Province	Jun 27, 1969
Danny J. Petersen	Specialist Fourth Class	Co. B, 4th Battalion (Mech), 23rd Infantry	Tay Ninh Province	Jan 9, 1970
Russell A. Steindam	First Lieutenant	Trp. B, 3d Squadron, 4th Cavalry	Tay Ninh Province	Feb 1, 1970

25th Division Awards Ceremony – Cu Chi, October 1968

Vietnamese III Corps Commander Awards
Gallantry Cross to Division

CU CHI On Tuesday, January 28, 1969, Lieutenant General Do Cao Tri, Vietnamese commander of the III Corps Tactical Zone, presented the Vietnamese Cross of Gallantry with Palm to the men of the 25th Infantry Division. Tropic Lightning commander, Major General Ellis W. Williamson accepted the award on behalf of the men of the 25th.

The Cross is a tribute to the men who served with the Lightning Division between December 1965 to August 1968. Their efforts on the battlefield and the intense civic action programs were cited as major contributions to the preservation of freedom in the Republic of Vietnam.

Essay | By John H. Tidyman

Badge of Courage

Recognition for the few, the proud, the fighters

When I see a Vietnam service ribbon on the license plate of a car driving by, I look for a chance to yell to the driver, "What outfit?" When I spot a car with the plates in a parking lot, I stop to talk to the owner. I feel as if I'm speaking a language only we understand. Maybe I am.

These people tell me they were everything from chaplain's assistants to door gunners. Not many say they were infantrymen. I wonder why, 30 years after a spectacular loss, we wear our ribbons.

Then I saw it, at the Army Navy Goldfish Store on Prospect Avenue downtown, a new display: All manner of miniature medals from recent wars. The one that caught my eye is a replica of the CIB, the Combat Infantryman's Badge. On a blue rectangular field 1 inch high and 3 inches wide rests an old musket. A wreath if set in the middle.

The decoration was created in 1943. Most of the credit for the badge goes to Lieutenant General Lesley J. McNair, who wanted to call it "the fighter badge." The general had a special place in his heart for the grunts, the dogfaces, the Queen of Battle, the infantry.

Henry M. Stimson, secretary of war at that time, said, "It is high time we recognized in a personal way the skill and heroism of the American infantry."

There is only one way to be awarded the CIB: Be an infantryman in the U.S. Army and experience combat. My friend Joey Ebenger once told me it was the one decoration he wanted and believed he deserved. He was a radioman for an artillery forward observer. He traveled and fought with the infantry, but he was in the artillery and that meant he couldn't wear a CIB.

For my generation, a CIB is the membership card to a most exclusive fraternity. If you have one, no one can take it away. The CIB is a memory of young boys and sticky blood, of dope and beer, of courage both accidental and serendipitous, of water buffalo and monkeys, of frantic voices screaming "Medic!," of thumping Huey helicopter rotors and the bright, tight chatter of an M-16, the lightweight plastic and metal rifle that looked like a toy and killed better and faster than our father's M-1.)

Where in a war do young boys act like such cool and calm men?

The lapel pin is a bond between those who wear it and the men who fought World War II. Vietnam was not Guadalcanal or Iwo Jima or Normandy or the beach at Anzio. But our uncles and fathers had pictures from that war, black and whites of themselves in uniform. Fighting men. Gallant men. I used to think all we wanted to do in Vietnam was be gallant men. Gallantry was what we learned at our fathers' knees, after all. If we fooled ourselves into believing combat was a rite of passage, it was one of a hundred tricks we played on ourselves.

Our own pictures are different from our fathers. We wore T-shirts in battle, a pair of bandoleers crisscrossing our chest. Resupply, after all, was rarely a problem. Our helmets had written on them, FTA (F*& the Army, or Fun, Travel and Adventure, depending on the rank of the person who asked), or "short timer." A cigarette pack, holding only four smokes and included in every C-ration box, often was secured to our helmets.

*Yet the CIB is more than a memory. **It is a frantic grasp for the** past, a way of silently screaming, "Hey, I was there! I was part of that ... that ... that." We're still unsure what it was, but it was ... that.*

The lapel pin is also ego, a way of saying, "Yeah, I'm in my fifties, and yeah, this is my beer gut, and no, I can't outrun or outshoot anybody or anything. But when I was in the infantry, you should have seen me run and shoot and ... "

What evocative power our icons have. Our fingers absently trace the outline of the CIB. We recall the zip that an enemy bullet made as it passed over our heads. We wonder why some boy died and others lived. Why some left behind limbs and others their sanity. We realize the enormous role luck played.

Luck. Sometimes generous, sometimes miserly, but always there. With all of that, the memories are not bad memories. Lots of laughs. Lots of living. For most of us, an indescribably intense year.

We wonder if our memories can be trusted. The CIB says yeah, you were there. It was a long, long time ago, but yeah, that kid was you. n

When John H. Tidyman returned from a one-year tour of duty in Vietnam in 1969, the nineteen-year-old trooper wore sergeant stripes ... and a combat infantryman's badge.

Our Purple Heart Veterans

I know that the incomparable General George Patton once said, "No son of a bitch ever won a war by dying for his country. He did it by making some other poor bastard die for his country." I admire Patton, but he was extremely arrogant and full of bravado—which one almost has to be in that position. I'm sure Genghis Khan, Alexander the Great, Caesar, Napoleon, Attila the Hun, and Ho Chi Minh carried the same traits.

But a lot of good men died before they were awarded Medals of Honor and Purple Hearts so that WE COULD PREVAIL!

The United States of America's oldest military decoration dates back to August 7, 1782. General George Washington named it initially as the Badge of Military Merit. It was renamed by General Douglas MacArthur in February 1932 as the Purple Heart.

There are not very many of these guys still living these days. *VFW Magazine* estimated in an editorial back in September 2010 that just over 1.5 million Americans have been awarded this unique and very well-known medal.

The Purple Heart is awarded now only to those in uniform who were wounded or killed in combat or similar hostilities. Its original intent was to be an award for wartime meritorious service, including wounds received in action against an enemy. Then, in the October 2011 issue of *Purple Heart* magazine, they published an article which estimated that at that time, there were slightly more than 500,000 living veterans from these wars who are Purple Heart recipients:

World War I	Persian Gulf War
World War II	Afghanistan War
Korean War	Iraq War
Vietnam War	New Dawn

My dear patriot brothers and sisters, to say that you are a rare gem in the American society today is a major understatement. The most current USA population estimates show there are approximately 315,000,000 living Americans ... and **less than 500,000 living Purple Heart recipients.**

However, of those 500,000 living recipients of the Purple Heart, recent statistics from *Purple Heart* magazine state that less than 20 percent of those half-million wounded veterans are subscribers to the *Purple Heart* magazine. I believe the Military Order of Purple Heart (MOPH) welcomes your participation and your support, dear fellow patriots.

It is interesting to read the history of this unique medal. Of course, the image on the face of it is George Washington. General Washington had always tried to maintain a high level of personal involvement with his Army. As he witnessed their bravery, their valor in the heat of battle, he would distinguish those acts of courage in battle.

One problem back in those days—the rewards for valor were generally hoarded by officers or men of stature and royalty. It was that way in Europe … the common soldier was rarely recognized. General Washington's Badge of Military Merit would not be awarded to someone based on his rank or economic status in life. The enlisted or noncommissioned veteran—the regular guy—would be honored as well if the medal was earned.

Purple Heart Recipient

General Washington once said this about his regular soldiers: "The road to glory in a patriot army and a free country is thus open to all."

Although the Vietnam War statistics show that more than 58,000 Americans died and over 300,000 Americans were wounded during the war, there were just 200,676 Purple Heart recipients who were wounded or killed during an engagement with a hostile force or enemy of the United States. **Be proud of your Purple Heart, dear brothers and sisters … my Grandpa Trimmer was … and so am I.**

Name: John William Trimmer
Hometown: York Springs, PA
Branch of Service: Army
Conflict: Spanish-American War 1898

Typical Day of a 25th Infantry Soldier!

A soldier is usually a member of land forces for his/her own country. If one is hired to perform for another country or a private firm, he/she would be considered a mercenary.

Noncommissioned and commissioned officers can be called soldiers for a nation's ground military. Other terms that could be included with "soldier" might be: infantry, grunt, trooper, Marine, paratrooper, ranger, sniper, engineer, medic, gunner, rifleman, recon, tanker, commando, Seabee, SEAL, sapper, Green Beret, artilleryman, Red Legs, and GI.

- **12:01 – 2:00 AM:** Most days began with a probe of mortar rounds by Viet Cong just to keep us honest. Every other week or so they might launch a human wave attack on our perimeter—with the help of their North Vietnamese cohorts. Most times, we fought it off with minor casualties—but not always. Pull guard duty otherwise.

- **2:00 – 5:00 AM:** Sleep—maybe.

- **5:00 AM or so:** Take malaria pills, followed by a breakfast of C-rations of beans and meatballs—"breakfast"? And maybe a shave. If it is dry enough, lay out an extra pair of socks (if you had an extra pair) and our one pair of boots for a chance to dry out. We did not bother with underwear—they just rotted away and made our jungle rot even worse where it hurt the most. Personal hygiene was not the best in an Army Infantry Unit. Sometimes we received a change of clothing every thirty days or so. Yes, I said EVERY THIRTY DAY OR SO, SOMETIMES LONGER—just before they were ready to rot off our bodies. Showers were not possible in the field. An occasional bath in a B-52 crater or a highly polluted river—where Agent Orange leaked into and where the Vietnamese actually dumped their human waste—was a luxury for us! We had few other options to find a way to cool off. After being resupplied, everything was divided up, and anything left over that we couldn't carry was burned so the enemy wouldn't get it.

- **6:00 – 7:00 AM:** Discuss our search-and-destroy mission for the day, which usually meant running into an "ambush," and my job as the point man was to prevent it from happening … if I saw it in time!

- **7:30 AM – 5:00 PM or so:** Three-five click sweep through Nam's exciting countryside, which could include swamps, jungle, rice paddies, unfriendly Vietnamese villages, booby traps, poisonous wildlife, heat exhaustion/dehydration, and most likely a firefight with who we were searching for.

Most of us carried a fifty- to eighty-pound pack, which usually included the following:

- Pack frame if you were lucky to get one
- The pack itself

- Canteens of water (3-4) and 1 canteen cup
- Pistol belt
- M-16 rifle or M-79 grenade launcher or M-60 machine gun
- Ammo bandoleers (3-4) with seven 20-round magazines per bandoleer
- Grenades (2-4 each). They were supposed to be five-second fuses, but sometimes they exploded in four seconds or six seconds, causing much anguish.
- Poncho—a MUST during **monsoon season**
- Poncho liner—our blanket—if you had one
- Air mattress. Some guys had one—mine was shot up.
- Gas mask, if you were lucky. I covered my face with a dampened towel when I needed **protection from napalm fumes**.
- C-rations ... or we ate local food like rice, bananas, monkey, pineapples, and fish from the natives
- Towel, which usually rotted away in 7-10 days
- First aid kit ... never enough of those
- Extra pair of socks (a luxury)

Radio telephone operators (RTOs) and medics had it worse, as they carried extra stuff which was critical to our survival. RTOs and medics' loads could be eighty to a hundred pounds. I also carried a machete, either Army issue or handmade by Vietnamese. I brought one of the latter home. Personal items included a watch (if you could keep it), writing paper/pens in plastic bag, and a camera if you had one—usually a small instamatic type. Lots of guys also carried cigarette packs in plastic bags, a wallet for money, military ID, ration coupons, and maybe a picture or two.

- **7:30 AM – 5:00 PM or so:** We would usually run into some or all of the following on our mission each/every day:

- <u>Red ants</u>, which seemed to hit all of us at the same time—their bites felt like bee stings, and they could stop an entire company. We would have to redirect our mission to get around them. As the point man, I would see them first and alert the others. Black ants had a worse bite, but red ants were far more aggressive, much worse than fire ants back in the USA.

Thank God we were never ambushed by VC or NVA while we were fighting off the red ants—just imagine that, because they attacked our eyes and ears!

- <u>Leeches</u> in the swampy areas had to be contended with on most sweeps—night or day. They didn't hurt so much, but sometimes they took so much blood that their size tripled to a foot long … really!

- <u>Scorpions, centipedes, and spiders</u>—most were poisonous, take your pick. Funnel web spiders were the worst. These spiders were very aggressive and could easily bite through our jungle boots. (So could the cobras and bamboo vipers.)

I have awakened in the morning with a scorpion or centipede or spider on me somewhere. We always checked our boots before putting them on—and I still do!

- <u>Snakes</u> were very common, even the poisonous ones like the bamboo pit viper, Malayan pit viper, and cobras. I did not have many close encounters with them, but others did. Usually a snakebite would get a soldier evacuated from the field **permanently**.

Big load in the bush

Here is what we were told to do if any of us were ever bitten by a snake in Vietnam: Identify the snake. Better yet, kill it, cut off the head, and bring it with you and the snake-bitten soldier to a hospital. Or bring the entire dead snake in with you. A cobra looks like any other large harmless snake when it is sliding through the grass. It does not look like the famed hooded cobra until it sits upright in the strike position. North of Saigon, the Malayan pit viper is more common. Areas closer to Saigon, the bamboo viper is more common. The rice paddies harbor more cobras. All of them are most active when the monsoon rains arrive.

- <u>Combat assault or eagle flight</u> … was a daily routine for all combat infantry warriors in 1968. This is where six to twelve Hueys would fly to our location—with hardly any notice—pick us up, and drop us off into a hot area in swamps where another unit was under attack. When the battle was over, we were eagle-flighted back to where we were picked up to finish our search-and-destroy recon mission or prepare for a night ambush patrol … with no break in between. This is **WAR!**

Sometimes more than one combat assault was demanded of us, so we would engage the enemy in a major firefight twice that day, and if we were really lucky, we would run into them again at night on an ambush. Yes, that would be a very full day … IF you survived it!

- <u>Booby traps</u> … from finding razor blades in Coke bottles to trip wires and poisonous pungi stakes in covered pits, the VC were always into our heads.

- <u>Rats</u> … nearly three feet long were a problem. Obviously, a bite from one of them would cause a disease, and sometimes we had to get a plague shot. I felt rats running over me at night a lot of times and even during battles.

- <u>No mail</u> … while we were out in the bush, as the big supply choppers couldn't get to us—either because of the jungle or because of enemy fire. Or someone back at base camp didn't do his or her job.

- <u>No warm meals</u> … while in the bush for the same reasons as above. But every so often a friendly Vietnamese showed up ready to sell us something that looked better than C-rations, and maybe he/she had a few Cokes in a bucket of ice to sell. (We had to be very careful here—very careful of potential booby traps in their buckets.)

- <u>Drinkable water</u>—HA! It was scarce and questionable when we found it. Most drinking water in Vietnam contained high levels of arsenic—which could cause neurological problems and extreme hypertension.

Over 50,000 cases of malaria were treated in U.S. troops between 1965–1970 along with over 100 deaths. Cholera and meliodosis were also experienced by some.

- **5:00 – 7:00 PM:** Wind down from the day's "fun." Dig foxholes if need be—chow down and get ready for the exciting events that awaited us later. (Squeeze a letter out if time and weather permitted—though it would not get mailed for a week or so. It took a week to arrive, too.)

- <u>Ambush patrol</u>. Every evening one or two squads take their turn to try and conduct a successful ambush on an unsuspecting enemy. Many times we were outnumbered, so we called in artillery for support. **Sometimes we were ambush victims.**

One evening we sprang a successful ambush on some Viet Cong in sampams, paddling down a river, who were inevitably on an ambush mission of their own on our brothers. That was literally like shooting sitting ducks on a pond. We killed them all and **WE LIKED IT!**

Those who stayed back at the perimeter set up their defenses, pulled all-night vigilance, and were either hit with VC mortars and M-51 fire or they were ambushed themselves. The 51-caliber machine guns could rip through most of our vehicles.

Sometimes going out on ambush patrol was the scariest thing possible. One night out on an ambush patrol, we were surrounded by a hundred or so North Vietnamese, and there were only eleven of us. We hid and kept quiet all night—turning off our radio and therefore breaking off communications with the rest of Bravo Company. None of us got any sleep that night. How could we, as we could have been detected at any moment and wiped out in minutes? We heard them talking and laughing all night, and we just lay there frozen stiff till daylight came. After the NVA left, we were able to turn our radio back on and eventually hook up with the rest of Bravo Co. but it left us in a horrified state of pure shock for quite a while.

Another day our combat assaults took us into the jungle, pineapple swamps, and rice paddies to counter an enemy ambush. The next day we were dropped into Saigon's Cholon area, where the Tet Offensive of May had heated up. House-to-house fighting would be the procedure for a successful mission, then back to the jungle and swamps, back to the regular routine ... with no rest in between.

That is pretty much what one full day was like, day after day, night after night. One full year of total discomfort, horror, uncertainty, and sorrow ... equivalent to ten or twenty years in real life back home. And I have stayed away from the gore of battle in this book!

Napalm ... For Lunch?

You smell that? Do you smell that? Napalm, son. Nothing else in the world smells like that. I love the smell of napalm in the morning.
                                    - Robert Duvall
                                    Apocalypse Now (1979)

Cool movie in some ways. A bit far-fetched in other ways. Most people remember that specific phrase referencing the smell of napalm in the morning. Unfortunately, if you were close enough to fresh napalm to smell it, you were close enough to die from it ... <u>fact</u>.

"Napalm burns are the most terrible pain you can imagine," said Kim Phuc. She was the naked Vietnamese child in the June 1972 photo that many Americans who watched the Vietnam War happening on TV seem to remember most when the subjects of napalm or Vietnam are mentioned. With the help of our buddies in the media, that day was connected with the American military. **There were no Americans involved with that incident near Trang Bang in III Corp that day!**

Sometime in May or June 1968, the 1st and 2nd Platoons of Bravo were combat assaulted (from where I can't remember) to some place in the Michelin rubber plantation just a few miles outside of our outpost, Dau Tieng. Our recon intelligence had reported a large and quite active congregation of VC in the area, and one of our sister companies had been ambushed with severe casualties in this same area a couple of days earlier. By this time, the VC movement was detected before they could ambush anyone, and we were on our way there by choppers to block their advance.

During our combat assault flight to be dropped into the Michelin's thick woods, which was also near the dreaded Iron Triangle VC hotbed, the powers that be back at 3rd Brigade headquarters made the call to hit the advancing VC with napalm!

Napalm will find you, even if the targets are dug in, as it flows into holes, bunkers, and ditches. But these VC were not dug in; they were on the move with a mission. This was just an ordinary day for us, as doing combat assaults into suspected enemy havens was the norm for us during these months, later to be coined as Tet II.

These VC never had a chance. It was impossible to get an accurate body count based on what was left of them. Napalm can kill a man in a variety of ways or all of them, such as fourth- and fifth-degree burns, suffocation, smoke exposure, hyperthermia/heat stroke, dehydration, carbon monoxide poisoning, asphyxiation, unconsciousness, and unbearable pain before death.

If one survives a napalming, he or she could suffer from the following after-effects: damage to the nervous system, horrible scars called keloids, and cancer.

The vegetation was still burning, and of course, the ground was still hot by the time we were delivered and dropped into the intended battle zone. **MAJOR PROBLEM!**

I was walking "point" that day, so the burning in my eyes and my mouth probably hit me first, but I think we all started coughing and choking together. I can still remember Jenner saying, "Holy f——, it's napalm!" Platoon Sergeant Maines yelled at all of us to hit it and cover our faces with our towels. (We always had a towel.) There was nothing else we could do—the napalm fumes had engulfed us completely. I can still feel the burn we felt that day. Good thing there were no live VC left to ambush us—they were all wasted, and I mean literally wasted.

We lay there for maybe a half hour with our dirty, mangy, rotted towels covering our eyes, noses, and mouths. Our hands and necks still felt the burning sensation, but it was just napalm fumes, and we would all be okay except for a few incidents of nausea.

Napalm was a treacherous weapon. At first, we used it mainly to destroy vegetation, but it soon became a primary weapon against a determined enemy. The NVA used napalm with handheld flamethrowers, like in Korea and WWII, but they used it to destroy entire villages of innocent civilians ... to which the Ameri-Cong media rarely, if ever, gave any attention. Later in the war, after America had left Vietnam, the NVA used napalm throwers from their Russian-donated tanks.

What does napalm smell like? Stick your nose into your auto's fuel tank for at least ten to fifteen minutes to get a good dose of it. That would be a close comparison, and if you are lucky, you may not get dizzy enough to pass out. I think a couple of our guys passed out on that day in the napalmed Michelin woods. We sure had a full load checking in to sickbay that day.

The afternoon ended the way it started. We were picked up and combat assaulted to our next destination, which would be very close to the Cambodian border, where more enemy activity was reported.

Day after day, week after week, for months and months, this was life in Nam. And day after day, every week, every month, for the remainder of the Vietnam War, our battles with the enemy and the environment would be covered by the biased left-wing media and sent back to Americans, but NOT as the events actually happened.

We, the soldiers who lived the experience of this ghastly nightmare called the Vietnam War, were being forgotten as the news sent back home was almost always distorted with atrocities, burning villages, and napalmed women and children, and the American soldier was portrayed as the villain.

Some of the books that were written about the Vietnam War were written by unqualified individuals. Oh, they certainly had the credentials to write "a book" as they were scholarly individuals. Some of them were even Vietnam veterans. Those who were based in places like Saigon or Cam Ranh Bay were just writing about what the biased media was reporting. Get the picture?

Coverage of the war in some written books was authored by professional historians, but they were not "real" Vietnam combat veterans. Who knows? Along with all the damage done to us by Agent Orange, I wonder if Vietnam combat veterans have experienced any after-effects from **napalm for lunch**.

What Were We Paid to Do This?

On May 6, 1968, the announcement came from Washington that a new pay rate increase was expected to go into effect on July 1, 1968. This new monthly raise would bring a $6.60 monthly increase for active duty recruits just entering the U.S. Army. Therefore, the new private E-1 base pay went from **$95.70 to $102.30 PER MONTH! We were there for the money, right?**

Our Sister Battalions in Action ...

February 1968
Tan Son Nhut Air Base was in danger of being overrun by several hundred Viet Cong, who were also fighting from Tan Son Nhut village's houses near the strategic airfield. The 25th Infantry's 3rd Squadron, 4th Cav, and ground troops from the 2nd BN, 27th Infantry Wolfhounds fought the VC from house to house until every enemy invader was destroyed or escaped through their extensive tunnel system. Several U.S. Army and Air Force vehicles were destroyed or damaged by the enemy anti-tank rockets. This battle was continued in an assault by the enemy's North Vietnamese 5th Army Division, but they were also overcome. Enemy KIAs estimated at 150.

April 1968
The 1st Brigade, 4th Battalion, 9th Infantry Manchus encountered multiple Viet Cong units approximately eight kilometers north of Saigon. They had to fight the enemy in such close quarters in between villages that neither artillery nor airstrikes could be called in. This battle was fought in swampy mud for two to three days. Snipers were everywhere: trees, village hooches, bunkers, sugarcane fields, rice paddies. Several infantry groups had to be combat assaulted into the area. This was a two-day battle, which found 169 enemy bodies when it ended.

May 15, 1968
The 3rd Squadron, 4th Cavalry pulled a reversal on a would-be ambush by Viet Cong's 7th Battalion in the Ho Bo Woods region near Trang Bang. Over 100 enemy bodies were found.

May 27, 1968
The 4th BN Mechanized, 23rd Infantry, and the 3rd Squadron, 4th Cavalry stopped a major attack of several Viet Cong battalions just two kilometers outside of Saigon's city limits. This was a major assault on Saigon that could have produced mass chaos and destruction in the capital city. With the help of accurate artillery and air attacks, the onslaught was halted just in time. Approximate enemy killed was reported at 218.

May 6, 1968
The 2nd BN, 27th Infantry Wolfhounds ended a fifty-nine-day vacation in the bush and received a well-deserved five-day rest in Cu Chi. Some of their activity included these accomplishments:

- 382 Viet Cong killed
- 576 enemy bunkers destroyed
- hundreds of small arms captured
- 42,000 rounds of ammo captured
- 17 tons of rice/salt captured
- 100 rockets/mortars captured

The Wolfhounds' main area of operation during those fifty-nine days in the field ranged from outside Tan Son Nhut Air Base to Hoc Mon.

25th Rangers and Recon Soldiers

It seems as though whenever I engage in a conversation with a non-military person about special forces or elite combat troops, they will automatically mention Green Berets and, of course, Navy SEALs due to their recent fame in the Middle East wars. Every so often someone mentions the U.S. Army Rangers. Thank goodness, how deserving.

We would run into Rangers/LRRPs (or LRPs) every so often when we would work out of the same fire support base out in the field. They always intrigued me with their tiger-striped fatigues and the fact that some of them preferred an M-14 over an M-16.

Under normal circumstances, you had to graduate from Ranger school in order to be a LRRP or LRP (Long Range Recon Patrol or Long Range

Patrol). But the Vietnam War was different. Special guys could volunteer, and since there weren't very many volunteers, chances were better than average that you would be accepted. I thought about it once or twice, but I had all I could handle as a basic grunt.

Actually, one of those "what do I want to be when I grow up" things was becoming an Army Ranger. Ever since learning about Major Robert Rogers and his Rogers' Rangers in the French and Indian War and later, in the American Revolutionary War, they have been on my radar.

Trust me on this, I have the highest respect and admiration for our Rangers Recon Patrol and Green Berets, but it always amazed me that their fatigues looked fresh and their boots (though a little worn) were polished. On the other hand, my brothers and I always looked like GRUNTS.

Our Rangers/LRPs went on patrols that usually lasted six to ten days. They were as far away from us as they could get. They would be flown to a drop-off site in helicopters and then hump for a few hundred clicks to gather information—information that might be able to save our lives.

Jungle Sweep – June 1968

We were truly brothers.

Firefight at Trang Bang

Hunziker, 1st Platoon – Oklahoma

Washing in Agent Orange

Rainy Season (Monsoon) – 1968

Our buddy, the Claymore

Join LRRP?

This was a request printed in the 25th Infantry's newspaper called *Tropic Lightning News*:

If you can lie still in grass for a couple hours with 12-50 Viet Cong less than 50 feet from you without giving your presence away, then call the Leap Frog switchboard as the LRRPs are looking for men like you.

You will train long and hard, physically and mentally. You will learn to detect hidden booby traps, disarm them, and learn how to assemble your own traps.

Infantryman, Ranger, Airborne, or Recon training preferred. However, men without such special training can be accepted and trained.

Volunteers will be accepted on a two-week attachment. If you do not meet the stiff qualifications required, you will be returned to your original unit.

Actually, most combat infantrymen became proficient at performing reconnaissance for the 3rd Battalion, 22nd Infantry if they lived long enough. One night, Smokey, George, and I sat down with a couple of LRPs at a fire support base and had a few warm (almost hot) Blatz beers together. One of the topics in our conversation as I kind of remember it went like this:

We said, "We know LRPs/Rangers do reconnaissance deep into enemy-held territory with only six to ten men. You move by night—when Charley is also moving. We know that our life expectancy as infantry grunts is not very high, but how about you guys?"

One LRP answered like this: "We have no life expectancy. The VC know we are different and that we are spies. Sometimes they offer a bounty for killing us—higher bounty for capturing one of us."

NO LIFE EXPECTANCY … how would you like a job that offered you a future like that?! A few more warm beers and we were becoming old friends. Then one of the Ranger/LRPs asked us how long we usually stay out in the bush without a secure fire support base to which to return. Remember, the Ranger/LRP's goal for a successful mission was not to engage the enemy. The goal of a combat infantryman was to SEARCH AND DESTROY! Our answer froze them. Their mouths opened wide and their jaws dropped when they heard our answer … **"Oh, usually thirty to forty days straight." But our record for the 25th Division remained intact till the war's end at <u>eighty-eight days</u>!**
We loved our Rangers and Recon guys, but they would never trade their job for ours, and most of us would trade with them in a heartbeat—those who were qualified.

Those Amazing Seabees!

I just couldn't put out a book about Vietnam's veterans without some mention of those "Fighting" Seabees—made famous by the John Wayne movie. Personally, I did not fight with any Navy Seabees. In fact, I'm not sure if I ever met one. We had our own combat engineers who built things.

Two of my Nam brothers back in Ohio were Seabees in Nam. Billy Mac-Donald, whom I have known since my earliest years in Twinsburg at age thirteen, and J.R., whom I've become a comrade with through another Vietnam brother, Rich "Rambo" Loska, who served with the 4th Infantry Division.

The stories from Mac and J.R. about what the Seabees accomplished in Vietnam have been impressive, but just like my experiences, they have more than a fair share of horrible memories that still haunt them.

Oh sure, the Seabees built roads, hospitals, airfields, base camps, and bridges. They also rebuilt schools and villages, and they helped to win the hearts of the Vietnamese people, which was a powerful weapon against the Viet Cong, who killed their own countrymen and destroyed their villages.

Our American Seabees left a legacy in Vietnam that few other American combat veterans were able to. They taught the South Vietnamese how to build, and God knows they had a monstrous task of reconstruction before them after the war ended.

When the 1954 Geneva agreements recognized a North Vietnam communist country and a democratic South Vietnam, our Seabees were sent to help, as there was a mass exodus of the North Vietnamese populace emigrating to the south. This was called "Passage to Freedom." Reception centers were set up throughout South Vietnam to accommodate the exodus of one million North Vietnamese by building huge refugee camps, and our Seabees were elected. Remember, this was 1954!
(Source: www.history.navy.mil)

During the Vietnam War's early years when our Army Green Berets were being sent over as advisors to Vietnamese military, the access roads and airstrips were built by the Seabees—who else?

Yes, they were builders all right. But they had to fight too ... this was Vietnam, not Florida. There was a huge battle in 1965 at a Special Forces camp just fifty miles outside of Saigon where the Viet Cong overran over 400 defenders. Casualties were high. A fighting Seabee named Marvin Shields earned the Medal of Honor from that battle posthumously, unfortunately. The story told was that he destroyed an enemy machine gun bunker and carried severely wounded comrades to safety before losing his life.

Mac and J.R. rarely engage in Nam talk, but when they do, it is worth one's time to pay close attention. It won't happen around non-Vietnam veterans, and that's pretty much my rule as well—with very few exceptions.

I know that the Seabees mostly worked in remote areas of the I Corp Zone in 1965 or so. Before the war had ended, they would have left their mark from the Mekong to Cambodia's borders to the east coast to the DMZ. Those 20,000 to 30,000 "Fighting" Seabees were generously shared across the entire country.

If you ever run into someone who served as a Seabee—in any war—I guarantee you will have met a proud Seabee … if he is a *real* Seabee.

J.R. and Mac told me how they often worked with the Marines, and I'm sure the Marines were glad to have them by their side. Places like Chu Lai, Phu Bai, Hue, and, of course, Danang are mentioned often. I wish that I could add more to this part, but Mac and J.R. have difficulty talking about their experience over there. I understand and I respect that. I took the liberty of inserting this small blurb about the "Fighting" Seabees on my own. I'll probably hear about it from both of them when they see this book, but they'll get over it.

They Fought Too … 25th Combat Engineers

Some would say their jobs were to build things, tear down things, and blow up things. They were shot at too, and they shot back. Thus the name "combat engineer." The accomplishments of America's combat engineers in Vietnam are too numerous to cover in this short story. Just like the Navy Seabees, the Army and Marine combat engineers' total contribution to the Vietnam War was superb.

I had the honor of "walking point" on several occasions while our combat engineers were sweeping secondary roads ahead of our tanks and armored personnel carriers. I had the pleasure of watching them blow up tunnel entrances and enemy bunkers and build bridges, and I had the distinction of fighting side by side with them during ambushes.

When the Tet Offensive of 1968 heated up, combat engineers and Seabees were forced into more direct combat with enemy forces as most combat infantry units were spread thinly on massive search-and-destroy assaults. More than once, the 554th Engineers Battalion hooked up with the 3rd 22nd and 3/4 Cav Armor Unit and fought together in overwhelming victories against the enemy. What I remember best about the 554th Engineers from hearing about them, as an eyewitness, and reading about them are things like this:

Recon lookout

- Infantrymen of the 3rd 22nd Infantry and 554th Engineers teamed up on a sweep through the HoBo Woods and destroyed a decades-old sanctuary for the Viet Cong.

- ARVNs, 25th infantrymen and engineers from the 554th combined to destroy a ten-year-old Viet Cong haven in Trang Bang.

- 554th Engineers completely resurfaced Vietnam's Highway 19. In order for this valuable project to be completed ASAP, we the infantrymen had to keep ambushers away from the construction project.

- In November 1968, our own U.S. Army's 554th Engineers teamed up with ARVN engineers to construct a replacement bridge across the Saigon River, where it was nearly a football field's length across.

- The Phu Cuong Bridge itself, which we had protected earlier in the year, had been partially destroyed by Viet Cong sappers. It took the 554th and the ARVNs approximately one full day to complete this critically important project. Actually, several engineer units teamed up that day.

- A tiny Vietnamese eleven-month-old child was saved by a surgeon of the 554th Engineers.

- 554th Engineers hosted a Christmas party for 250 Vietnamese children, ages ranging from just two years to sixteen years. Steak dinners were provided with ice cream for dessert. The ice cream was far more popular. At the end, Santa Claus handed out presents.

Things like this were going on in the Vietnam War while Americans were protesting our presence over there, and while people like Hanoi Jane Fonda and Hanoi John Kerry were doing their best to discredit American soldiers in the line of fire. Go figure!

Chapter 4

BRAVO COMPANY 3rd 22nd REGULARS

In the fall of 1966, the 3rd Battalion, 22nd Infantry left Fort Lewis by sea for the country of Vietnam. A place called Vung Tau was the initial landing place, but not for long, as Cu Chi was the next destination. Dau Tieng followed and Tay Ninh was our last base camp of operation.

Earlier in the book, I mentioned that the 3rd 22nd was in heavy contact with the enemy, especially in 1967 and 1968, where the unit earned a reputation that spread across Vietnam. Very few combat units that fought in the Vietnam War at any time would experience as much direct contact and inflict as many casualties to the enemy as the 25th Infantry's 3rd 22nd Regulars did. Unfortunately, the same held true for their own casualties.

When I first touched the shores of Vietnam, I heard about two of the battles—Soui Tre and Soui Cut—fought by the Regulars (2nd 22nd and 3rd 22nd) along the Cambodian border. Over 1,000 enemy died and over 400 American casualties were suffered in just those two single night battles. The horrors of those battles became legendary to all 25th Infantry combat soldiers, and the battles grew in size and horror as the bloody years of 1968 and 1969 came. Every time there was an enemy ambush, many of us were scared out of our wits that we could be in for another Soui Tre or Soui Cut, and you just never knew if you would survive one of those ordeals.

During the bloodiest year for every combat soldier in Vietnam—1968—the 3rd 22nd ended up being one of the most highly decorated units of the entire Vietnam War. Here is an article from the *Tropic Lightning News*, the 25th Infantry's official newspaper:

Regulars' 1968 Record Reveals Host of Honors, Valor Awards

In September of 1966, the 3rd Battalion, 22nd Infantry set sail from Ft. Lewis to the shores of Vietnam. Shortly after landing at the present R&R center of Vung Tau, the 3/22, under the operational control of the 25th Infantry Division, took part in operations Bremerton, Attleboro, and Cedar Falls, driving the Viet Cong out of War Zone C, and keeping a constant surveillance on the old Viet Cong stronghold. During 1967, the 3/22 took part in numerous campaigns and battles, notably, Operation Junction City, which includes the largest single-day battle of the Vietnamese War, Soui Tre, where 640 Viet Cong and North Vietnamese were killed in an abortive attempt to overrun the 3/22 perimeter at Fire Support Base Gold.

Few combat units that fought in the Vietnam War experienced as much contact with the enemy during the peak years of this war (1967–1969) as the 25th Infantry's 3rd 22nd Regulars did … fortunately or unfortunately. Here is a brief recap about some of the encounters between the communist terrorists and Tropic Lightning's Regulars, and again, this is a "brief" recap.

DAU TIENG – During the bloodbath year of 1968, the 3d Battalion, 22d Infantry has proved to be one of the most decorated units in the Vietnam War.

Since the middle of March 1968, the Regulars have been awarded 52 Silver Stars, four Distinguished Service Crosses, more than a hundred Bronze Stars for valor, and more than 150 Army Commendation Medals for valor.

Colonel Lewis J. Ashley, commander of the 3d Brigade, has heaped praise on the battalion's awards and decorations section.

"The 3d of the 22d deserves the high number of awards they are receiving. Since the beginning of this year the battalion has borne a large part of the fighting burden in our area of operations and has done outstanding work," said Ashley.

Third Brigade Records Another Bountiful Year

January 3, 1969 (From 25th Division Yearbook)
DAU TIENG – The 3d Brigade has drawn the curtain on a year in which the Tropic Lightning infantrymen killed more than 4,200 enemy in 1968.

In 12 months of fighting which ranged from the streets of Saigon to the jungles of War Zone C the brigade captured more than 426,000 lbs. of rice, countless weapons and ammunition.

The year was highlighted by counterpunches at Soui Cut, where more than 350 enemy died in a single night; near Saigon in the enemy's abortive Tet offensive; around Trang Bang and Tay Ninh City during the enemy thrusts in May and August, and in the area near Dau Tieng base camp during the closing months of the year.

As the year began, the brigade's forces were positioned in Fire Support Base Burt, on the Soui Cut, a small stream 60 miles northwest of Saigon.

In the second largest single day of action of the entire Vietnam War, forces of the 2d Battalion (Mech), 22d Infantry and 3d Battalion, 22nd Infantry dealt death on enemy human waves hurling themselves out of the jungle on the night following New Year's Day.

Aided by guns of the 2d Battalion, 77th Artillery, helicopter gunships and tactical air strikes the infantrymen killed 382 enemy.

During the days following Tet, the brigade's forces were split between the areas around Dau Tieng and Saigon.

While the 2d Battalion (Mechanized), 22d Infantry Triple Deuce ranged Dau Tieng to Trang Bang in road sweeps and combat operations, the brigade's other two battalions fought in areas between Cu Chi and Saigon.

In fierce fighting less than 10 miles from Saigon and in Cholon, infantrymen of the 2d Battalion, 12th Infantry and 3d Battalion, 22d Infantry, dealt with enemy in house to house fighting and in battles across rice paddies.

In March – saw the end of Operation Saratoga and the end of tri-brigade action between the Saigon River and Cu Chi. Two hundred forty three (243) enemy died in the first week. The 3d/22d took to the water north of Cu Chi and eliminated 100 enemy. Then they swept from west of Saigon to Cambodia, into the long time communist stronghold … the always dangerous Hobo Woods.

In April, Regulars of the 3d of the 22d, backed by the Triple Deuce, killed 137 enemy in a night battle near the edge of war Zone C.

April's pace continued with the arrival of Operation Quyet Thang. In some of the most bitter fighting since the January-February Tet Offensive, 25th Division elements and ARVN forces teamed up to kill 470 enemy in one week near Highway One district, stopping an NVA offensive against Saigon.

Directly after the "Battle of Good Friday," April 12, 1968, the 1ˢᵗ Platoon was reorganized. Area of Operations started around Dau Tieng, which was also our Base Camp. During the next three months, the A.O. expanded. First Platoon remained out in the jungle for an astounding 63-day operation. These actions included many sweeps, search and destroy missions, ambushes and many combat assaults by chopper. Oh! Yes, we remember the red ants, flies, mosquitoes, leeches, mud, rain, and dysentery. Ha! Yes, the good C-rats! Despite adverse conditions, the 1ˢᵗ Platoon held up remarkably and encountered and repelled the enemy "Charlie."

As the enemy tried yet another offensive in May, Tropic Lightning organized a Task Force, bringing numerous units of the Division under operational control of the 3d Brigade.

May saw the second Saigon Offensive begin. A task force of infantry and armored cavalry killed 134 NVA in a two-day battle, 10 kilometers from downtown Saigon. Then, just eight kilometers south of Cu Chi, four battalions of infantry and one armored Cavalry troop backed an NVA battalion to a swamp and decimated them … killing over 350 NVA in just three days.

Another NVA battalion lost 220 killed, attempting to get away from the 25ᵗʰ Division's Task Force.

In 13 days the Task Force killed more than 800 enemy in sweeps ranging from Hoc Mon and the Saigon area toward Tay Ninh City. In all, the force accounted for more than 1,200 enemy killed.

*August will always be remembered as the month the NVA launched massive human wave attacks near Dau Tieng and Tay Ninh. At Fire Support Base (FSB) Buel an estimated regiment sized force attacked the 25ᵗʰ Infantry's 3d brigade troops during the last week of August. **That week nearly 1,000 enemy NVA were killed.***

At the conclusion of the summer operations the brigade held the enviable record of not allowing a single enemy rocket or mortar round to be fired from its area of responsibility. Earlier the area has been notorious as part of the enemy rocket belt.

With its return to Dau Tieng near the edge of war Zone C, 45 miles northwest of Saigon, the brigade concentrated on thrusts into the Boi Loi Woods.

In June, near Cu Chi, over 134 VC were killed in two single day battles near Trang Bang. Third Brigade uncovered "tons" of enemy mortars and rockets. June ended with the 3d/22d Infantry killing 70 NVA just 12 kilometers north of Saigon.

After the brief stint around Cu Chi, Base Camp on Bridge Security, the 1ˢᵗ Platoon of the 3/22ⁿᵈ moved their Base Camp to Tay Ninh. The Platoon was then beefed up with replacements and sent out to find "Charlie."

Many encounters ensued with the enemy, but the 1ˢᵗ Platoon was not to be dishonored with whatever they did. The 1ˢᵗ Platoon made over 100 combat assaults. We remained in Tay Ninh Province until we left to go back to the "real" world.

While on OP's, 1ˢᵗ Platoon covered places like the Iron Triangle, Boi Loi Woods, HoBo Woods, HocMon, "The Catholic Village", Trang Bang, Cholon, The Pineapple Delta, Phu Cuong, Michelin Rubber Trees, Nui Bau Den,"The Black Virgin Mt.", FSB Buell, Rawlings, Mitchell's and Cambodia.

Does Everyone in Nam Get a Bronze Star?!

On Memorial Day of 2007, I put on a dress green uniform, loaded it with my medals, and marched with a local VFW/American Legion-sponsored Memorial Day parade. This was the first time that I had put on a uniform or displayed my medals in a public fashion since the day I came home from Fort Hood in the fall of 1969.

Please take note of the fact that I had to explore about a dozen different Army/Navy stores in several different states before I could hook up with a pair of U.S. Army trousers and a dress jacket that I could fit into! Weighing a svelte 165 pounds in 1969 versus 195 pounds in 2007 (more now) was quite an awakening for me when I tried on a few remnant uniforms.

I wanted to and had intended to participate in a formal parade before that, especially when John Kerry opted to run for President. In fact, since I had dug up those medals from a box in the closet, I decided to post them on my wall in my office, where there was very little public traffic. One day, a UPS man walked into my office and he made the following comment about my medals to my secretary: "Whose medals? Was he in Vietnam?" My secretary replied yes, of course. Then he said, **"Well I was there too. I wasn't in combat, but I see a Bronze Star of Valor there. I understand that they gave those out quite generously."** When I was told that, I thought about what a cheap shot it was. I wasn't showcasing my medals to anyone. In fact, one had to walk around a corner into my office to view them on the wall next to my desk. This wasn't an issue for me, but it was to one of my other Vietnam combat vet brothers, and he told me this: "Dusty, you earned the right to display those medals, and you should do so proudly. Oh, by the way, here are some facts you can share with that UPS driver next time you see him—if you choose to address him."

In the entire Vietnam War, where approximately 3,000,000 men and women from the USA served, here are the numbers of Bronze Stars that were awarded:

★ Bronze Star – Achievement/Service	28,474
★ Bronze Star – Valor	6,215
TOTAL:	34,689

Even my math tells me that if just 6,215 Bronze Stars for Valor were awarded during an eleven-year war where approximately 3,000,000 troops had served, every Bronze Star recipient, whether for Valor, Achievement, or Service, should be awfully proud to have earned one of them. **So I think I'll keep my medals posted on my wall till the day they bury me. And so should everyone else!**

South Koreans – June 1968

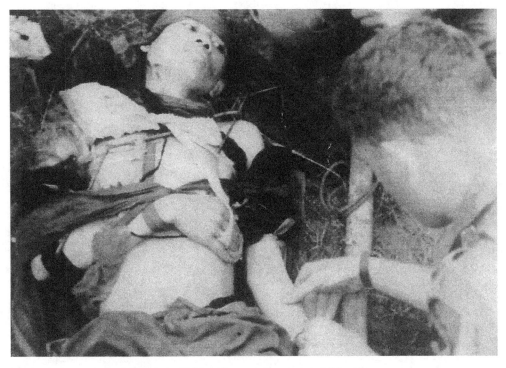

Wounded VC—Our medics helped them too.

South Vietnam Rangers (I think)

South Vietnamese Army – August 1968

The Heavy Shit!

March 21, 1967   Soui Tre (One-Day Battle)

| - Communist Casualties | 647 Dead | 1,200 – 1,800 Wounded |
| ★ American Casualties | 31 Dead | 187 Wounded |

(Vietnam War's largest one-day battle)

The Mother of Battles ... Soui Tre

March 21, 1967

Fire Support Base Gold, also the battle of Soui Tre ... a brief recap as told by members of Bravo Company 3rd 22nd:

Since Vietnam, March has always been a tough month for me to get through. Forty-six years ago, my life changed forever, just as it did for a lot of guys.

- Ted Rowley
Chaplain, Bravo Company

The battle of Soui Tre lasted "just" four hours, fifteen minutes, but it turned out to be the most intensely sustained fighting of the Vietnam War up to that day. There were approximately 450 American and South Vietnamese soldiers present that day, about forty percent or so of them comprising Bravo Regulars, 3rd Battalion/22nd Infantry 25th Infantry Division.

The enemy force would be approximately 2,500 seasoned professionals from the Viet Cong Army who were "dug in" and waiting to pull a surprise ambush on our guys. It has been said that a VC spy had learned of the position of the 25th Infantry units at Soui Tre, and the encounter was unavoidable.

The Battle of Soui Tre began at approximately 6:30 a.m. The VC sent wave after wave, storming the compound on two sides. The howitzers were leveled to fire horizontally, loaded with canisters of thousands of pellets, fired point-blank at the masses of Viet Cong. As one Mario Salazar wrote, "As our unit, the 2nd 22nd Mechanized reached the 3rd 22nd positions, the scene that they witnessed was worthy of an outrageous Hollywood set." So indeed, the movie *Platoon* was based on a composite of this battle and a later battle at Soui Cut, also fought by the 25th Infantry's 3rd 22nd.

When the 2nd 22nd arrived, Bravo of the 3rd 22nd was virtually out of ammunition and bayonets became active. It was like the cavalry in a western movie, riding in to rescue the encircled wagon train.

A total of 678 men died during the four-hour battle of Soui Tre, an average of nearly 170 per hour. The units that fought at Soui Tre were awarded the prestigious Presidential Unit Citation, the highest honor a unit can receive, comparable to a collective Medal of Honor.

So many who fought at Soui Tre and survived it have passed away prematurely since coming home. The battle of Soui Tre, Oliver Stone's *Platoon* … that was the Nam.

January 2, 1968   Soui Cut (One-Day Battle)

- Communist Casualties	401 Dead	1,000 – 1,200 Wounded
★ American Casualties	23 Dead	153 Wounded

(Vietnam War's second largest one-day battle)

April 11, 1968   Battle of Good Friday (One-Day Battle)

- Communist Casualties	206 Dead	500 - 700 Wounded
★ American Casualties	16 Dead	47 Wounded

Total Casualties: 4,411 – 5,174 in three battles

The above-mentioned battles were the BIG THREE for the 3rd 22nd 25th Infantry up till then. However, the next several months in 1968 would prove to be the bloodiest of the entire Vietnam War, with III Corp receiving the brunt of enemy attacks as the NVA's main focus had shifted away from the northern provinces—with Saigon on their mind.

The battle at the ARVN Compound (as my letter to Rick and Frank mentioned earlier) was a startling and stressful introduction to Nam for us new guys. Surely we would be given a badly needed rest after that … or so we thought.

About the same time our battle was going on, just a few miles away at 4:00 a.m. or so on April 11, 1968—Good Friday—the 3rd Battalion, 22nd Infantry Regulars of the 25th Infantry Division were being bombarded by an unknown number of mortar and rocket rounds. As the intensity of the attack increased, a human wave attack of several thousand North Vietnamese and Viet Cong swarmed toward the 3rd 22nd perimeter.

The Bravo Company sector received the main brunt of the attack, and the situation looked bleak for them in the early going. It became impossible for Bravo Company to hold their position as the intensity of the human wave attack got worse.

Later in the day, a recon platoon reinforced Bravo Company, and they were able to retake their original positions and stand their ground until more reinforcements arrived from their sister unit, the 2nd Battalion, 22nd Infantry Mech. Unit. They had worked their way through approximately six kilometers of pure jungle to reinforce their brothers of the 3rd, 22nd Infantry.

Together, the 3rd 22nd and 2nd 22nd fought off the communist attackers. Sixteen Americans lost their lives that day and forty-seven were wounded; most of the casualties were inflicted upon Bravo and Charley companies. The 1st Platoon of Bravo was decimated with casualties. They had just three or four sound bodies left. Replacements were needed ASAP!

The next day the news came. Several of us were being transferred to Bravo Company of the 3rd 22nd Infantry immediately. That very night we were given no rest. We were sent out on patrol to search for the enemy at night, and unfortunately, they found us first. They ambushed us with small arms and a .51 caliber machine gun. A .51 caliber round could rip palm trees in half. It was another long, long night for our new unit and us new guys.

Almost instantly, we new guys became veterans of war … and our indoctrination would not be getting easier any time soon.

For days and weeks after, we heard the stories from our new brothers about the Battle of Good Friday. It remained a terrifying experience for them—and as I now can relate, it remained with them for the rest of their lives.

Some of them had also been at the Battle of Soui Cut, which was even worse than the Good Friday Battle near Ap Cho in terms of casualties on both sides. *No one* who has never been in these situations can possibly comprehend the experience or the long-lasting trauma afterward … no one.

Richard Beck, Don Pringle, Paul Gipson, and Bobby Best were there. We could see the horror in their eyes every time they told us their stories about Friday the 13th. All four would become a casualty before their tour ended … one dead, three wounded.

Toan Thang I

The 25th Infantry was the driving force in the multi-division campaign, which lasted about two months from April 12th to May 31st. Toan Thang I was the largest operation in terms of total troops which the Vietnam War had known. Toan Thang I included U.S., Vietnamese, Australian, South Korean, and

Thailand armed forces. My buddies and I met many of them, particularly in Saigon's Cholon district, where the "Mini-Tet" offensive would take place in May.

No Tropic Lightning campaign has more dramatically demonstrated how we were going to take this war smack into the enemy's backyard than Toan Thang I. One moment we probed the triple-canopied areas of War Zone C. The next moment we were guarding Tan Son Nhut Air Base. Or we would be combat assaulted to the extensive Michelin rubber plantation. Moments later on the same day, we would be fighting our way across rice paddies and pineapple swamps.

Toan Thang I brought 3,542 communist soldiers to their death by the 25th Infantry Division alone ... and we were just warming up.
(Source: *25th Infantry History Book*)

Toan Thang II

June 1, 1968 begins ... It's not like we could tell the difference between Toan Thang I and Toan Thang II as one operation was the same as the other with a different name, in our minds.

At this point, I cannot begin to describe our state of mind. Just a couple of months ago we were writing letters to our loved ones back home. We talked often amongst ourselves about how we would all get together back in the States—ALL of us—and our friendships would last forever. So we thought.

In June 1968, just over three months after landing in Cam Ranh Bay, South Vietnam, we had slowed down in writing letters to home, as we no longer had any positive news to report. You could just say that we weren't motivated anymore. In fact, many of us seemed to have lost the will to survive—or we just stopped believing we were going to make it. Even I was getting there and didn't know it.

I walked "point" most of the time during the Toan Thang Operations. Because I wanted to. In fact, one of our second lieutenants insisted that only I walk point for him—that was fine with me, just fine.

It was late in May or early June, so I don't know if this happened during Toan Thang I or II ... We were camped in the Boi Loi Woods when our perimeter was starting to be probed. First we heard the Viet Cong talking to themselves—or they were talking to us, I am not sure. Didn't have time to sort it out ... First the mortars and rockets came, followed by a good old-fashioned "human wave" onslaught.

Nothing fancy about this attack—we fought it off, took a few casualties. We killed enough of the enemy to send them off into the night ... surely to return another day.

Of course, there would be no sleeping that night. We were all too scared to sleep. When morning came, and this is what I remember most about this particular battle, many of the dead were not VC, not NVAs. **They were CHINESE!**

Like we really needed to add Chinese Regulars into our worry equation, and believe it—we did add that fear into our minds. All of us did for the rest of our tour in Nam.

June and July were quieter months for most combat units—no sirree, not the 3rd 22nd Regulars. We traveled from Dau Tieng to Saigon to Cu Chi to Go Dau Ha to Hoc Mon to Tay Ninh, often touching the Cambodian border. We might as well have been called Airborne Regulars because we flew over 100 combat assaults or eagle flights during May, June, and July.

AMBUSHED ... Take Cover ... DIE?

Almost been there ... almost. Ever since I've been back from Vietnam, I've pretty much been a living example of an "accident waiting to happen" as I have seemingly walked into one physical mishap after another almost blindly ... or maybe intentionally?

People closely associated with me often wonder how I could have been successful at what I did in the Vietnam War. I was trained to be prepared, brainwashed into being alert and on guard at all times over there—twenty-four/seven for nearly a full year. I did not let my war buddies down over there, but the nonstop stress has affected many of us to this day. Even though I am still very vigilant, I can't react and respond like I did in Nam. But ... I remain vigilant just the same.

As anyone might be able to figure out, when one is ambushed, the ambusher usually enjoys a tactical advantage. They have the advantage geographically and they have the element of surprise in their favor. They just don't play fair in an ambush. The enemy doesn't give you the courtesy of an advanced warning of their intentions. No shit!

We were like cats in Vietnam, too dehydrated to be fat, too leery of every sound and movement to ever take our next step for granted. At least that is how I remember most of the 1st Platoon ... one very lean, mean, and vigilant T-E-A-M of damned good soldiers.

Walking point in the rubber plantations and jungle canopy around Dau Tieng, HoBo Woods, Boi Loi Woods, and the Iron Triangle did not allow us to smoke dope or fall to sleep on watch ... not ever, and I did neither on my tour. Viet Cong ambushes were worse than North Vietnamese ambushes. The VC rarely had the numbers that the North Vietnamese had, so the VC planned their ambushes, each and every one of them, as though it would be their last. Many times it was, but not always.

I don't know how anyone could have anticipated an ambush in the terrain we plowed through in Nam. We were told constantly to **Stop, Look, Listen**. Right. I'm swinging my machete at hummingbird speed for a short time— at least and for sure, every smart VC within 100 meters knows we are coming and when we will reach their **KILL ZONE!**

Still, we had to remain aware, vigilant, ever so observant of every leaf or bush that was moving ahead of us—while I slashed with the machete or walked head-on into an **AMBUSH**!

Every combat infantry unit was ambushed in Vietnam. It was part of the day—fortunately, not on most days. How you reacted or responded to the ambush would determine the outcome of your day … if you would see another day and another and another. **What a routine!**

When the 1st Platoon walked into an ambush at Hoc Mon in 1968, yeah, sure, we all hit the ground (mud) and took cover—for a few seconds. But instinct would save many lives. As I remember (barely), in the next few seconds, while the enemy's ambush was very much in progress, this happened …

- Haywood "George" Taylor and Don "Bug" Jenner advanced their position.
- I advanced my position over to the men who were the immediate casualties of the ambush.
- John "Babyson" Martino advanced his position up to the area I made it to, where wounded men were pinned down.
- Billy "Farmer" Loftis advanced his position.
- Others attempted to advance, but failed.

I believe that our instinct to advance our positions and **ATTACK THE ATTACKER** helped save many lives that day. Several members of the 2nd Platoon also advanced their positions and so the ambushers could not improve their tactical positions. The rest of that afternoon would become one big *blurrrrr* for me, and my platoon brothers would have to explain the details to me at the day's end, and the next day, and the next, and for several years later as well.

What we learned from getting ambushed was that as important as it was to keep your head down, it could be just as important to **COUNTER AMBUSH** and put your ambushers on the defensive. Easier said than done, of course. However, if we had not done the **COUNTER AMBUSH**, a lot of guys would get picked off one by one … and that was the enemy's plan.

Catholic Village, Hoc Mon Province

June 15, 1968

Bravo Company was on a recon mission in an area where Charley Company had been badly mauled in an ambush the day before. The setting was just another hot, humid day in the Nam, but the heat and humidity were enhanced substantially by the canals and pineapple swamps we were operating in that day. Man, it felt like 120° and 100 percent humidity. Heck, our jungle fatigues and our jungle boots were already rotting right off our bodies, and the Hoc Mon pineapple swamps just made it more uncomfortable.

Most of us were experiencing severe cases of the "creeping crud" or jungle rot. Okay … these were painful, itchy sores on our bodies caused in large part from what was being sprayed all around us from above … AGENT ORANGE. And the tropical vegetation it was sprayed over was rotting our bodies away.

The 1st Platoon was the lead platoon on this day, which I was part of. It seemed pretty quiet and then … all of a sudden, we were AMBUSHED and our left file point man was calling out, "Help me, help me, help me." I was talking to him from about thirty yards away when—don't ask me how or why—I jumped up (with bullets flying everywhere) and ran (kind of plodded as it was swampy) with my goal to reach Paris at the front of the second squad. John Martino (M-60 ammo bearer for the second squad) was already there, I believe, protecting Paris, but he could not move him alone.

Hey, no way am I talking hero stuff here. I just reacted or responded to a brother who was in need as so many American soldiers have done since the Revolutionary War. Anyway, when I reached Paris, he was understandably delirious, in shock, and pretty much out of his mind with pain. I think he had many bullet wounds. As I recall, his shoulder or ribs were exposed from the bullets. I don't know for sure as I was starting to freak out. I used all of my M-16 ammo, all of Paris' ammo, I threw my grenades, I threw Paris' grenades … and my M-16 jammed!

Well into the battle, I heard one of our guys cry out to me. I think it was Jenner, who we called Bug. George was out of ammo. He was our M-60 gunner for the 1st Platoon's 1st Squad. So … out of my mind with the situation Paris was in, I had two or three lines of M-60 ammo, and I ran (or plodded) back those thirty yards of swamp as the battle raged on … and dropped off the lines of M-60 ammo I had.

Oh crap! I had to run (plod) back to where Paris and Martino were, and by the way, there were seven more wounded soldiers pinned down in those godforsaken swamps behind Paris, and everyone was trying to get to them.

So … when I plodded over to drop the M-60 rounds to George and …

then ran (plodded) back in between bullets to where Paris was and the wounded guys were behind him, here is what Haywood (George of the Jungle) did: He stood up, exposing himself to enemy fire, and fired relentlessly at the enemy terrorists!

At least two of our guys tried to make it up to us to help Martino and me carry Paris back for a med-evac. We couldn't drag him on the ground; he had too many wounds—it would have killed him. The only way to keep him alive and get him to a med-evac chopper was to drag him through a canal—gently!

As I said, a couple guys tried to get to us, but never made it. Then a third man finally made it by crawling up a canal to Paris, Martino, and me. His name was Loftis. He was from North Carolina, as Paris was.

WHY ... WHY ... WHY ... were we here? Why were we even in this horrible situation? What purpose did it have?!

Martino, Loftis, and I dragged Paris very gently through a canal, sucking scum/swamp water for a short distance. Then Martino and Loftis finished the deed, along with other comrades who came up to help, while I had to scramble back to the forward position behind the cemetery stone and cover our asses to prevent an enemy charge. I looked down at my boots. My left foot was bleeding. (I would discover later that both feet were so badly infected with cellulitis that I would be hospitalized for over a week. But I walked on them until the day I fell to the ground, unable to walk another step!) Blood was also trickling down from my head, but I didn't feel any pain—NONE!

We still had guys back there, lying in the swamp, bleeding ... bleeding ... bleeding, moaning to get them out of there, and God only knows what was going through their minds. Would we ever get out of this place? Would we even live to see our families again?

The adrenaline was flowing with my brothers (who weren't dead or wounded), and it happened without any exchange of words. **We had to go back and get all of our wounded brothers ... We HAD to!**

We were doing a search-and-destroy mission this day, something we had done for countless days before, and I think we had become numbed by the day-after-day of this routine. And then all of a sudden ... **clack, clack, clack—the sound of AK-47s.** In seconds our left file, the second squad, went down as they took the brunt of the ambush.

To this day, I don't know how many casualties the 2nd Platoon took in coming to our aid. I just know that over half of the 1st Platoon was never seen after that day ... Casualties were heavy.

Okay, the battle was still on. This was a Viet Cong type of ambush, as North Vietnamese and Chinese Regulars like to just come right at you with a full human wave onslaught ... in your face, hand-to-hand.

Oh my God, the screaming, the crying from our guys from the second squad … it was unbearable, but we—the first squad of just thirteen or fourteen guys—were pinned down and couldn't do anything except protect ourselves and keep the enemy from advancing.

Crazy thoughts raced through my mind that day, while the firefight went on and on and on. Seemed like we were there for days—or so it seemed. Why were we even there, living like scum-sucking maggots? Was this where all of our lives would end on this day? I thought that and I dreaded it! But we fought on, hiding behind the cemetery stone, returning shots at invisible attackers, and tossing a grenade every so often.

At my far forward position, it was impossible to see all of the heroic acts that took place in evacuating every wounded man that day. Broussard, Best, Loftis, Martino—I think these four were the main guys who got the wounded out of there. After we moved Paris into the canal and the others carried him out of harm's way, I returned to the forward position behind the cemetery stone and stayed there until all the wounded were rescued.

Please understand, in a hotly contested battle for your life, everyone involved is going to remember what went on around his or her immediate position. Paying attention to anything else could end your life in seconds. My participation that day has been explained to me by others in the 1st squad of the 1st Platoon—George, Jenner, Smokey, Loftis, Martino, and Daniels—from what they can remember. My wife has heard it in their words.

It's hard, *very* hard, to describe events like this in a low-key manner. I did what had to be done. And I am grateful to God that I was able to perform. I guess that I am also grateful that the opportunity was offered to me.

And, while horrors like this were taking place everywhere in Nam, those who sent us here were living in pure luxury back in Washington, not caring about us—not in the least.

It was a nightmare. How long the whole event lasted, I really don't know, but I know it was too long, and it didn't make any sense—none!

While I was trying to run (plod) back to where Paris was, the many, many wounded behind him were crying for a medic. Our medic was hit trying to reach Paris, Martino, and me at the front of the battle; we never saw him again. I believe there was a sniper in a palm tree and someone nailed him when I was running (plodding) back to Paris.

The battle wasn't even halfway over. It seemed like we had been five or six hours into it by then. It could have been fifteen minutes—I just don't know. Did I mention that we were in a cemetery? Well, Paris, Martino, and I were actually lying behind a cemetery stone—that was our cover. (Martino still remembers what color it was.)

I wish there was a way to soften things up here, but I cannot. As I mentioned earlier, Paris had several wounds, and he was not mentally in control. He was in unbelievable pain—as were many of our brothers behind us. We had to get these guys back for med-evacuation.

Clack, clack, clack … all of a sudden my helmet flew off my head and I mean it flew—landing about ten to fifteen feet away from me. Keep in mind that ten to fifteen feet in swamps is like thirty to fifty yards on Astroturf today.

To this day, I do not know if the bullet grazed my head or not. It surely parted my hair though. There was a trace of blood dripping from my head later on, but **"it don't mean nothin'!"**

I was clearly dazed. I actually went into shock and just sat there behind the cemetery stone while Paris was in an urgent situation to get the hell out of there, as were the wounded guys behind us. I don't know how long I just sat there until I finally heard the guys behind us saying, "Dusty, wake up, snap out of it—THEY'RE COMING UP ON YOU!" (meaning the VC were advancing).

Oh no … I snapped out of my dazed state and crawled back to grab the helmet; **it was still smoking**. I put it back on my head and started returning fire at the VC using our medic's M-16. **Thank you, dear God!**

Clack, clack, clack … the sound of the Viet Cong's AK-47s continued. They weren't going anywhere because they had us pinned. They had superior strategic position, or so they thought.

Oh, by the way, we owed our lives to that guy named Haywood Taylor, who was our 1st squad M-60 machine gunner. We called him "George of the Jungle."

When the ambush at Catholic Village was finally over and every wounded man had been successfully rescued and med-evac'd, Lieutenant Graves and Sergeant Daniels both approached me and said: "Trimmer, that was a fine thing you did today. In fact, pretty much the entire 1st and 2nd Platoons rose to the occasion in order to save a lot of lives. We are recommending you for the Silver Star and several others for Bronze Stars for heroism."

I remember those words precisely to this day. Later that same evening, we bombed the area with a massive B-52 attack. We also went out on ambush patrol with just seven or eight men, and a few days later, the "new guys" started to filter in.

Today, when I think back at the ambush at Catholic Village, I figure that I went through twelve to sixteen bandoleers of M-16 ammo. I had nothing left by the time Loftis made it up to help us drag Paris out of there. Oh, that had to be so painful for Paris; he looked so mangled from the multiple bullet wounds. It was hard to imagine that he would survive that day—but he did.

I brushed aside a sinister-looking snake during our crawl through the canal. Could have been a bamboo viper, but I didn't care. I told it to get the #*@^ out of our way.

Our brothers in the rear covered our rescue of Paris like a whole platoon of John Waynes and Audie Murphys—they had to or else the three of us would still be in that leech-infested swamp.

I think many of us were different after that day. I know that I had a much better opinion of some soldiers who I did not care for previously, and I am sure those who weren't too fond of my cocky attitude looked at me in a more positive way from that day forward.

We managed to get Paris to a med-chopper. Luckily, it landed and took off safely as the firefight wasn't over yet. We heard later that he was okay. He had been sent home to Walter Reed Hospital, where he received the extensive rehab care he needed.

Actually, we did hook up with Paris once again … many, many years later at a platoon reunion in Massillon, Ohio. It was the platoon's second reunion since leaving hell in 1969. Paris looked and sounded fine. I am relieved for that. I was happier to see him than he was to see me, I think, but I doubt if he could remember much about that day as he was utterly delirious most of the time we were pinned behind the cemetery stone.

"George" and I became special friends after that day.

Tet I, II, III Offensives

While the world watched the dramatic siege of Khe Sanh, North Vietnam and their Viet Cong brothers were well on their way to bigger goals. They were drifting down the Ho Chi Minh Trail through Laos and Cambodia, setting the stage to attack more strategic locations around Saigon, including Saigon.

Despite what the American media reported, including Walter Cronkite's highly inaccurate suggestions that the NVA/VC were actually winning the war, Americans dealt the enemy a succession of defeats in every major confrontation.

The enemies' Tet Offensives of 1968—I, II, and III—would be the last concerted attempts against America and our combined free world forces in Vietnam until the end of the war seven years later. And yet, back home Americans were becoming more reluctant to support a war that the media kept insisting was being lost!

While 1968 was the bloodiest year of the war, especially for the enemy, 1968 could also be remembered as **the beginning of the end of the Vietnam War, but nobody knew it at the time!**

Clearly, the third offensive in the fall of 1968 brought the most sustained fighting of the war to III Corp in Tay Ninh Province, also known as War Zone C. The 25th Infantry Division bore the brunt of the enemy's last major onslaughts in that bloody year.

NVA human wave attacks and counterattacks became the calling card of the enemy. These nighttime battles were the epitome of what the pure horror of war was all about. By August, Army intelligence had estimated that 40,000 additional hard-core NVA had infiltrated Tay Ninh Province alone. The stage was set for the enemy's final attempts to defeat us.

Historians, biased by false media reporting, have not shown how decisively we beat the communist forces back then. While we fought off the NVA's human wave attacks repeatedly, we also took after them and carried them right to the Cambodian/South Vietnam border—and beyond.

The South Vietnam military gained new confidence because of these victories. The civilian population of South Vietnam did not rally to the cause of the NVA, and the depleted Viet Cong army was never the force it once was. North Vietnam's General Giap was shocked at what was happening. But the growing peace movement and anti-war marches back in the U.S. were just what General Giap's battered forces needed to carry on with the war … and they did that. **THANK YOU, AMERICAN MEDIA … THANK YOU, WALTER CRONKITE!**

It has been well documented, but sparsely promoted, that the mass distortions by the Ameri-Cong liberal media relied heavily on our enemies' propaganda for their stories. This has not been restricted to just the Vietnam War, but the lies of enemy defeats told to Americans as victories took place during the Persian Gulf conflict as well as the Afghanistan and Iraq wars. Add more insult to injury as our Ameri-Cong liberal academic Americans have also distorted the facts about all of these wars … to show favor to our enemies so that future generations of Americans will remain misinformed. Basically, the Ameri-Congs have not only stolen our valor, but our history as well.

N E W S F L A S H … AMERICA DID NOT LOSE THE WAR IN VIETNAM!

I am not the expert here—I don't claim to be. But having served there, having fought in daily combat for most of my time over there and survived, I do take a personal interest in what has been said about the Vietnam War, and what continues to be said. And continues to go unsaid! The Viet Cong and the North Vietnamese armies were soundly defeated by Americans and our allies from 1961 through 1973 … **FACT! If we lost that war, then the British won the Battle of New Orleans!**

Author, June 1968
After ambush in Hoc Mon Province

Remnants of 1st Platoon
The Day After an Ambush in Hoc Mon Province
(Hunziker, Gainey, Loftis, Me, Pringle, and Maines)

Riding Shotgun on 3/4 Cav Armored Personnel Carrier
July 1968

Armored Personnel Carrier down from Rocket Propelled Grenades (RPGs) – July 1968

Helicopter down

Transport plane down

Firefight from the air – 1968

BRAVO COMPANY
3rd Battalion 22nd Infantry

Vietnam Memorial Wall ★ Panel & Line Information

Name	Panel	Line	Name	Panel	Line
Jessie Gomez	13E	52	Rodney Weed	16E	117
William Madison	13E	59	Thomas Dando	16E	111
Scott Webber	13E	60	Fred Patterson	16E	114
James Harris	13E	63	Herman Anders	16E	127
Edward Brock	13E	66	Kenneth Blanton	16E	129
Marvin Hughes	13E	67	James Hintz	17E	5
William Mullins	13E	68	Brian Gibbons	17E	3
Norman Toennies	13E	69	Charles Greer	17E	4
Vincente Zuniga	13E	70	Virgil Ledford	17E	7
Louis Wandler	14E	65	Edward Muller	17E	9
Marlin Eversgerd	16E	110	Thomas Talmadge	17E	14
Jack Gosnell	16E	111	Larry Warnock	17E	15
Robert Linn	16E	112	Allen Mican	17E	86
Paul McGowan	16E	113	Jimmy Harper	17E	122
Louis Sas	16E	115	Salvador Nava	18E	11
Donald Schroeder	16E	115	Albert Graham	21E	34
Donald Walters	16E	117	Jerry Beebe	23E	16
Baxter Ellis	25E	16	Richard Beck	60E	8
James Watanabe	27E	17	Edward Crow	60E	9
Larry McDuffie	28E	50	George Mundy	60E	15
Louis Armstead	28E	107	Eldon Coldren	44W	22
Bertmann Miller	39E	4	Lonnie Lundy	44W	27
Darrell Morey	30E	102	Daniel Persons	43W	47
George Duplessis	31E	23	Roger Dixon	34W	22
Odell Stokes	33E	23	Guiseppe Magri	34W	15
Kenneth Howell	34E	53	Randall Wicklace	34W	19
Earnest Martin	34E	54	Franklin Lanier	29W	21
Thomas Watts	34E	55	Louis Castro	27W	71
Charles Irby	34E	54	Roger Hood	27W	73
Richard Walker	34E	56	Michael Howard	27W	74
Luey Holland	36E	15	David Trinkala	25W	56
Robert Gray	38E	67	William Crusie	23W	84

Name	Panel	Line
Donald Roemer	40E	30
Bobbie Sikes	40E	31
John Milanowski	40E	25
Louis Martinez	40E	74
Edward Beckwith	49E	29
Alan Butkus	49E	28
John Cunningham	49E	30
Robert Ellsworth	N/A	N/A
William Maxwell	49E	34
Robert Melton	49E	34
Glenn Moller	49E	35
Reynaldo Orozco	49E	36
David Strupp	49E	37
Donny Tidwell	49E	37
Douglas Weiher	49E	38

Name	Panel	Line
Bruce Eamick	20W	112
Walter Hogaus	17W	41
Elvis Mullen	17W	42
Florencio Marquez	17W	117
Luis Le Bron	14W	81
George Boatwright	13W	18
Bobby Swanson	12W	53
Gary Metz	07W	28
James Duckworth	07W	26
William Allsbrook	07W	105
Bruce Stickel	07W	107
David Tinsey	07W	108
Jimmy Westbrook	07W	109
Stephen Kaster	06W	35
Robert Gumm	06W	56

Chapter 5

PLATOONS OF BRAVO COMPANY

U.S. Army platoons … all infantry units have typically used the same basic doctrinal principles, operating from a standard organization, except in VIETNAM!

Only a complete dork or geek would try to force his platoon to go by the rules he was taught in officers' candidate school or noncommissioned officer school and try to apply them in Vietnam. There were few rules over there that would keep you alive other than to keep your head down, stay alert, and never underestimate our enemy.

A combat infantry platoon in Vietnam at full strength would be twenty to twenty-seven men. In the World Wars and in Korea, a full-strength platoon was more like thirty-five to sixty men. In Nam, a combat infantry platoon was often asked/demanded to accomplish things that would normally require a full company of 200 to 300 men to carry out successfully.

- We had to be our own LRRPs—Long Range Recon Patrol!
- We had to set up and conduct ambushes on much larger forces, and if we did not succeed, being outnumbered three or four to one could guarantee death for all of us.
- We were all very young and in the absolute best physical condition any man could be—we had to be. Every so often, we would be forced to engage the enemy in a battle more than once in one day, then shake it off and be ready for the same thing the next day.

As I read it, a platoon in WWII or today in one of the Middle East wars would have a lot of titles within. It was literally a bureaucratic element, with their men having almost as many titles as they had bodies. Not so in Vietnam. Our creed was versatility. Point man today … forward observer tomorrow … flank security the next day … rifle squad leader the next day … machine gunner the next … radio telephone operator (RTO) the next … and back to point man. We had to be flexible—on the spot—every day.

In Vietnam, the platoon needed to quickly become a cohesive unit like a football team's offense or defense. Learning and anticipating each other's next move during crunch time was obviously a mandatory requirement—*mandatory*!

Whenever I think back as I am doing right now, I think … **GOD, HOW I LOVED THE 1ST PLATOON AND HOW IT FUNCTIONED BACK THEN!**

104

None of us had the slightest idea back in 1968 that we were going to be part of a history-making unit—the same unit Oliver Stone fought in and on which he presumably based his Oscar-winning movie *Platoon*.

Bravo Company, 3rd Battalion 22nd Infantry Division had been referred to as **the worst fighting unit in the 25th because it took the highest casualties, or the best fighting unit in the 25th because it took the highest enemy body count**—take your choice.

In March of 1968, my new family of brothers and I were elected as the replacements for most of that unit that Oliver Stone fought in during those dreaded months of October 1967 to February 1968 ... Those were THE Tet months.

Regardless of whether or not you are a fan of Oliver Stone and/or his movies, make no mistake about it ... he survived some of the most intense combat situations ever experienced in the jungles of Vietnam. Captain Robert Hemphill was the commander of Bravo Company 3rd 22nd of the 25th Infantry during Oliver Stone's tenure in Nam. Captain Hemphill was quoted in his own version of the book, *PLATOON: Bravo Company:*

Oliver Stone was a good soldier. He earned a couple of good medals and a righteous Purple Heart.

Unfortunately, this good Captain Hemphill passed away in 2012 at the young age of sixty-nine. In his 1998 book, he also wrote this about combat infantrymen coming home from Vietnam:

The Vietnam combat veteran has faced two enemies because of his service—the enemy in the field in-country and the indifference and occasional hostility of his own countrymen. The combat soldier feels the effects of this second enemy—the failure of his fellow Americans to appreciate his efforts, including his constant willingness to place his very life in mortal danger—to the greatest degree, more so than others who served in Vietnam but who saw little or no significant direct combat.

Many folks perceived Stone's movie *Platoon* to be on the harsh side, even some Vietnam veterans who saw it. Apparently, maybe they were shielded from combat during their tours in Vietnam. *Platoon*, the movie, actually modified many of the combat scenes because the real-life violence and horrors would have been too difficult for some viewers to handle. While I did not participate in the two largest single-day battles of the entire Vietnam War, Soui Cut and Soui Tre, I did research their stories tirelessly and will mention them again. They were battles that no Hollywood movie could ever do justice to. Bravo

Company 3rd 22nd's 1st Platoon was deeply involved in these two horror events, and their casualties were devastating to the unit.

The 3/22nd Infantry was the last 25th Division battalion to leave Vietnam in 1971. Since that time, there have been numerous reunions of former Bravo Company members. I have been to several for the 1st Platoon. *Bravo Regulars* is a society I belong to, consisting of former Bravo Company brothers who fought in Vietnam … many at different times. *Bravo Regular* is also a quarterly newsletter for our society of former combat brothers.

There was a special bond over there back then, as there is now a special bond with some former members of Bravo Company 3rd 22nd of the 25th Infantry Division who fought in the Vietnam War. I believe that we Bravo Regulars who followed those in the 1967–1968 time frame were given a lot more room to do our job because of what our pioneering brothers did before us. When the batons were passed on to us in March/April 1968, Bravo Company 3rd 22nd had become known as the best fighting unit in the 25th Infantry Division and possibly in all of Vietnam. We had a legacy to follow, and I believe my brothers and I lived up to the task.

Oliver Stone fought in the 2nd Platoon. I fought in the 1st Platoon a few months later. Both platoons earned an abnormal amount of battle citations … and I mean they **earned them**.

Here is a true story, which I borrowed from a current edition of our unit's newsletter called *Bravo Regulars*:

AMBUSH (January 15, 1968) – First platoon was under heavy fire when Oliver Stone and his buddies from second platoon saved the day. First platoon was ambushed shortly after we had stopped to eat our c-rations around noon. Lt. Richard Walker was the first to get it. He walked right in on an enemy bunker and was killed by machine gun fire. Shortly afterwards, my squad leader, Sgt. Thomas Watts, was hit along with several other guys. I heard our Platoon Sgt. Ernest Martin, yell at his RTO Gary Payton to "tell them to get that god damn artillery off us!" Then a second later, in came an artillery round right over my head, landing on Sgt. Martin. He was killed instantly. About that time, an AK grazed my head. Those of us that could, low crawled back about 50 feet and got behind some big anthills for cover. We continued to fire until we ran out of ammunition. About this time, a very heroic Medic, Spec. 4 Dick Reisch, jumped up from behind his anthill and ran out into the firing to pull Tom Watts back behind my anthill. Tom had been hit with AK fire about 5 or 6 times. He was still alive and I tried my best to comfort him. Twice, the medic tossed me morphine syringes to give Tom shots to ease his pain. Unfortunately, Tom died on his way back to the field hospital. First platoon was completely out of ammunition. We could hear the gooks chattering about something or other and we thought they were going to get out of their bunkers to finish us off. About that time, Oliver Stone and four of his buddies came crawling up behind us. I told them to be careful, that there were a lot of VC in front of us. Stone said they would go get them. Stone and second platoon members crawled forward toward the enemy bunkers and all we could hear was a chorus of AK and M16 fire. Stone and the others came crawling back.

Most of them had been wounded including Stone. What this did for first platoon was to let the enemy know we still had live bodies with live ammo, thus dissuading them from getting out of their bunkers to execute us. For this I will always be grateful. Stone and his buddies saved the day because it bought us enough time for the 2/22nd APCs to come to our rescue. They clambered up behind us firing away with their 50 caliber machine guns.

- Larry Robinson
1st Platoon, Bravo Company
3rd 22nd 25th Infantry, 1967-1968

1st Platoon's Minor "Skirmishes"

March 1968
I was with 2nd 12th this day when an ARVN compound attacked and captured. We counterattacked and destroyed the compound, killing all enemy Viet Cong. I saw my first American casualty—name unknown, and yes, I remember how he looked to this day.

April 1968
Also with 2nd 12th this day. While on point along the Cambodian border, we were confronted by NVA. We yelled "Chieu hoi" to two NVA, but they reached for their weapons. Both died fast! Remaining NVA attacked us. The firefight left twenty-two enemy dead.

April 1968
Now with 3rd 22nd. Numerous encounters near Trang Bang, Boi Loi Woods, Iron Triangle—thirty-two KIA. Two Americans were wounded.

May 1 – 29
Included daily search-and-destroy missions, several combat assaults and nightly ambushes. The 3/22nd 25th Infantry killed more than 600 enemy soldiers in this May Tet Counter Offensive Phase II. (One hundred twenty enemy were killed in the vicinity of Cambodia.)

May 1968
While on point during a night ambush mission, we were ambushed by VC with 51-cal machine guns. We lost another American that night. Oh, what the 51-cal rounds did to a man; it was an indescribable dose of the reality of war.

Even heavy camouflage didn't help a VC sampan (a flat wooden boat used by the Viet Cong to travel mostly at night) escape night ambush by the Regulars.

Having set up along the bank of the Saigon River, Bravo Co's 1st Platoon proceeded to intercept two communist sampans during the course of the night. The first came downriver soon after dark, only to meet a hail of fire from the Plat's machine guns and small arms. Two VC bodies were recovered. Undeceived by the camouflage, the Regulars cut loose on the floating "greenhouse" and scored seven more Viet Cong killed and another sampan put out of commission for good. Found nine KIA.

May 14
Ho Bo Woods combat assault into ambush by NVA on Americans. Enemy repelled. KIA unknown.

May 15
Human waved in Boi Loi Woods by NVA and Chinese Regulars. Attack repelled. Morning sweep found seven KIA and many blood trails. Three Americans were wounded.

May 21
Acting as reactionary force into pineapple swamps in Hoc Mon. Ambush was sprung successfully. Found eleven KIA.

May 28
Ambushed by VC outside Go Dau Ha Village. Repelled enemy. Four KIA.

May 29
Attacked Go Dau Ha Village around 4:00 AM. Casualties included civilians and eleven KIA.

June 4
Set up perimeter and LP outside Go Dau Ha. VC attacked again. Seven KIA and many blood trails. One American officer was killed and several soldiers wounded.

June 15
Hoc Mon Province/Catholic Village—ambushed while on recon in support of sister company under ambush by unknown force. We were ambushed from two directions. I took a round in my helmet—grazed my head. Called in B-52 strike—blood and body parts were everywhere. Enemy KIA unknown. One American dead and eight wounded.

June 26

While on recon ambush patrol, we were ambushed outside of Cu Chi. Ambush repelled. Enemy KIA unknown. Two Americans were wounded.

June 27 – July

R&R to lick our wounds and wait for replacements. Worked with Mobile Riverine Patrol and guarded Phu Cuong Bridge under repair. Several encounters with VC while doing these patrols … no big deal.

July 3

After an ambush at Trang Bang, I fell or was knocked off an Army vehicle and knocked unconscious. Med-evac'd to Dau Tieng base camp for observation and treatment. I was never treated.

July 4 – Dau Tieng Siege

Dau Tieng was our main base camp at the time of this event. At approximately 2:30 AM on July 4, 1968, back-to-back predawn ground attacks by two NVA companies supported by Viet Cong followed a barrage of fireworks that lit up the skies and could be seen for several miles despite the thick woods and jungle terrain. More than 400 enemy rockets and mortar rounds rained in on Dau Tieng, destroying or damaging several buildings, including the clinic and several hooches. This was the largest attack on Dau Tieng in its history up to this point.

I had been carried to Dau Tieng the previous night with a concussion due to a mishap of my own, falling from or getting knocked off a vehicle at an ambush near Trang Bang. I think "Bug" Jenner was with me, but it is foggy to me now. The combined NVA/VC force overran Dau Tieng on two different sides with the west perimeter getting hit the hardest. Suicide squads were sent by the VC in an attempt to blow up Dau Tieng airfield.

The 3rd Battalion 22nd Infantry took the brunt of these attacks. Before dawn, "Puff the Magic Dragon" aircraft began circling the battle, dropping flares and, of course, providing much appreciated firepower onto the attacking enemy.

On the east perimeter, at least ten enemy KIA were found with blood trails leading into the woods. The roar was deafening for the entire morning as artillery pounded the attackers still trying to get inside the base camp. Seventy-three enemy KIA were left inside Dau Tieng when the battle had ended sometime by midday on July 4th. Countless enemy body parts and blood trails were found outside the perimeter. American casualties were five KIA and fifty-three wounded, eighteen seriously. I was nicked by shrapnel that night, and sent back to the field on/about July 5th. I was never treated for the head bump/concussion on July 3rd or the shrapnel nick on the 4th—no medic available. Several others received nicks that night but were not treated that I can remember. I know, too, that our hooch was destroyed—sure glad we weren't in it. We were already in a bunker when the attacks began. **THIS WAS NOT A MINOR SKIRMISH!**

August 16
Combat assault to Saigon/Cholon to repel VC ambush. Enemy dispersed. Blood trails found. KIA unknown. Several Americans wounded.

August 28
Tay Ninh, working with 3/4 Cav, was ambushed by VC supported by unknown NVA force. Enemy KIA was twelve. Three Americans were wounded.

September 11
Human wave attack on Fire Support Base Buell by NVA and Chinese Regulars. Some positions were overrun, but eventually all enemy were beaten back, but not without a huge price. Enemy KIA was 112. Three Americans died; ten were wounded.

September 13
Human wave attack #2 on Fire Support Base Buell. Enemy got inside the wires but did not overrun perimeter. Enemy KIA was seventy-seven. Eleven Americans were wounded.

October 10
Tay Ninh's Nui Ba Den Mountain—ambushed. We counterattacked enemy into the jungles of Cambodia. Blood trails everywhere. KIA unknown. Three Americans were wounded.

November 8
On recon on edge of Cambodia, ambushed again by large NVA force. Repelled and found thirteen KIA. One American dead; five Americans wounded.

(Source: This brief list of smaller skirmishes was prepared by our 1st Platoon brothers John "Babyson" Martino and Robert "Smokey" Ryan for our 1988 reunion for which they and their wives were the workhorses in coordinating.)

A Warrior's Last Day!

Fire Support Base Buell – FSB

As described by John Martino, fellow 1st Platoon brother of Bravo Company, 3rd 22nd :

On September 10th – 11th, a temporary lull in the Vietnam War ended abruptly for units of the 25th Infantry Division and South Vietnamese (ARVN) forces in Tay Ninh Province. Base camps, fire support bases, and numerous outposts came under heavy enemy assaults as several forces of Viet Cong and North Vietnamese were determined to overrun our positions outside Tay Ninh and within the city itself.

Initial action was triggered as an ambush patrol from Delta Company, 2d Battalion, 27th Infantry spotted an estimated enemy battalion three miles northeast of Tay Ninh City. As they let the enemy force deliberately pass their ambush site, they engaged the enemy's rear elements while coordinated artillery fire blasted away at the front of the column. Many VC were killed in our attacks.

At Support Base Buell II, only three and a half miles to the northwest, base personnel were alerted by the ambush and were aware of the imminent danger. They were ready when at 1:23 a.m., 75 to 100 rounds of 82mm mortar and 12 rounds of 107mm rocket fire crashed into their perimeter.

Moving under the cover of the rockets and mortars, another enemy battalion made a vicious ground attack on the base, hitting first in the direction of the 7th Battalion, 11th Artillery. During the following four-hour battle, the firebase was hit from the southeast and northwest. Massive automatic weapons fire plagued the U.S. defenders. The 105mm howitzers from Bravo Battery, 7th Battalion, 11th Artillery, and the 155mm guns of Alpha Battery, 3d Battalion, 13th Artillery retaliated with point-blank fire. Elements from the 3d Battalion, 22d Infantry, 4th Battalion (Mechanized), 23d Infantry, and 2d Battalion 34th Armor delivered a devastating fire into the VC as they pushed their attack.

Additionally, elements of the 9th NVA Division attacked from the shelter of a nearby banana plantation to the northwest, Base Coordinator Lieutenant Colonel Alexander H. Hunt, battalion commander of the 3d Battalion, 22d Infantry directed the artillerymen to use direct fire on the approaching enemy.

Our own brigade commander, Lieutenant Colonel Hunt, used flare ships and called U.S. Air Force tactical air strikes within 150 meters of the perimeter. Helicopter gunships from Delta Troop, 3d Squadron, 4th Cavalry, and Bravo Troop, 25th Aviation Battalion continually strafed the enemy with machine gun fire and rocket attacks. They were assisted by the 187th Assault Helicopter Company, under the operational control of the 25th Infantry Division.

Heavy fighting continued until 4:40 a.m. when the enemy started retreating after suffering heavy casualties from the combined Infantry, Artillery, and Armor team at the fire support base. Eighty-three enemy were killed while American forces suffered one killed and twenty-six wounded.

Meanwhile, Tay Ninh base camp was attacked during the enemy operation from 82mm mortar rounds and 107mm rockets hurled inside the perimeter.

During the coordinated attacks, Tay Ninh City was hit as the VC mortared the district headquarters in an attempt to move into the city itself. An unknown size enemy force was reported in the city.

Another target for the coordinated enemy advance was the communications center atop the 3,200-foot Nui Ba Den Mountain near the fire support base. The small signal relay station received fire from small arms, automatic weapons, and RPG rounds, beginning at 2 a.m. The sharp conflict continued until dawn. At one point, four bunkers were occupied by enemy troops. Ten Viet Cong were killed while eight Americans died and twenty-three were wounded.

On the morning of September 10th we went on a company-size patrol to and partway up the black Virgin Mountain (Nui Ba Den). It was not a search-and-destroy patrol, however. We were to patrol in an area near a no-fire zone containing a monastery or something of that nature and see if we could draw fire. There was intelligence that there was a large NVA unit somewhere in the area. We conducted the patrol but were unsuccessful (or maybe very successful) as we were not shot at.

While heading back to and upon arriving at Fire Support Base (FSB) Buell, we noticed a very obvious absence of any local indigenous people—no farmers, no vendors, no kids—a sure sign that the enemy was in the area. First Platoon had four bunker positions, each about eight to ten meters apart, starting in the corner facing towards Nui Ba Den and running to the left. The corner bunker had a 50-caliber machine gun. Dale Nowakowski, Billy Loftis, Dean Coldren, and I were in the next bunker with the M-60 (and I think Dean had an M-79). I don't recall who was in the bunker to our left—it could have been Smokey, George, and Dusty.

At dusk, Nowakowski came up to me carrying a roll of concertina wire and said we should put this out. I helped him and we laid it out about ten meters to our front. Ski felt it was important to put it out. Events soon proved his feelings to be very correct. We also set up additional trip flares in the area between the concertina wire and the regular perimeter fence.

I should note at this point that from the beginning of my tour in country, I was blessed with a "sense" that would wake me if something was going to happen. I would suddenly wake up and know we were about to be attacked. Well, in the early morning hours of September 11th, that sense went off. I woke the others and told them to get in the bunker, and we did so just as the mortar rounds began to fall inside the perimeter. While mortar rounds were still coming in, there was a loud explosion to our front. I suddenly felt that we had to get out of the bunker, and when I said so, everyone did, despite the incoming mortar rounds. Moments later, an RPG round slammed into our bunker through one of the firing slots, ripping up the inside of the bunker. At the same time, we observed enemy soldiers to our front inside the perimeter wire. They had blown the outer perimeter fence (the earlier explosion to our front) but were then stopped when they came to the unexpected roll of concertina wire. They had not known it was there as we did not put it out until almost dark (thank you, Ski). We were all firing everything we had at the enemy, who were trapped behind the wire. We burned out the M-60 barrel that night.

At some point, I noticed that the 50-caliber machine gun in the corner bunker to our right wasn't firing. I yelled over and found out that all but one of the guys manning the bunker were wounded, and the one remaining soldier was giving first aid. I responded to the bunker to assist with the injured and to get the 50 firing again. I remained there until the 50 became inoperative due to a jam that I wasn't able to clear in the dark.

The bulk of the attack was just heating up as there was still plenty of activity going on. Dean Coldren had a Starlight Scope and could see some NVA in the clump of bushes to our right front. He handed me the scope and told me to direct him as he fired an M-16 at the enemy soldiers.

In any event, we all (the four of us in our bunker) made it safely to morning. As it continued to get lighter, we observed numerous bodies to our front, both inside and outside the perimeter. We were shocked when one of the bodies up against the concertina wire suddenly sat up. He had been only ten meters from us all night and was somehow still alive! His sudden movement was not a good idea, however, as all three bunkers facing him opened fire.

A short time later, the company set out on patrol to check bodies and retrieve weapons. It was during that patrol that Dean was killed when an NVA soldier stood up with his weapon over his head in the surrender position, stating "Chu Hoy." Like many others, I knew there was something wrong with the apparent "surrender" but couldn't immediately identify what. We had all been awake most of the night, involved in prolonged intense fighting, and were suffering from adrenaline withdrawal, so we were not as mentally quick as we should have been. Still, seeing the event in my mind, I have long since recognized the problem. There was a magazine in the AK-47. There should not have been if he was truly surrendering. In any event, in a split-second, he lowered the weapon and fired a burst towards the CP group, and Dean had the misfortune to be standing in front of the group. The "surrendering" NVA soldier was cut down immediately, but the damage had been done. **Dean lay dead on the ground.**

One hundred seventy-nine VC/NVA died and hundreds more were wounded on these two days!

Core Members of 1st Platoon After Buell—8 out of 27, September 1968
Taylor, Gainey, Martino, Nowakowski, Turner, Trimmer, Ryan, Loftis

Remembering Smokey Ryan

As I mentioned elsewhere in this book, another platoon brother passed away prematurely on June 13, 2012. The cause was Vietnam War related … AGAIN!

As I was flying home on June 16th from Smokey Ryan's funeral, I was reminiscing about some of the memories Smokey and I shared together. Although we had fallen out of close contact during the last several years, my love and admiration for this gallant warrior will always remain strong.

Smokey and I first met in early April 1968. We were assigned to the 2nd 12th Infantry, formerly part of the 4th Infantry Division. Our stay there was brief, maybe three or four days. One day after we fought in a battle to recapture a South Vietnamese army compound which was overrun by Viet Cong, we were both transferred to a unit in the 25th Infantry Division which had been decimated by their third major human wave attack by North Vietnamese Regulars. This battle was named the Battle of Good Friday, staged on April 11th. Our new unit was the famous and infamous 3rd 22nd of the 25th Infantry— famous for their whopping high body count of enemy soldiers, and infamous (as I have mentioned earlier) because of their own high casualty rate.

We thought that just maybe we would be given the night off on our first night with our new family since everyone had been in a battle the previous day. Plus, our entire platoon, the 1st Platoon, had *all new guys* who started together in April. NO SUCH LUCK! We were told to saddle up and lock and load because the 1st and 2nd Platoons were going out on an ambush that night. This would be the first night ambush for Smokey and me. Unfortunately, we never made it to our destination for an attempted ambush because we were ambushed by a Viet Cong force with the formidable .51 caliber machine gun in their arsenal. We were badly over-matched and we took casualties as a result. We had to pull out and retreat … to come back another day, which we would surely do.

Smokey was one of our eight wounded during the battle at Catholic Village near the town of Hoc Mon in mid-June. We pulled Smokey out that day. This would be his first of three hard-earned Purple Hearts, requiring hospital care each time. In contrast, none of my little nicks and scratches required hospital care except when my knee and foot became badly infected.

Two men led Smokey out of the Catholic Village battle, straight to a medevac helicopter. But it took three men to make him get into the chopper! Smokey wanted to stay and help rescue the other wounded men in spite of the fact that he was suffering from his own wounds. He finally gave in as we assured him that NO ONE WAS BEING LEFT BEHIND this day. All eight wounded were rescued. Most we never saw again … EVER.

Smokey returned to us a few weeks later as feisty as ever, and he proved it rather quickly as soon as he got back to the field. He was a holy terror on the VC; they did not have a chance.

A couple months later in the fall, he and I were in Cu Chi together, heading over to an Enlisted Men's Club to have a few beers. We had to stop at the PX first, so I went ahead to grab us a table and have a beer waiting for him. It was a rowdier bunch than I expected. Some Special Forces guys were acting like they owned the place, and one of them charged to the front of the line.

Everyone else ignored his rude move, but I would have none of it, and I asked him to get to the end of the line.

A push here, a push back, and then we were rolling on the floor. I was getting the better of him when two of his Special Forces buddies jumped in to help him. I was outnumbered three to one! In walked Smokey just in time. Now the odds were in our favor—two to three! Smokey dusted off the other two in lightning quick fashion, and my opponent decided to leave, taking his buddies with him.

Smokey ... Smokey ... Smokey! You were one tough Irishman! Smokey traveled to more Vietnam veteran coming home parades than any other ten Nam vets that I knew.

Robert Smokey Ryan was a great soldier for America and the American people. He did not deserve to die at age sixty-five from the war he fought so bravely in. However, now Smokey is one of **God's soldiers**. They are both in good hands.

On my way home from Smokey's funeral, it stood out in my mind how many of our platoon members who were still living were unable to travel and honor our fallen brother due to health problems—or they had also died prematurely. I was able to make the trip to honor Smokey, fortunately—but barely. I cannot drive much more than a couple of hours at a time or I will literally black out, and I never know when it will happen. This is caused by the Agent Orange diabetes Type II disease.

Many of us have died quickly and suddenly after coming home from Vietnam. And many of us are dying right now as I write this book about the Vietnam War. **We are still fighting not to become CONDEMNED PROPERTY of the Vietnam War!**

Smokey attended coming home parades all over the USA. He even marched with me in Cleveland, Ohio's coming home parade. We have gone our separate ways, but many of us in the 1st Platoon have maintained some contact with each other. Nearly all of us have health issues that are directly related to Vietnam: PTSD, Agent Orange cancers, diabetes, heart problems. It's a long list.

Smokey was a soldier once and young. **I will always remember him as one tough Irish man—but mostly I'll remember him as a patriotic soldier still!**

Smokey Ryan and Dusty Trimmer – October 1968

Early picture of some 1st Platoon members – March/April 1968

Sweep outside Cholon District near Saigon – May 1968

A short breather after a sweep
Shelton & Trimmer

Checking Viet IDs

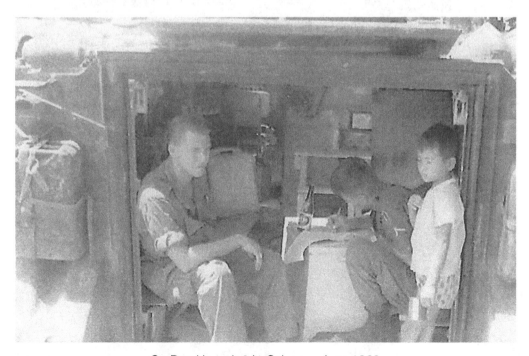

Go Dau Ha with 3/4 Calvary – June 1968

Go Dau Ha – April 1968

Overnight accommodations

Author, April 1968

Broussard and Best – 1968

Local GI Recovers From War Wounds

Pfc. Robert Wayne Best, 20, has advised his parents, Mr. and Mrs. M. H. Best of 311 Windsor Place, that he is recovering satisfactorily from wounds received in Vietnam on April 12.

Serving with a unit of the 25th Infantry Division, Best was one of 47 Americans wounded in five hours of close quarter fighting in War Zone C, 49 miles southwest of Saigon. He was hit in the head by shrapnel and is being treated at a field hospital.

. The battle took place when enemy troops stormed U.S. positions and left 128 enemy dead

inside or near the edge of the U.S. perimeter. Sixteen U. S. troops also died in the fighting which the men have tagged "The Battle of Good Friday."

Best has been in Vietnam almost exactly one month when he was wounded. A 1967 graduate of Southern Wayne High School, he enlisted in the Army last Sept. 5. He received basic training at Ft. Bragg and advanced training at Ft. Jackson, S. C. where he made the highest score in his unit on the physical fitness test. He left California for Vietnam on March 10.

Smokey, Loftis, and Best

Smokey and George

Twice ... Very Lucky!

One of the guys in our second platoon of Bravo Company, 3rd Battalion, 22nd Infantry experienced one of those lucky days—like I did with the bullet that removed my helmet from my head. Only this guy was hit squarely by an enemy round ... not once, but TWICE during the same ambush!

Jerry Hunziker, from Oklahoma, was walking point for the second platoon on September 4, 1968 as I was walking point for the 1st Platoon. When Jerry stopped suddenly, there was movement in the bushes ahead and not very far away either. Then suddenly we heard a familiar sound. It was an M-79 grenade round, but this one wasn't launched from our own guys. It originated from an unseen enemy. "Thud" Hunziker was hit and stunned, but amazingly, the grenade did not explode; fortunately it was a "dud."

A firefight followed with Sergeant Daniels leading the counterattack. All of a sudden, Hunziker screamed out as he was hit again by an enemy M-79 grenade, and one more time it turned out to be an unarmed dud ... WOW! Jerry was hurt and had to be evacuated by Dustoff helicopter to Tay Ninh Hospital to recover.

What a lucky day that was for him, and September 4th just happened to be his anniversary. By all odds, both of those rounds should have gone off, but this was Jerry Hunziker's lucky day, and he was happy to be alive.

Hunziker in Tay Ninh
After being wounded by two M-79 rounds – September 1968

Wall of memories stirs old pain

By MARK CURNUTTE

The Register Star

*Marlin Coldren buried his grief over the death of his nephew, Eldon "Dean" Coldren Jr.—
"my little buddy"—for 19 years before letting it out at a reunion of Dean's platoon in August
1988.*

    Now, the second step in Marlin's healing process is happening this weekend at the Moving Wall, which was brought to Rockford for Fourth of July weekend.

Two members of Dean's platoon—Dale "Ski" Nowakowski, Milwaukee; and Dusty Trimmer, Aurora, Ohio—have come to participate in the ceremony.

Out of a sad situation some good did come, I guess." Marlin says.
After the reunion in Norton, Mass., Coldren, his wife, Sue, and their three children drove to the Vietnam Veterans Wall in Washington D.C., where they traced the fallen soldier's name.

"It was something … like touching him again." Marlin recalls. "But having the Wall in Rockford was even more emotional because this is where Dean lived."

LAST WEEKEND at the Moving Wall, Nowakowski, Trimmer and Coldren and his family each wore reunion t-shirts. Members of the platoon treat Marlin and his family like part of their family.

Platoon's 1988 Reunion—Boston

The Platoon pulled it off—a twenty-year reunion just like we used to talk about back in 1968. How they did it impresses me to this day—I still think about it. We were missing quite a few of the originals, but a couple of guys and their wives managed to scrape up a total of fourteen survivors and get us out to Boston to "Shorty" Martino's home. Spouses and children, where applicable, also joined in. Two very special guests joined in and shared this highly emotional event with us:

- **Major General Flynt**, who was the 3rd Brigade commanding officer in 1968, known as Colonel Flynt back then. The general said this in a speech to us one evening: "It is one of my greatest honors to be a part of this reunion, to see some of the men who fought so bravely under me. In fact, they even made a movie about you (*Platoon*)."

- **Marlin Coldren**, who was the cousin of Dean "Babyson" Coldren, who died in Vietnam in 1968.

The 1st Platoon has had a couple of get-togethers since 1988, but none of them could ever compare with the first one, our first meeting since we fought together in the swamps of Vietnam in 1968–1969.

I have to mention this because it remains one of the highest compliments ever bestowed upon me in my entire lifetime, and I mean EVER! Curtis Daniels was one of the sergeants who we followed and looked up to back then. It was he and a 2nd lieutenant who recommended a Silver Star for me for something I did during a June 1968 battle where we were ambushed.

The 1st Platoon was a special unit, one that never left one of its own behind—never! We had guys like Dusty Trimmer who would charge up to our wounded and protect them before our medic could even get there.

Sorry, I had to mention that. My wife was there and she heard those words exactly as I wrote them here. Oh dear God, that made me so proud.

The Platoon's first ever reunion ended after three days of crying, laughing, more crying, and vows to remain in touch, which we have done to some degree. Remember, we were in the tensest of environments over there, literally thrown into each other's laps, and we did not always get along—just like some marriages. **The Platoon's twenty-year reunion was an overwhelming success—one that none of us will ever forget!**

Trimmer & Tetting (Deceased)
1988 Reunion

Martino & Gainey (Deceased) – 1988 Reunion

1988 Reunion

Haywood Taylor and Me – 1988

Major General Flynt, Author, and Martino – 1988

Platoon Group Picture – 1988

Special Thanks

There were many people who helped me get through this book, way too many to list here. They know who they are, and I have thanked them over and over again.

I am eternally grateful to all who fought in Vietnam, those who died over there, those who came home wounded physically and mentally, those who died prematurely because of Vietnam, those who are dying right now, and those who are still attempting to come home spirit-wise.

This book would not exist if so many had not made such **unbelievable sacrifices for their country.** Nor would it have been necessary to write it. This book would never have been possible if Smokey Ryan and Shorty Martino had not arranged and pulled off the amazing reunion for the 1st Platoon of Bravo Company 3rd 22nd of the 25th Infantry in 1988.

Our hooch in Dau Tieng was blown up twice in 1968, destroying everyone's personal belongings, including hundreds of pictures that were taken in the early months of that year. Smokey, Shorty, and their wives gathered pictures and articles from all of the remaining members of the 1st Platoon (who were still living and reachable), made copies for all of us, and put together scrapbooks for about a dozen of us. Many of the pictures in this book resulted from their efforts. **THANK YOU, SMOKEY AND SHORTY!**

*THEY Won't Believe This!

The Goliath in this war was not America. David was not the Viet Cong. Goliath was in the form of North Vietnam, China, and the Soviet Union— the real aggressors. David was in the form of the South Vietnamese, who were only trying to protect their freedom from the communist invaders. The anti-war protesters in America fell right into the communist plan for victory. In the background of this war, the communists were committing atrocities against South Vietnamese civilians, but America's left-wing media overlooked this, as they took isolated incidents like My Lai and blew them out of pro-portion. To this day, many Americans recall the name My Lai and the way in which our Ameri-Cong media covered it in 1969.

Chapter 6

WHERE WAS OUR IWO JIMA?

There was no Iwo Jima, Gettysburg, Yorktown, or Bunker Hill in the Vietnam War. While I am not a degreed historian or a certified researcher, I have prepared some comparisons to the Battle of Iwo Jima and the Battle for South Vietnam, as I refer to it:

Iwo Jima (February 19 – March 25, 1945) has been immortalized in the minds of every patriotic American with the famous image of the U.S. flag on top of a volcanic mountaintop, being raised by five Marines and one Navy Corpsman. This picture has pretty much become the symbol of the WWII veteran, particularly the U.S. Marines.

- Iwo Jima's battle lasted 35½ days.
- Combat Marines on the ground totaled 70,000+.
- Combat Japanese soldiers on the ground totaled 22,060.
- Iwo Jima was an island, offering no means of a retreat for the Japanese.
- America owned the air and the seas around Iwo Jima, sending devastating rounds of fire and bombs onto the heavily fortified Japanese positions.
- Defeat was inevitable for the Japanese. Victory was certain for America.
- The Japanese fought ferociously with no intention of surrendering; they had no avenue of retreat available.
- The Japanese had built more than ten miles of underground tunnels where many Japanese would end up buried alive.
- Mines, booby traps, and snipers were placed everywhere by the Japanese. Every Japanese soldier had to be killed or wounded for a total American victory to be achieved. That end was carried out.
- Originally, it was believed that most of the 22,060 Japanese died, except the unconscious or crippled who were taken prisoner.
- American casualties totaled more than 26,000 of which nearly 7,000 died. The strategic importance of Iwo Jima has always faced criticism and still does to this day, even though it became an emergency landing point for B-29 bombers later in the war, as well as those B-29s that carried atomic bombs to Japan in 1945.

After the battle for Iwo Jima, it was discovered that there remained several thousand (maybe 3,000) Japanese still living in the caves and tunnels. Most of

136

them eventually committed suicide, but a few of them did surrender. The last of these gave up in 1951 ... nearly six years after the battle—AMAZING!

In some ways, the Vietnam War itself resembled one very long Iwo Jima, but they were vastly separate in most ways:

- In Vietnam, the enemy always had sanctuaries to escape to ... tunnels to and from Cambodia, Laos, and North Vietnam.
- In Vietnam, the Viet Cong and North Vietnamese chose when and where a major engagement would occur. Those rarely lasted beyond a few days or few hours with the exception of the siege at Khe Sanh.
- In Vietnam, the enemy was supported by China and the Soviet Union (Russia). In WWII, America, China, and Russia fought on the same side.
- Most of the casualties on both sides during the Vietnam War resulted during ground battles, ambushes, and search-and-destroy missions, while heavy casualties in WWII resulted from air and naval battles. There were few of those in the Vietnam War.

Obviously, the major difference between WWII and the Vietnam War is that the United States military was attacked at Pearl Harbor by Japan, and North Vietnam did not initiate an attack on American-owned soil.

Were there any battles in Vietnam as bloody as the likes of Iwo Jima? Ask a WWII veteran and a Vietnam War veteran, and the same answer is highly unlikely. I know ... I've asked many WWII veterans, and their typical reply is like ... you have to be kidding!

Okay, here is a myopic comparison of the Battle of Iwo Jima in WWII and the one-day Battle of Soui Tre fought by units of the U.S. Army's 25th Infantry Division in 1967:

Year	Iwo Jima (1945)	Soui Tre (1967)
Duration	36 Days	1 Day
Enemy KIA	21,844	647
Americans KIA	6,800	31
Kill Ratio	3.2 – 1	19 - 1

Had Soui Tre lasted thirty-six days, estimated KIAs on both sides might have been 23,292 enemy and 1,116 Americans, purely hypothetical.

We Never Lost a Battle in Vietnam—Maybe?

Anyone who believes this false cliché needs to do his or her homework. Sure, we were overwhelmingly dominant over our adversaries in most of the largest engagements like Soui Tre, which was the largest one-day battle of the entire Vietnam War.

Without going into the entire long and detailed list of significant encounters that our military commanders claim as victories in Vietnam, but were in fact defeats for our side, I have provided a small sample that can be researched from several sources for verification. But first, who keeps saying that we never lost a battle over there?

The United States won every major battle of the Vietnam War ... every single one.
- Barrack Obama
President, United States
August 30, 2011

The United States never lost a battle in Vietnam.
- David Petraeus
Major General, U.S. Army
1986

We all know the government lies. That doesn't exclude high-ranking military officers as General Petraeus (retired) has recently proven in 2012. I don't know which did the greatest cover-up jobs, the biased left-wing media on our victories or the high-ranking military officers—on our losses? Trust me, we did not win every battle or every major battle—which is nothing to be ashamed of, except for the cover-ups.

Never Lost a Battle—Here Are a Few!

Pleiku's Airbase (1962) – Over 300 Viet Cong overran the perimeter guards and swept through the base camp, killing and wounding Americans and ARVN soldiers at will. After they withdrew with few casualties, they left behind the following damage:

- 25 aircraft damaged or destroyed
- 134 American casualties

Dong Xoui (1965) – Navy Seabees were still doing construction when mortar shells rained in followed by NVA human waves. The base camp was overrun despite the presence of American Special Forces supporting ARVN units and American air strikes.

- Hundreds of casualties; exact total never reported
- Dozens of helicopters damaged and many MIAs!

Cu Nghi (1966) – Battalions of the 7th and 12th Cavalry, 1st Cav Division including Colonel Harold Moore's 3rd Brigade. This "victory" as we labeled it, resulted in the following:

- 10 helicopters shot down
- 140 Americans KIA
- 220 Americans wounded

Xa Cam My (1966) – Charley Company, 2nd Battalion 16th Infantry, 1st Infantry Division was separated from its two sister companies as a ploy to bait a large NVA unit into an engagement. The NVA obliged them, surrounded the 134 men of C-Company, attacked, and overran the perimeter. During the battle, American artillery went errant and hit C-Company's perimeter rather than the NVA-VC attackers. This allowed the enemy to finish off some of the wounded Americans as they cut their throats. Eventually, C-Company's sister companies arrived, but it was too late. The damage was done:

- Of C-Company's 134 men, 108 were casualties in this single-night massacre.
- Two Medals of Honor were awarded ... posthumously.

A Shau (1966) – This Special Forces camp near Laos was heavily fortified and defended by several hundred troops, including mercenaries, ARVNs, and Americans. A Shau was attacked and overrun by an estimated five battalions of NVA. Five Americans escaped by helicopter, and twenty Americans were killed or MIA. Over 90 percent of the local troops were left behind; their fate was inevitable.

Operation Paul Revere IV (1966) – This American loss is as grisly and depressing as any of our losses. The 2nd Brigade 4th Infantry and the 3rd Brigade of the 25th Infantry Division engaged in and completed a twenty-three-day operation of being in the field and exposed to constant combat. This operation was considered an overwhelming victory as approximately 1,500 enemy were killed. However, two battalions sweeping the Cambodian border for NVA and Viet Cong were ambushed themselves and overwhelmed in the thick jungle terrain. Again, complete details of this battle are difficult to find, but one account stated that at least two full platoons were overrun, leaving only one survivor.

- 130 Americans KIA (estimated)
- 666 Americans wounded (estimated)

Dak To (1967) – This so-called victory by American generals involved units of the U.S. Army's 4th Infantry and 173rd Airborne. During the Americans' advance up this hill, a series of disastrous events happened. American artillery rounds hit and killed some of their own. A Marine jet accidently dropped a 500-pound bomb on the Americans. The NVA counterattacked, causing confusion and almost complete chaos. Eventually, the NVA withdrew and the Americans took control of the top of an empty hill.

- 570 Americans fought in this battle; total casualties were 340!

Prek Klok (1967) – Operation Junction City, a successful multi-division effort, except one lone company from the 1st Battalion/16th Infantry that was searching for and hoping to destroy an NVA force reported to be nearby. They found each other. Specific records of this engagement were never found, but individuals who survived that day stated that they were surrounded, badly outnumbered, and had no way to retreat. Fortunately, a sister company came to their rescue, and all had to be extracted by helicopter. Army generals proclaimed this retreat a victory? The company commander was awarded a Silver Star. Damage done to a 400-man battalion:

- 25 Americans KIA
- 128 Americans wounded

An Khe Ambush (1967) – A U.S. Army convoy with thirty-nine trucks, returning from delivering ammunition and supplies to Pleiku. The area was secured by elements of the 1st Cavalry Division and yet a Viet Cong company ambushed this very large convoy in broad daylight! Damage done:

- 7 Americans KIA
- 27 Americans wounded
- 30 of 39 trucks damaged or destroyed
- NO enemy casualties
- Convoy destroyed in less than an hour!

Operation Swift (Several Encounters 1967) – Along the DMZ border, several NVA units of unknown strength moved across the border to attack Americans and inflict casualties—period. Two Marine companies in the Que Son Valley were ambushed and overrun. Two more companies of Marines were sent to save them from annihilation, but they were cut to pieces. The result of this battle was:

- 127 Americans KIA
- 362 Americans wounded
- The NVA accomplished their mission and withdrew, leaving nearly 600 of their own dead behind them.

Attleboro ... A Victorious Defeat?

(1967) - This one has been described with different accounts on what actually did happen, depending on whom you talk to and which source you read. The real story is somewhere in between, so I will try to tell it as objectively as I can with a natural bias to our guys ... the American combat veterans.

It was near the end of 1966, and I would not touch the sand of Vietnam's Cam Ranh Bay for another sixteen months in March 1968. War Zone C or III Corps is where it began, a small "training exercise" for the 196th Light Infantry Brigade. However, about halfway through the planned training exercise, somehow elements of the following units were called into action: 25th Infantry, 1st Infantry, 173rd Airborne, a Special Forces unit, and some Republic of Vietnam (ARVN) battalions. At this time and after it ended, Operation Attleboro, as it was called then, would end up as the largest U.S. operation of the war to that time frame of September 14 to November 25, 1966 ... about nine weeks.

Tay Ninh and Dau Tieng were the specific areas in which this operation took place. It all began with a few probing searches and sporadic firefights with Viet Cong. Eventually, combat air assaults were made to probe deeper into suspected VC-held territory. There is much more to be said about this "training exercise" than I can dedicate in this book, but there are several sources available on this operation for anyone interested.

As the combat assaults increased and intensified, so did the contact with enemy forces. There are accounts of separated units because of the dense overgrown jungle. (Agent Orange spraying would hit this area hard in 1967 and 1968.) Heavy, close, face-to-face fighting became common for the rest of the operation, with VC snipers firing from well-concealed spots including trees. The 25th Infantry's Wolfhounds were heavily active in these battles, but the VC kept up their attacks as the Americans attempted to rescue their wounded.

In early November 1966, several different engagements with the enemy took place. There were several human wave assaults attempted by large VC units. At least two officers, a first sergeant, and several platoon leaders were killed during the November 4th and 5th engagements. Several more infantry platoons lost their way in the dense jungle and could not reach their destinations. Several radio operators had also been killed, so there was a major breakdown in communications between various companies. During this nine-week "training exercise," there were two Medals of Honor bestowed for uncommon bravery. Those men were Captain Foley and Pfc. Baker. Operation Attleboro left 1,106 dead Viet Cong on the battlefield. However, it was clearly evident that some of the senior officers in command had lacked a good understanding of how to attack and counterattack a highly elusive and very determined enemy force in jungle landscape. Many of the attempted maneuvers failed, and ground communication was not well planned or well executed, for which the officers in command have been criticized. Yet, the stories of heroism and bravery during this series of battles would make any American proud. **Total American casualties—653.**

Battle of Hue (1968) – This one really exemplified the Tet Offensive of January–February 1968. Although American commanders claim a win here, it is easy to argue with them. The costly battle took heavy casualties of American and South Vietnamese forces as ten battalions of NVA and VC sprung a surprise attack on a very weakly defended city. Hue should *not* have been poorly defended as its logistical value was priceless. Who is to blame? Whose job is it to make sure a military force is COMPLETELY PREPARED? The top brass!

I was not at Hue in 1968, nor do I personally know anyone who did fight and survive the five-week battle. History books are not kind to those who were in charge, but then again, hundreds of military leaders were caught completely off guard when Tet hit all of South Vietnam in 1968.

Eventually, the brave and determined Marines and South Vietnamese dispersed all communist forces after endless days and nights of bloody street-by-street and building-by-building battles. When victory was declared, it did not seem like it. The Battle of Hue's costs were:

- 216 Americans KIA
- 452 ARVNs KIA
- 1,584 Americans wounded
- 2,123 ARVNs wounded
- 5,000 civilians KIA
- 9,375 total allied casualties
- 80% of Hue City destroyed

This "victory" did not sit well with Americans back home, compliments of the Ameri-Cong media via television (CNN) and newspapers. Although the rest of 1968 would be bloodier yet, the Vietnam War's popularity back home had peaked, and the next five years would be a period of getting out of there.

Kham Duc (1968) – This was a large Special Forces base camp that was surrounded and assaulted by an NVA regiment-sized force and then reinforced by a Viet Cong regiment. Despite reinforcements from other American infantry units, this battle was a devastating defeat for the U.S.

- Total casualties unknown
- Base camp abandoned
- Hundreds of civilians and military personnel left behind

Ambush near Khe Sahn (1968) – A forty-one-man platoon from the 26th Marines was sent out on a night ambush patrol. Spotting some Viet Cong scouts, the Marines pursued them and were led into an ambush. The Marine platoon was destroyed.

Lang Vei (1968) – SURPRISE! An NVA force brought tanks, compliments of the Soviet Union, to overrun a supposedly well-defended Special Forces camp. U.S. artillery support and our firepower did not prevent massive losses to the base camp's defenders. Damage done:

- 500 Montagnards KIA
- 7 Americans KIA
- 3 Americans captured (POW)
- 11 Americans wounded
- 90 North Vietnamese KIA

Ben Cui (1968) – Dau Tieng was the 25th Infantry base camp associated with Ben Cui. A mechanized unit (1st BN 5th Infantry) had left Dau Tieng for a search-and-destroy mission. Not far out of Dau Tieng, an NVA force ambushed the badly outnumbered column of armored personnel carriers (APCs), destroying five APCs in minutes. A quick retreat was ordered, but the damage was done:

- 17 Americans KIA
- Dozens of Americans wounded
- 5 APCs destroyed
- The dead had to be left behind in the retreat

Nui Ba Den (1968) – The Black Virgin Mountain (images shown in this book often) had been attacked often—and overrun often. Most times, we were victorious, although Americans back home never heard about those victories. In May 1968, several hundred NVA assaulted the top of Nui Ba Den and destroyed the outpost completely. The attack was so quick and unexpected that most of the casualties died without a weapon in their hands. Damage done:

- 24 Americans KIA
- 55 Americans wounded
- 2 Americans taken prisoner (POW)
- Base camp burned to the ground

Hoc Mon (1968) – There have been many ambushes in this area. I know from experience, as half of our platoon was mauled at Hoc Mon. On this ambush, it was a ninety-two-man company of the 4th Battalion, 9th Infantry, 25th Infantry who were on a search-and-destroy mission for Viet Cong who were rocketing Tan Son Nhut Air Base and then … AMBUSH! In less than ten minutes, the ninety-two-man company was cut to pieces.

- 78 of 92 Americans were casualties

Dai Do (1968) – This battle took place near the DMZ. Reports are sketchy; however, there are various accounts from some of Dai Do's survivors. Basically, this battle took place between a Marine infantry battalion that was sent to destroy a much larger NVA force. The NVA force was at least a full regiment, so the Marines were badly outnumbered. Some results of the battle were:

- 81 Americans KIA
- 400 Americans wounded
- Several hundred NVA KIA

Khe Sahn (1968) – This was the village just three kilometers away from the famed Khe Sahn Marine base. The village was defended by 160 ARVN troops and fifteen American advisors. NVA attacked the village, leaving few survivors. Khe Sahn base sent a company of reinforcements, but they were also ambushed with few survivors. Records are incomplete regarding the total casualty count for our side, but estimates have been put at hundreds!

Firebase Airborne (1969) – There are too many vague and different accounts on how this base camp was overrun by NVA. Viet Cong sappers

Chinook

On Nui's Top – 1968

On Top of Nui Ba Den

Bottom of Nui Ba Den

slipped inside the defenses and blew up the ammunition dump, killing all within range. The NVA proceeded to kill or wound everyone in their path, destroying big artillery guns.

(Americans hid until the NVA left just before dawn.) Firebase Airborne was never officially classified as captured even though it was destroyed by the NVA.

- Casualties not reported ... few survivors

Hamburger Hill (1969) – At this time, following the bloodiest year of the war (1968), Americans back in the States were very tired and frustrated with the continuance of the Vietnam War. When the news of this battle arrived, public support dropped to an all-time low. Several battalions of the 101st Airborne Division were sent to take this meaningless hill from the NVA encamped on its top. Eventually, the enemy evacuated the hill, probably through tunnels, and that allowed our guys to take the empty mountaintop— then they vacated it. Damage done:

- 84 Americans KIA
- 480 Americans wounded
- **564 casualties for what?**

Firebase Ripcord (1970) – This 101st Airborne firebase was being evacuated when it was attacked by a massive force of NVA. Ripcord was completely surrounded by thick jungles, and the only means for supplies was by helicopter. It was 1970 and the war was in its winding-down mode, but no one told North Vietnam. A twenty-three-day siege followed the NVA's initial human wave attack, which was repelled. Some reports estimated the NVA force had a 10:1 advantage in troops over the Americans. Eventually, the evacuation was completed. Heavy casualties were inflicted onto the enemy, but they kept up the attack. In the end, American damages were high:

- 75 (at least) Americans KIA
- 463 (estimated) Americans wounded
- Dozens of helicopters shot down
- ALL major equipment left behind
- Several soldiers were reportedly left behind

Dau Tieng Falls!

During my tour in Vietnam, the main base camps of the 25th Infantry were attacked often. Dau Tieng, where I was initially assigned, was overrun three times, once while I was inside the base camp on July 3-4, 1968.

When the North Vietnamese Army was rumbling, almost unopposed, over and through every South Vietnamese Army stronghold in 1975, I was paying particular attention (from back home) to the area of Dau Tieng and Tay Ninh. My heart sank when I heard that both base camps had fallen in April 1975.

By March 1975, the North Vietnamese had overrun and captured all the provinces in I and II Corps as well as most other tactical zones around Saigon, except for Tay Ninh Province. Dau Tieng-Chon Thanh stood in the way to Tay Ninh. Xuan Loc would follow them both. This was the last stronghold for the South Vietnamese Army, still under advisement by the American military.

Dau Tieng fell to the onslaught of several NVA regiments. As most of the defenders of Dau Tieng had retreated to Tay Ninh and Xuan Loc, the NVA onslaught left over 2,000 dead South Vietnamese. Surprisingly, this time the NVA were merciful, as they allowed nearly 500 captured prisoners to live.

Xuan Loc Falls ... War Over!

Tay Ninh was given up without a fight, setting up what would be the final major battle of the Vietnam War between April 9 – 21, 1975. Up till then, North Vietnam's forces literally ran through the northern provinces of South Vietnam with little opposition. But the battles at Dau Tieng-Chon Thanh were not so easy.

Xuan Loc was South Vietnam's last-ditch attempt at stalling the inevitable conquest of South Vietnam by the communist forces. Stories abound about how the South Vietnam 18th Infantry Division (guys we taught) fought a heroic battle at Xuan Loc, despite being heavily outnumbered 12,000 to 40,000! I have read the accounts of this battle over and over again. It makes me proud to know that the South Vietnamese fought the way they did when all seemed hopeless. It makes me feel somewhat proud that their valiant, defiant, last-ditch effort gave some meaning to our being there for ten years!

Saigon Falls ... To Viet Cong?

One newspaper after another from New York to Los Angeles printed headlines that read something like this:

"SAIGON SURRENDERS TO VIET CONG"
- The Washington Post
April 30, 1975

My fellow Vietnam War buddies know the truth. South Vietnam was not conquered by a bunch of militia, terrorist-type peasants with homemade weapons. And there was never a unified uprising by the civilian population of South Vietnam as Hanoi Jane Fonda and John Kerry would like Americans to believe. South Vietnam's final defeat, well after we left, was conducted in full force in the same manner Genghis Khan ran through Asia, as Hitler steamrolled Europe. It was another media myth that Vietnam vets had to live with all these years when the truth was that **Saigon fell to seventeen North Vietnamese divisions, fully equipped, trained, and supplied by the Soviet Union and China!**

Xuan Loc's "capture at all costs" mentality was just that. The South Vietnamese forces suffered with 2,036 casualties, while the North Vietnamese paid a much steeper price with over 18,000 casualties. Yes, indeed, the South Vietnamese did not turn and run this time. However, Xuan Loc did fall, and this opened the gates with a clear path to Saigon. The war was over shortly after that.

The sources of this information are quite numerous. More details can be found from U.S. Army or Marine records, their various websites, various books written about some of these lesser-known battles, and from Oliver North's war stories. It is all public information.

The Vietnam War was not about fighting farmers with pitchforks and shovels as some of our WWII veterans claimed. It was not about killing women and children or babies either. Every war has innocent victims, but our war was showcased to the world by the highly biased TV sitcoms. Saigon, Xuan Loc, Dau Tieng, Hue, I Corp, and II Corp were all conquered by a North Vietnamese Army with modern Soviet and Chinese technology. But the Ameri-Cong media and their left-wing comrades would leave Americans with the belief that the Viet Cong had prevailed ... They did not.

In 1975, when the communists paraded victoriously through Saigon, the ragged remnants of what was left of a once-proud Viet Cong Army marched at the end of the victory parade. They carried one flag for The Democratic Republic of NORTH Vietnam. During the last years of the war, most of the Viet Cong's ranks had been replaced with North Vietnamese. Even though they fought side by side with the remnant Viet Cong Army, they marched with their North Vietnam brothers.

Months after the North Vietnamese made it official, when Pham Hung, a communist leader in North Vietnam, informed all of the remaining Viet Cong leaders that they were no longer needed, the Viet Cong's final demise came at the hands of those they fought for and sacrificed their lives for: North Vietnam.

Hey, Hanoi Jane, where were you and all your buddies when this happened? This war was never about a revolution for independence—it was always about COMMUNISM!

I did not enjoy writing this particular part of the book, but I felt people should know what we were faced with over there. The Vietnam War was a savage, in-your-face horror show where death happened at any time from any direction. There was no rest for those who fought there then and died there, for those who survived and came home to die here, or for those of us still living today.

Of course, we won most of our battles in Vietnam. We did not win all of them, despite the lies told by bureaucrats, politicians, and high-ranking military officers. Maybe now, after reading this section, more Americans will finally realize why we rarely talked about it with non-Vietnam veterans!

I regret if I have brought up old wounds for some and if I have hurt anyone's feelings. I fought there, too. I know the horror. I know the pain. **"ALL GAVE SOME ... SOME GAVE ALL."**

Even "They" Disrespected Us!

The majority of Vietnam veterans who I have known agree with what I am going to mention again here:

- One of the most degrading and disheartening insults that we Vietnam veterans ever received came from the so-called "greatest generation"—WWII veterans. They banned us from most of the mainstream service clubs such as Veterans of Foreign Wars, American Legion, etc.

They would say things like this to us: "We won our war" ... "Yours wasn't even a war" ... "Oh, you were those baby killers!" Never mind that when we came home, there was no parade, no disability compensation, no counseling, and no system in place to find a job. PTSD was not yet acknowledged, and we were treated like outcasts from those we used to look up to who fought in WWII—our dads and uncles.

As a result of this treatment, many specialized Vietnam War veteran organizations were formed independently, such as Veterans of the Vietnam War Inc., The Veterans Coalition, Vietnam Veterans of America, Viet NOW, etc.

This was a necessary move. NOW HEAR THIS ... when I go online to search for Vietnam War organizations, this option *immediately* is thrown up first ... **"Also try ANTI-VIETNAM WAR ORGANIZATIONS"!** This is 2013 and they are still giving them space?

Everyone ignored Vietnam vets, and people wonder why we rarely talked about Nam. One would think that WWII vets (many fought in Korea, too) should have known better than to believe the smear being told by our Ameri-Cong media and people like Hanoi John Kerry. Not so, as many of them chose to believe the lies.

Banned from mainstream veterans service organizations by the "greatest generation" because of our so-called "undeclared war," we had to stand alone. Now, fewer (much fewer) of us stand at all!

Hail the Conquering Heroes ... Seriously!

As shocking as the My Lai Massacre was, here is what will undoubtedly be a very controversial comparison to some other attacks on innocent and defenseless civilians by our own American military:

Battle of Okinawa, WWII (April – June 1945) - This was an epic eighty-two-day battle between mostly American forces, supported by Great Britain, Canada, Australia, and New Zealand with 183,000 forces against Japan and 120,000 forces. This strategic battle resulted in the highest number of deaths of any battle up until then, as follows:

- 95,000 Japanese military KIA
- 12,513 American/Allied military KIA
- 100,000 – 150,000 civilians, women and children KIA

Bombings of Hiroshima and Nagasaki, WWII (August 6-9, 1945)
The Germans had surrendered back on May 8, 1945, but Japan fought on despite their massive losses at Okinawa. With the rest of the world as America's ally, the end for Japan was inevitable. On July 26, 1945, the United States, Republic of China, and the United Kingdom called for a surrender of Japanese forces or an ultimate invasion, which would have meant tens of thousands of deaths on both sides. But the outcome would be an Allied victory. Japan ignored the ultimatum. On August 6th and again on August 9th, the United States delivered the final blow of WWII and dropped atomic bombs on the cities of Hiroshima and Nagasaki respectively. Casualties were as follows:

- Hiroshima: 100,000 – 170,000 killed
- Nagasaki: 60,000 – 80,000 killed
- Total: 160,000 – 250,000 civilians killed (mostly women and children)

Compare the civilian deaths from these actions to this highly publicized act:

My Lai Massacre, Vietnam War (March 16, 1968)

- 300 – 347 civilians, women and children KIA

President Truman's Study

In July 1946, President Truman authorized a study by the U.S. Strategic Bombing Survey Group that came to this conclusion:

*Based on a detailed investigation of all the facts and supported by the testimony of the surviving Japanese leaders involved, it was the Survey's findings that prior to December 31, 1945 and in all probability, prior to November 1, 1945, **Japan would have surrendered even if the atomic bombs had not been dropped**, even if Russia had not entered the war, and even if no invasions had been planned or contemplated.*

General Dwight Eisenhower, Supreme Commander of all Allied Forces, had said, "The Japanese were ready to surrender and it wasn't necessary to hit them with that awful thing."

When asked his opinion about dropping the atomic bomb, General Douglas MacArthur was quoted as saying, "I saw no military justification for the dropping of those bombs." **Many now believe the atomic bombs were dropped because it was important to impress Russia!**

To this day, the civilian deaths on Okinawa and the civilian deaths at Hiroshima and Nagasaki are debated for ethical reasons as Japan was going to be defeated anyway.

- Okinawa/civilians killed: 100,000 – 150,000
- Hiroshima/civilians killed: 100,000 – 170,000
- Nagasaki/civilians killed: 60,000 – 80,000
- My Lai/civilians killed: 300 – 347

And the Ameri-Cong media labeled Vietnam veterans as "baby killers"?

Hey, before anyone gets their blood pressure up over what I've just mentioned here, please understand that I love our WWII heroes as much as anyone does, but they also took civilian casualties. *They had no choice*. In fact, various sources estimate thirty-five million civilians died in WWII, while there were twenty-five million military deaths overall. After the A-bombs did their immediate destruction, it has been estimated that tens of thousands of Japanese civilians died from radiation exposure.

The death of innocent civilians is a tragic happening—one in which those who inflict it or witness it might carry a traumatic memory for life. Killing another human can strip one of his/her innocence, especially killing an innocent civilian.

War has always threatened civilians, even the ancient wars. With more modern and powerful weapons being used, civilians have become more vulnerable to becoming a casualty from battle.

To our credit, Vietnam War veterans have often vowed, **"Never again will U.S. veterans be treated the way we were."** We have held strong to that promise. It is largely due to the Vietnam War era veterans' efforts that our war brothers and sisters coming home from the Gulf War, Afghanistan, and Iraq are being treated with more respect than we were ... and they deserve the recognition.

In fact, many who opposed the Vietnam War put forth great energy to demonize Vietnam vets. For those too young to remember the truth, or it was never made available to them, I'm afraid those lies have been too often repeated and generally accepted *still*! What a despicable act.

The Amalekites Are Destroyed ... 3,000 Years Ago!

As the United Kingdom of Israel and Judah, its first king was Saul, who ruled from 1047–1007 BC. Enemies of Israel were the Amalekites, who attacked constantly whether they had a reason or not. One of these raids on Israel happened after a major planting of crops; the plantings were destroyed (1 Sam 15:2-3).

God saw reason for severe actions against the Amalekites, and so he commanded Saul to destroy them. That included innocent women and children.

1 Samuel 15:2-3 (New International Version)
²This is what the LORD Almighty says: 'I will punish the Amalekites for what they did to Israel when they waylaid them as they came up from Egypt. ³Now go, attack the Amalekites and totally destroy all that belongs to them. Do not spare them; put to death men and women, children and infants, cattle and sheep, camels and donkeys.'

A few years later (about 1,000), Genghis Khan and his Mongols rampaged most of the known civilized world with their "rape, pillage, and destroy" mentality. Before Genghis Khan would depart from this world, OVER ONE HALF OF THE WORLD POPULATION (forty million) would perish under his army's merciless acts.

Napalm was first introduced in WWII in 1945. Just two and a half weeks before Germany's inevitable surrender was to come, the allies hit Dresden with heavy bombs and napalm, killing an estimated 30,000 to 40,000 innocent civilians and a few hundred German soldiers.

The main reason for this section is not an attempt to diminish the glorious memories of our fathers, uncles, etc. who fought in WWII. My point is to show just how powerful the media is, whether it leans to the left or the right. Unfortunately, for the Vietnam War generation, it was a left-leaning media, and they were relentless in creating a negative perception about America's brave, very young men who fought in America's most unpopular war ... for ten years.

Baby Killers? Damage Done!

To be deliberately shunned socially or mentally can be the worst form of rejection. We received both. Shunning a person is usually a method for punishing them for doing something shameful. **Were we "baby killers"? Are we losers? Are we crybabies? HELL NO!**

Every year since the My Lai Massacre, the media makes sure to re-mention this day in history, usually with front-page headlines. Is this to make sure that generation after generation of Americans never forget that one isolated incident when a few brainwashed and thoroughly stressed-out American boys lost it in severe combat conditions? Here is a description of something I found on the Internet:

Baby Killer: a derogatory term used to identify Vietnam veterans returning from the war in the late 1960s and early 1970s. "Look what's getting off the plane. Friggin baby killers!"
(Source: www.urbandictionary.com)

Women and children died in Vietnam, as they have in every war. It is sad and deplorable. In the Vietnam War, Americans did everything possible to prevent innocent civilian deaths. We thought most of the kids were great. As mentioned elsewhere in the book, we built schools and hospitals and rebuilt entire villages in Vietnam.

The real baby killers were the Viet Cong, and worst yet, they were killing their own kind. It was part of their plan to defeat us by putting the civilian population in a constant state of unrest. There are no pictures of dead babies in this book; however, I could display many of them that resulted from Viet Cong massacres of women, children, and the elderly, as it was common … too common.

In closing this chapter, I would say this to our WWII brothers and any other American who may have shunned Vietnam veterans when we came home—**we were no better than you were, and you were no better than we were!**

*THEY Won't Believe This!

The Vietnam War was not about booby traps and homemade weapons against American high technology. North Vietnam fielded one of the largest hard-core armies in the world. China contributed over 300,000 personnel and $20,000,000,000 in aid, and the Soviet Union was sending tanks, artillery, and $1,000,000,000 annually to North Vietnam. From 1968 on, most American casualties were inflicted by Soviet-made technology, not mines and booby traps. Heck, even the Viet Minh's defeat of the France military at Dien Bien Phu in 1954 was led by, supported by, and directed by … China!

Chapter 7

BOB HOPE & CHRIS NOEL ...
AMERICAN HEROES

Every Nam vet's girlfriend is still hanging with us! Hey Nam bros, never had a date with that cute blonde who used to talk to us on Armed Forces Radio-Vietnam? She is still around and she is still fighting for us.

CHRIS NOEL was America's first female disc jockey for Armed Forces Radio since World War II. Her show was called *A Date with Chris*, which was aired to more than 300 military stations in Vietnam until 1971.

While Hanoi Jane and Hanoi John were disrespecting us, Chris Noel was teaming up with Bob Hope to spread good cheer to the forgotten warriors in Vietnam. If you were lucky enough to be near a radio and lucky enough to be in a safe area to listen to one, you were one of those who dreamed of having a date with Chris.

Hey guys, it's not like Chris was hard up for a date or something. Her list of former boyfriends would make all of our wives dislike Chris; they included the likes of the following: Jack Jones, Edd Byrnes, Hugh O'Brien, Steve McQueen, Gary Lockwood, Richard Chamberlain, Chad Everett, and Burt Reynolds. I have talked with Chris about this book, and she wishes us the best of luck with our mission to help all veterans, not just Vietnam veterans. That mission is shared by Chris to this very day.

Think about this, fellow Nam vets ... Chris gave up the Hollywood scene and all the glamour it offered because she fell in love with the soldiers of Vietnam—literally. Chris was America's answer to Hanoi Hannah. Unlike Hanoi Jane Fonda, Chris visited with the "good guys" in country while Hanoi Jane fraternized with the enemy in North Vietnam.

Chris was a New York Giants cheerleader, a model on the cover of *Good Housekeeping* at age sixteen, a beauty pageant winner, Miss Palm Beach, and she turned down an offer from *Playboy*. She appeared in more than a dozen movies.

How/why does a person give up things like appearing in movies and TV series to volunteer to go to Vietnam and travel on her own to hospitals, base camps, and remote outposts? Some say—and Chris agrees—that her destiny was altered in 1965 when she visited a VA hospital. Since then, Vietnam veterans became her primary mission in life. Twice, Chris was traveling in a helicopter that was shot down!

Chris was touched by the Vietnam War like most Vietnam veterans were touched. She married a U.S. Army Green Beret who took his own life in 1969, suffering from battle stress. He had been wounded three times.

Chris Noel was as courageous as any Vietnam combat veteran was. She had to be, as our terrorist enemy, the Viet Cong, actually placed a sizeable bounty on her … to bring her in "dead or living."

Today, Chris Noel is as remarkable and determined to help veterans as she runs two shelters in Florida for homeless veterans. She fought the unpopular fight with us over "there," and she continues another unpopular fight for our homeless brothers back here. **She could use your help.**

In 1985, she co-starred with Don Johnson in the movie *Cease Fire*, which detailed the trauma faced by Vietnam veterans. This gave her the idea to open her homeless shelters in Florida.

Chris has had to deal with her own Vietnam War-related problems, such as the unfortunate suicide of her first husband, flashbacks, migraines, and stress disorders. Chris chose to serve her country rather than herself, unlike many other egomaniacs in the entertainment industry. She has been rewarded tenfold in ways that no amount of riches could possibly buy.

Now, my brothers/sisters, Chris Noel could use our help as CEASE FIRE HOUSE is kept running from donations from patriotic Americans. **Please support our hero, Chris Noel, if you are able.**

CEASE FIRE HOUSE
291 NE 19th Avenue
Boynton Beach, FL 33435
Phone: (561) 736-4325
Email: vetsville@aol.com

Vetsville Cease Fire House

The Mission of Vetsville Cease Fire House, Inc. is to help disabled, homeless, and hungry veterans by providing emergency residential lodging, food, clothing, and employment opportunities regardless of race, color, creed, sex, or age; providing referral service to other appropriate human service agencies, and working cooperatively with these agencies to help our clients return to the community as responsible, productive, self-sufficient citizens.

Vetsville was started by Chris Noel. Any Vietnam veteran will know who she is and how much she meant to us.

A Date With Chris Noel

When Hollywood turned stridently against the war and the men who fought it, Chris Noel stuck with the GIs—and she's still with them.

A model-turned-actress in the early 1960s, Chris Noel was a young blonde bombshell with a number of movies and TV guest appearances under her belt when she first started entertaining the troops in Vietnam. She received the Distinguished Vietnam Veteran award in 1984 from the Veterans Network for her work during the war. In an interview, Noel recalls her life-altering experiences and her ongoing efforts in support of Vietnam veterans.

Excerpts from The Vietnam Interview
By Claudia Gary and David T. Zabecki
Originally published by Vietnam Magazine in 2008
Re-published here by consent of Chris Noel

Vietnam: Tell us a little about your Hollywood career before Vietnam.
Chris Noel: When I first went to Hollywood, I was put under contract to Universal for one month, and then they fired me. Their head of casting said I had the worst voice in the world, and said to "send that girl back where she came from, she's atrocious." So I cried a lot, until three weeks later I was under contract to MGM. In the first film I did, I played the girlfriend opposite Steve McQueen, in Soldier in the Rain. Jackie Gleason and Tuesday Weld were in the film. I guest-starred in almost all of the television shows of that year. I did a lot of beach movies and motorcycle movies and just a little bit of everything.

What was the turning point for you?
The 1965 Christmas tour that I made with California's Governor Pat Brown and various celebrities. That year, my boyfriend was over in Vietnam with Bob Hope. Then I had the opportunity to go to the VA hospitals. When I went into the gangrene ward of double and triple amputees, I was stunned. I remember the very first guy I saw there said something really nasty to us.

Then Sandy Koufax took and threw a ball to a guy who had only one arm, and he reached up and caught the ball. He was laughing, and the other guys were laughing. I thought, "Wow, I have to find a way to learn to make them happy." My girlfriend and I sang "Diamonds Are a Girl's Best Friend," and we were absolutely terrible, but it was kind of cute. When I walked out of the ward, I was still very, very stunned. Those moments changed my life and made me realize that I had to make a difference.

How did you get the disk jockey job with Armed Forces Radio?
My boyfriend came back from his tour and he had to put in Reserve time. He was at Armed Forces Radio and Television Service in Hollywood, and he found out that they were looking for someone to put on the radio. So I called, made my appointment, went in and did my interview—and they chose me. I started off doing a show called *Small World* with George Church III. I became really popular. The colonel called me in one day, and said, "Well, Chris, I hate to tell you this, but you've been fired." I said, "Fired? What did I do wrong?" And he said, "Well, you've been fired, but you've been hired to do your own show." It was pretty exciting. They came up with the name, *A Date With Chris*. They would record it to be put on 33-1/3 records, which would be sent to all the outlets throughout the free world.

What did you think about your radio show being called America's answer to Hanoi Hannah and Saigon Sally?
Something that just blew me away was when Hanoi Hannah stated that she really didn't know how the GIs all felt about her until she got a video of the movie *Good Morning, Vietnam!* Isn't that weird? I never really knew what Hanoi Hannah looked like until 2007, when CSPAN was showing an interview with her. It was fascinating. I had heard just a little tiny bit of her voice a couple of times in Vietnam, but usually I was so busy that I wasn't really tuned in to her.

How did you get on Bob Hope's tour?
After I started my radio show, I knew that the holidays were coming and Bob Hope would be going back over again. I asked, "Is there any way that you could get Bob Hope to let me go with him to Vietnam?" The answer came back: No, I wasn't considered a big enough star to go with him. But a few weeks later, I got a telegram from the Pentagon asking if I would go over and entertain the troops.

How was your first trip to Vietnam?
The first time I went over was in December 1966. I was very excited, but I didn't have the foggiest idea of what to do, because all I knew was how to be an actress on radio and television. I took a portable record player with batteries, and a little record case. I think I had the top 100, or maybe only the top 50 songs. They said, "You're going to be there at Christmas time, so take some kind of Santa Claus outfit." I was only being paid $200 a week by MGM, so I didn't have a lot of money. I went to Hollywood Boulevard and I saw a little silver miniskirt and little silver top, and that's what I bought for my Santa Claus outfit.

They sent me to one of the bases to get my shots, and I had to stand in this line, just like all the guys. I had never been anywhere outside of the United States except one time to Mexico. When we landed in Vietnam and I walked down the steps at Tan Son Nhut, it was stifling. They took my suitcase and we got into a van. The windows were open, but there was mesh on the windows, which they said was to keep grenades out.

What was it like being on Bob Hope's 25th Anniversary show in Cu Chi on December 25, 1966?
My escort officer said to me: "Chris, Bob Hope is going to be doing a show on Christmas Day. How would you like to be in his show?" I wasn't very far away from Cu Chi, so they just helicoptered me in. When I first got there so many cameras were clicking, it sounded like a field of locusts. We went to this tent, and they had fans going, and makeup artists, and hairdressers. Some GI had given me a poem, something about the Night Before Christmas, only it all had to do with the Vietnam War. It was that whole poem I did onstage.

I kept hearing all of these show business people complaining—they complained about everything! They complained about how hot it was—"I can't go out there if I'm sweating like this," and "You must do something better with my hair." I'm sitting there thinking, my gosh, I can't stand these people! They're all just prima donnas. They don't have the foggiest idea of what it's really like over here. They're in air conditioning as much as they can, and they've got the best of everything, and all they do is complain!

Some big acts were restricted to base camps for security, but you sometimes went alone to the more isolated firebases. What was that like?
I'm so thankful that I was able to have that opportunity—to just drop down out of the sky in a helicopter, and to see the guys come out of the boonies, exhausted, and already with that stare in their eyes. I feel really blessed that I could be there for a few moments with them, just to sign some pictures, just

to say hello, just to let them know that, yes, people do care about you. Along with Maggie and a few female war correspondents, I was one of the only women who ever traveled the entire scope of South Vietnam. I really think I got to have one of the most incredible experiences, to see that it wasn't the same war for everybody.

You kept doing this even though the Viet Cong had a $10,000 bounty on your head and you had a fear of heights?
I didn't think they'd ever really get me. I felt really protected. And once I started getting into those helicopters, I just loved it. What's weird is that now, when I get into helicopters, I freak. Back then, one time the hydraulic system went out in a helicopter and we went down ... that was scary.

Did your helicopter ever come under fire? Were there any close calls on the ground?
I only remember one very serious time in a helicopter, while trying to leave a mountaintop. Being in places that were being mortared—maybe three times. And ground fire—maybe twice.

You are a hero to GIs, but in show business, openly supporting the troops was the equivalent of professional suicide. How did you keep doing the hard right over the easy wrong?
Whenever I talk to young people, I always leave them with one thought: Do the right thing. Actually I never really thought of it that way, but when I started hearing it a lot—"do the right thing"—I realized that that's how I went along in my life, just always trying to do the right thing. I cannot imagine anybody having grown up in this country ever betraying it. Yet I've met so many people who are somewhat like that. And I've had to endure their conversations and sit there politely, and excuse myself when the time was up.

Your book A Matter of Survival is subtitled The War Jane Never Saw. How could you and Jane Fonda, coming from the same Hollywood culture, see things so differently?
I went to see a psychiatrist in New York who was doing work with PTSD, and I was just hoping that maybe she could help me because I really needed some help from somebody. Something came up about Jane Fonda. The doctor looked at me and asked, "How can you possibly even consider yourself in the same breath? She was born with a silver spoon, and you weren't. Why would you even bring her up? You don't have anger against her, you just have anger, period, and your own hostility. You're just using her as a catalyst."

I was in a pretty fragile state as it was, and I thought to myself, "Man, then if I have these thoughts that are so misdirected, are you trying to say to me that all these thousands and thousands of men and women who know the truth about Jane Fonda and feel the same way that I do—that we're all screwed up? That she was fine, but we're all the ones who are screwed up?"

Did you ever meet with Jane Fonda?
Yes. In the 1970s a girlfriend said, "Come on, I'm going to this event—Jane Fonda is talking, at Warner Brothers Studio." They had it set up in a big room. She was talking, and I was thinking, "I can't believe I'm here listening to all of this." So finally, I stood up and told her: "I don't even know where you're coming from. How can you say these things? You know, you went over to the enemy side in the Vietnam War, and I didn't. I stayed with our troops, which I felt was the honorable thing to do. How can you live with yourself, having done what you did? And how can you be saying today all the things that you're saying about our government and the oil industry? I can tell you right now, I'm married to an independent oil producer, and it's costing him more money to get the oil out of the ground than he's getting for it. He's losing everything that he owns and he's going under. And I'm sitting in this room, listening to these disgusting things that you're saying. You don't know what you're talking about."

She said: "You and I need to talk. Would you come up afterwards? Because you and I just need to talk." Well, that went nowhere. Everybody in the room looked at me like I was some kind of lu-lu.

You married Ty Herrington, whom you met in Vietnam, but that went terribly wrong?
Ty Herrington was a very charming, good-looking guy. I was madly in love with him, and it was so incredibly romantic. I was this Hollywood star, and he was this warrior. He was able to slip out of Vietnam a couple of times. I met him on R&R in Hawaii.

Then we decided to get married, but things started happening right before we got married, things that scared me. I realized that something was very, very wrong—but I went ahead and married him anyway. It was a horrible mistake. He used to put a gun to my head, and a knife to my throat, and he used to strangle me until I passed out. He would get this look in his eyes. I was scared, but I didn't know how to get out from underneath it.

We moved to Nashville because he had a contract with Monument Records. They recorded him singing "When the Green Berets Come Home" and "A Gun Don't Make a Man"—isn't that something? I was able to get him to go see a psychiatrist once. The psychiatrist told me that he was a paranoid-schizophrenic manic-depressive, and that he was very dangerous. Then one day he put a gun to his head and he was gone.

So many of those fighting this war are children or, in some cases, grandchildren of Vietnam veterans. What more can be done to ensure we take better care of these new veterans?
Just keep fighting for them. Just keep fighting for the veterans' issues. Keep fighting to make Walter Reed a better hospital—with more doctors. Sometimes our vets are fortunate, and they get a really good doctor; at other times, they are not so fortunate.

What enduring lessons did you gain from your experience during the Vietnam War?
I just think that war is hell, no matter who is fighting or where the wars are. But I think sometimes you have to have war in order to have peace. I mean, I'm just a retired movie actress. What do I know? I just keep fighting for what is my truth, trying to make it a better world for as many people as I come in touch with. I try to give the best of myself whenever I'm around other people, and try to be the best person I know how to be.

Claudia Gary is senior editor of Vietnam *magazine. David T. Zabecki is senior military historian for* Vietnam *and all of Weider History Group's other magazines. For more about Chris Noel and her work, see* www.chrisnoel.com.

One of the most eagerly anticipated events by Americans in Vietnam was Bob Hope's annual Christmas show. Mr. Hope remembered his first Vietnam soldier audience like this: "I looked at them; they laughed at me, and it was love at first sight."
What would Christmas in Vietnam be like without Bob Hope and friends? Once again, our hero finished off the Tet year in Vietnam with a standing ovation from 12,000 to 15,000 soldiers at the 25th Division's headquarters of Cu Chi on December 25, 1968. Accompanying Mr. Hope ... Raquel Welch, Barbara McNair, Rosey Grier, and more.
Like father, like son, and they both loved Bob Hope. Harry L. McNeer III of the 25th Infantry followed his father's footsteps when he was introduced to Mr. Hope in 1968. In 1944, Mr. Hope was touring France when Harry L.

Chris Noel – 1988
Coming Home Parade, Cleveland Ohio

Bob Hope

McNeer, Jr. and he met each other … twenty-four years earlier. That man, Bob Hope … a true American hero to all war veterans. **God bless Mr. Hope!** Sure, it was only a small portion of the 2.8 million troops who served in Vietnam that actually got to attend Mr. Hope's shows. But those who did—and many of us got to see taped versions later—were given a real lift and a terrific memory for our lives. **THANK YOU, BOB HOPE!**

Chris Noel, though certainly less famous, also left an acting career to try and cheer the troops up in Vietnam … and she is still taking care of us today! Chris was a successful Hollywood actress who appeared in films with Elvis and Steve McQueen. She left that limelight to become a field entertainer and basically served with us—often in very unsafe conditions. Chris wrote a couple of books titled *Vietnam and Me* and *Matter of Survival: The War Jane Never Saw*.

Bob Hope Vietnam Years 1964 – 1972

The legend of Bob Hope entertaining America's GIs started in May of 1941 when the country was at peace. When World War II broke out, Bob Hope, with a band of "Hollywood Gypsies," took off for Europe, North Africa, and the South Pacific—wherever our men in uniform were training or fighting. Throughout the war Bob's weekly radio shows were performed before GI audiences. The tradition of spending Christmas with the troops began in 1948 when Bob, with his wife Dolores, flew to Europe to entertain Americans involved with the Berlin airlift, and continued to entertain them through each Christmas through Desert Storm in 1990. Among Bob's most cherished memories are those holidays he shared with our troops in Nam.

1964	Guam, Okinawa, Korea, Thailand, and Vietnam
1965	Guam, Thailand, The Philippines, Wake Island, and aboard USS *Ticonderoga*
1966	Danang, Saigon, USS *Franklin Delano Roosevelt*, and USS *Bennington*
1967	Saigon, Long Bihn, Danang, and Cam Ranh Bay
1968	Hope's 18th Christmas abroad and his 5th Tour of Vietnam
1969	Europe and Southeast Asia
1970	England, Germany, Thailand, Guam, Korea, Vietnam
1971	Honolulu, Wake Island, Okinawa, Thailand, Vietnam, Spain, Cuba
1972	Japan, Korea, Thailand, Diego Garcia Island, Philippines, Guam, Wake Island, Shemya Island, Vietnam, and the USS *Midway*

Other Well-Knowns Who Supported Us

Martha Raye narrowly escaped a Viet Cong ground attack on Nui Ba Den mountaintop, as she was the lead entertainer of the USO-sponsored show "Hello Dolly." She was protected by 25th Infantrymen and Special Forces as helicopters rescued her and the other members of the USO troupe. They were delivered safely to Tay Ninh, another 25th Infantry base camp.

There was another recollection of Martha's bravery and loyalty. It was in 1967 near Pleiku after a deadly battle had cancelled another of her popular shows. There were many KIA and WIA from the battle. Martha, who had nurse training, not only helped carry the body bags of dead soldiers, she helped tend to the wounded. Martha Raye is buried at the U.S. Army Special Forces cemetery at Fort Bragg. **God bless Martha Raye!**

Joey Bishop, Tippi Hedren, and Mel Bishop made visits to Vietnam in December 1968 as a morale booster for the soldiers. Joey Bishop was made an honorary "Regular" of the 3rd Battalion, 22nd Infantry. Bishop hosted a late night show on ABC television in America.

Reverend Billy Graham finished one of his morale-boosting tours in 1968 with his last three stops at 25th Infantry fire support bases on Christmas Day, 1968. He succeeded in lifting the spirits of a lot of men.

My war buddies before me and after me were also entertained and motivated by other well-knowns, such as Nancy Sinatra with her walking boots, Anita Bryant, Joey Heatherton, Les Brown and his Band of Renown, Danny Kaye, Vikki Carr, James Drury, the New Christy Minstrels, and Phyllis Diller.

One popular group that made it to Cu Chi was Stan "The Man" Musial, Hall of Famer of the St. Louis Cardinals. Stan "The Man" was accompanied by other baseball favorites ... Brooks Robinson, Henry "Hank" Aaron, Joe Torre, Harmon Killebrew, and Mel Allen, a famous broadcaster.

Oh shucks, I left out one very sweet dignitary we all love—Bob Hope's lovely wife, Dolores, accompanied him a couple of times and sang "Silent Night" for my brothers.

*THEY Won't Believe This!

There is a Vietnam Memorial in Canada, a Mexican-American Vietnam Memorial in Sacramento, California, and a Vietnam Memorial in the "Isla Del Encanto," Puerto Rico. There is a National Memorial to Australian Vietnam Forces in Canberra. Thailand has the Clock Tower Vietnam War Memorial. Even New Zealand and American Samoa have memorials in honor of Vietnam veterans.

Canada, as a nation, did not officially fight in the Vietnam War. They were "neutral." I was not aware of this when I fought over there because I met several Canadians serving with our Army—met them on R&Rs in Vung Tau and Australia. Yes, of course, Canada was the preferred sanctuary for American draft dodgers and deserters as well—approximately 30,000. However, trumping those Americans were an estimated 50,000 Canadians who volunteered for U.S. Vietnam era forces. **Bottom line ... we owe those Canadian brothers much gratitude.**

The North Wall in Windsor, Ontario, is Canada's only gesture of appreciation for their own who went off to Vietnam, and it was two Americans from Michigan who donated their own money to construct this memorial. Unfortunately, Canadians were treated just as poorly as we Americans were when returning from Vietnam. It may have been more difficult for the Canadians as they did not have the numbers we had in the U.S.

Eighty Canadians died in the Vietnam War, and—get this—345 Puerto Ricans died in Vietnam. There were four Medal of Honor recipients from Puerto Rico ... while home-born Americans were draft dodging and deserting? **I STILL CANNOT BELIEVE THIS!**

Thank you, Puerto Rico, Canada, Australia, New Zealand, Thailand, American Samoa. Thank you, thank you, thank you.

Chapter 8

FONDA & KERRY, HEROES ...
IN NORTH VIETNAM

It is common knowledge that John Kerry was honored by the communists in Vietnam as a hero in their victory over the United States and South Vietnam. In the Vietnamese War Crimes Museum (now called Communist War Remnants Museum), a photograph of John Kerry hangs in a room dedicated to the anti-war activists ... who helped the Vietnamese communists. That photograph shows John Kerry as a senator of the U.S. being congratulated by General Secretary of the Communist Party of Vietnam, Comrade Do Muoi.

It is also common knowledge that John Kerry's testimony before the U.S. Senate Foreign Relations Committee in 1971 contributed to the false image of Vietnam veterans as being a bunch of "baby killers" and barbarians. This message was repeated over and over by the Ameri-Cong liberal media for decades.

Each of Kerry's prestigious medals awarded to him in Vietnam has met controversy and has been questioned by other Swift Boat veterans who served during that period; however, they were awarded to him authentically. Allegedly, there were documents showing that Kerry met with representatives of the Viet Cong and the North Vietnamese government more than once.

Kerry was also quoted as saying, "American troops routinely committed war crimes, that they were the rule rather than the exception." In the end, it became evident that many of Kerry's so-called Vietnam veteran supporters **were never in Vietnam**. They turned out to be liars and valor thieves. Maybe Kerry was the victim of deceit?

Other documents from a 1971 meeting in Detroit showed that the Vietnam Veterans Against the War and their spokesman, John Kerry, had been working toward similar goals that were being pursued by the communists of Vietnam. I need to mention again that in WWI and WWII, mass bombings of civilian population centers was common by American military. In Vietnam, it was not. On a 1971 TV show hosted by Dick Cavett, John O'Neill accused John Kerry of attempting the murder of the reputations of the 2.8 million Vietnam veterans who fought and died over there. On that TV show, John O'Neill presented facts which stated that none of Kerry's colleagues who made verbal accusations about American war crimes in Vietnam was ever willing to sign a deposition regarding their allegations.

O'Neill also said:

The country does not know it yet, but it has created a monster in the form of mil-lions of men who have been taught to deal and trade in violence, who have returned with a sense of anger and a sense of betrayal, which no one has yet grasped.

In *Stolen Valor*'s chapter entitled "Atrocities: The Good War Versus the Bad War," Hanoi Kerry was described as a hippie type, wild-eyed activist who was directly involved in organizing protests against the Vietnam War. It was in one of those protest rallies where he threw his precious medals (including a Silver Star, Bronze Star, three Purple Hearts) over a fence in the capital city of America.

Unfortunately, millions of Americans accepted Kerry's words and his actions at face value, looking past the Hollywood act that Kerry was putting on for his political gains. Amazingly, it was reported that Kerry's discarded medals were replaced and displayed on the wall of his office after he was elected to the Senate.

To give Kerry some benefit of doubt, back then he probably did not know that many of his followers in those protest rallies were phony imitations of "real" Vietnam veterans. Even today, the streets are filled with phony wannabes who never served in Vietnam.

During the last six months of Kerry's election run, I borrowed thousands of dollars, purchased several databases of names on disks, and started campaigning against him via direct mail and email. One of those databases I acquired contained nearly 50,000 mailing addresses (with some email addresses), and they would be the primary target of my anti-Kerry propaganda onslaught. **Those nearly 50,000 names were Purple Heart war veterans.**

Remember, I had to do this the old-fashioned way, with letters, envelopes, and stamps … tens of thousands of them at my personal expense. I felt it was worth it as the mere thought of Kerry becoming President and Commander in Chief of the USA military force made me lose a lot of sleep every night for those six months up to election night. Bottom line—Kerry lost, but he almost won, and that is still a horrible afterthought for most Vietnam veterans.

The year of 2004 was a time of waking up for a lot of Vietnam veterans including many of the Swift Boat veterans who served with John Kerry's unit. *Unfit for Command* is a 2004 book about Kerry by John O'Neil and Jerome Corsi. That book's timing was critically important to the contribution of Kerry's defeat. It was a *New York Times* bestseller upon its release in August 2004. The book was released at the time that ads by Swift Vets and POWs for Truth, a group founded by O'Neill to oppose Kerry's campaign, were being aired on U.S. television.

Yes, there were a few Swift Boat veterans who remained loyal to Kerry. But the final count would show that 85% or more of those who served directly with Kerry did not believe he was qualified to be Commander in Chief of the U.S. armed forces.

To Set The Record Straight, by Scott Swett and Tim Ziegler, is a more recent publishing also dedicated to American veterans of the Vietnam War who served with courage and honor. This book should be a must-read for any real patriotic American ... non-veterans included. It tells how the Swift Boat veterans and POWs of the Vietnam War united to defeat John Kerry in his presidential run.

Honestly, I have never met another Vietnam veteran who felt anything positive about John Kerry, and I have met with hundreds of Vietnam veterans across the United States. My own little political campaign against Kerry may or may not have had much of an impact on his defeat, but it sure left me with a pretty good feeling.

Since that time in 2004, I have become more active in marching in parades in a dress green uniform with all of the medals that I earned. THANK YOU, JOHN KERRY for helping me come out of hiding in the background and no longer being ashamed that I am a Vietnam veteran. Today I will shy away from NO ONE if they initiate conversation about Vietnam and Vietnam veterans ... NO ONE! **So, congratulations to John Kerry for being acknowledged as a hero ... in North Vietnam!**

Communist Vietnamese honor John Kerry, the war protestor, as a hero in their victory over the United States in the Vietnam War.

Many Vietnam veterans still refer to him as Hanoi John Kerry, and he is responsible for this statement when he referred to conversations he had with other Vietnam vets:

They told stories at times they had personally raped ... cut off ears ... cut off heads ... taped wires from portable telephones to human genitals and turned up the power ... cut off limbs ... blown up bodies ... randomly shot civilians ... razed villages in fashion reminiscent of Genghis Khan ... shot cattle and dogs for fun ... poisoned food stock and generally ravaged the countryside of South Vietnam in addition to the normal ravage of war and the normal and very particular ravaging which is done by the applied bombing power of this country.

> \- John Kerry, Representative of Vietnam
> April 22, 1971
> Veterans Against the War

Hanoi John is very notably remembered for throwing his medals over a fence in Washington D.C. Actually, he did not throw the medals themselves. He threw ribbons, which are representative of one's medals for dress uniforms.

Thousands of Vietnam Vets Rally Against Kerry!

(From: SOLDIER OF FORTUNE, January 2005)

The patriotic country-western music of Ray Cornelius blasted across Capitol Hill in Washington D.C. as an estimated five to eight thousand Vietnam Vets gathered from across the country to join the rally organized by Captain Larry Bailey, USN (Ret).

"I'll never forget heroes crying ... these hurtful memories will haunt me till I die," the deep voice chanted.

The timeless lyrics applied to a different time and a different place—30 some years ago. The memories of the pain brought by John Kerry and other anti-Vietnam War activists' actions in the early seventies had brought his group together.

"I waited for this moment for 34 years" one of the speakers, nurse Captain Donna Rowe told me. "He (John Kerry) called us a generation of monsters and baby killers."

"I recovered from what the North Vietnamese did to me" Dexter Lehtinen, former U.S. attorney, who addressed the crowd later, told Human Events. Lehtinen, whose face was disfigured by a mortar, said "the next thing I remember is people telling me, 'that guy is calling you Genghis Kahn.'"

POW Jim Warner told of being tortured ruthlessly and of being forced to read statements made by Kerry that called him and his fellow prisoners and U.S. soldiers baby killers.

B.G. Burkett, known for his extensive research in his book Stolen Valor that exposed fraudulent Vietnam Vets said, "Leave John Kerry to command the largest vessel he's ever competently handled—his surfboard." The peaceful rally lasted two hours. Once more, the

Vietnam Vets were drawn together to defend their service to their country and to vindi-cate those that had fallen.

What John Kerry did for this crowd may not have been intentional and may not be recognized by those who felt betrayed. In making his Vietnam War record a calling card for his presidential race, in glorifying himself, he glorified all who served in Vietnam.

'Hanoi John' Gets Unwelcome Reception From Veterans

By Robert B. Bluey
CNS News.com Staff Writer
July 29, 2004

Boston (CNSNews.com) – Hours after Sen. John Kerry sailed into this city with his Vietnam swift boat crewmates Wednesday, about a hundred other veterans gathered near the Democratic National Convention site to protest the anti-war positions of Kerry's past.

"He's a phony and he's a traitor," said Vietnam veteran Rich Burke, 66 of Boston. "He returned from Vietnam and testified in Congress that the military were baby killers and war criminals. He aban-doned and left all of his comrades to put up with that sort of statement. He's no good."

The veterans gathered near Kerry's Boston office at 1 Bowdoin St. around 6 p.m. and marched toward the FleetCenter where the convention is taking place. Vietnam veterans were joined by Korean veter-ans and Vietnamese-Americans, many of them from Boston and its suburbs.

The protest was designed to counter Kerry's use of Vietnam, including his war medals, as a campaign issue. Even before Kerry's arrival in Boston with 13 veterans Wednesday, the Democrat had routinely enlisted some of his former comrades to boost his presidential campaign.

"They're in the minority," said Korean War veteran Richard Creccr, 70, of Brighton, Mass. "These are the veterans right here. We're the ones who count. We'll be the ones voting. Let's hope he doesn't make it, but in this country, you never know."

Kerry's repeated mention of Vietnam in his presidential bid has irked some veterans because of the anti-war positions he took once he returned from his four-month tour of duty. Kerry became an influ-ential leader of Vietnam Veterans Against the War, aligning himself with activist Jane Fonda. One sign on Wednesday compared "Hanoi Jane" to "Hanoi John."

John Kerry testifies before the U.S. Senate Foreign Relations Committee in 1971.

Then there is Jane Fonda, aka Hanoi Jane Fonda. Due to her perceived traitorous actions, the attention she still deserves in this book would require more room than I am able to afford her. Hanoi Jane and Hanoi John Kerry are extremely unpopular people to Vietnam veterans. However, had John Kerry not become a candidate for President and Commander In Chief of the United States, I personally would still be a closet Vietnam veteran, and I would not be writing this book.

Fonda (Hanoi Jane) and Kerry (Hanoi John) are viewed as traitors to the large majority of Vietnam veterans to this very day and *they both know it*. Both are perceived to be instrumental in helping North Vietnam overcome disastrous defeats in battle with the American military.

Movie star Jane, with the support of her family's fortune behind her, made several personal visits to North Vietnam in support of their efforts to defeat America and South Vietnam.

Hanoi Jane and ... Kent State!

Yes indeed, our pretty Hanoi Jane had something to do with the Kent State riots in April 1970, although not directly. President Nixon cleared the way for an invasion into Cambodia for American and South Vietnamese troops so that we could "finally" pursue the hit-and-run North Vietnamese terrorists into their so-called sanctuary. Shortly after the invasion into Cambodia, Hanoi Jane let out her feelings publicly and called the President a "warmonger"!

I guess it was okay for Jane when North Vietnamese killed American boys. But when we defended ourselves by pursuing the aggressors, Jane's feelings were hurt.

Those Lovely Students

At their peak, the far-left antiwar group called Students for a Democratic Society (SDS) had between 400 to 450 chapters in the USA. SDS members rejected organized religion, capitalism, and those good old-fashioned, traditional family values. The Vietnam War proved in their eyes that the USA was an imperialist bully, fighting an immoral war for power—and that the USA was a racist country.

SDS participants were more common on such college campuses as California-Berkeley, Michigan, and Wisconsin, but gained much of their fame at the Kent State riots. Draft avoiders made up a large portion of their membership, and they helped to popularize burning draft cards. Although SDS disappeared before the Vietnam War had ended, a similar group of activists appeared in 2006 in response to the Iraq War. Their future is doubtful.

Enter the Kent State riots ... shortly after Hanoi Jane stirred things up with her public comments about the President. Having grown up near the Akron-Kent area, I know many people who were present before, during, and after the unfortunate Kent State horror.

This "peaceful demonstration" did some of the following before the Ohio National Guard was called in:

- Broke hundreds of windows
- Set fires, including the destruction of the ROTC building
- Attacked reporters and photographers
- Cut the firemen's fire hoses
- Assaulted several policemen and firemen

Here are some little known or not very often mentioned rumors about what happened there and why the shootings occurred:

- Weapons were found in several students' apartments after the violence had ended, leaving four dead and at least nine wounded.
- Shots were heard before the National Guard shooting and identified as originating from a .38 revolver and M-1 rifle.

Before the young and inexperienced National Guard troops fired on the rioting students, which turned into an out-of-control mob-type attack on the Guardsmen, the rioters were screaming the words KILL ... KILL ... KILL! Then the attack began with the attackers pummeling the American Guardsmen with dozens of deadly objects such as baseball bats, golf clubs, bricks, rocks, bottles, pipes, protruding spikes from golf and baseballs, slingshots, launched objects, wood clubs with razor blades, and bags of excrement. Several Guardsmen were struck and very badly cut and bruised, but the Ameri-Cong media barely mentioned this.

Before the riots began, local business owners were threatened and forced to display anti-war signs in their windows. It was later confirmed that many of these radical youths were NOT students enrolled at Kent State. As many as three to four dozen were members of the radical left Students for a Democratic Society, sent in by their leaders and supporters to instigate violence. One radical left leader, Jerry Rubin, was quoted with this statement at the time of Kent State's riots: ***Until you are ready to kill your parents, you're not ready to change this country.***

Ohio's Governor James Rhodes referred to the mob rioters as being similar to Nazi brown shirts, communists, vigilantes. These participants weren't just your everyday students. They were well-organized, well-trained militants with a mission of revolution on their minds.

Hanoi Jane's public bashing of President Nixon's authorization to invade Cambodia's sanctuaries for North Vietnamese Army regulars, Jerry Rubin's chilling statement to Kent State "students," and the militant influence and participation of the far left group, Students for a Democratic Society, made Kent turn into the ultimate nightmare.

Kent State's aftermath? Hanoi Jane's infamous statement with a clenched fist, "power to the people," became a battle cry for rioters across America. More than 800 campus demonstrations took place in 1970 with more than 400 of them being forced to shut down due to the massive protests and demonstrations by these far left radicals. Included in this violent display was the bombing of the National Guard's Headquarters in Washington.

ROTC enrollments were reduced substantially across America, diminishing the number of and decreasing the quality of commissioned officers available to serve in Vietnam. Millions of Americans were turned against the Vietnam War after Kent State. I think it could be said that hundreds, if not thousands of America's casualties in Vietnam that occurred after the campus riots in 1970 could be attributed to the Kent State war protest and the hundreds that followed at other universities.

The term "baby killers" became commonly used by the rioters, and, of course, the media carried the torch even further. Soon, most of America had been brainwashed into believing that most Vietnam War veterans were "baby killers."

Eight Guardsmen who were prosecuted for violating civil rights of students were acquitted. Reasons stated, "The evidence was insufficient for prosecution."

I believe that every year since the Kent State riots, there have been ceremonies held by radical left members in memory of the fallen students and a reminder of how evil America is. In the end, and this is also little known information, J. Edgar Hoover told White House officials, "Many of the Guardsmen at Kent State would have been killed if they had not fired." **God bless J. Edgar Hoover!**

This is the Jane Fonda some people chose to dislike:

March 1975 – In Moscow, Hanoi Jane told the Soviet *Litirachurnayc Gazeta*, "I would like to use this opportunity to thank the Soviet people for the assistance they're rendering to North Vietnam." At the same time, the North Vietnamese Army was mowing down columns of fleeing South Vietnamese civilians on Route 7 called "This Convoy of Tears" and Highway 21, "The Trail of Tears." The estimated slaughter was 50,000 women and children. (Source: www.americong.com)

March 1975 – *(New York Times)* Robert Reinhold reported that as Tom Hayden and Jane Fonda watched the refugees' flights of death and dismay, Jane Fonda said, "The suffering and turmoil have been going on for decades—this is just a pittance."

Just a pittance, says Hanoi Jane! The so-called liberation of South Vietnam was under way, and America stood by as the bloodbath was just beginning. In South Vietnam, Cambodia, and Laos, millions would be wiped from the earth, and this was also just a pittance. Jane?

In April 1975 when the North Vietnam Army rolled into Saigon, the Hanoi generals' celebrations were allegedly shared by Tom Hayden, Jane Fonda, and John Kerry as they were thinking how gloriously happy the South Vietnamese people would be. However, their ecstasy was not shared by the Saigon civilians, as Saigon (later renamed Ho Chi Minh City) was referred to as "Saigon's Streets Without Joy." The NVA took over a dead city without a sign of gratitude, as there were no cheering crowds to welcome them. To this day, many Vietnamese still call the city by its former name … Saigon.

Also in 1975, an offshoot of the North Vietnam Army, the Khmer Rouge, assumed control of Cambodia, led by a communist dictator and soon to be the slaughterer of millions. He was an understudy to the great Ho Chi Minh … His name was Pol Pot.

Many years later, another American supporter of Hanoi, Joan Baez, changed her colors after she had invested $200,000 investigating the civil rights of Vietnamese after the communist takeover of South Vietnam. She basically condemned the new Socialist Republic of Vietnam and asked the North Vietnamese to stop torturing and imprisoning the scores of civilians from South Vietnam. In particular, she asked them to stop using Vietnamese as human sacrifices for clearing Viet Cong planted minefields. Hanoi Jane and hubby, Tom Hayden, were furious with Baez, as many stories report. Jane even referred to the Vietnamese refugees (prisoners) as "misfits."

Loyal to Country or Enemy to It?

The do-gooders of the far left had to be shocked at the attempted mass exodus of Vietnamese by the millions. People like Fonda, Hayden, Kerry, etc., had convinced themselves and others like them that Americans had been fighting on behalf of only the wealthiest Vietnamese. They expected only those elite rich would bother to leave Vietnam after the communist North took control. Instead, an estimated 2,000,000 fled. There would have been more if they could have found something to float on. Unfortunately, another 1,500,000 of the fleeing Vietnamese would never reach their destinations.

Joan Baez changed her allegiance not because of hearsay, but by her own personal experiences or discussions with "real" Vietnamese refugees who were the victims.

This is how Joan Baez described things:

- A grim mosaic.
- The jails are overflowing.
- People are disappearing, never returning.
- People are shipped to re-education centers, fed a starvation diet.
- People are forced to squat, bound wrist to ankle, suffocated in "conex" bores.
- People are being used as human mine detectors, clearing live minefields with their hands and feet.
- For many, life is hell; death is prayed for.

(Source: www.phoeniciatimes.com/archives)

Joan Baez' reversed judgments about the human rights travesty in Vietnam under the communists were based on her own independent judgments. Remember, she was on the side of the Fonda/Kerry types beforehand. In October 1979, Joan Baez was quoted as follows: "This tragedy will rival the holocaust if we don't act now."
(Source: *Newsday*; October 6, 1979)

Before the end of December 1979, Joan Baez had been responsible for raising $1,250,000 for the Vietnamese refugees. That would be exactly $1,250,000 more than Hanoi Jane or Hanoi John probably ever raised for these "real" refugees. **A Salute to Joan Baez.**

On the other hand, Hanoi Jane has never really repented for her blatant support of the communists during or after the Vietnam War … NEVER.

This is how Dr. Roger Canfield, PhD, describes Hanoi Jane's "unrepentant" history in *Comrades in Arms*:

Jane Fonda the Unrepentant

- Though she made much of American use of chemicals in Vietnam, thereafter Jane Fonda did not protest either North Vietnamese use of chemicals in Laos, or "yellow rain chemicals" by the Soviet Union in South Yemen, Afghanistan, and Angola.

- Five years later, Jane stated that she was more profoundly committed to what she believed in now than when she was considered a traitor. (Source: *McCall's*; January 1978)

- Ten years later, Jane said, "I don't regret going at all (North Vietnam). I'm proud I did." (Source: *Los Angeles Times*; December 6, 1978)

- Thirteen years later, Hanoi Jane claims she was not wrong for her actions. She was a scapegoat while America's leaders were fundamentally the enemies of everything this country stands for.

- Twenty-five years later, Hanoi Jane's PR person stated, "It was extraordinarily unfair to say that Jane supported the other side." (Source: *Army Times*; August 17, 1987)

- In 2005, Hanoi Jane tried to dust off her established anti-war reputation by insisting that she loved the troops and hated the war in Iraq … yeah, right, Jane!

Why do these people maintain a residence in the USA if they detest what it stands for?

To my knowledge, Hanoi Jane has never shown remorse for the millions of defenseless civilians in Southeast Asia who were massacred by the communists after the war in South Vietnam ended. I have already given Hanoi Jane way too much mention, but it is extremely difficult to ignore her history with Vietnam.

How Hanoi Jane "earned" her nickname: On October 28, 2011, reporter Mike Ives published an article entitled "Hanoi Hotel Unearths Vietnam War Bunker That Sheltered Jane Fonda, Joan Baez."

Roberts wrote about how it was nearly forty years later since Nixon's bombing (erroneously labeled Christmas Bombings) in December 1972 when a war bunker near the Metropole Hotel was reopened. North Vietnamese Nguyen Thi Xuan Phuong, age 83 in 2011, remembers staying in the bunker during the Christmas Bombings of December 18-29, 1972 with anti-war activist Joan Baez. Others who sheltered there included Jane Fonda, said Phuong.

Fonda's visit ignited fury at home. She criticized U.S. policy on North Vietnamese radio and earned the nickname "Hanoi Jane" after posing for a photo atop an anti-aircraft gun.

(Source: www.militaryrecords.us.org)

THANK YOU, Hanoi Jane!

Vietnam War Veteran Defends Hanoi Jane?

Unfortunately, for some mind-boggling and inexplicable reasons, there has been some published material floating around over the past few years that attempts to imply that Hanoi Jane's displays against Vietnam War veterans weren't actually so unpatriotic. You can refer to Jerry Lembcke's book called *Hanoi Jane: War, Sex and Fantasies of Betrayal*. He has also written material on the "myth of the Vietnam War," which many of us have read, but not with complete approval.

Hanoi Jane was more than just an anti-war activist. She did visit with the North Vietnamese Army, but never with the American troops in South Vietnam. Commie sympathizer, or what?

Of course, we did not lose the war because of Hanoi Jane's public support of the "enemy" of America, just as we did not lose due to Hanoi John Kerry's statements and public displays. But North Vietnam exploited both of them to gain sympathy and a more favorable opinion by American citizens ... THAT LOST THE WAR!

Jerry Lembcke is unquestionably an accomplished writer and apparently a bona fide Vietnam veteran. However, much of his writings in this book givve Hanoi Jane way too much slack, and I don't understand why. In fact, in his 1998 book, *The Spitting Image: Myth, Memory and the Legacy of Vietnam*, the sociologist/author disputes that any of us were ever spit at or even jeered by anti-war protesters when we came home. He actually stated that it was all an urban legend to discredit the anti-war protesters. Really? Was he there for all ten years, greeting all 2.7 million Vietnam veterans when they came home—at all hours of the day, night, and morning?

My memory of the night I came home from Vietnam through Oakland, California, is still very clear. We were booed profusely, and yes, we were called disgraceful names by the longhaired greeters. I don't need to write an eighteen-page report on that ... IT HAPPENED!

Back to Hanoi Jane. She was a major contributor of financial support to Vietnam Veterans Against the War, for which John Kerry was a spokesman. Hanoi Jane married Tom Hayden, a major supporter of Students for a Democratic Society (SDS), many of whom just happened to be at the unfortunate Kent State horror show in April 1970. Oh, by the way, Hayden also visited North Vietnam, who was at war with us, and used much of the communists' propaganda in his lectures. He openly called for an American defeat in Vietnam and a socialist America by whatever means possible.

Nguyen Van Troi was a convicted Viet Cong terrorist who was executed by a firing squad on October 15, 1964 in Saigon. He was captured by South Vietnamese while attempting an assassination of the U.S. Secretary of Defense Robert McNamara *and* Henry Cabot Lodge Jr. in1963. As would be expected, Troi's arrest and his crime were ignored by the left-wing Ameri-Cong media ... surprise. Of course, he was viewed as a martyr by the communist bloc and, obviously, Tom and Jane, as they named their son Troy Garity (now an actor) in honor of the deceased Viet Cong terrorist.

In 1972, Hanoi Jane visited North Vietnam and was quoted as saying on one of her radio broadcasts, **"AMERICA IS THE COMMON ENEMY!"** Hanoi Jane and Tom were both honored by North Vietnam as "comrades-in-arms." On that note, I urge every American, especially Vietnam veterans, to purchase *Comrades in Arms: How Americong Won the War in Vietnam Against the Common Enemy—America,* by Roger Canfield.

Finally, in 1973 when American Prisoners of War (POWs) complained of their torture, Hanoi Jane called the POWs "hypocrites, liars, and pawns."

Hanoi Jane called them hypocrites and liars, and she said there was no reason to believe they tell the truth—they are professional killers, referring to American POWs. Some of the POWs responded to Hanoi Jane's comments as follows:

Liars, hypocrites and pawns are we? Men died at the hands of our captors. I hope the ghosts of those men come and haunt her.
                                        - Roy Ziegler II, 5 Year POW

I challenge her (Fonda) to look at the scar still visible on my arms from the torture and tell me to my face that I am a liar and a hypocrite.
                                        - James Ray, POW

I was the one she said was a liar. I was in the hospital ... had a broken arm and paralyzed. My experience with brutality, starvation and torture was no lie.
                                                                    - Bud Day, POW

As many of the POWs of the Vietnam War began to open up about their experience and about the effect of the anti-war movement, comments such as these came forth:

John Kerry's speaking before J. William Fulbright's Senate Foreign Relations Committee was the most effective propaganda my North Vietnamese captors had to use against us ... Kerry bombarded us with anti-war quotes from people in high places back in Washington.
                                                                    - John McCain
                                                                    U.S. Senator/POW

(Source of POW comments: *Comrades in Arms* by Roger Canfield, PhD, author)

NOTE: 114 VERY YOUNG AMERICAN POWS RETURNED FROM NORTH VIETNAM IN CASKETS!

Is She Really Sorry?

I have listened to Jane's apology over and over from 2000 and 2005, which went something like this:

I will go to my grave regretting the photograph of me in an anti-aircraft carrier, which looks like I was trying to shoot at American planes. It hurt so many soldiers. It galvanized such hostility. It was the most horrible thing I could possibly have done. It was just thoughtless.

As I listened to her and watched her online, I thought she was genuinely remorseful. But then ... Jane was a great actress. I did not have an opportunity to hear any of her radio broadcasts where she was also very genuine sounding with statements such as these in August 1972:

This transcription, dated August 22, 1972, was made from her Hotel Especen broadcast in Hanoi at 7:11 PM.

This is Jane Fonda. During my two week visit in the Democratic Republic of Vietnam, I've had the opportunity to visit a great many places and speak to a large number of people from all walks of life—workers, peasants, students, artists and dancers, historians, journalists, film actresses, soldiers, militia girls, members of the women's union, writers.

I visited the (Dam Xuac) agricultural coop, where the silk worms are also raised and thread is made. I visited a textile factory, a kindergarten in Hanoi. The beautiful Temple of Literature was where I saw traditional dances and heard songs of resistance. I also saw unforgettable ballet about the guerrillas training bees in the south to attack enemy soldiers. The bees were danced by women, and they did their job well.

In the shadow of the Temple of Literature I saw Vietnamese actors and actresses perform the second act of Arthur Miller's play, All My Sons, and this was very moving to me—the fact that artists here are translating and performing American plays while U.S. imperialists are bombing their country.

I cherish the memory of the blushing militia girls on the roof of their factory, encouraging one of their sisters as she sang a song praising the blue sky of Vietnam— these women who are so gentle and poetic, whose voices are so beautiful, but who, when American planes are bombing their city, become such good fighters.

I cherish the way a farmer evacuated from Hanoi, without hesitation, offered me, an American, their best individual bomb shelter while U.S. bombs fell nearby. The daughter and I, in fact, shared the shelter wrapped in each other's arms, cheek against cheek. It was on the road back from Nam Dinh, where I had witnessed the systematic destruction of civilian targets—schools, hospitals, pagodas, the factories, houses and the dike system.

As I left the United States two weeks ago, Nixon was again telling the American people that he was winding down the war, but in the rubble-strewn streets of Nam Dinh, his words echoed with sinister (words indistinct) of a true killer. And like the young Vietnamese woman I held in my arms clinging to me tightly—and I pressed my cheek against hers—I thought, this is a war against Vietnam perhaps, but the tragedy is America's.

One thing that I have learned beyond a shadow of a doubt since I've been in this country is that Nixon will never be able to break the spirit of these people; he'll never be able to turn Vietnam, north and south, into a neo-colony of the United States by bombing, by invading, by attacking in any way. One has only to go into the countryside and listen to the peasants describe the lives they led before the revolution to understand why every bomb that is dropped only strengthens their determination to resist. I've spoken to many peasants who talked about the days when their parents had to sell themselves to landlords as virtually slaves, when there were very few schools and much illiteracy, inadequate medical care, when they were not masters of their own lives.

But now, despite the bombs, despite the crimes being created—being committed against them by Richard Nixon, these people own their own land, build their own schools—the children learning, literacy—illiteracy is being wiped out, there is no more prostitution as there was during the time when this was a French colony. In other words, the people have taken power into their own hands, and they are controlling their own lives.

And after 4,000 years of struggling against nature and foreign invaders—and the last 25 years, prior to the revolution, of struggling against French colonialism—I don't think that the people of Vietnam are about to compromise in any way, shape or form about the freedom and independence of their country, and I think Richard Nixon would do well to read Vietnamese history, particularly their poetry, and particularly the poetry written by Ho Chi Minh.
(Source: www.1stcav/medic.com/hane_fonda.htm)

Bob Hope and Chris Noel took 180-degree paths from what the Fonda/Kerry pair chose. Wonder WHY? Mr. Hope, a true American hero in every American's eyes except the most ultra-left liberal or "commie pinko," took years away from his career back in the USA to make dozens of stops at military bases and ships from 1964–1972. He never forgot Vietnam as his presence was enjoyed and appreciated at places like Saigon, Long Binh, Danang, Cam Ranh Bay, Cu Chi, Guam, the Philippines, Thailand, Korea, and many, many other locations.

How could these four highly successful celebrities take such opposite paths with opposite views of the Vietnam War and the American troops that fought and died there? Bob Hope relished his military shows. He genuinely loved his military audience. Chris loves her Vietnam veterans and what they did in Vietnam—to this day.

Did Fonda and Kerry actually betray us? Probably not. However, neither has ever been embraced by Vietnam War veterans as warm and fuzzy people like John Wayne, Bob Hope, Chris Noel, and Martha Raye. Nor have either of them ever reached out to Vietnam War veterans with any memorable endorsements that we did what we were asked to do and that we did not deserve the cold shoulder from Americans when we came home … **WE DID NOT!**

The anti-war leftists and their left-wing media did contribute to a North Vietnamese victory as they helped direct the rage of many Americans onto US! We were sent halfway around the planet to fight for what our government told us was a just cause … and then treated with hatred and contempt when we came home … those of us who survived to make it home. Many of us wish to this day that **we had died over there!**

Some Vietnam veterans feel that the last battle of the Vietnam War may have been fought and *won* on November 2, 2004 when Hanoi John Kerry was defeated in his attempt to become Commander in Chief of the United States military as President of our country. That battle was fought between America's mainstream, heavily dominant left-wing media and that very large group of Vietnam veterans who served with or even commanded Hanoi John … the Swift Boat veterans and POWs for Truth.

These Vietnam veterans were fighting this battle for all of us who were dishonored by the media and the war protesters of which Hanoi John was a staunch supporter. So that was the real last battle of the Vietnam War and this time **WE DID NOT LOSE!**

To John Kerry's credit for Vietnam veterans, he was quoted in *Vietnam: A History* by Stanley Karnow as follows:

There I was, a week out of a jungle, flying San Francisco to New York. I fell asleep and woke up yelling from a nightmare. The other passengers moved away from me—a reaction I noticed more and more in the months ahead. The country didn't give a shit about the guys coming back or what they'd gone through. The feeling toward them was 'Stay away—don't contaminate us with whatever you've brought back from Vietnam.'

Obama Nominates Kerry for Secretary of State

The Secretary of State is an important senior position on the President's Cabinet and National Security Council. It is also the highest ranking appointed executive branch official, both in the presidential line of succession and the order of precedence. Secretary of State ranks as one of the four most important Cabinet members, with Secretary of State being rated as a Level 1 position.

Kerry will be the 68th Secretary of State since the creation of this position in 1789, succeeding Hillary Rodham Clinton, who was only the third woman to hold this position.

Time will tell, but I would expect Kerry will be able to fill this position quite adequately. My perception of him, shared with most Vietnam veterans because of his history with us, does not need to be clouded by what he is being asked to do for America today. However, my feelings for the Kerry I saw back in the Vietnam era have not changed. **GOD BLESS AMERICA.**

Believe this? One of the first important decisions by our new U.S. Secretary of State, John Kerry, was to provide approximately $60,000,000 in aid to Syrian rebel fighters in their armed civil war against so-called radical forces in Syria. Personally, I would not have a problem with this if these two significant contradictions did not exist:

1) The Vietnam War (which Kerry protested after his service) began with the U.S. sending only "advisors" and aid. (We all know where that went.)

2) The U.S. is in a major budget crisis, looking to cut useless spending, and there goes another mere $60,000,000 out the door, compliments of you and me … American taxpayers.

John Kerry sitting behind Jane Fonda during an anti-war rally at Valley Forge, PA in September 1970. (Source: www.snopes.com/politics/kerry.asp)

Another major problem, aside from giving away money which we borrowed ourselves, is the war in Syria, which at the time I wrote this wasn't just one war. It consisted of several small wars at once, and each group was well represented by Islamic terrorists! Don't hold your breath waiting for Kerry's next questionable move (supported by our President, of course). Mr. Secretary has vowed to help our "friends" in Egypt fix their economy in the form of economic assistance from our wealth of borrowed money! This will be old news when *Condemned Property?* publishes, but worth a reminder. Hey … maybe I should have written this book about our country itself as being **Condemned Property?**

Democrats. Republicans. Loyalists. Whigs … they are all the same. Are there any true American "patriots" left in politics?

As this book was going through its final proofing in September 2013, Kerry and Obama were pushing for a military strike on Syria. Americans need to be told why a military attack on Syria is morally justified and our attacks against North Vietnam and Iraq and Afghanistan were not. It will be interesting to see how history professors view these events.

*THEY Won't Believe This!

"Hell no, we won't go!" "Making money burning babies!" "Stop the war, feed the poor!" "War is not healthy for children!" Those were some of the anti-war slogans used by protesters. The left-wing media back home would show combat infantrymen on a "search-and-destroy mission" and then show images of a burning Vietnamese village, allowing Americans to make an incorrect, disgusting assumption.

Another major error of perception created by the biased media was that only during WWI and, of course, WWII did Americans faithfully and bravely go to war as "volunteers." Truth is, over 70% of Vietnam veterans volunteered, while most WWII veterans were drafted. How about **draft dodgers**? Our lovely media has had people believing that draft dodging or deserting was rampant during the Vietnam War. Truth is, only 40,000 Americans illegally defied or refused the draft during Vietnam's war. In WWI, 337,649 faithful, brave Americans dodged the draft.

Chapter 9

TRADING A BUNKER FOR A HOOCH!

When we were out in the bush, every couple of months we were given a taste of what base camp living was like (for a day or two) opposed to the bush. Even though I have been to neither, it was like heaven versus hell.

During my seven or eight days of rehab at Tay Ninh Hospital in the fall of 1968, I had a lot of time to think about the last eight months or so. I was kind of getting to like Tay Ninh. But I knew as soon as my foot and knee infections healed up, I would be back out there. Maybe that is where I belonged, I thought.

My brothers were hit with some serious stuff while I was sitting back at Tay Ninh Hospital and doing some clerical work for our first sergeant. Man, that bothers me to this day, even though I more than did my part while I was out there in the bush.

Last Night in the Field – October 1968

It was sometime in October 1968, I think, when the first sergeant (Top) came to me, and to this day I don't know why he chose me. But he said this: "Trimmer, there's a job down at division headquarters in Cu Chi working as an aid in the adjutant general's office. But you will have to earn the job in an actual interview with a colonel. Are you interested?"

Oh my God! A chance to never go back to the bush, a chance to live base camp life for the rest of my tour, a better chance to **COME HOME ALIVE!**

I almost said NO! That night I got drunk on Carling Black Label beer with George, Smokey, Boone, and

Sergeant Daniels, and they told me, "Trimmer, go for it. You might be able to help us down there at division headquarters."

The next morning I jumped on a chopper to Cu Chi for the interview with the colonel at division headquarters. By this time Cu Chi was massive, bigger than Dau Tieng and Tay Ninh combined.

The Interview

The colonel was my interviewer in the office next to the division commander's office. I was scared to death. "Specialist Trimmer," the colonel started off with, "I see you were with the 3rd 22nd. My God, man, that is the 25th Division's most highly decorated unit—are you aware of that, Trimmer?"

"No sir. I was not, Colonel, but it's great to know. Thank you for letting me know that, sir."

"Trimmer, you can type of course—right? But I hope you can drive a jeep as you've been out in the bush for a long time now. Trimmer, I also see that you are from Twinsburg, Ohio. Are you an Ohio State Buckeye football fan?" (The colonel was also from Ohio.)

"YES SIR!"

"Well then, Trimmer, you will be able to listen to the Ohio State – Southern Cal Rose Bowl game on your own radio … *you've got the job!*"

Cu Chi Hilton – December 1968

The Next Few Months ...

The next few months I lived better than I had ever lived up to that point in my life—I'm dead serious. I had not seen or experienced ANY of the following out there in the bush:

- A cot with air mattress and a blanket!
- A locker to hang fresh clothes!
- Fresh clothes—even underwear!
- Warm/hot meals ... three times every day!
- Dinner at the officers' mess hall on Fridays!
- A PX with all the amenities I needed!
- A shower ... EVERY DAY!
- No more crapping in the jungle and wiping with tropical plant leaves ... OUTHOUSES WERE PURE LUXURY TO ME!
- A protective bunker to run to every time we got mortared—yes, that still happened—but most of the time I lay on top of the bunker with a beer and laughed at the base camp warriors scrambling and falling down, knocking each other over, trying to get into the bunker first!
- Entertainment at EM Clubs, although I usually just stayed back at my hooch (hut) and appreciated the hooch itself, which had a ROOF OVER MY HEAD!
- R&R's! I got two of them in my last four months as a base camp warrior ... Sydney and Vung Tau.

I was turned down twice when I put in for a so-called R&R out in the bush to be with my buddies ... What's wrong with this picture?

I was able to get back out to see some of my old platoon brothers via courier chopper when the adjutant general had to go to Saigon for a pow-wow. Then I visited with Tex Daniels, George, and Smokey a couple of times, and that just magnified my guilt complex even more because they were still living in **THE OTHER VIETNAM!**

Eventually I was able to help a couple of my brothers get base camp jobs, and that gave me some satisfaction. I also heard that most of the remaining guys were pulled out of the bush and given some pretty good base camp duties in Tay Ninh—thank you, dear God!

I never did drugs over there. Not in the bush and not in base camp. It was like an epidemic in Cu Chi. Everyone got high pretty much every night.

As the adjutant general's aide, I could pretty much do whatever I wanted. I had my own jeep at my disposal, and the general was usually off to Saigon a lot. I had to drive in a couple of convoys, and we were ambushed each time. I felt more secure back in the bush with my combat brothers than I did pinned on the highway during a convoy ambush. I got nicked in one of those ambushes, nothing major. One advantage the boonies had over the base camp life was that there was no racial problem out there. All combat units were racially integrated and mostly color-blind in combat. But I always heard there was another war going on back in the base camp between blacks and whites. As a result of this, racially motivated killings were not uncommon in the rear, but not well publicized.

Back in the base camp, it could also be very unsafe because of the number of Vietnamese civilians employed there. After all, most of them were VC at night, weren't they? The Vietnam War had no safe places because of the Viet Cong's incredibly successful, unconventional warfare tactics. No one could let his guard down and so no one had time to grieve. WHAT A FRICKING MESS!

I have been back from Nam for over forty years, and except for my mother's death, I have found it difficult to grieve for the loss of a loved one or a family member's passing ... WHY? Here might be one very good reason. Over there we were never allowed the time to grieve for our dead. They were here and gone just like that. WHAT THE HELL WAS THAT ALL ABOUT?

An American soldier who wept for a fallen brother in Nam was usually warned to keep his mind straight or stuff those tears. Open grief over a death was clearly not acceptable in Vietnam, as it may have been in previous wars.

My God! As I look back on this, I feel hatred for those who sent us to Nam and then abandoned us—unscrupulous people, guilty of whole-scale murder! If grieving was considered unimportant over there, then no wonder many of us came back with seemingly cold emotions ... NO WONDER!

I guess this is how we Nam vets came up with the phrase **It don't mean nuttin'!**

Let's Ambush a Convoy Today, Tomorrow, and the Next Day!

There were two ways that I could attempt to visit my platoon brothers who were still operating out of Tay Ninh after I was sent to Cu Chi—courier helicopter or by one of the daily convoys. Supply convoy runs operated almost daily during the peak years of the war, 1967 to 1970. Helicopters could only deliver so much in the way of heavy supplies, so the importance of trucks was paramount.

Unfortunately, the ground convoys were routine, and the enemy was completely aware of this. On the other hand, we operated in the field very non-routinely, allowing us to catch the Viet Cong by surprise sometimes.

Vietnam was a unique war in which everyone could be exposed to some combat action on a daily basis. Even the so-called rear unit base camps could become a battlefield ... there just were not any defined front lines. During the bloodbath year of 1968, truck convoys were hard-pressed to have escorts by military police (MP) units as they were scarce and spread thin in those years. As I understand from late 1969 into the 1970s, more MP units were sent to Vietnam, and convoy escorts became a large part of their workload, making them somewhat safer.

Volunteers to ride shotgun in one of the jeeps were welcomed in 1968–1969, and I volunteered twice. After all, volunteering brings satisfaction, they say. Both of those convoys were ambushed. It was a December-January time frame, and I had just two months left on my tour in Nam.

Most of our battles in the bush took place after dark. At least the convoys did their thing in the daylight hours when enemy forces were more visible. But land mines took their toll in the daytime too. Unfortunately, land mines took more civilian casualties then than U.S. and Vietnamese soldiers.

New Base Camp Job – Cu Chi

Cu Chi to Dau Tieng Convoy Ambush Thwarted!

It was in January 1969 when an estimated battalion of NVA and Viet Cong attempted a double ambush on two convoys coming from Cu Chi to Dau Tieng and Tay Ninh. One convoy had just split off from the other, on its way to Tay Ninh.

One ambush took place just nine miles from Dau Tieng, heading for Tay Ninh. The second convoy was ambushed a mere five miles away from Dau Tieng—headed for that city. This was the second and third attempt to destroy a convoy within a three-week period. The first one took place at the end of December 1968 just one mile outside Dau Tieng, where approximately 100 enemy died.

The January 1969 ambushes were just as aggressively fought by the enemy as the first one was. Once again, our sister unit of the 2nd Battalion Mechanized 22nd Infantry of the 25th Infantry was part of the convoys' guard, and the enemy attackers took heavy casualties. Supported by artillery and helicopter gunships, there were 132 enemy bodies lying dead when the two ambushes ended unsuccessfully. There were dozens of blood trails leading away from the ambush sites. American and South Vietnamese losses were minimal, but many were wounded.

In the second of those convoys I rode in that were ambushed, one of our fuel tanker trucks was hit by a Viet Cong rock-propelled grenade (RPG). Our gun trucks and their .50 calibers were smoking the wood line as were our mounted M-60s from the jeep. We also called in some air support, and after we passed around the blazing fuel tanker, we made it. This seemed awfully primitive, but convoys were economically more feasible than an armada of Chinook choppers, I guess. I took minor shrapnel in that convoy ambush— just a few stitches and a few Band-Aids. That was my last act of volunteering to participate in a ground convoy. I felt my chances were better with riding in the small but quick courier choppers. Maybe my experience in those 100+ combat assaults by air gave me a false sense of confidence to visit Tay Ninh by air rather than by land. I guess it was a coin flip.

As the war continued to heat up in 1969, the convoys were usually escorted by some of the Mechanized Infantry's tanks or APCs (armored personnel carriers). Sometimes chopper gunships would tag along. After all, the ground convoys often carried thousands of tons of supplies and **badly needed ammunition for the guys in the bush.**

When January 1969 came, the word was that most of my original platoon from Bravo Company 3rd 22nd had been given more secure assignments in Tay Ninh, which made me rest more at ease over their situation. Then again, I had two R&Rs coming (Australia and Vung Tau) and just six weeks left in country. I pretty much kept a low profile those last few weeks. In fact, some-times I joined the other base camp warriors (which I was one of now) and ran to a bunker for protection when Cu Chi was being hit by mortars and/or rockets. **After all, I was no longer living in a completely hopeless situation. I had reason for hope.** My former platoon buddies were relatively safe now, and I was counting the days and hours till the day I was going to board that Freedom Bird for Home Sweet H-O-M-E!

Australia, Here We Come ...

Bondi Beach, Australia - January 1969

Warning ... warning ... look out, Sydney! Messmer and Trimmer are coming, and we have not seen a white woman in nearly a full year. LOOK OUT!

I think it was in January of 1969 when Messmer and I were granted an R&R to Sydney, Australia, and we were going together. Two absolutely wild and crazy Americans from the Vietnam War were coming to the "land down under" after ten months of Nam ... and we were ready!

Kings Cross, Whisky Au Go Go, Mandy Beach, Bondi Beach ... we already had our geography lined up for the next seven days and six nights. I never made it out of the Kings Cross area, and the Whisky Au Go Go in Kings Cross was my starting point every night, and most nights (or mornings) it was my finishing point.

I think Messmer and I shared a hotel room across the street from Bondi Beach, where we would sleep most of the day, resting up from our evenings and mornings in the Kings Cross area. I remember there had been some shark attacks while we were there ... the great white shark types. I don't think we even went into the ocean the entire time we were there.

It was only my second evening of R&R when *she* walked into the Whisky Au Go Go. She was the closest thing to a Natalie Wood look-alike that any of us had ever seen. She was with a wedding party (not the bride-to-be), and I had to meet her. I asked her for a dance, and the next five days were a *blur*. Next thing I knew, it was time to report back to Vietnam—OR I could go absent without leave (AWOL) and face a court-martial!

Miss Natalie Wood look-alike insisted that I return and fulfill my obligation to the U.S.A., and if God willed it, we would meet up sometime later in our lives. We wrote to each other a few times, but as would be expected, she was grabbed up and married an attorney. So I settled back into my Vietnam lifestyle ... *just like that*. It was time to think about going HOME next month.

By the time I was getting close to departing from Vietnam in February of 1969, Cu Chi had matured into a semi-permanent base camp and one of the Army's most vital installations. It was now virtually impossible to overrun via a ground attack, but continued to get mortars and rocket rounds, **and casualties continued.**

Living conditions were still rather ascetic compared to stateside life. But Cu Chi was making progress. Before I left, we had the following luxuries available to us:

- Red Cross field office
- Improved PX
- Couple of swimming pools
- Couple of chapels
- A barbershop
- EM Clubs with "cold" beer
- Movie theatre (outdoors)

Even more impressive was the talk that semi-permanent latrines were coming. I left before that happened.

In general, Cu Chi was becoming a secure place where a soldier could get some rest and relaxation without too much fear ... completely opposite of what our life was like in the bush.

Earlier in 1968, resupplying Cu Chi was risky business, especially since it was done primarily by road. Convoys were ambushed often. As late as October – December 1968, the Viet Cong had attacked several convoys, but our retaliation was massive, and the VC were overwhelmingly defeated each time. Earlier in 1968, some convoys had been destroyed by the VC.

Cu Chi was surrounded by a large cleared area, including a man-made lake backed up by Ann Margaret Dam, which was built by the 65th Engineer

Battalion. The bunker line consisted of observation towers, firing positions with overhead cover, an earth berm, barbed-wire entanglements, spotlights, and minefields. The support battalions camped at Cu Chi were assigned sectors of the defensive perimeter with very specific rehearsed plans for reinforcement and counterattack. Artillery, counter-mortar fire, sensors, communications, reconnaissance, combat patrols, air support, and pacification all worked together to permit a large logistic and command complex to survive in no-man's land.

Complete books have been written about Cu Chi, and I could elaborate in much greater detail in this one. But I have a far more important goal for this book. By the end of my tour in Vietnam, Cu Chi had become better than a stay at a Holiday Inn. It was an in-country R&R destination for the combat soldier in the bush.

Armed Convoy

*THEY Won't Believe This!

When our Australian allies left for Vietnam, they left as a group in front of a parade. When they returned as a group, they did so in a welcome home parade in major cities such as Sydney, Brisbane, Melbourne, Adelaide, etc. Dozens of these parades took place … to deafening cheers. While approximately 20,000 American draft dodgers fled bravely off to Canada, living off their rich parents in the States, 40,000 Canadians were volunteering for American military service.

Every anti-Vietnam War protester during that war owes every "real" Vietnam War veteran an apology. It won't happen, and I doubt that very many of us would listen … but an apology is the least they owe us.

Chapter 10

COMING HOME FROM HELL!

Dusty Trimmer To Return Home

Spec. 5 Roland E. Trimmer, better known as "Dusty" Trimmer is expected home after serving our country. He served 1 year in Viet Nam with the biggest part of his time in combat.

While serving with Co. B, 3d Battalion, 22nd infantry, he distinguished himself by heroic actions while on a reconaissance mission. He received the Bronze Star for heroism and the Purple Heart for wounds sustained as well as citations for exceptionally meritorious service in Viet Nam.

We were flying to Long Binh from Cu Chi in late February or early March of 1969. There were two of us together from the 1st Platoon of Bravo Co. 3rd 22nd on a small courier chopper. Dale (Ski) Nowakowski from Wisconsin was with me. Ski was our M-60 gunner for the second squad, and he was pretty messed up in the mind from the past year ... really messed up.

I guess it was appropriate that we received some enemy fire shortly after we airlifted from Cu Chi. Guess it was a farewell and "don't come back" message from the enemy. NO WORRIES ABOUT COMING BACK ... AIN'T GOING TO HAPPEN! Fortunately, they missed our little chopper, as it wouldn't take much to bring one of those down.

On the flight home, I constantly thought about the "transition period" that I would be guided through by the U.S. Army. After that, everything would go back to a somewhat normal state like it was before I went to Vietnam ... RIGHT?

Almost forty-four years later, I am still looking for the "normal state" in my life.

The next day I heard that a convoy on its way from Cu Chi to Saigon was ambushed with heavy casualties and they had to go back to Cu Chi. If I had one or two more days to go in Cu Chi, I could have been in that convoy— EASILY! **What a send-off from HELL!**

To this very day I cannot even begin to comprehend why anyone would extend or re-up and return to Vietnam. Unless they had a cake base camp job waiting for them or they had absolutely nothing to go home to. Oh, by the way, on the plane, we were told to change into civilian uniforms ASAP after landing so that we would not be accosted by American protesters.

None of our original platoon members went back to Nam, and those who did make it home safely were wounded physically, mentally, or both. NO WAY JOSE … we wanted to get home on that Freedom Bird and to see all those smiling faces that would be welcoming us home from the longest and most horrifying year of our lives. Yup … couldn't wait for the welcome home greetings back in 1969. **IT'S 2013 AND I AM STILL WAITING!**

Surprising Mom … I'm Home!

Ski and I were granted the opportunity to leave Nam a few days earlier, and this would allow me to "pop in" at home and completely surprise Mom and family. We came in through Oakland with a forgettable stop in Guam. In fact, the entire flight to Guam—Oakland—Cleveland is a blur to me—except for the reception at Oakland!

We landed just before midnight in March 1969, and all I can remember was the reception of people when we walked off the plane. They booed us, and they threw eggs at us! Man, that was a bummer … Americans booing American soldiers coming home from a yearlong struggle to survive one of the most horror-filled wars in history. I shake my head to this day as I write about it … nearly *forty-four years later*!

The temperature at Cleveland's airport was in the twenties with light snow. Since no one knew I was coming home, there was no one waiting for me at the airport. The reception by the passersby at Cleveland Airport was one of indifference. No one welcomed me home; no one said thank you. In fact, no one talked to me … but I did get a lot of unfriendly stares.

I had to carry all my world belongings crammed into a huge U.S. Army duffle bag that had to weigh over one hundred pounds. I did not have an overcoat. Just thin, summer-type dress greens on in 20° temperature—I had just left a 100° climate a couple of days earlier.

Cleveland had a Rapid Transit System then (still does). It's like a streetcar or subway system. I took it to downtown Cleveland from the airport. From there, I hopped on another one to Shaker Heights/Warrensville Heights. From there, I had about thirty miles left to find my way home … hitchhiking in the snow! I stood there in the same spot on Chagrin and Van Aken Boulevard in the snow … in my Army uniform … for three and a half hours before someone stopped to asked me if I needed a ride. It was a huge black Cadillac. The inside felt like a palace to me. Just a few days earlier I was in a rat-infested, mosquito-plagued base camp in Southeast Asia.

"Young man, you look tired. Did you just come home from Vietnam?" one of the two men in the Cadillac asked me.

"Yessir," I replied. Then they asked me where I was going. "Home," I said. "I live in Twinsburg."

They said, "That's a long walk. Mind if we drive you there?"

"Yessir—I mean, no sir, I do not mind—I would really appreciate it. But I don't have very much money to pay you," I said.

They laughed and then one of them asked me, "Have you had steak or lobster for dinner lately?"

"Man, I mean, sir, you have to be kidding. Heck, no," I said. Next thing I remember from that day was getting out of the Cadillac in front of a restaurant in Maple Heights, Ohio, called The Post & Paddock. We went in and they ordered me a steak and lobster dinner—NO LIE! They both had a salad and watched me with a humorous look as I gobbled down everything in what seemed like seconds to me … Man, was that good. And I had a scotch and water for the first time in a year!

I remember that they owned a business (that no longer exists today). I think it was called the Rayco Cover Company or Inc. or something like that. We talked about Nam a lot while they were driving me to Twinsburg. I tried to describe the entire year over there in the next forty-five minutes or so. (There was no freeway from Maple Heights to Twinsburg in 1969.)

When we arrived at Glenwood Drive in Twinsburg, it was late evening and still snowing lightly. I asked them to drop me off at Ravenna and Glenwood—I wanted to walk the final two to three miles down Glenwood to my family's home.

I think surprising my mom like that almost gave her a heart attack, as she went hysterical on me when she saw me at the door.

That was how my trip from hell went. It started out a little rough, continued to be NOT what I had expected and hoped for, but in the end, it was a BEAUTIFUL DAY!

New Year's Eve Party—Back From Nam

December 31, 1969 – January 1, 1970

When I was fresh out of the service after a few months of boredom at Fort Hood, Texas, I decided to attend a party, my first since entering the U.S. Army in 1967. It seemed like a good idea. After all, everyone there would be people I knew, and certainly they would be understanding that I had just been turned loose on society, wouldn't they?

My date was Madge Beck, my girlfriend from high school who waited for me during my forced vacation with the U.S. Army. However, it was a different me that came home to Madge, and she would not stay with me for very much longer … I couldn't blame her, as I offered no future for her and me at that time. What a shame. She stuck with me for almost ten years, and most everyone in our hometown of Twinsburg figured they would be attending our wedding some day. It wasn't meant to be.

The New Year's Eve party went well for most of the evening, and a good time was seemingly had by all—seemingly. But something was brewing in the air, and it would cause a major disruption of the party before it was supposed to end.

As it turned out, one of the party's guests was Jack Bellemy from nearby Solon, Ohio. Jack and I knew each other before Nam, but we were only acquaintances till now. To our mutual surprise, both of us had spent some time in Vietnam at some of the same locations and at some of the same battles. Each of our descriptions of certain events at places such as Trang Bang, Boi Loi Woods, Go Dau Ha, Hoc Mon, Cu Chi, etc. were mirror images of what we both had to say. We had fought together over there—WOW!

Unfortunately, a couple of the other guests at this party did not respect or appreciate the things Jack and I were discussing about our experiences in Vietnam, and a very unfriendly exchange of words began to take place between several of them and us. The basis for the other's views about the Vietnam War was based on a book one of them read. The author had spent five years in Vietnam, and his narration of the Vietnamese people, American military, and the Vietnam War itself was almost 180 degrees different than how Jack and I were describing it … Tempers began to heat up.

As I mentioned earlier, our friends at the New Year's Eve party boastfully threw it at Jack and me that the person who wrote about Vietnam in the book they referred to did not spend just one measly year there … he spent a whole five years there in a place called Cam Ranh Bay! So what we could possibly know about Vietnam paled miserably to what the author of that book thought he knew about Vietnam. **Happy party sours immediately!**

The next event that took place is not being exaggerated to any degree. In seconds, Jack Bellemy flew through the air in an almost perfect parallel position, as though he had wings. At the front of his missile-like attack were his outstretched arms, and his hands landed perfectly with a death grip around one of the verbal assailant's neck. It took three of us to pry Jack's death grip from his target's neck. Finally, cooler heads prevailed. We actually did receive an apology from them for their comments. We accepted the apology, sort of, but in everyone's best interests we agreed to banish ourselves to the kitchen and finish the party in seclusion from the others. Jack and I talked till the morning hours about Vietnam.

Madge and Me – October of 1969

Jack Bellemy and Me at My Wedding – 1984

To this day, Jack Bellemy, who was a combat engineer assigned to the 25th Infantry Division in 1967–1968, and I are still the best of friends—true brothers, in fact.

Next, I would like to share some excerpts from a recent email I received from The Combat Infantryman's Association:

Excerpts From
The Warrior's Code of Honor
(Written by: Unidentified Wounded Soldier)

The "Warriors Code of Honor" author wishes to remain anonymous. His experiences an as 18 year-old rifleman in a infantry rifle platoon of the U.S. Army 7th Infantry Division in Korea and his experiences coming home led him to write this Code. He is also a Purple Heart Medal recipient and a life time member of both the Military Order of the Purple Heart (MOPH) and the disabled American Veterans (DAV).

I wrote it because my coming home expectation that things would be more or less the same was so unrealistic that it crashed and burned, along with my heart. This happened because: I had no idea that I was so emotionally numbed-up/shut down that I could not feel my feelings.

I had no idea that I had changed so much that my High School friends would now be merely acquaintances.

I had no idea that I came home an adrenaline junkie, which made me consider those who were not willing to engage in dangerous but thrilling activities, not OK people. The only people I wanted to relate to were other combat vets. It is a fact of life however, that in virtually every social circle, the numbers of authentic combat veterans are few and none. This was true in my case; consequently, there was nobody I wanted to talk to. The feeling of isolation, of being apart from anyone, of being alone in a crowd, made me consider myself deficient for being that way. I had no idea that my way of being was not unusual for a combat vet, but the usual. And so on. In short, coming home was hell for me.

Thanks to the G.I. Bill and multiple, simultaneous part-time jobs, I graduated from university and became a successful professional by day and alcoholic and junkie by night.

It is my life desire that my words will forewarn combat veterans about the danger of coming home with un-realistic expectations. If they return with realistic expectations, all will be well. If they do not, they will be in hell.

Ancient wisdom teaches that to be forewarned is to be forearmed. I came home un-forewarned, was thus unarmed, in hell, and bleeding—shot thru the heart by un-realistic expectations. And on that bloody hook, thereby hangs this tale.

More Excerpts From
The Warrior's Code of Honor

As a combat veteran wounded in one of America's wars, I offer to speak for those who cannot. Were the mouths of my fallen front-line friends not stopped with dust, they would testify that life revolves around honor.

In war, it is understood that you give your word of honor to do your duty—that is— stand and fight instead of running away and deserting your friends.

When you keep your word despite desperately desiring to flee the screaming hell all around … **you earn honor.**

Earning honor under fire changes who you are.

The blast furnace of battle burns away impurities encrusting your soul.

The white-hot forge of combat hammers you into a hardened, purified warrior will-ing to die rather than break your word to friends—your honor.

Combat is scary but exciting.

You never feel so alive as when being shot at without result.

You never feel so triumphant as when shooting back—with result.

You never feel love so pure as that burned into your heart by friends willing to die to keep their word to you.

And they do.

The biggest sadness of your life is to see friends falling.

The biggest surprise of your life is to survive the war.

Although still alive on the outside, you are dead inside—shot thru the heart with non-sensical guilt for living while friends died.

The biggest lie of your life torments you that you could have done something more, different, to save them.

Their faces are the tombstones in your weeping eyes, their souls shine the true cama-raderie you search for the rest of your life but never find.

You live in a different world now. You always will.

Your world is about waking up night after night silently screaming, back in battle.

Your world is about your best friend bleeding to death in your arms, howling in pain for you to kill him.

You did your duty, survived the dance, and returned home. But not all of you came back to the civilian world.

Your heart and mind are still in the Warrior's World, far beyond the Sun. They will always be in the Warrior's World. They will never leave, they are buried there.

In that hallowed home of honor, life is about keeping your word.

People in the civilian world, however, have no idea that life is about keeping your word.
They think life is about ballgames, backyards, barbecues, babies and business.
The distance between the two worlds is as far as Mars from Earth.
This is why, when you come home, you felt like an outsider, a visitor from another planet.

Many combat veterans—including this writer—feel that the war was the high point of our lives, and emotionally, life has been downhill ever since.

Another reason why we did not leave Vietnam with the perception of winners was that our military was largely a draftee force, and when the war peaked in 1968–1969, over twenty thousand men per month were being taken out of their homes from pretty comfortable environments and then sent to HELL! Most were given a very fast basic training, even less advanced training, and BANG … you're in the Vietnam War—**deal with it!**

In 1968 and 1969 the coffins were coming home—over one thousand dead young Americans every month. Initially, our fallen brothers were viewed as fallen heroes—like in previous wars—and the military had America's support. But when the coffins kept coming and coming, people—mostly in small-town America—began to ask: "How long is this going to last? When is it going to end?"

After the Tet Offensive, which we won overwhelmingly except in the view of the media, Americans had changed their minds drastically. The end was seemingly inevitable because of those two bloody years in which over 30,000 Americans died. I hate to be redundant here because I've said this already over and over, but it is a disgrace how Americans could or would not separate the Vietnam War from the young men they sent involuntarily to fight in a war in hell. It was shameful.

One of my favorite all-time Presidents and Commander in Chiefs of our great country's military once said this:

A man who is good enough to shed his blood for his country is good enough to be given a square deal afterwards.
                    - Theodore Roosevelt

Most Vietnam vets have not yet been given the "square deal" America owes them. We continue to be viewed as *Condemned Property*? So why even bother with us?

Fort Hood—Corpus Christi ... AWOL?

Usually after a combat troop had finished (survived) a full year's tour of duty in a W-A-R, soldiers would be given some slack and sent home if they had only a few months remaining to serve. NOT for us Vietnam veterans ... we weren't going to be let off the hook that easily. So I had to go to Fort Hood, Texas, and play war games ... **PLAY WAR GAMES?**

To this day, I have a hard time understanding how I almost ruined my life at Fort Hood, Texas, which was my last tour as an "active" United States Army soldier.

I had made it! Or so I thought. If I could handle that year of horror in Nam (which seemed like ten years), what could five months be like on home turf in Fort Hood, Texas? Piece of cake, I figured. WRONG!

Right off the bat, because I could type, they made me a supply sergeant for headquarters company. Lucky break. I had several squads of men at my disposal to perform the menial duties that needed to be done for the bureaucrats at the top of headquarters company. I was a model soldier, a highly decorated combat vet, and I was in great shape, so they made me part of the headquarters company honor guard and I got to march in front of majors, colonels, and generals.

PROBLEM! I couldn't do *this* for five months ... spit-shine my boots, stand at attention, salute every fricking 2nd lieutenant, make inspections, etc. I couldn't handle it—JUST COULDN'T! I came close twice to getting **court-martialed** for insubordination (or worse) because of the chicken crap they were asking me to dump on the troops in my details—and **I just could not do it.**

My weekends were spent with non-coms in Waco and Travis Lake if we could get away from Killeen and Temple. I had to get away from the jerks who stayed at Hood in their spare time. I was down to about thirty days to go and I would be a FREE man ... just thirty days. Surely I could stay clean for one more month, right? However, my head was spinning. Another day of taking orders from some simple s—- E-6 "lifer" was just not going to happen— or I would end up with a dishonorable discharge and maybe some time in a military prison for assault!

Why were they still messing with us Nam veterans? WHY, WHY, WHY? Okay, it was August 1969 and just as hot at Fort Hood as it was in Nam without the humidity and the jungles. In fact, I believe we went dry for the entire summer that year—for two or three months. We also had an invasion of crickets that year. They called it a "cricket plague." There were millions of them.

I gotta get out of here NOW! Since I was the supply sergeant, I had access to records, including my own. So I changed my ETS date, moved it up a full month, and no one knew any different. My plan was to head down to Corpus Christi and just be a bum for the next thirty days. Basically, I ordered up my own R&R after the war—and why not?

A few of those days at Corpus Christi I stayed at a Days Inn when I needed a shower and a real bed to sleep in. Most of the time I slept on the beaches like a bum ... like I did in Vietnam. I was right at home with a blanket on the beach. Those thirty days zoomed by. There were plenty of prostitutes down there to keep a twenty-three-year-old male content—and I learned to rely on prostitutes in Vietnam and the R&Rs. I never saw a prostitute in my life until I entered the military. **THANKS TO THE U.S. ARMY!**

I returned to Fort Hood on my official ETS date to get my things that a buddy was taking care of for me and "sneak out" of Fort Hood in the night. I called a taxi to take me to town—Killeen or Temple—can't remember which. As I was about to jump into the cab I heard this: **"Hey, Trimmer, what are you doing here? I thought you ETS'd?!"** I was being addressed by a sergeant first class Korean War veteran "lifer," and I figured I was going to get fried ... Fort Leavenworth Prison, here I come!

"Trimmer, talk to me. What the hell is going on?" he asked. So I told him my entire sob story on how I just couldn't take the bulls—— of playing war games—not after *the* Nam—and that I temporarily fudged my ETS date and snuck down to Corpus Christi and Padre Island to give myself a chilling-out R&R.

Son of a gun, the sergeant first class actually commended me on my creativity and on the risk I took to get some piece of mind. Heck, if I hadn't, I would have killed someone—and I was sure trained or brainwashed well enough to do that. He was so impressed and so understanding of what I did, he drove me to the bus station himself and never said a word to anyone that he saw me again!

I could have never done anything like that had I not experienced what I did in Vietnam ... NEVER! We came home from Nam and just didn't have any fear of anything anymore. It was going to take me a long, long time to chill out from Nam. So here I am in 2012, and **WHY AM I STILL PROPERTY OF VIETNAM?**

Freedom Bird

Great Freedom Bird, climbing so fast,
Leaving this war-torn land at last.
With silver wings shining so bright,
Screaming up into the morning light.
Taking home the happy ones who fought,
And long this one last ride have sought …
But think again of those left behind,
Or those who sudden death will find.
For those you see, Great Freedom Bird,
The captain's voice will not be heard.
So tip your silver wings to either side,
For those who will never take this ride.
Then once more, before the clouds you meet,
Think of the poor souls, the enemy keep.
For they, lost men, know not when,
They'll ride your winds into the wind.
So carry on your load of human life,
But show pity for the weeping wife.
So Great Freedom Bird, fading out of sight,
Seem not so proud in your long, long flight.
For every long mile that you shall fly,
Somewhere, a poor lonely GI will die.
And he, through no fault of his own,
Will never take your long flight home.

-Ken Harrington (1969)
War-torn South Vietnam

Author as Honor Guard
Fort Hood Headquarters Company – July 1969

*THEY Won't Believe This!

The day I was scheduled to leave Vietnam for good, I was on a small courier chopper from Cu Chi to Long Binh. There were three of us going home that day. We didn't say a thing to each other on the ride, but we all looked at each other like we were thinking the very same thing … **WHAT DID WE JUST DO IN THIS COUNTRY?** We remained silent until the end of the ride. I knew then that very few of us were going to talk openly with anyone except another Vietnam veteran about what we did over there.

The movie *Apocalypse Now*, in which Marlon Brando repeated these words over and over, will always depict the Vietnam War for me … **THE HOR-ROR … THE HORROR!**

Chapter 11

THRILL JUNKY AFTER VIETNAM!

Rattlesnakes are vipers too ... In Vietnam we used to say, "There are one hundred types of snakes in Vietnam. Ninety-nine are poisonous and the other one could swallow you after it squeezes your breath out of you." Actually, sources verify that there are approximately thirty species of poisonous snakes in Vietnam, including the famous king cobra. The danger for tourists in Vietnam was low (if you were stupid enough to tour Nam in the sixties and seventies), but for the mud-sucking combat infantry grunt, our risk was substantial.

Many times I heard stories of snakes crawling over guys while they were on the ground. It never happened to me, but then I was not a very stationary guy, my machete was always with me, and it was active.

The most common poisonous snake over there was probably the sinister-looking green bamboo viper. It was potent all right, so we didn't try catching any. Once during a firefight in the swamps of Hoc Mon Province, one of those little green devils crossed my path as I was crawling. Fortunately, Mr. Bamboo Viper was just trying to get out of the way, and I wasn't about to put a delay in its intentions ... there was a battle going on at the time. Writing this book has refreshed my memory of those few seconds in my life.

With all that expert jungle training in the Nam and Fort Polk, Louisiana, I became infatuated with exotic snakes, particularly the venomous kind. So I took up the challenge of becoming a rattlesnake hunter just two years after returning from Nam—in between auto accidents, of course.

Let me introduce one of my buddies to you ... Lee Manning. Lee Manning is a very tough, hard-drinking "redneck" born in St. Marys, Pennsylvania. He was everyone's mentor when it came to rattlesnake hunting. Like the rest of us who hung with Lee, his word meant something. Proudly I say that Lee and I are friends to this day.

When we were younger, we even ventured to Texas to catch western diamondbacks, a much bigger rattler than the timber rattlers in Pennsylvania. One year we bagged over 100 pounds of westerns. We even brought two six-footers home to Ohio where we kept them as "pets."

Lee has slowed down a bit (we all have). He was bitten a few years ago and has not recovered yet—but he still goes into the Pennsylvania mountains two or three times a year to catch and release those little devils.

It was 1972, in fact, when I caught my first timber rattler. It was about forty-two inches—big enough. My buddy Lee Manning and I caught three that first year. I still have a picture of the first one in my hands. This was during some major car accident recovery time, so I skipped a year, only to make up for it by going back several times in the mid-1970s. One day we hit the mother lode. We bagged seventy-seven snakes that day. Back then we caught them and threw them into sandbags. Did anyone ever get bitten? Sure! That's another story—another time—but I was never bitten. I came close though. Was my experience in the exotic jungles of Nam directing me to things like this, or was I just born to be a rattlesnake hunter? I think Nam contributed heavily to this hobby. Forty years later in 2012, I still participate in organized rattlesnake hunts. After all, rattlesnakes are vipers too, as were Vietnam's bamboo vipers, and they never hurt me.

Anyway, my VA shrink just shakes his head when I tell him that I am still doing this stuff … 'cause I'm not a young buck anymore. **WHY in God's name am I still doing things like this?! Is it because I am still CON-DEMNED PROPERTY? OF THE VIETNAM WAR?**

Rambo Trimmer's first rattler – 1972

Rattlesnake hunters (Tough Group) – Early 1980s

Rattlesnake hunting – 2002

This one chased me – 2010

Reflecting on Vietnam via the Everglades and the Amazon!

It didn't take long for me to figure out that I craved a bit more out of every-day life since coming home from Vietnam's ultimate challenge ... the combat arena. Florida's Everglades and Louisiana's bayous always intrigued me. Since it was the 1970s, it was still considered a dangerous expedition to venture into either, especially solo—which was my style, and that's why I loved being a point man in Nam.

I wouldn't be looking for any confrontations with drug pirates or anything like that. All I really wanted was a peaceful experience with nature where I could just hang out and think ... think ... think. I thought the tropical envi-ronment of Florida's Everglades offered me the best opportunity in the win-ter months from December through March. I had heard of other Vietnam combat vets living in the southernmost part of Florida's Everglades, and I was hoping to find one and rap with him. But I also heard they might be living like hermits and might not be open to making new friends, whether it be with fel-low Nam combat vets or not.

It took a couple years of rehab to get back into shape after destroying the Pantera back in 1972. A few surgeries on my head, nose, and wrist required in and out hospital time and rehab physical therapy, which my insurance covered most of, but not all of the expense. And I wasn't able to work full time even if I tried. I was still going to college part time, having to take some classes over due to my time in the hospital.

It was 1975 when I first ventured into the Everglades. I went in by way of Chokoloskee and the Turner River. I lucked out as a friend of mine knew another Nam vet who lived down that way and he had a canoe, so I was able to do my very first Everglades trip with his experience as a benefit. His name was Rusty ... yeah, *Rusty*. He was with the 1st Cav in Nam in 1969. He knew of abandoned Seminole shelters where we could camp out mainly from protection from the rain and mosquitoes. It was a nice three-day, two-night trip that made me want to do it again and again and again by myself. And I would do just that again and again—till this very day. So from 1975–2012, I have been doing the Everglades, but it's not the same anymore ... way too much population down there now.

I have never run into any of those Nam vet hermits I heard of, although I have found abandoned huts or hooches, which may have belonged to hermits, and I have used them as shelters a few times. They beat the open sky.

In the late 1970s, I-75 had not reached Fort Myers or Naples yet. So believe me, the southwestern coast of Everglades National Park was not a convenient place to camp out. But I enjoyed it.

The closest near-death experience I faced down there was in 1977. I walked into a bar in a very remote area (it's no longer there), and the cold stares that greeted me should have made me turn around and scurry right out of there without looking back. But I stayed and drank rum and Coke—what else? This place looked like it belonged in the movie *Treasure Island* as it seemed like half of the men and some of the women had a black patch over one eye. After five or six rum and Cokes, I was feeling quite feisty, which was *not good*. As I was about to order another spirit, one of the chicks in the bar (who had a pirate-looking bandana on) sat down next to me and said, "This one's on me, mate." She looked pretty good aside from the one tooth missing and a few scars on her face, and of course, she was wrapped in leather, including a leather vest with no shirt underneath. Her name was Sandy. I wasn't sure if I had ventured into the fantasy of my life, the twilight zone, or Alice in Wonderland!

Turns out, it was the twilight zone! It was not apparent to me at the time, nor did I care after seven or eight rum and Cokes, but my life was in serious danger. She said, "You are not from around here. What's your business here?" It was obvious that she did not believe my answer, which was an honest one; that I was just looking for some peace of mind and adventure in the Everglades. We talked some more, had a couple more cocktails, and before I knew it, she and I had become very close friends and I was about to leave the bar with her—to go to her place, I thought.

The rest of the patrons in the bar knew my name by now, and they were buying me drinks too … so I was up to ten to twelve rum and Cokes. The only weapon I had was a machete, handmade in Vietnam, which I still have to this day, but my ESP was telling me that I was outgunned that night.

Just before Sandy and I were about to leave arm in arm and madly in love (RIGHT!), in walked Rusty—the same 1st Cav Nam vet I canoed with back in 1975. It turns out, I was walking out the door with his sister … indeed I was. It also turned out that Rusty's entrance at that time was a pure life saver … **MINE!**

I had entered a bar that was a hangout for drug runners. And anyone else who came in there and was a stranger was automatically pegged as a federal agent. The little pirate look-alike miss I was leaving with, we were definitely heading back to her place together. However, if Rusty had not shown up when he did, that would have been my last night as a living human in this world, as the plan was to cut my throat and toss me into the Everglades, where I would have become "gator meat."

Okay, Vietnam combat vet, "thrill-seeker," once again my path of self-destruction had failed … or should I say succeeded since I had survived?

Back to the bar, Rusty, his sister, and I went for a few more rum and Cokes. He assured everyone in the bar that I was cool, and several guys bought me more rum and Cokes. The point of this part of my Everglades excursion was that I went home with Sandy, we kind of fell in love that night, and we stayed in touch afterwards. Unfortunately, she was shot to death in 1978, and Rusty died of cancer in 1979, thanks to Agent Orange. So the adventure of Dusty, Rusty, and Sandy ended.

I want to move on, as the aftermath of Vietnam is far more important than my personal escapades—even though they are Vietnam related or induced. My next most exciting thrill in the Everglades happened in 1982. After canoeing the Turner River and offshoots of it, I pulled my canoe to shore to hike a bit. Unfortunately, I trekked a bit too late and found a surprise awaiting me when I returned to my canoe. It was MAMA GATOR (I guessed it was a she) lying right next to my canoe, and she wasn't letting me get into my canoe, not just yet. When I threw some rocks, she hissed, so I aborted that tact.

The sun was just beginning to set, and I had another hour or so of canoeing left to get back to my camp (a hermit's hut). I was not prepared to stay the night at this location … HOLY S—, WAS THIS VIETNAM ALL OVER AGAIN OR WHAT?! I threw some logs at her, which just pissed her off more. Okay, I figured that she had a nest nearby (if gators had nests) and that I was a threat. I had to start looking for a shelter or the means to construct one, because this Mama Gator was seemingly staying put.

I found a soft, dry place where deer or wild hogs might have lain. That was where I was going to stay. To hell with the wild hogs, I had my machete and it was them or me, because I couldn't get that gator to leave. Oh, by the way, she was easily a ten-footer—enough said?

The sun had not disappeared yet, and I was sitting on a rock about thirty feet from my canoe and Mama Gator when all of a sudden she backed up, sank into the river, and disappeared. OH WOW! I jumped into my canoe so fast I almost rolled it. I paddled my butt off, kind of laughing all the way and saying to myself, *No one will believe this story!*

It didn't matter if it was day or night—the Everglades brought me back to Nam, and not only did I like it … **I needed it!** WHY did I need it? I still don't know. It was just me and the Everglades. Once or twice, sometimes three times a year. Just me and my trusty machete … déjà vu the Nam. The more I did the Everglades, the more I wanted something better.

The last really good canoe trip in the Everglades that stands out in my mind happened just five years ago. Remember, I am married now, supposedly mellowed and settling down—right? It was the same area off the Turner River. I had been canoeing most of the day, enjoying fantastic scenes of wildlife—eagles, gators, otters, a multitude of birds, fish jumping all over the place. I never tired of this—all by myself! I pulled over to rest and then could not believe what I saw, absolutely could not believe it. In front of me, maybe fifteen feet ahead, was some kind of Florida native duck standing on shore. Cute, I thought. But just five feet away from the duck was a submerged gator, and it was a twelve-footer by my estimation. The duck was completely unaware, and the gator kept moving forward slowly but surely. This was like *National Geographic* to me. I was in my glory with nature … wondering how this was going to end. I was not going to interfere, although I had thoughts about warning the duck. That wouldn't have been fair to the gator and his hard work.

Foot by foot, the gator slowly moved forward; the duck's back faced the gator. I took pictures one after another, hoping the clicking would not disturb what I was witnessing. As I was taking one more picture, the gator lunged with all his might, water flew up in the air, and as the duck responded, I swear the gator's jaws grasped the duck's feathers as the duck escaped to live another day.

I felt sorry for the gator, but I did not dwell on that feeling as I was more concerned about how the pictures came out. And now I had to wait for this big twelve-foot gator to quit pouting and move on so I could get back into my canoe and get these pictures developed. *National Geographic* quality ... that is what everyone who has seen the series of pictures of that event with the duck and gator has told me.

I still go back to the Everglades from time to time, but it's not like it was back in the 1970s and 1980s. And I'm not thirty-five years old either. That's it for the Everglades and my weak attempts to recapture Vietnam—I was hoping for more.

My trips to the Everglades were beginning to become routine to me. Even though I had a few close calls down there with gators, wild pigs, snakes, and drug runners, I still needed something else. Geez, that would have been enough for most rational humans.

Off to the Amazon

Early Everglades Camp – 1979
Better than what we had in Nam most nights

Gator on the attack after stalking its prey – 2005

1983

After having several discussions with an assortment of "unique" people about joining up with some mercenaries in South America or Angola, I made a commitment to meet with some people in Peru. I'm not sure that I planned to come back, either by my choice or someone else's. But it appears that the higher power had other ideas for me, as a young lady named Virginia (Ginny) Brancato entered my life just a few weeks before I was to leave for the Amazon. Ginny Brancato (my future first and only wife) would impact my life forever like no other human being ever did before. Anyway, I did the Amazon trip, but canceled the meeting with the mercenaries and just explored the jungle at my leisure.

Here are some notes I wrote to Ginny while I was down there.

Notes to Ginny Brancato and to Myself in the Amazon

September 1983

Hi Ginny!

It's alright here! Honest!!! This is a love letter, and in case you're wondering, I miss you!

My personal guide is "just like me," independent, sarcastic, feisty, a maverick, good-looking (ha ha), a "fighter," and he likes you already. His name is César Rojas. He's a leader among his friends, is very honest, sincere, has compassion for people, and I think he would make a good adoptable son or brother. He's 22, but very mature with common sense.

It's H-O-T, oh so very hot, but so serene, yes, and beautiful. I've heard sounds that scare the shit out of me, but nothing has presented itself so far, except a pet ocelot, a six-inch millipede; many, many, many, many ants of all sizes, and they can be mean; big spiders and other things.

Ouch!!! That cute little damn ocelot just bit my ankle. Wait 'til you see the pictures of this little guy. He's six months old and a real hellion, and very wild.
Ginny, this is so much like Vietnam I could cry, but no shooting! No bombing! This

Captured ocelot cub

is what I've been looking for; I don't know why, but I need this. I'm crying right now ... I can't help it! It's so much like Vietnam ... I need this!

Gosh, I get a bit embarrassed when we talk about money, the economy, etc. Peru is just like Vietnam in so many ways. The people are dark, small and so poor. César earns just $100 a month. His apartment rent in Iquitos is $25 a month; not much is left ...

César and I have already talked about communicating thru the mind. He believes!!! He's seen "Magic Men" do things that are indescribable.

Ginny, I love you. Wish I could bring you down here, but rattlesnakes and bushmasters aren't the same, and bushmasters are a real problem here. There's no cure if one bites you—you're a goner.

They say there's a tiger of some sort down here bigger than a jaguar; hope we don't see it! (But I think it's a tale or joke they are playing on me.)

Just arrived at another village on the Nappo River 50 miles deeper in the jungle. The people are really primitive.

We fished for some piranha on this trip and we're going to fish for them again, also the piache fish later. I'll tell you about it!

The piache is good eating, have had it twice already, and lots of rice just like Vietnam ... Oh God!

We may go spear fishing tonight in a small flat canoe. They also use bows and arrows with sharp wooden tips. I'll bring some home.

Caught dozens of piranha this afternoon. Tomorrow we're having them for lunch. Better that way than the other way!

Golly, the sounds down here. It's peaceful, not like Vietnam where shooting, bombing and crying were in the background.

More rice for dinner and a few other odds and ends – WOW!!! "Piranha Soup" – even the head is in the bowl! What a sense of humor these people have! They actually put the whole darn thing in my bowl ... what a sense of humor!

Just came back from night fishing. One of the Indians speared three fish, all through the head, right between the eyes and without any flashlights—must have taken him a lifetime to get that good. Tomorrow night it's my turn to try it!

WOW, do I ever itch.

Earlier I had a parakeet drinking beer from my glass—funny! It sure is a feisty thing ... yells at everyone, even the little ocelot ... but he keeps his distance. We gave the little ocelot a dead piranha to eat and whenever anyone went near it, it growled!!!

Every night I have slept either well or very well despite the discomfort of heat, dampness, and sounds of things moving in the trees and on the ground all around us. But the other sounds are just too much to even begin to describe—we didn't have these sounds in Vietnam, just boom, boom, boom, and crack! And the smell of death is not

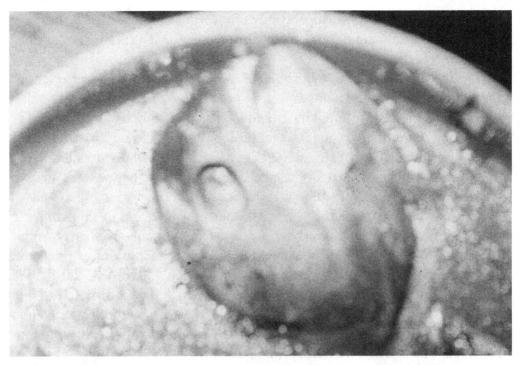

Piranha chowder?

here either; it's relaxing, not tense.

I hated war before and even more now after seeing what Vietnam must have looked like once, and what it looked like when I left.

Many of these people are so happy and yet they live like people did thousands of years ago. Vietnam was like that. I'll never forget Vietnam.

This was some experience; how did I ever do this for a full year! This was Nam all over again ...

I guess the fight for survival in Nam made the inconveniences unnoticeable, but my memory is coming back now! It was definitely a hardship.

Mercenaries or Drug Pirates?

The same night that I had originally planned to meet with some mercenaries, which I decided not to carry through with, I went out with César and Andres instead ... *to search for bushmasters*! Bushmaster hunting at night! Hell yes, nighttime action was Vietnam all over again—man, was I looking forward to this, but WHY?!

The bushmaster is the largest viper in the world and the second largest venomous snake in the world, second only to the king cobra. An ordinary mature bushmaster would range from six to ten feet in length, but larger ones have been recorded.

Just like the Viet Cong, a bushmaster is able to lie in one site for a long time, waiting to ambush its unsuspecting prey along lonely routes in the jungle. The bushmaster can smell its intended prey, and I swear the VC could as well. César and Andres warned me that bushmasters would seek us out and we would have to be so very extra alert. Oh great ... We had just inhaled a gallon of raw rum, compliments of a local Yagua Indian tribe we were staying with, and we had to be very alert the next day. RIGHT!

We walked oh so cautiously—just as cautiously as we did in Vietnam, one step at a time with flashlights. (No flashlights in Vietnam—we had starlight scopes.) It was about 2:00 AM when we heard a lot of chatter on the river, and at that moment, César whispered to me, "DOSTY, PLEASE HIT IT!" (They called me Dosty, not Dusty.) "Drug pirates," César whispered to me. And they would kill us all if they caught us. We lay there for at least a couple of hours. Mosquitoes were tormenting us—but we had to wait this one out. Seems like I had been here before, in a place called VIETNAM!

The only weapons we had were machetes, and the drug pirates were loaded for bear. I would have given up my life savings for an M-16 and three or four bandoleers of ammo right then ... and maybe a grenade or two. Obviously, since I am writing this book, we made it that night, but it could have gone the other way.

OH MY GOD ... it was 1983, fourteen years after I had come home from the horror of Vietnam, and here I was—on this trip where I almost joined a mercenary unit and I almost had my throat cut by drug pirates! We returned to the Yagua Indian village to catch some zzz's until our next jungle expedition. **So much for our hunt for the mighty bushmaster. Oh, by the way, if we had found a bushmaster and if I had been bitten, this book would not have been published!**

The next day I was going to get a professional and personal training session on how to hunt with blowguns, and our success with them would dictate what we had for dinner that night. It would hopefully be monkey meat!

The remainder of my trek in the Peruvian Amazon Basin was fairly routine, except for the mosquitoes. I thoroughly enjoyed every minute of the day and night. We saw many Caymans, too many very intimidating-looking arachnids (spiders) and one small (twelve-inch) anaconda. We caught and ate lots of piranha and even hit a two-inch lizard of some kind with a blowgun—never could hit one of those black monkeys in the trees.

On the day I was supposed to fly back to Miami from Iquitos, there was an unstaged, real-life firefight going on with the Peruvian army and some rebels or drug runner soldiers. My flight was delayed a couple hours, and I made it home, having fulfilled my dreams.

Well, although I promised my lovely wife that I would try to curtail activities

Nam-like trekking in the Amazon

Author in the Amazon – 1983
Blowgun practice

Yagua Indians – 1983

Amazon boat people

Happy Amazon kids look like Vietnamese

Trekking the backwaters

Amazon lily pads

Day's Catch – Piranha Snacks

Me Tarzan! – 1983

Home Sweet Home

Everglades Python –2013

like this—rattlesnake hunting, etc.—I did go to Florida in January 2013 to check out their FIRST PYTHON CHALLENGE with my trusty machete by my side.

*THEY Won't Believe This!

Living primitively in Vietnam's jungles was a shocking lifestyle change. We were suddenly thrown into a hostile wilderness environment and forced to live as primitively as our Stone Age ancestors did. Time of day or night was no longer important to us for a year. My trips into Florida's Everglades and Peru's Amazon have been therapeutic for me, strange as that sounds. It reminded me to appreciate simple things like a hot meal, clean clothes, fresh water, clean sheets on a bed, a roof over my head, and all the other things that are not available in third world countries.

In the bush, our attitudes were critically important for survival. When we got up each morning, we had to encourage ourselves. No one else could do that ... I guess the primitive lifestyle of Vietnam helped mold some of us into real-life "survivors."

Chapter 12

A GENERATION ... BETRAYED!

Betrayal (or backstabbing) is the breaking or violation of contract, trust, or confidence that produces moral and psychological conflict within a relationship amongst individuals, between organizations or between individuals and organizations. Betrayal is also the act of supporting a rival group.

Betrayal is the worst form of a lie, especially when it is a blatant scheme or plot. I can list dozens of examples of how America's media and its politicians betrayed, deceived, lied to, backstabbed, broke trust, and robbed the Vietnam War's warriors.

One example stands out in my mind as it does in many of my brothers from that war. That example would be **$$$$$!** Money was made by the few who could have ended the Vietnam War in half the time that it lasted. Instead, it dragged on and on, and good, solid, patriotic American soldiers died by the hundreds of thousands during and after the war. Then, they (media and politicians) made us continue to suffer by putting unbearable inner guilt ON US!

In the earliest months of the Korean conflict, psychiatric casualties accounted for 25 percent of all evacuations from the battlefield. When the Vietnam War began in the early sixties, supposedly, the U.S. military had learned from its mistake in Korea on handling the psychological casualties. The plan in Vietnam was to treat the patients quickly and return them to combat quickly. In the early going, this seemed to work. And then in 1968, the TET Offensive emotional trauma cases rose at shocking rates.

The American psychiatric community became more vigilant of what was happening to the combat warriors in Vietnam. One of those was Robert Jay Lifton, a Yale psychiatry professor and a former Air Force psychologist in Korea. Lifton began suggesting that Vietnam would create worse trauma on the soldiers than that of all previous wars. He even implied that military psychiatrists in Vietnam were taking orders from the U.S. military to treat soldiers and get them back to combat as quickly as possible.

That "Other" Generation!

I think it was Tom Brokaw who coined the WWII era "The Greatest Generation." And who could argue that? They survived the Great Depression and they fought in WWII ... *the* big one, as WWII vets call it. That generation made hero worship fashionable, and our country became the ultimate superpower of the world after the big one.

What is a hero? My heroes are the young men who faced the issues of war and possible death, and then weighed those concerns against obligations to their country. Citizens to soldiers who interrupted their personal and professional lives at their most formative stage in the timeless phrase of the Confederate Memorial in Arlington National Cemetery, 'Not for fame or reward, not for place or for rank, but in simple obedience to duty as they understood it.'

Who suffered loneliness, disease and wounds with an often contagious élan. And who deserves a far better place in history than that now offered them by the so-called spokesman of our so-called generation.

　　　　　　　- James Webb
　　　　　　　Former Secretary of the Navy

Although 70 percent of WWII veterans were drafted, their generation was still credited for voluntarily going off to war because it was the right thing to do ... which it was. That generation had the likes of Audie Murphy, Patton, Bradley, Eisenhower, MacArthur, and Doolittle. They were truly great heroes.

Then comes that "other" generation, the one into which I was born. Some of us were too young to make it in The Greatest Generation and too old to make The Baby Boomers Generation.

How could our country betray us? How could those from The Greatest Generation abandon us?

Personally, I will proudly go to my grave as being part of That "Other" Generation. We were not baby killers, we were not crybabies; we were and are **Ultimate Survivors.**

"Real" Vietnam War veterans living today are as unique as any American veteran group in our great country's history from 1775 to the present. Who else returned home after risking their lives for their country and its people ... were abused, scoffed at, ignored, defamed, vilified, unappreciated, and worst of all, DISHONORED?

We Vietnam War veterans who are living today are some of the most unique Americans our country has ever had, but there aren't many of us left.

Regardless of which generation a soldier was born into, there should have been heroes whose names were recognizable to most average Americans, but I doubt that any non-Vietnam veteran can name one from the Vietnam War. Other than Oliver North, who became so well known after the war, or maybe Westmoreland's name might pop up, but who else? How about this guy ... General H. "Stormin' Norman" Schwarzkopf? Sure, he will be remembered as the hero of the Gulf War, but he also spent considerable time in the Vietnam War ... then again, nobody equates any heroes from Vietnam's war. By the way, Stormin' Norman died prematurely at age seventy-six of complications from pneumonia and a previous bout with prostate cancer—Agent Orange related from Vietnam maybe?

WWII and Vietnam were both substantially represented with Medal of Honor awardees, as follows:

Congressional Medal of Honor Award Recipients

	WWII	Vietnam War
Army	324	160
Marines	82	57
Navy	57	16
Air Force	0	13
Coast Guard	1	0
Total:	464*	246**

* 266 awarded posthumously (57%)
**156 awarded posthumously (63%)

I have read in many books about WWII and Vietnam—that WWII veterans rarely suffered (after the war ended) from inner guilt. Vietnam vets, on the other hand, came home with inner guilt abounding because **THE WAR IN VIETNAM WAS CALLED IMMORAL.**

We who went there did not start that war! Most of us did not want to go there, but over 70 percent of us enlisted and less than 30 percent were drafted. Why would a man agree wholeheartedly to leave the comforts of home, march off to fight an unpopular war—later to be labeled an immoral war—and then come home (if he did come home) to a shattered world completely unlike that which he was taken from just a couple years ago? **Because he believed it was the right thing to do!**

The Communists Said This in the 1950s

North Will Absorb South ... The directing force behind the effort to conquer South Vietnam is the Communist Party in the North, the Lao Dong (Workers) Party. As in every communist state, the party is an integral part of the regime itself. North Vietnamese officials have expressed their firm determination to absorb South Vietnam into the communist world.

Through its Central Committee, which controls the government of the North, the Lao Dong Party directs the total political and military effort of the Viet Cong. The Military High Command in the North trains the military men and sends them to South Vietnam. The Central Research Agency, North Vietnam's central intelligence organization, directs the elaborate espionage and subversion effort.

Under Hanoi's overall direction the communists have established an extensive machine for carrying on the war within South Vietnam. The focal point is the Central Office for South Vietnam with its political and military subsections and other specialized agencies. A subordinate part of this Central

Office is the Liberation Front for South Vietnam. The front was formed at Hanoi's order in 1960. Its principal function is to influence opinion abroad and to create the false impression that the aggression in South Vietnam is an indigenous rebellion against the established government.

For more than ten years the people and the Government of South Vietnam, exercising the inherent right of self-defense, have fought back against these efforts to extend communist power south across the 17th parallel. The United States has responded to the appeals of the Government of the Republic of Vietnam for help in this defense of the freedom and independence of its land and its people.

(This editorial was taken from Aggression from the North, which was published by Armed Forces Information and Education, Department of Defense.)

(Source: http://www.25thida.org)

Earliest Betrayals

There are those who believe that the war in Vietnam or some place in Southeast Asia was planned by our government shortly after the end of WWII in 1945. There are those who claim they can prove it, but the mainstream media won't touch that story. There are some who believe that after America entered the Vietnam War, our country or its corporate world was still selling war technology to Russia (Soviet Union). Some of these weapons would then be turned over to the North Vietnam Army and would be used to kill AMERICANS!

In 1959 or 1960, most of America had no idea of what a Vietnam was. They would know the word from Maine to California, Alaska to Hawaii by 1965 or so. Vietnam became a hot (not necessarily popular) topic of discussion around the world in 1968 and 1969. After the Vietnam War ended for our participation, few Americas wanted to talk about it, especially those who served there. It seemed as though most Americans just wanted the memories of the Vietnam War to dissipate into the air, go away somewhere, anywhere— just **GO AWAY!**

Which President Deserves the Credit?

To his credit, among the many great things he did, President Franklin D. Roosevelt would have nothing to do with France's repeated requests for aid to help them recolonize Vietnam. President Woodrow Wilson also declined requests from Ho Chi Minh and France to back both of them.

Amazingly, many liberal Democrats still remember Richard Nixon's invasion of Cambodia as one of the major escalations of the Vietnam War. The war was all but over by then. Nixon was just trying to stop the "hit-run-hide" attacks by the North Vietnamese on American military bases. Nixon deserves NO CREDIT for escalation of military activities … everything he did was to protect Americans as we were attempting to de-escalate the war, for which Nixon was responsible.

Presidents Truman, Kennedy, and Johnson deserve much credit for the Vietnam War … non-debatable. Harry Truman's initial aid to France against the Vietminh continued to escalate as France continued to beg for more support. As I see it, Truman (America) was "paying France" to fight in Vietnam long before America physically entered the scene. In fact, Truman was sending money, supplies, and non-combat troops to Indochina during the Korean War. Who remembers that? Just check your history books.

President Eisenhower also deserves some credit for the beginning of American participation in Vietnam, when he sent military advisors to train the South Vietnamese Army in 1955. From there, it was all Kennedy and Johnson. Enter the U.S. Army's Green Berets to South Vietnam in 1960 under Kennedy.

Unfortunately, also in 1960, the National Liberation Front (NLF) or Viet Cong was organized, and the Soviet Union pledged support to the NLF. The big chess game was on. Under Kennedy, in 1961, herbicidal warfare (Agent Orange) was tested; it was called "Operation Trail Dust." When Kennedy became President, there were less than 1,000 Americans in South Vietnam. Just before he was assassinated in 1963, there were 16,000 American troops in Vietnam.

President Truman set the stage. President Eisenhower began our commitment and made it almost mandatory for Kennedy to continue involvement in Vietnam. By 1963, President Johnson was hearing the "domino theory" from all around him. And he did believe that Vietnam was the place where the advance of communism needed to be stopped.

President Johnson underestimated the will of the Viet Cong, the North Vietnamese, and the support that came from China and the Soviet Union. Or … he was just flat-out caught with his pants down! Johnson had once called North Vietnam a "raggedy-ass fourth rate country" and said that they would be defeated very quickly. Maybe it was American arrogance that prevented our total victory.

My take on this little scenario is that it does not matter which political party is in power. They are both full of themselves with elite attitudes that they are the chosen ones. Democrats or Republicans—it matters not who is in power because they both drink their water from the same polluted well … think about it.

When France was crushed by the Viet military, now there were two Vietnams, both free. Ho Chi Minh had his North Vietnam, and South Vietnam remained a non-communist country. Ho Chi Minh was not satisfied with this arrangement, as he wanted South Vietnam under his rule. Here is an interesting fact that I'll bet most of this book's readers were unaware of, which is:

Ho Chi Minh's main resistance in South Vietnam originated and continued from the million or so North Vietnamese who migrated to South Vietnam—running away from communism!

Many of these North Vietnamese were people of stature, so they became heavily supportive of the non-communist South Vietnamese government. In fact, one North Vietnamese anti-communist named Ngo Dinh Dien became the prime minister of South Vietnam. He was a Roman Catholic and bitterly hated the communists.

Amazing and hard to believe? Sure it is because the American media never told the whole story and neither do the present-day history books.

Here are a few juicy tidbits for you to mull over, and *please* mull them over:

Should I become President, I will not risk American lives by permitting any other nation to drag us into the wrong war at the wrong time at the wrong place through an unwise commitment that is unwise militarily, unnecessary to our security and unsupported by the American people and our allies.

- John F. Kennedy
Presidential Candidate
New York Times, October 31, 1960

The betrayal begins officially? You make the judgment after you read the following statements:

We now have a problem in making our power more credible and Vietnam is the place.

- John F. Kennedy, President –1961

We are not about to send American boys ten thousand miles away from home to do what the Asian boys ought to be doing for themselves.

- Lyndon Johnson, 1964

Do the math. Never has there been a war engaged by America that was never supported by its people back home, its home media, nor its own government. **No wonder so many Vietnam veterans find it extremely difficult to sleep at night.**

The betrayal continued on the battlefield. On July 28, 1965, President Lyndon Johnson committed additional combat units to the Vietnam War (over 175,000). One year later, Johnson more than doubled our military commitment by raising troop levels to 385,000, and by the end of 1967, our total troop presence had been elevated to 490,000. And then … to a record high of 546,000 by the end of 1968. **Where and when was it going to stop?**

We were winning battles everywhere. We searched and destroyed in 1968. It was almost impossible to stop us, as dead Viet Cong and NVA bodies were being found everywhere.

We took the fight into Cambodia, destroying their base camps and hospitals, cutting off their supplies from North Vietnam and China from the Ho Chi Minh Trail. And then on October 31, 1968, President Johnson stopped the bombing on the Ho Chi Minh Trail, and the handwriting was on the wall for us. We would never win this war. Our own country would ensure that we lost. The beginning of the end was in progress, even though the war lasted a few more years and another 20,000 Americans would die for virtually nothing. Here are some quotes from North Vietnam's leader:

Our forces had been nearly wiped out. It took us a couple years after our devastating losses in 1968 to re-establish our forces back to full strength.

If the Americans had not begun to withdraw under Nixon in 1969, they could have punished us so severely we would have had no choice but to surrender.

Oddly, the American generals could never (or wouldn't) seem to deploy a maximum force at one time, which could have given them a great military victory.

General Giap was a brilliant, highly respected leader of the North Vietnam military. The following quote is from his memoirs currently found in the Vietnam War memorial in Hanoi:

What we still don't understand is why you Americans stopped the bombing of Hanoi. You had us on the ropes. If you had pressed us a little harder, just for another day or two, we were ready to surrender! It was the same at the bat-

General VoNguyen Giap after the War

tle of TET. You defeated us! We knew it, and we thought you knew it. But we were elated to notice your media was helping us. They were causing more disruption in America than we could in the battlefields. We were ready to surrender. You had won!

General Giap has published his memoirs and confirmed what most Americans still don't know. The Vietnam War was not lost in Vietnam—it was lost at home in America.

A Taste of All-Out War – 1972 – Too Late!

Most Vietnam War generation people around the world are aware that Vietnam combat veterans were forced to fight a formidable enemy with one hand tied behind our backs. We pretty much fought a war that we were not supposed to win. However, for one very short period of less than two weeks, under President Nixon, the American military removed the white gloves and unleashed all of its firepower on North Vietnam, especially Hanoi itself. This happened because North Vietnam backed out of the 1972 Paris peace talks— again! They also relayed this message to America: "Peace was indeed at hand—under our terms—or there would be no peace at all."

North Vietnam had no idea that Nixon was unlike his predecessor, Johnson. President Nixon reacted immediately, giving North Vietnam an ultimatum for Hanoi to return to the negotiations or face severe consequences. Having watched American forces pulling back in the 1970s, North Vietnam called Nixon's bluff … this time it was no idle threat. This President would follow through in grand fashion.

On December 18, 1972, our Air Force unleashed maximum force onto the country of North Vietnam. Unbelievably, this was the first time our powerful B-52 Stratofortresses were used (allowed) to attack North Vietnam directly during the entire war. Had we done this under Johnson in the fall of 1968 when the Viet Cong had been almost completely annihilated, it is quite possible that the Vietnam War would not have made it into 1970. Instead, Johnson stopped the bombing on the Ho Chi Minh Trail, and that move gave North Vietnam new life, so the war dragged on.

Linebacker II was the name of the military operation in 1972 that scared North Vietnam out of its wits, and they rushed back to the bargaining table with America. However, this unleashing of hell from above shattered North Vietnam back to reality and gave them a look at what an all-out war effort could have and should have looked like from their end … They did not like what they saw. And China and the Soviet Union did nothing about it.

In *The Lessons of Vietnam*, British military expert authority Robert Thompson wrote, **"Those B-52 attacks on Hanoi had basically won the war."** If America had opted to, they could have walked in and mopped up. North Vietnam could have been done in right then and there. Again, had we taken such initiative when we counterattacked North Vietnam during the Tet Offensives in 1968, South Vietnam and Laos would not be communist countries today. Nor would Cambodia have suffered the millions of casualties dealt to them by the communist-instigated and communist-supported genocides that occurred after the Vietnam War ended.

When this short but awesome eleven-day attack ended, North Vietnam's damages included the following:

- 1,000 missions logged
- 1,600 military installations crippled
- 42,000 bombs fell
- 80% of Hanoi's electric power was out
- Dozens of airfield and roads were crippled
- Hanoi Hannah's radio broadcasts were shut down
- Civilian casualties were considered light, at less than 2,000

North Vietnam was on their knees. One month later, they signed the Paris Peace Accords on January 27, 1973. Of course, the communists broke their promises made on that day, and two years later, they marched into Saigon.

The primary goal of the bombings was to unleash maximum destruction of military targets, not civilian life. However, inflicting severe stress on Hanoi's civilian population was part of the plan.

Nixon's plan was successful. American POWs have since confirmed how they danced around in their cells, yelling, cheering, and crying with pleasure. They saw North Vietnamese guards so terrified that some screamed, trembled, and "wet their pants." North Vietnam had never experienced anything like this in decades of war with the French and other nations before, including China and Japan.

Of course, the anti-war mob back in America claimed many thousands of defenseless women and children were massacred. Joan Baez told a reporter, Tsugoshi Doki, "Nixon is a madman. I will do my utmost so that the antiwar movement can be united and become more powerful."

When the bombings had ended, North Vietnamese reported that 1,318 civilians died in Hanoi and 305 in Haiphong. A reminder ... **the carpet-bombings of Tokyo in March 1945 killed 85,000 Japanese civilians!** However, many of Hanoi's 1,318 civilian deaths were caused by the 1,242 SAM missiles and artillery shells fired by North Vietnam, which fell back into the civilians on the ground. The North Vietnamese admit to this day that the bombings had almost completely destroyed their will to continue the war.

One rumor that has appeared in several sources has said, "American anti-war activists urged the mayor of Hanoi to fabricate an accelerated death toll of 10,000, but Mayor Tran refused. The "suspects" for this cruel intended lie were ... Joan Baez, Jane Fonda and Barry Romo.

Oh, by the way ... also in 1972, the North Vietnamese Army turned its military firepower on fleeing, innocent civilians in Quang Tri and An Loc, killing 15,000-20,000. And yet ... **there was no outrage by the American media or Americana anti-war supporters!**

There is unquestionable documentation today that shows there was no indiscriminate carpet-bombing on Hanoi's civilians during the December 18–29, 1972 B-52 bombings. Aerial photos are available that prove this. There are. In fact, many civilians were sacrificed as "human shields" by their own North Vietnam military.

The American media coverage of the 1972 bombing came through once again in support of the enemy—NOT America. In fact, it is documented that ABC, NBC, CBS, AP, and UPI consistently provided negative coverage about the South Vietnam government, and yet most of their stories about the "enemy" were favorable. A study of CBS by the Institute for American Strategy showed that 83.3 percent of CBS stories were negatively biased against the government of South Vietnam, while 57.3 percent of CBS coverage of Hanoi's regime was positive.

After the Vietnam War ended, Hanoi Jane Fonda and Hanoi Joan Baez had differences that became public. They pertained to the cruelty of North Vietnam against their conquered South Vietnamese "brothers and sisters."

Throughout the Vietnam War, when villagers were attempting to escape battle scenes and move to safer areas under government or American protection, the North Vietnamese routinely bombed, rocketed, mortared, and mined roads for absolutely no military advantage. It was documented in several historical books on the war that between the years of 1968 and 1972, the number of civilians sent to hospitals from communist-inflicted injuries averaged 30,000 every month or 360,000 each year ... or 1,800,000.

Dan Rather and Walter Cronkite, of CBS, reported to the American people what Radio Hanoi had told them to report.

No event in American history has been more misunderstood ... misreported and misremembered than the Vietnam War. Rarely have so many people been so wrong about so much for so long. Never have the consequences of their misunderstanding been so tragic.
- President Richard Nixon

A Decade Later, Many Viet Vets Still Think They Were Betrayed

April 30, 1985 | MARK I. PINSKY | Times Staff Writer, Los Angeles Times

The 14 Vietnam veterans from Orange County who gather each Tuesday night at the Vet Center in Anaheim have a great deal in common: most come from working-class or lower-middle class backgrounds, they served in ground combat as young enlisted men and they suffered nightmares or flashbacks when they returned, and from time to time since. Many have lost wives and jobs.

They are the "grunts," the people who fought the war and survived. Sort of.

In the years since, they said, newspapers and magazines have continued to identify people accused of violent or anti-social acts as Vietnam veterans, perpetrating what Ken Flint called the "walking time bomb" stereotype, reinforced by its cinematic counterpart, "the super-hero crazy person."

Vietnam vets betrayed again – Pentagon bureaucrat wants to abridge 50ᵗʰanniversary ceremonies

Posted by Twana Blevins on November 12, 2010 at 10:02 pm in *Support Our Troops and Veterans; The Washington Times*

The 50ᵗʰ-anniversary commemoration of the Vietnam War should be a time of reflection and redemption, when a grateful country pays a long-standing debt to veterans who nobly fought in the conflict but came home to scorn and spit. But if a Pentagon bureaucrat has his way, the Viet vets will be denied their rightful honors once again.

Enter Michael L. Rhodes, director of administration and management at the Pentagon. His office has been given oversight over the anniversary commission, which he has down-graded to a "planning staff." Mr. Rhodes has made meaningful work by the commission next to impossible and has sought drastically to scale back the planned commemorations. According to an August action memo prepared by Mr. Rhodes for Secretary of Defense Robert M. Gates and obtained by the Washington Times, *he urged Mr. Gates to reject the proposed commemoration program and adopt instead a "targeted" $30 million program. The memo describes the new approach as "a dignified and meaningful DoD Program of national recognition [that] need not be tied to the full time frame of the U.S. military involvement" and that will "provide nationwide participation, while utilizing the resources involved in the most effective manner."*

Mr. Rhodes' plan cuts the time frame of the commemoration down to 2015–18 and inexplicably features a kickoff in his former home of Honolulu, which is not exactly a resource-effective location. Hawaii is inaccessible for most veterans and is in a time zone where most Americas could not watch the event live on television.

The misinformation about the Vietnam War is massive. It exists in many so-called scholarly books, government reports, documentaries, and magazine articles.

Numerous credible sources say that less than one million American Vietnam veterans are living today, although 2.8 million served in Vietnam. Many more millions of people are still suffering from the Vietnam War and the aftermath around the world. Scars of war never heal; they are taken to the grave.

When did we get to grieve for our dead? Long-term obstruction of grief can lock one into chronic rage. If our government and country don't care about our emotions and our need to grieve—then why should anyone be shocked at our rage when we are sent back to civilian life?

There is no emotion more intense than the bond between soldiers in combat. Not having the opportunity to grieve over losing a comrade is torture.

PTSD, like diabetes, is a serious illness, where the chance of a total recovery is highly unlikely. Returning to normal cannot happen, as symptoms will remain active to some degree forever. In both PTSD and diabetes, CONTROL is a must in order to survive.

It was once believed that psychological casualties of Vietnam were lower than that of WWII. That has been proven incorrect. The average combat time of a combat soldier in Vietnam for one year was considerably longer than the average combat time a WWII veteran faced in four years of duty.

Our government was in a state of denial for many years after the Vietnam War ended in regards to facing the reality of that war's damage to combat soldiers over there. NO ONE who has ever been in combat (traumatic combat) can even begin to understand the closeness of true combat brothers in the heat of battle. It's closer than any family member, even your parents. You covered each other's backs in the worst hell possible!

Stolen Valor: How the Vietnam Generation Was Robbed of Its Heroes and Its History

A self-published book by B.G. Burkett and Glenna Whitley in 1998 asserted the once-popular view of Vietnam War veterans as broken men and psychos. It also documented the "wannabes" or phonies who lied about a Vietnam War experience they never participated in. B.G. Burkett is a Vietnam War veteran himself who served with the 199th Light Infantry Brigade as a company grade officer. Glenna Whitley is an investigative journalist.

Burkett is one of our champions. He exposes the truth of how the bias of the media promoted the myth that these phony "wannabes" were representative of the "real" Vietnam War veteran. THANK YOU, B.G. BURKETT! Fact is, B.G.s book, *Stolen Valor*, led to the 2005 Act itself.

The Stolen Valor Act of 2005, signed into law by President George W. Bush on December 20, 2006, is a U.S. law that broadens the provisions of previous U.S. law addressing the unauthorized wear, manufacture, or sale of any military decorations and medals. It makes it a federal misdemeanor to falsely represent oneself as having received any U.S. military decoration or medal. If convicted, defendants may be imprisoned for up to six months, unless the decoration that they lied about is the Medal of Honor, in which case imprisonment could be up to one year.

The Act was first introduced in the U.S. House of Representatives on July 19, 2005 by Representative John Salazar, from Colorado, as R.R. 3352. It was introduced into the Senate by Senator Kent Conrad from North Dakota on November 10, 2005, as S. 1998. The Senate version was unanimously passed on September 7, 2006

Stolen Valor Act Upheld

The 10th U.S. Circuit Court of Appeals in Denver upheld the constitutional validity of the 2006 Stolen Valor Act on January 27, 2012. The federal law makes it illegal to lie about being a war veteran and to make related false statements.

The three-judge panel reversed in a 2-1 vote the earlier decision of a U.S. district judge claiming the law violated the First Amendment.

Their ruling was clear: "As the Supreme Court has observed time and again, false statements do not enjoy constitutional protection, except to the extent necessary to protect more valuable speech. Under this principle, the Stolen Valor Act does not impinge upon or chill protected speech, and therefore does not offend the First Amendment."

Stolen Valor Act Ruled Unconstitutional

The Stolen Valor Act is being treated like a yo-yo as it was ruled unconstitutional by the Supreme Court on June 28, 2012. Once again, it became legal for someone to lie about military service never fulfilled or military awards never earned.

I guess if it is okay for our country to allow illegal aliens to cross our borders by the millions, a few white lies about "stealing valor" couldn't be that big of a deal ... regardless if many actually deserved their valor awards—OR DIED FOR THEM.

I guess protecting the integrity of a "real" veteran has once again reached a new low of importance with our illustrious, arrogant, highest court in America. However, we should all stay tuned on this one, as this subject is very likely to be reversed *again*.

(Source: American Legion Newsletter)

Stolen Valor: States must rectify the federal government's gross lapse in judgment

By Major General James E. Livingston, USMC (Ret.)

The federal government failed us all on June 28th, and in more ways than one. Days before Americans celebrated the anniversary of our nation's hard-fought independence, the Supreme Court of the United States declared unconstitutional the Stolen Valor Act. Overshadowed by its decision to uphold the constitutionality of the Affordable Care Act (aka Obamacare), the Court's decision was a landmark blow to a definitive feature of American culture: The prestige and honor we bestow upon sacrifices made by few while protecting the freedoms enjoyed by all.

(Source: http://americaneedsfatima.blogspot.com/2012/07/ gen-james-livingston-speaks-out-on.html)

Will Stolen Valor Roller-Coaster Ride End?

[September 13, 2012] Less than three weeks after a resolution passed at the 94th National Convention of The American Legion called on Congress to introduce and approve a new Stolen Valor Act, the U.S. House of Representatives has done just that.

The revised legislation, which replaces a law signed in 2006 but struck down last June by the U.S. Supreme Court, sailed through the House by a 410-3 vote Thursday.
(Source: www.legion.org/legislative/212032)

December 3, 2012—The Stolen Valor Act of 2012 became officially official when it passed the Senate as an amendment to the 2013 defense authorization bill. Senator Jim Webb's (a Vietnam veteran representing Virginia) proposal makes it once again a federal crime to make false claims about having served in the military or having received a military decoration ... for personal gain. An example would be an employer who hires alleged veterans ahead of non-veterans.

February 5, 2013—The Stolen Valor Act received another antidote shot in the arm as the U.S. Senate introduced revisions that enhanced the current law. On June 3, 2013, the latest version of the Stolen Valor Act was signed into law by President Obama. Some have labeled the Vietnam War as the "anti-hero's war." I presume this uncomplimentary term comes from the fact that there are so many phonies claiming to be Nam veterans—pure liars about fighting in combat, risking their lives to save their buddies, et cetera, et cetera, et cetera. I guess this helped these poor soulless creatures gain some prestige.

Maybe we "real" Vietnam veterans should in some way find consolation that millions have been imitating us. What a turnaround from the way we were looked at in the 1970s and 1980s.

Another feather in the Vietnam vet's cap is this—there were more Canadians who went to Vietnam than there were American DRAFT DODGERS who slid over the border to Canada to avoid Vietnam. Now that is very interesting.

I wonder how many of the cowards who ran away to Canada have returned home. I have never met one—maybe this book will reach some of them.

The "real" Vietnam combat veteran's bond with the men they fought next to was at the highest level of any American soldier that ever fought before them—in any war.

We had to invent our rules in order to survive. There was little leadership from our elite politicians who sent us here—no goals, no strategies, no moral rewards for courage and strength.

Vietnam veterans had to dig down deep just to get up every morning because we already knew it was probably going to be another rotten day and the day after that as well ... IF that day came.

It didn't take long for a combat soldier/Marine to begin feeling alienated, forsaken, abandoned, and powerless to change that feeling of doom. We became helpless, forced to face and deal with repeated exposure to the ongoing situations that caused our stress to begin with!

How do you climb out of darkness when there is no avenue of escape other than the unthinkable?! The only way a person has a chance to climb out of the black hole of depression and oppression is by maintaining some level of **H-O-P-E!**

Writing this book has been a double-edged sword for me. On the one hand, it has been good, but on the other hand, it has been bad. The writings have brought back so many memories that I had tried to repress over the last few decades. Some of my nightmares similar to those in the 1970s and 1980s have returned, including lifelike hallucinations. Writing this book has renewed and strengthened my vows with some of my Nam veteran brothers.

Other Things We Did Over There ...

While Americans were trashing Vietnam veterans, in country and at home, and while Hanoi Jane and Hanoi John were motivating the protesters, here are a few examples of some other things we were doing over there when we weren't fighting for our lives:

- Bau Dieu District Festival, sponsored by a 25th Division Civic Action Office, provided food, gifts, and entertainment for over 150,000 Vietnamese villagers in December 1968. At the same time, 25th Division Support Command was treating several hundred patients who needed medical care.

- 2nd 22nd Infantry worked very hard to rebuild schools that the Viet Cong had destroyed. The local villagers were quick to recognize the good intentions of the U.S. Army, and many chimed in with full support. Requests to learn English were common.

- I heard this one about the 25th Infantry's 725th Maintenance Battalion. There was this detail that went out on most days in 1969; their mission was to provide comfort and aid to the Catholic Rose Orphanage in Hoc Mon. These soldiers had to work very hard at repairing and painting buildings, building additions, constructing playgrounds, swing sets, and other recreational equipment. Food was also brought for the children and their livestock. Every day the heads of these details were faced with the same problem—each and every day, **there were too many volunteers for the details!**

Medics and Corpsmen Saved Enemy Lives!

Our "Docs" were combat soldiers too. They killed and they saved lives on both sides. I can vaguely remember our first three medics with the 3rd 22nd in 1968, but not their names. None of them lasted long enough to get acquainted with, and NO ONE wanted to become intimately acquainted with them—reasons are obvious. So we just referred to them as "Doc." Their counterparts for the Marines were Navy corpsmen.

I read on a website that there are 2,096 Army medics and Navy corpsmen listed on the Vietnam Memorial Wall. They did not wear red crosses on their helmets or carry armbands—those would have been targets for our enemy ambushers. These heroic men did it all on the run in the heat of severe, life-threatening battle. They bandaged wounds, treated amputations, set splints, treated head injuries, shock, CPR, and seizures, and applied tourniquets. They did it all while they were being shot at in close quarters.

While left-wing protesters back in America were doing their thing, the medics and corpsmen were doing everything possible to keep Americans living. It is quite obvious that the Vietnam War's medical wonders were very good. In WWII, less than 85 percent of wounded soldiers had a chance to live if treated within one hour. In Vietnam, the expected survival rate for a wounded soldier was almost 98 percent if treated and evacuated within one hour of being wounded. They carried everything we carried, plus enough medical supplies to treat at least a dozen men.

Call it reverse psychology, or maybe it was just good old-fashioned American compassion. I remember how our MEDCAP teams used to treat family members of known Viet Cong renegades in the small villages outside of Cu Chi

... by the thousands. Medicines, vitamins, cold pills, cough syrups, injections, bandages, and splints for broken bones were shared with Vietnamese adults as well as their children. And teenagers could fill the role of Viet Cong very easily. No matter, we were the Americans and that was what we did.

- Tay Ninh MED treated thousands of Vietnamese villagers, including administering plague inoculations. In fact, at one time in January 1969, over six hundred patients were being treated per hour. Nearly 40,000 patients were treated under a new program called MEDCAP'S Civic Action Program.

Obviously, Hanoi Jane and Hanoi John never saw this part of the war or refused to see it.

We learned how to save our own lives and the lives of those around us. We had to become unbelievably callous in a very, very short time. That's why we used to say, "Ain't no big thing" after a battle. Or "Don't mean nothing." Or "Sorry about that." (Xin Loi). **BETRAYED? Xin Loi (Sorry about that or Tough s#%@!)**

The Kids ... Forgotten—Also Betrayed!

Maybe some of us allowed ourselves to become too attached to the Vietnamese children during our short visit to their country. But we were Americans, and helping others in need was the American way—wasn't it? Isn't it? Some would say America was the big bully over there, picking on those patriotic Viet Cong, and maybe from their standpoint, they were somewhat correct—"somewhat" at best.

Sure, some of the kids we talked to and kidded with during the day changed into their "Mr. Hyde" Viet Cong outfit when night came. Some—but not most—and we know that to be true. **The Vietnamese kids loved the American GI and we loved them back!**

I don't know how many Nam vets stayed over there or returned to Vietnam after their military obligations were completed; I would guess several thousand. I thought about returning for good. Most villages and their inhabitants were friendly and quite happy to see us—but not all of them to be sure.

I saw some of the damage that our firepower did to some of the villages, but most of our contact and communication with the natives had a positive goal and result. Unfortunately, many times when we came to a village, they had been hit by the Viet Cong—who either abducted their able-bodied males or left them without a leg or arm. Their surgical process wasn't up to the same code that Walter Reed or the Cleveland Clinic maintained—the results were ugly. So our medics would try to help them or we would get them to a hospital. Well, we came and we left. What we left behind us was **CONDEMNED PROPERTY!**

The children of the Vietnam War were exposed to the same traumas that cause PTSD as we Americans were, but they got a dose of it for a full decade. They were also victims of *our* Agent Orange/dioxins. Vietnam officials have estimated that several million of their people in South Vietnam were exposed to our spraying, from which they say tens of thousands of birth defects have resulted.

There should be little doubt that our government should provide more assistance to the children of those who were exposed to our spraying. Even several senior members of Vietnam veterans of America have been quoted as saying they felt Washington and the Agent Orange manufacturers, Dow Chemical and Monsanto Company, have a moral duty to compensate or assist the Vietnamese people who have suffered from Agent Orange exposure—as many Americans have suffered.

American Nam veterans back home are still fighting their own war to be compensated and/or taken care of for Agent Orange-caused health problems. As I have already mentioned, my claim for Agent Orange-related type II diabetes was filed in October 2010 … and was still pending as of February 28, 2013!

The Children of Vietnam Veterans Health Alliance states that they have compiled a list of 194 reported illnesses that the biological children of Vietnam veterans are suffering from, although no official claims have been proven or disproven at this writing (www.covvha.net/second_generation_health). Other reports have indicated that there could be up to five hundred illnesses and conditions that the second generation suffers from. Many were born with these problems to veterans between the ages of twenty and forty-five.

At this writing, the U.S. government is still unwilling to recognize that Agent Orange causes birth defects or illnesses in the children or grandchildren of male Vietnam veterans. An excellent read about the children of Vietnam and the children of American Vietnam veterans was published in the *Plain Dealer* newspaper on January 30, 2011. It was called "Unfinished Business: Suffering and Sickness in the Endless Wake of Agent Orange" by Pulitzer Prize winner Connie Schultz.

Honestly, I miss the little Vietnamese kids saying this to us: **"GI, YOU NUMBER ONE … YOU ARE BUCU NUMBER ONE!"**

Paul Gipson, me, and the kids

Broussard & Nowakowski herding kids to safety – 1968

Author and Vietnamese children

The sadness …

America betrayed them, too.

Loyalty Rewarded With Betrayal

Undying loyalty to a friend, family member, employer, sports team, state, or country is a strong virtue. Vietnam combat veterans gave their blind loyalty to their country and the American people. Our unwavering allegiance to America was rewarded twofold:

1) We made ultimate sacrifices!
2) We were betrayed by the disloyal!

Shouldn't those who were disloyal have been punished? Those disloyal Americans who fled to Canada were forgiven and welcomed back with open arms, while those who remained loyal and fought in Vietnam **are still being punished.**

Dwight D. Eisenhower—34th President of the United States from 1953–1961, former five-star general, U.S. Army Supreme Commander, Allied Forces; World War II, Europe—openly opposed getting involved in Vietnam, saying it would be the type of war America could not win. **NOBODY LISTENED, OR THEY REFUSED TO LISTEN!**

As I have mentioned earlier, and it warrants repeating, betrayal is a violation of trust. It is an act of backstabbing at the lowest level, whether that trust was broken between individuals or an organization. Betrayal causes extreme distress on the recipient that is often long term. It becomes betrayal trauma. Betrayal trauma and PTSD appear to be similar. Both are deadly and can cause fear and severe anger. PTSD with combat veterans is very likely to be much greater when the element of betrayal is higher.

Vietnam combat veterans have a special bond with each other, having fought side by side *together* in the most hated war in America's history. Vietnam's combat veterans were betrayed *together*, and forty-plus years later, many of us are considered to be **CONDEMNED PROPERTY of the Vietnam War! But not all of us.**

More worst-case examples of American media bias toward their own country during and after the Vietnam War:

- During the war, North Vietnam and the Viet Cong executed/slaughtered tens of thousands of innocent South Vietnamese civilians, including women and children.

- The Viet Cong's primary tactics to destabilize South Vietnam was absolute and totally brutal terrorism. Their plan icluded mass abductions, assasinations, bombings, public murders, and village burnings ...

This was terrorism at the highest level. Clearly, a large proportion of the population did NOT favor the Viet Cong nor did they have the slightest desire to come under the rule of the communists in North Vietnam.

- Many North Vietnamese in the communist party had become very unenthusiastic about continuing a longer war with a doubtful outcome. The economics would not have been possible without the massive support from China and the Soviet Union. And the casualties being inflicted by the Americans were traumatizing their entire society. However, because of the U.S. anti-war movement and support from public figures like Fonda and Kerry, the war dragged on and Americans kept coming home in body bags.

- After the war, the North Vietnamese executed between 60,000 and 80,000 people and imprisoned nearly one million more in concentration camps. It was estimated that 80,000 to 100,000 people died in these camps. Many who remained alive were kept in prison for fifteen to twenty years.

- The "Reign of Terror" in Vietnam by the communists caused a mass exodus in the millions, from the south and the north.

- Communist Vietnam sent several divisions into Cambodia and colonized much of that country. Under the communist leader Pol Pot, nearly 25 percent of Cambodia's entire population was slaughtered.

- Laos also remains a communist country to this day, while Cambodia deposed of the communist Khmer Rouge murderers.

Oh, by the way, the massive population reduction of able-bodied men, the duration of the war, and the economic cost of the war left North Vietnam exhausted. Their endeavor into Cambodia and a major falling out with China left North Vietnam completely incapable of trying to force communism onto any other Southeast Asian countries. They had all they could handle with managing South Vietnam.

FYI—the Soviet Union's support of North Vietnam put a devastating strain on their economy. And their losses in the invasion of Afghanistan made it impossible for them to provide any more support to North Vietnam—essentially, North Vietnam was on its own.

Eventually, the Soviet's empire fell to pieces. The **Domino Theory** was a real threat. The Vietnam War stopped it in its tracks, and America won that war ... on the battlefield as well as off the battlefield after the war ended.

Was the **Domino Theory** invalid or not? There is tons of evidence that substantiates that it was valid and that our presence in South Vietnam definitely prevented it from escalating. And it deserves further coverage later on in this book.

The single most amazing thing about ALL of what I have just stated here is **the complete lack of media coverage by America. It's as though they wanted Americans to believe forever that the fall of South Vietnam was a warm and fuzzy happening that brought peace, love, and liberty to all of Southeast Asia!**

I guess Americans were happy and content without knowing the truths. But my brothers and I and our families were victimized casualties of that war in more ways than a few. Some of us remain in constant vigilance of our health problems as a result of the Vietnam War; therefore, we are in constant vigilance of not becoming **CONDEMNED PROPERTY?**

The barrage of books about the Vietnam War took place in the 1980s and even the 2000s. One of the most popular topics of these books was **betrayal**. Here is a short list of some of those books I researched for my readers:

Wounded Warriors Chosen Lives (healing for Vietnam veterans)

Tears of Blood (betrayal of America's veterans)

An Enormous Crime (the definitive account of American POWS abandoned in Vietnam)

War Trauma (lessons unlearned from Vietnam to Iraq)

Nothing Left to Lose (the Vietnam veteran)

Partners in Power (Nixon and Kissinger; betrayal in Vietnam; veterans of today)

America's Betrayal and Treason (1964 to 1975)

Uncertain Warriors (Lyndon Johnson and his Vietnam advisors)

A Grand Delusion (America's descent into Vietnam)

No Peace, No Honor (betrayal in Vietnam)

Vietnam's Forgotten Army (heroism and betrayal)

The Betrayal (a Marine is the author ...)

Hanoi Jane (war, sex, and fantasies of betrayal)

Betrayal (Will Stone in Vietnam)

War Stories (danger, grief, betrayal in Vietnam)

Not Enough Tears (combat infantry soldier's war with PTSD)

Wrong War: Why We Lost in Vietnam

To Bear Any Burden (Vietnam War and its aftermath)

Achilles in Vietnam (combat trauma and the undoing of character)

Glory Denied (saga of Vietnam vet, prisoner of war)

None Came Home (the War Dogs of Vietnam)

Dereliction of Duty (Johnson, McNamara, and the lies)

The Protected Will Never Know

Kill Me If You Can, You SOB (soldier's diaries through three decades)

Wounded Men—Broken Promises

Corruption (U.S. corruption and betrayal in the Vietnam War)

Those are just a few; there are many more. I'll guess that there remain many Vietnam veterans who are not aware that so many books have been published about the wrongdoing to us in Vietnam and back home. I find it gratifying that there are those who stepped up and **TALKED ABOUT IT!**

Betrayal is the work of the devil. I surely hope there are very few who read this book who would disagree.

Gratitude Expressed From a Patriotic American— Quang Nguyen

July 24, 2010

I just want you all to know that the American dream does exist and I am living the American dream. I was asked to speak to you about my experience as a first generation Vietnamese-American, but I'd rather speak to you as an American.

If you hadn't noticed, I am not white and I feel pretty comfortable with my people.

I am a proud U.S. citizen and here is my proof. It took me eight years to get it, waiting in endless lines, but I got it, and I am very proud of it.

I still remember the images of the Tet Offensive in 1968, I was six years old. Now you might want to question how a 6-year-old boy could remember anything. Trust me, those images can never be erased. I can't even imagine what it was like for young American soldiers, 10,000 miles away from home, fighting on my behalf.

Thirty-five years ago I left South Vietnam for political asylum. The war had ended. At the age of thirteen, I left with the understanding that I may or may not ever get to see my siblings or parents again. I was one of the first lucky 100,000 Vietnamese allowed to come to the U.S. Somehow, my family and I were reunited five months later, amazingly in California. It was a miracle from God.

If you haven't heard lately that this is the greatest country on earth, I am telling you that right now. It was the freedom and the opportunities presented to me that put me here with all of you tonight. I also remember the barriers that I had to overcome every step of the way. My high school counselor told me that I cannot make it to college due to my poor communication skills. I proved him wrong. I finished college.

This person standing tonight in front of you could not exist under a socialist/communist environment. By the way, if you think socialism is the way to go, I am sure many people here will chip in to get you a one-way ticket out of here. And if you didn't know, the only difference between socialism and communism is an AK-47 aimed at your head. That was my experience.

In 1982, I stood with a thousand new immigrants, reciting the Pledge of Allegiance and listening to the National Anthem for the first time as an American. To this day, I can't remember anything sweeter and more patriotic that that moment iin my life.

You see, America is not just a place on the map, it isn't just a physical location. It is an ideal, a concept. And if you are an American, you must understand the concept, you must accept this concept, and most importantly, you have to fight and defend this concept. This is about Freedom and not free stuff. And that is why I am standing up here.

Brothers and sisters, to be a real American, the very least you must do is to learn English and understand it well. In my humble opinion, you cannot be a faithful patriotic citizen if you can't speak the language of the country you live in. I still struggle to come up with the right words. It's not easy, but if it's too easy, it's not worth doing. I learned of the 500,000 Americans who fought for this little boy. I learned of the 58,000 names scribed on the black wall at the Vietnam Memorial. You are my heroes. You are my founders.

At this time, I would like to ask all the Vietnam veterans to please stand. I thank you for my life. I thank you for your sacrifices, and I thank you for giving me the freedom and liberty I have today. On behalf of all first generation immigrants, I thank you for your services and may God bless you all.

- Quang Nguyen
July 24, 2010
Creative Director/Founder
Caddis Advertising LLC

Notice that he referred to himself as an American, NOT Vietnamese-American. How good it would be here in America if all of the immigrants—no, EVERYONE—felt like Quang Nguyen.

What Domino Theory?

The reason that President John Kennedy sent more troops to Vietnam was the same reason that he took a stand in Cuba and in West Berlin. Kennedy thought he was taking a stand to stop the spread of communism. The end of

WWII saw communist governments installed by Russia in half of Europe. The formation of the Soviet Union isolated those countries from our influence and threatened the U.S. militarily. Our former ally, Nationalist China, fell to the communists in 1949. The Korean War stalemated with the communists still in control of the northern half of the country in 1953. Cuba went communist in 1959. Communist takeovers were also attempted in Africa, the Middle East, Latin America, South America, and Asia.

The free world was shrinking, and communist countries vowed to conquer the entire world. Vietnam, divided after WWII, was communist in the north and had its sights on the democratic south. Several other countries in Southeast Asia were leaning toward communism. Kennedy took a stand in South Vietnam against communism as did Lyndon Johnson after him, and he upped the ante. All of these descriptions of what type of war Vietnam was have merits.

When China fell to the communists in 1949, the U.S. was forced to become dedicated to try to prevent further expansion of communism in Asia. It was the **Domino Theory** threat that convinced President Kennedy to increase America's presence in South Vietnam, and later, President Johnson decided to commit more military presence in South Vietnam.

What happened after the war in Vietnam ended has been blatantly ignored by the American media. Maybe in a future decade, some noteworthy right-wing researcher will document how the **Domino Theory** was ever so real and almost threw Southeast Asia into turmoil.

The **Domino Theory** threat has been proven—it was real at the time of the Vietnam War and for many years after that war ended. For instance:

- **Vietnam Invades Cambodia** – While the Vietnam War was on, North Vietnam's communist regime had formed an alliance with the Khmer Rouge communists in Cambodia. In December 1978, Vietnam invaded what was then Democratic Kampuchea (Cambodia) and overran the country in just two weeks. In January 1979, a pro-Vietnam government was established, which lasted for ten years.

- **Laos** – In 1975, two years after America exited Vietnam, Laos became a communist-controlled country. Laos could not avoid being dragged into the Vietnam War. North Vietnam had become its big brother, and so they allowed North Vietnam to use its land at will as a supply route to South Vietnam. Laos is a People's Democratic Republic in 2012.

- **Vietnam's Attacks on Thailand** – Vietnam's defeat of Democratic Kampuchea (Cambodia) in 1979 forced the Khmer Rouge to seek refuge in Thailand, which was no friend to communist Vietnam. They squared off often after the Vietnam War ended, well into the 1980s. The main reason that Thailand teamed up with the U.S. against North Vietnam was because of the **Domino Theory** threat, which the Thais feared with a passion. Thailand was in constant fear of Vietnam's threat to infiltrate the Thai government internally with their communistic goals. When Vietnam's military began their occupation of Cambodia, Thailand stepped up their defenses toward Vietnam. Many believe that Thailand remains a Democratic Republic today because of our stand against North Vietnam during the Vietnam War. Vietnam continued its border attacks on Thailand and Cambodia for fifteen years after the Vietnam War officially ended. They ceased in December 1989.

Everyone who was an anti-Vietnam war protestor should repent or go to confession. The Vietnam War was ALL about preventing communism. The problem is, many anti-war protesters are left-wing socialists anyway. North Vietnam was communist all the way, supported and prodded by the entire communist bloc from Cuba to China. **The Domino Theory was real.** Our intervention stalled the communists' advance and allowed the rest of Southeast Asia to strengthen themselves, which they did.

Hanoi Jane and her entire lot were used by Hanoi back then. This is NOT JUST MY OPINION. The communists have admitted to this many times. They have also admitted to this:

- From 1950–1978, China "gave" (not a loan) North Vietnam about $20,000,000,000 (billion) in aid plus …
- China sent more than 300,000 military and private personnel during the peak of the war. We who fought there saw some of them.
- The Soviet Union was sending at least $1,000,000,000 (billion) annually to support North Vietnam.

Get the picture NOW of what we were up against? Heck, even the Viet Minh's resounding defeat of the French at Dien Bien Phu in 1954 was led, directed, and supported militarily by China.

So, was the **Domino Theory** a hoax? Not at all. It appears that it was right on. Many of the Southeast Asian nations that exist today remained free from the communist threat because of the U.S. commitment to the Vietnam War. **Arguably, the Vietnam War was one of THE turning points against communism!**

One of the theories at the earliest stages of the Vietnam War was that it would be far better to fight communism on the battlefield of Vietnam—on China's doorstep—than fight them years later in Hawaii!

The original **Domino Theory** was based on South Vietnam falling to communist North Vietnam, who was backed by communist China and communist Soviet Union. If that happened, which it did, then Cambodia and Laos would ultimately fall ... and they did. The only reason Thailand held strong was that they had twenty-plus years of American buildup and training, and their economy was strong. Their government was also very popular with the Thai people.

The Other Domino Effect ... Fragging!

Destroy the morale of an army, and that army will not function effectively for very much longer. There were so many things that helped to destroy the morale of our soldiers in Vietnam, aside from the actual war itself. Here is my short list, not in any order of importance:

1. Frustration of being shot at by invisible enemies.
2. Frustration from not being fed or clothed properly and treated as though we were expendable.
3. The loss of lives, watching body parts fly, and watching men being evacuated in body bags.
4. Frustration/depression with lack of support at home and hearing how our war buddies were being treated (when they came home) by other Americans.
5. Frustration from not being allowed to fight with maximum force and always having one hand tied behind our backs.
6. The media bias. We heard what they were saying about us; it never seemed like they actually wanted us to win.
7. The corruptness of the South Vietnamese government; it seemed like they were perfectly willing for us to carry the load in the war.
8. Americans who actually supported Hanoi could have been the ultimate blow to our morale; as a result, many American soldiers reverted to **fragging their own leaders!**

Having worked and fought in the business jungle world of sales for over forty years, I have developed a fairly good understanding of how valuable morale is to a team ... especially a military team in severe combat situations.

I often wonder how many men died in country during battle because their morale had gone south and they just weren't 100 percent focused on the task at hand … of staying alive. I often wonder how many Americans were killed in Vietnam by other Americans because of their state of mind, depleted morale, etc.

To this day, I think of how we lay in stinking, polluted Agent Orange-sprayed swamps while being shot at, and at the same time, there were Americans lending sympathy and support to Hanoi! **This will piss me off till I die. In fact, that anger just might contribute to my demise as it has to so many of my war buddies … so many.**

Morale is what holds a team together and gives them the edge they need to compete at a higher level. In a combat arena it gives you the edge to live another day. In Vietnam, our platoon managed to stay together and withstand the morale problems that were magnified during and after the bloodbath year of 1968. We supported each other, the core group that is, but we could see the attitudes changing as the new guys came in.

In 1964, there were North Vietnamese regulars fighting with the Viet Cong. In 1966, the American approval rating of bombing of North Vietnam was 62 percent in favor, as a Harris Survey of July 11, 1966 revealed.

There were underground groups with underground newspapers that offered "bounties" to frag a very unpopular officer. Very few of those who carried out these murders were ever prosecuted.

Please understand my position. A deliberate assassination of one's own team is not something I ever witnessed, although the conversations were heard by most of us. I understand that the term itself, "fragging," was first used in the Vietnam War; however, the act goes back to the early 17th century, I believe. Lump all of the eight reasons for morale destruction, and they all equate to **A DISASTROUS ENDING!**

*THEY Won't Believe This!

The Vietnam veterans weren't the first to be betrayed by the anti-war left. Before and during the Revolutionary War (War for Independence), most colonists were loyal to England. In fact, in 1775, General Washington had to make do with a mere 3,500 highly untrained troops at his command to face one of the world's greatest powers at that time … England. At that time, 9,000 to 10,000 colonials (loyalists to England) either joined the British Army or scurried off to Canada. Sound familiar?

Those original anti-war loyalists, faithful to the enemy, were just the beginning. The War of 1812 was worse. Political battles became violent; parts of New England threatened to join England's side and secede from America. Fortunately, cooler heads prevailed, and they banded together to defeat England.

The Mexican-American War, Spanish-American War, even the Civil War, WWI, and Korea—all had their anti-war groupies to deal with. I think, just my opinion, there is a certain faction of people who NEED WARS TO PROTEST!

In regards to the "fragging," the website www.history.army.mil/books states the following:

The full extent of the problem will never be known; but it increased sharply in 1970 and 1971 when the morale of the troops declined. A total of 730 well documented cases have come to light. Fragging was symptomatic of an Army in turmoil.

Chapter 13

DENY, DELAY … TILL YOU DIE!

My first venture into Cleveland's Veterans Affairs Office was in 2005. I had heard so many negatives about the VA that I just didn't think it would do me any good whatsoever to seek help from them. Most Vietnam veterans I knew felt that way—many still do.

My initial orientation was a positive experience for me, much better than I had envisioned it. There were a lot of veterans there that day, all for their first visit … some younger vets from the Gulf War, a couple of Korean War vets, and about twenty Vietnam vets. I think they all came away impressed with what they heard that day and were quite happy to have finally taken this step … I was too.

Oh my, how I wish I'd had the guts and the initiative to visit the VA earlier than 2005—much, much earlier. But there wasn't anyone stepping up to encourage me to do so. That 2005 orientation lasted about two hours, and it could have extended itself for another few hours, as I was absorbing everything that day.

Little did I know, that eventful day would be the beginning of a whole new and revitalized life for me. I would not be writing this book had the events of that day not happened. The day's pleasant surprises were to continue for a few of us. As the orientation ended and as I was beginning to walk out the door, I heard one of the orientation's speakers say, "Hey, soldier, got a minute?" I turned around immediately, realizing that he could have been addressing any of the other dozens of veterans in that room, but he was talking to ME!

The man who reached out to me that day was a veterans services officer, and I did not even know that they existed till then. Nor was I aware of their function. How ignorant of me—or was it the way our government wanted us to be? His name was Ed Schaeffer.

"You talking to me?" I replied and sure enough, he had addressed me. He asked me to come into his office to talk for a while. He knew from the look on my face—and my age—that I was a Vietnam combat veteran and that I needed help. It was only a few minutes into our conversation before I had broken down and wept over Vietnam like I had never done since coming home (not in front of anyone) from Vietnam.

It is quite possible that I would not be there today had I not met with that Veterans Services commission officer back in January of 2005. As I mentioned earlier, he was doing an orientation at VA Medical in Cleveland that day, and I was in the audience. Why he singled me out after the meeting, I don't know.

Ed brought me into his office and listened to me for a couple of hours like NO ONE had ever done with me since I returned from Vietnam in 1969— no other non-veteran, that is. He listened and listened, never interrupting me until I was finished with my little story. Since that day, until he parted ways with the Veterans Services Commission a couple of years ago, he always made me feel as though I was his own brother and that Vietnam veterans were actually important to him. I believe he was genuinely concerned. He not only took great care of me, he also found time to assist every Nam vet I referred to him … over a dozen.

Even worse, he went out of his way to make me laugh with his weird sense of humor. Apparently, he thought that cheering me up was important therapy for my depression and moments of anger—**how rude and inconsiderate of him to care like that!**

Ed even came to the complete rescue of my Nam brother Curtis Daniels, who was on dialysis and pretty much confined to a wheelchair from his diabetes, caused by Agent Orange. Unbelievably, the VA-Houston did not even have Curtis at 100 percent disability and so he was paying for some of his expensive medication and treatment out of his own pocket. VA-Houston never told him he was entitled to more.

My Cleveland Vet Services officer got involved on Curtis' behalf, contacted VA-Houston, and in a very short time Curtis was receiving the full disability rating he should have had for many years.

He left Vet Services for unknown reasons, but he and I have remained great friends to this day and I expect we always will. I wish there were more people like him at VA … **WORKING FOR US!**

Nam brothers, our uniform may have changed, but our mission has not. We need to continue being soldiers as our country needs our service now more than ever. WE ARE SOLDIERS STILL! My Cleveland Vet Services officer is a great example. I could write an entire book on Ed Schaeffer and what he has done for Vietnam veterans, and for all types of veterans. Maybe I'll do that someday.

While I was describing Nam and my life after Nam to the Vet Services officer, he picked up a telephone and placed a call to someone else at VA, and I heard him say, **"I have a combat Vietnam veteran here in my office, and I would like to file a claim for him immediately for post-traumatic stress syndrome."**

SHOCKED … I was speechless. What was I doing? I was okay. Thousands of other veterans needed care and attention before me, I told him. He demanded that I listen to him and told me that Americans **OWED ME** for risking my life for them, that the American government was obligated to come to my aid—to my brothers' aid—and that we deserved it ... **WE EARNED IT!**

Okay, I agreed to follow through on it. He also cautioned me that Vietnam veterans were not a high priority at the VA. In fact, he told me that the mindset down there regarding Vietnam vet claims was pretty much DENY, DELAY ... TILL YOU DIE! Of course, I had never heard that cliché before, but it would not be the last time that I would hear it.

Cutting to the chase, I was given a compensation hearing for PTSD a few months later, and I was awarded a disability rating of 30 percent for PTSD. I was thankful for this and pleasantly surprised.

I became registered with the VA in 2005—some thirty-six years after leaving Vietnam. Plus, America was now going to send me a tax-free check every month for about $350 and change. Again, I was really grateful.

As I became more familiar and comfortable with the VA system, I learned that there would be some expectations of me from the VA in order to receive medical care and the monthly checks for PTSD, and I was ready to prepare myself for that as my family would be in better shape if I did. I received a letter from the VA's VARC/Intake Clinic on May 25, 2007. This I believe was the VA's psychiatry clinic for drug and alcohol abusers. I understood why I was being required to meet with someone there. I'd had considerable problems with alcohol since Nam during the 1970s , 1980s, and even in the 1990s, so I did go.

When I entered the VARC intake room, I had no idea of what to expect, nor was I prepared for the early moments of the interview that transpired, as follows:

"Mr. Trimmer, so you are a Vietnam veteran, right? We're getting a lot of you guys lately. Off the record, I would like to ask you a couple of questions about Vietnam because I, too, am a Nam veteran."

He asked me several questions, and I answered them promptly and thoroughly. Then he said:

"Oh my, you really are a Nam veteran. You can't believe how many phonies come into this office looking for a free handout, and I resent them. Mr. Trimmer, they don't care about you down here. Vietnam vets just aren't a high priority. In regards to your requests for help and compensation, the standing motto here is **DENY, DELAY ... TILL YOU DIE!"**

He asked me if I had an alcohol or drug problem. I said, "I used to, but not anymore." He entered my answers and told me that he was validating my statement in his records. Otherwise, I might have been required to be on twenty-four-hour call for a blood test for alcohol. He was waiving that requirement based on my word … from one Nam brother to another.

That gentleman of the VARC division of VA also arranged a meeting for me with a Social Services officer for further counseling, including professional counseling for my PTSD.

Names withheld, I met with three different psychological professionals at the VA, and each one seemed to genuinely care about my well-being. The next few years would prove to be an advantage for me—health wise—to have entered into this VA program.

However, during one session, one of the psychologists told me of his frustrations with his colleagues because Vietnam veterans were not being given the same priority as the present vets coming home from Iraq or Afghanistan. In fact, he told me that the philosophy with many of his colleagues toward us was **DENY, DELAY … TILL THEY DIE!**

Wow, there it was again. Now I had heard this from four different people who worked for the VA—I could not believe it!

Dear combat Nam vet brother, if you have several or all of these conditions—whether you know it or not—YOU MOST LIKELY SUFFER FROM PTSD AND/OR YOU HAVE TYPE II DIABETES because each and every one of these symptoms/conditions mentioned here can be caused by PTSD or type II diabetes.

Diabetes or Post-Traumatic Stress Syndrome?

- You suffer from increased blood pressure … cause?
- Your insulin levels are elevated … cause?
- Your cholesterol levels increase abnormally … cause?
- Your vision is deteriorating rapidly … cause?
- Your kidneys are malfunctioning … cause?
- Your mood disorders are worsening … cause?
- Your heart problems increase … cause?
- Your risk for heart attack or stroke is increased … cause?
- You are suffering from peripheral neuropathy … cause?

Many thousands of our brothers have already died prematurely from these BIG TWO KILLERS due to their severe combat-related stress and their exposure to dioxin TCDD and other toxic chemicals … in other words, Agent Orange.

If you have not filed claims with VA for either or both of the BIG TWO KILLERS of Vietnam combat veterans, then shame on you, my brother.

The sources from where my information originates are way too numerous to list here. Trust me; this is pure, unchallengeable FACT! If you have not filed your claims or you have not even registered with Veterans Administration, please keep this frightening thought close to you ... IT CAN TAKE A VA CLERK SEVERAL MONTHS TO PUT A COPY OF YOUR DD-214 INTO A FOLDER TO BE REVIEWED BY OTHERS WHO MAKE A FINAL DECISION.

My point is simply this ... WAIT NO LONGER! My brother, whether you have a life insurance policy, a pension, or both, or neither—IF you were on disability from either of the BIG TWO KILLERS from our beloved Vietnam War, and IF you die from either of the two ... **your spouse could receive benefits for her lifetime.**

Remember, my brother, **YOUR COUNTRY OWES YOU! You gave them a blank check with your life on the line as collateral. America has overspent that check from us—many times over!**

An example of what you could be going through can be made through my own claim into VA for type II diabetes:

- The date of my diagnosis by a VA primary care doctor was October 2010.
- The cause of my type II diabetes is an unchallengeable disease related directly to Agent Orange because I was a combat Nam vet plodding through the jungles where Agent Orange was sprayed. This has already been proven to the VA ... it is an unchallengeable FACT.
- The unthinkable horrors we as Vietnam combat vets suffered from over there (and now) is also a given. We should have to prove nothing else as WE WERE THERE!

And yet my claim for type II diabetes was over two years old in late February 2013.

My brothers, it is worth the hassle and the delay for you and your spouse. IT IS DEFINITELY WORTH IT! Remember, these VA clerks are federal civil service employees of the United States government who are paid by your tax money.

Next? The waiting game or the DELAY game. And it still might get denied, God forbid. Next? You may die during the DELAY process. Your claim could run the course something like this:

A. DELAY ... DENY!

B. DENY ... DELAY ... YOU DIE!

C. DELAY ... DENY ... DELAY ... **DENY TILL YOU DIE!**

Whether you die before the claim gets an approval, if/when it is approved, it is good to go and your spouse will be covered retroactive to your original filing date. So please, my brothers ... do not dilly-dally around in getting your claim filed, and whatever you do—no matter how long it takes—**DO NOT GIVE UP! You did not give up Vietnam. You came home physically, so why would you not continue the fight now?**

Government's Ongoing War Against ... Us?

Fellow Vietnam War buddies, did you know that there was a program available by Veterans Administration back in the 1960s that was supposed to assist returning Vietnam servicemen? Did you also know that in late 1967, this program was doing so well that VA expanded it? Supposedly, this program was launched with the full cooperation of the Department of Defense, as it was President Johnson's wish to help us make adjustments to civilian life. Yes, the same President Johnson who stopped the bombing of the Ho Chi Minh Trail in 1968, allowing the North Vietnamese Army to run rampant from North Vietnam to Laos, Cambodia, and South Vietnam.

I do not recall that program. I have yet to locate another Vietnam veteran who can recollect such a program. Oh well! I recently read about this program in the 25th Infantry's newsletter, *Tropic Lightning*. I found it on February 14, 2013, just a tad late after my return to civilian life in March 1969 ... forty-four years too late!

Well, our government tried to make up for this by taking better care of the Vietnamese aliens who came to America after North Vietnam conquered South Vietnam. In fact, our government at times seems to care more about the illegal aliens who keep flooding into America now in 2013.

In 1975, the fall of Saigon brought an end to the Vietnam War in Southeast Asia while our U.S. government generously welcomed more than 50,000 Vietnamese refugees onto American soil in southern California by sheltering, clothing, and feeding them.

Most all of the refugees arrived with no money or personal possessions, and very few spoke any English. Nonetheless, they were compassionately accepted and sponsored by volunteer families, churches, and corporations, eventually assimilating into our society. The vast majority became productive U.S. citizens.

In addition to this gesture of goodwill, our government also pro-vided shelter, beds, meals, TV, recreation, and health care for hardened criminals in our local, state, and federal prisons, and it offered the same safe and comfortable living conditions for violent thug terrorists at Guantanamo Bay, Cuba.

On the other hand, disabled and homeless veterans who selflessly defended our nation have been forgotten and dispossessed by the same government and forced to live alone, homeless, and hungry in back-alley slums.

By the VA's own admission, 47 percent of today's homeless veterans are from the Vietnam War era. Most of them are now in their sixties and seven-ties, and many are in frail and declining health.

Inexcusably, while the Vietnamese refugees were welcomed into our country, America's veterans who had fought to defend them in their native homeland were demeaned when they returned home to their own native country.

The fact that Vietnamese refugees were given immediate attention and support decades ago while tens of thousands of our Vietnam War veterans are still homeless and destitute is a national disgrace beyond comprehension.

President Obama (not a veteran) has failed to deliver on repeated promises that his administration would faithfully honor a sacred trust to care for our disabled and homeless veterans.

Vietnam veterans believed President Obama would honor his promises to end the shameful mistreatment of Vietnam veterans since nearly half of today's homeless veterans are from the Vietnam War era.

It is estimated that since the Vietnam War ended, more than twice as many Vietnam veterans have committed suicide than the 58,272 who were killed during the war.

The death toll amongst homeless Vietnam veterans will continue to climb as more commit suicide, overdose on VA drugs, are murdered, or die of hard-ship and old age while fighting against the domestic enemy.

Their solace is found in Plato's prophetic claim more than 2,500 years ago: *"Only the dead have seen the end of war."*

Think about it; the Vietnam War ended forty years ago, yet the U.S. gov-ernment seems to continue waging an ongoing war against the veterans of that war instead of defending them. And President Obama's administration, in its second term, continues to treat Vietnam War veterans with little respect or honor.

Forty-four Years Later VA Says
"Prove You Were There!"

The VA says I wasn't there … forty-four years later! The horror stories of the Veterans Administration's incompetence have been well documented and written about often over their existence. I know they are getting better in some areas and at some VA facilities. But the horror stories continue of lost records and erroneously recorded claims—causing untold anguish, anger, and premature deaths without earned compensation to the veterans or their families.

I personally know Nam veterans who were wounded over there, and their heads are screwed up beyond what the average person on the street can begin to comprehend. And yet, they cannot get the treatment or benefits due to them because their records have been lost, destroyed in fire, etc. Never mind the fact that these Nam vets can produce photos with brothers they fought with over there, and never mind the fact that these warriors can also produce statements from their Nam brothers who verify with unchallengeable credibility that **THEY WERE THERE**—never mind all of that. The beleaguered Vietnam combat veteran still has to fight, fight, fight, fight, fight several decades after that rotten war ended. **I THOUGHT WE SUFFERED ENOUGH OVER THERE … DIDN'T WE?**

Well, get this … almost eight years after my first visit to a VA facility in 2005 for an Agent Orange physical, and forty-four years after my participation in the 1968 Tet Counter Offensives in country, I was told on October 11, 2012 that VA records DO NOT show that I was exposed to Agent Orange spray in Vietnam. Essentially, this human error (I hope that it was a human error) was saying this to me: "*Mr. Trimmer, you need to prove to us again that you were in Vietnam when and where the herbicides were sprayed.*"

As I mentioned earlier, it was a VA doctor who uncovered this error shortly after he had to present the news to me that I might have prostate cancer along with diabetes (and other complications), which are all undeniably related to my heavy exposure to Agent Orange in Vietnam. I wonder if our brothers who fought in WWI, WWII, Korea, and the Gulf Wars had to go through these inconveniences. Putting it mildly, I wonder.

Okay, problem identified. Regardless of how frustrated and VERY angry I am about this … I have to take a few deep breaths and regroup some of the factual records I have—in case I have to prove all over again that I was, in fact, in the Vietnam War. Good grief! When will it stop? When will they stop messing with us? DENY … DELAY … TILL WE DIE!

I can't soften up the above statement. It is serious. It almost implies premeditated murder of an entire generation of warriors and their families.

Tough talk? You bet. Why not? Didn't my warrior brothers in Vietnam fight to preserve that freedom of statement? Of course we did ... so I will continue the fight and I will publish this book.

Okay, so how did I react to this recent and very troubling fiasco? Without any hesitation whatsoever, I prepared a letter to the Veteran Services representative who has been managing my disability claim for diabetes type II. Here is the gist of that letter:

October 12, 2012
Dear Ms. Jones,
Just came home from a couple of examinations at a local VA medical facility. They were relatively routine, such as:

- *They increased my meds **again** for my PTSD.*
- *They increased my meds **again** for my blood pressure, which is at a critical level.*
- *They noted that my cholesterol had increased **again**.*
- *They informed me that I had some prostate problems. PSA levels had zoomed upwards—close monitoring is required and possible biopsy in near future.*
- *My diabetes type II seems to have leveled off, although a lot of damage has already been done.*
- ***Last, but not least of importance, they informed me that the VA profile did not show that I was exposed to Agent Orange.***

*In other words, the last item was saying that **I WAS NEVER IN VIETNAM!** My DD-214 and DD-215 and other government records in regards to my service over there state this:*

- *Awarded ... **Vietnam** Service Medal with 3 Bronze Star*
- *Awarded **Vietnam** Campaign Medal*
- *Awarded **Vietnam** Cross of Gallantry with Palm*
- *Awarded Bronze Star – Valor for Heroism in ground combat in The Republic of **Vietnam***
- *Awarded the Purple Heart for wounds received in combat action in The Republic of **Vietnam***
- *Awarded Army Commendation Medal for Meritorious Service in The Republic of **Vietnam***
- *Awarded 2 Overseas Bars in The Republic of **Vietnam***
- *Foreign Service in Republic of **Vietnam**, 1968–1969*
- *Served in the Tet Offensive in **Vietnam***

- *Served in the Tet Counter Offensives of Phase IV and V in **Vietnam***
- *Served with Bravo Co. 3rd 22nd Infantry 25th Division in **Vietnam***

No wonder so many Vietnam vets remain so angry. Can you please look into this? Eleven times my U.S. Army records state that I served IN VIETNAM!
Thanks much,
> *Roland "Dusty" Trimmer*
> *Vietnam War Combat Veteran*

How DUMB is all of this? I have heard and read about things like this, and I have heard that they happen quite often. What kind of person works at a job where people and their families' lives are put in jeopardy by a simple mis-filing or NON-filing of a valuable record of someone's service in defending their FREEDOM?

- What kind of person hires these people?
- What kind of people allow these unforgiveable mistakes to continue?

At the end of the day, I still can't do without the VA, as there are many wonderful people there who genuinely care about us.

Small Town/Old Fashioned VA—Really?

I have spent five busy years driving over 10,000 miles to and from the VA located at Cleveland, Ohio's Wade Park facility. I never really minded the thirty- to forty-five-minute waits to see the designated medical professional. Plus, I was always reimbursed at $20.00 for travel even though I had to stand in line for another thirty to forty-five minutes for that $20.00 and change. Oops, I forgot to mention that thirty- to forty-five-minute wait once I entered the medical professional's office. A typical trip there could last pretty much a full day.

I truly didn't mind all that—the medical fees were "cheap" and I thought that I was in good hands—most times. At Cleveland's Wade Park VA facility, no one ever recognized me or remembered my name regardless of how many visits I made or to which department I may have visited—whether frequently or not. It was almost as if every time I walked into the facility, it was for the first time. Still, I did not mind it that much as I looked forward to mingling and chatting with other Vietnam vets, regardless of how sad their stories were, and they rarely wanted to hear my morbid stories—but I did not mind that either. So many good men in wheelchairs. **Sooo, this is what the guys look like now that we carried out of battles to medevac choppers!**

I have news for you … the Brecksville VA was even more unfriendly or less user-friendly than Cleveland's Wade Park VA. Brecksville resembled a huge prison complex. I hated going there, and I celebrated by myself when it was closed down.

Just over two years ago, one of the Cleveland VA medical professionals asked me this question,

Mr. Trimmer, I see that you live in Portage County and that you drive about forty miles or so and back to make your appointments here. Wouldn't the Ravenna, Ohio VA, which is also located in Portage County, be more convenient for you to be treated?

DUH! After five years of fighting Cleveland's traffic and the Cleveland VA's delays and after being seen by a different medical professional each and every time (I never saw the same person twice), I thought for a couple of seconds, and then I responded … HELL YEAH! However, I must give credit to the Cleveland VA's surgeons. I had two surgeries performed there for wrist and elbow problems. I am 100 percent satisfied with their work and the follow-up I received for both surgeries.

Having spent about half of my life in the city of Cleveland (yeah, I know—it wasn't Chicago or New York), I had done enough time in the so-called big city to understand its pluses and minuses—and balance them out.

When I arrived at the Ravenna VA facility, I thought to myself, *Oh my, what have I done—how could this little building have the quality medical professionals that my messed-up mind is in need of?* Small town/old-fashioned VA turned out to be precisely what my aching mind and body needed.

"Hi, Mr. Trimmer." That's how at least half a dozen medical professionals at small-town Ravenna, Ohio VA greet me when they see me walk into the building. ARE YOU KIDDING ME … I love it!

I suppose it will only be a matter of time before the Ravenna VA's reputation spreads around and more veterans will be asking to transfer their health care requirements over there … I don't blame them.

It's October 12, 2012 as I write this section, and I just had two appointments yesterday at Ravenna VA. While I could write an entire book about my two-and-a-half-year experiences at Ravenna VA (and I may someday), my experiences there have been AWESOMELY POSITIVE!

Ravenna VA has saved my life … in more ways than one. I can't thank them enough, therefore their mention in this book. I'll start with Dr. Robert Marcus, PhD, a psychologist. I could also write a separate book about him (and I may someday). Aside from the difference we had instantly—he is a Notre Dame fan and I am an Ohio State fan all the way—we got past that and have had remarkably productive therapy sessions. Of course, on the way out from every one of those sessions, I never fail to say, GO BUCKEYES!

Dr. Marcus has saved my life a couple of times. Finally, I had encountered a mental health professional who **believed** and understood the agony that so many Vietnam War combat veterans suffered from … and for so long.

Gee whiz, why did it take all these years for me to meet someone like this, someone who could help me, wanted to help me, and genuinely pushed me into allowing him and the VA to help me? At all times, he touted what the VA could do for me with his guidance. He was a company man all the way, but I was sold on him more than the VA itself.

As time went on, Dr. Marcus introduced me to others at Ravenna VA—doctors, nurses, medical techs, support personnel—and I have yet to be disappointed with any of them. Dr. Fantauzzo, Dr. Martinez, Judith, Tina, and many others … they all send out the message to me when I visit Ravenna VA … **TLC**!

Diabetes type II and all the problems associated with that, critically high blood pressure and cholesterol, optical problems, bone deterioration problems, neuropathy, excessively high PSA count/enlarged prostate problems, sleep disorders, PTSD (and all the problems associated with that, including suicidal thoughts) … I've been a handful for Ravenna VA, a small town, old-fashioned VA. **Bottom line: I stumbled onto a diamond in the rough here—a life-saving stumble!**

Oh, by the way, it was the medical professionals at Ravenna VA who discovered that my official profile with Veterans Administration did not have me officially posted as having been exposed to Agent Orange in Vietnam! Fortunately, they were able to get this ridiculous error corrected this past November after several frustrating attempts. This was almost comical—almost. **GOD BLESS THE VA AT RAVENNA, OHIO!**

It Wasn't So Bad … Was It?

In Vietnam, the usual tour of duty was twelve or thirteen months. In WWII it was determined that breakdowns rose sharply after one year of combat. During WWII the military officials did acknowledge that heavy, continuous exposure to battle could break a man, so to protect them from this, **they evacuated the entire unit after a battle of any nature. This would be the major reason that WWII veterans did not seem to suffer an equal proportion of psychological injuries as Vietnam veterans.** (Source: *VFW magazine*)

Then again, there was no evacuation system in place for psychiatric casualties in the Vietnam War. Nor was there a counseling program offered to them when they returned home. **They were just expected to blend in and**

deal with it. Because the typical tour of duty had been "just" one year, it was thought that soldiers who broke down in that time frame must have been damaged goods before entering the service … **THEY WERE WRONG!**

There was not a program in place for PTSD during or after the Vietnam War. What was called "shell shock" or combat neurosis during/after WWII simply was not understood or accepted as a problem for Vietnam vets. After all, we were only exposed to combat for one year or less, unlike WWII veterans, who were exposed to battle for three or four years … right? RIGHT?

Men who were seemingly broken in combat in Vietnam simply did not exist. They were ruled out as potential casualties by America's government and the American public. **Unfortunately, the military experts miscalculated something about the combat veterans of the Vietnam War, which has proven to be a costly error.**

- **In WWII, the typical combat infantryman saw an average of forty days of combat in a four-year tour of duty.**
- **In the Vietnam War, a combat infantryman saw an average of 240 days of combat in just one-year tour of duty.**

The combat infantry grunt's participation in the Vietnam War looks something like this:

- **Fifteen percent of all American soldiers who served in Vietnam had a combat infantry title.**
- **Eighty-five percent of all American casualties were suffered by the combat infantry veterans.**
- **One of the many unknown facts about the Vietnam War was the alarming rate of amputations or crippling wounds. In Vietnam, they were 300 percent higher than in WWII and 70 percent higher than Korea. Multiple amputation wounded also occurred at a much higher rate in the Vietnam War.**

(Source: Veterans of Foreign Wars – VFW)

Regardless of what America is doing for Vietnam veterans today, some forty-plus years after the war, America was not prepared then for what was coming home from Vietnam. While America ignored Vietnam veterans, their problems kept building, unattended to for decades.

Think about it; the typical combat infantryman in Vietnam was exposed to six times the horror of combat that his WWII brothers were … in one-fourth the time frame!

I fought with hundreds of combat Vietnam soldiers. I have been in touch with thousands of Vietnam veterans from every branch of service since the war ended. The overwhelming majority of us are still depressed about the war. Most will say they are proud to have served and they wish more Americans who did not serve there would also be proud of them.

Most of us have the classic symptoms of sleeping disorders, feelings of worthlessness, and difficulty in concentrating, and most of us have weapons in our possession—me included. Unfortunately, the possibility of suicide is and always has been present with many Vietnam veterans—I am no exception.

In WWII when a combat unit suffered from heavy casualties, the entire unit was usually removed from the battle area until it was back to full strength. In Vietnam, there was little or no grieving time allowed when casualties were incurred. Grieving was to be handled as quickly as possible. The unit remained in battle and continued their missions. Replacements would arrive just like nothing ever happened. I remember what that was like when I was one of the "new guys." The "new guy" wasn't trusted and was always given the worst jobs—and why not?

In WWII there were goals and battle plans. There would be a winner and a loser of the day. Vietnam-style combat held no final resolution of conflict for the combatants. Overall, the outcome was just an ongoing and endless production of killed and wounded with no measure of accomplishment for the battle. It did not matter how hard we fought, bled, sweated, or how bravely one died; the outcome was never any different. We gained ground—then gave it back—so we gained nothing.

Vietnam War combat troops were constantly mortared or rocketed or ambushed with human wave assaults, and Americans were almost always outnumbered numerically by the NVA and VC.

How does a man carry on for a full year knowing that each day is probably going to be a bad day and that there will be no time to rest and relax when night comes? The looks on our faces would give chills to each other ... that empty, hopeless stare at nothing!

Vietnam combat veterans received little support from home. The American media made sure of that. We deserved better. The Vietnam combat veteran felt helpless over there with no way out. Our return to the United States put us in another situation of helplessness. Except for a few family members, there were no open arms waiting for us. Our choices were limited; get on with our lives on our own or don't even bother. Many chose not to bother. I was almost one of those. **IT WASN'T SO BAD ... WAS IT?!** I have not gotten over that war, and I'm not so sure I ever can.

When night was upon us in Nam, we could not sleep; we dared not. We had to be even more vigilant. We had to prepare mentally for the inevitable; we had to be prepared for an attack night after night. So we developed a combat survival skill that NO ONE could possibly comprehend unless they lived it themselves. **GET OVER THAT WAR?**

When we slept, it was on our backs (as I do now) with our weapon across our chest or we slept sitting up. To this day, I sleep with my trusty machete hanging on my bedpost, ever vigilant of what might lurk in the dark of night. I still do this because of a war that I left back in 1969. But Vietnam refuses to leave me. In some ways, I am still **PROPERTY OF VIETNAM, but I refuse to become** *CONDEMNED PROPERTY?*

Those *Rambo* movies were really, really dumb, weren't they? How could an individual become so programmed into what the Rambo character portrayed? How? When an individual is brainwashed from his initial eight-plus weeks of basic training and then another eight-plus weeks of advanced infantry training and then exposed to continuous threats day after day, night after night for fifty weeks, his body will remain mobilized and prepared for battle … indefinitely.

Many of us who were broken by the experiences of combat in Vietnam have lost much of our capacity for self-respect and confidence. Seeking professional consultation is generally not an option that very many Vietnam veterans will choose. Many have died prematurely because of their unwillingness to seek the help that is now available to them through the VA. But it wasn't always available.

Most combat-hardened Vietnam veterans who have died prematurely probably never opened up to anyone about their combat horrors over there. Many more will die prematurely, having kept everything inside, which only accelerates their end to come sooner.

Oh sure, we know that it is no longer politically incorrect to discuss Vietnam openly in society today. I suppose that is the reason there have been so many books written about this war over the last dozen years or so. But the pain remains with most of us, and I just don't see a way to make it all better.

If I added up all of my little damages from the Vietnam War—a scratch on the head from a VC carbine round passing through my helmet, malaria, jungle rot for life, concussion from a fall, shrapnel in knee and foot, shrapnel on face, diabetes II/Agent Orange, PTSD—and multiply those minor inconveniences by ten thousand times, those little bumps and bruises would not measure up to the pain and suffering that any one of our Nam brothers endured when they died prematurely over there … or back home.

I guess the only way America will get over that war is when all Vietnam veterans have been put to rest. Maybe then all of the guilt will go away about what was done to us—or not done for us—when we needed it most! **NOW COME ON, DUSTY—THAT WAR WAS OVER FORTY YEARS AGO, SO GET OVER IT! Well, we are trying to do that, but many of us still need help from our loved ones.**

Burying the Past … Living the Present

Several Vietnam vets who are close friends of mine could not contribute even a short story about their experience in Nam or about other Nam vets they knew. I can understand and I can appreciate their reasons as I mentioned at the beginning of this important chapter.

In my PTSD therapy sessions, I have been advised to try and "live in the present" in order for me and others around me to live a happier life. During most of the last several years, I think that advice has been successfully carried out … for the most part. Understanding how to do this is quite difficult without help from others. My lovely wife, Ginny, and some darn good buddies have been there for me when I needed them most. Some of those good buddies are also Vietnam vets, and they also need support to help them live in the present rather than in the past. Unfortunately, many, if not most Vietnam vets I have known will not accept or seek out support from their own friends. I guess this sort of admits a sign of weakness in their makeup as I used to believe.

Why is it so difficult for many of us to stay focused enough on the present, like hitting a little white golf ball that is just sitting there motionless and daring us to hit it squarely? Because our minds wander off, even as we are whispering to ourselves, *Keep your head down, dummy!* If you've ever been in therapy, then you know that you were asked to relive some of your past experiences. I am being told now that this strategy is being reevaluated and that its value is questionable. So maybe my trips into the Everglades and the Amazon jungle to recapture Nam haven't been such a great idea. **I have been told lately, when our attention is stuck in the past, our quality of life will NOT improve! So maybe I need to get this book done with and move on.**

When it's time for your next shot on the golf course and you're coming off a really bad shot, which of these thoughts would work best for you:

- Dwelling on that last bad shot and what you did wrong
- Thinking about the next several holes and future shots and how you can make up for that last stinking shot

Of course the correct answer is to dedicate ALL the focus you can muster into the present shot! That's the only advice I am capable of and qualified for in helping to improve anyone's golf game. Except KEEP YOUR HEAD DOWN—just like they told us in Vietnam.

Most of us will never be able to completely wipe out all those bad memories from our experience in the Vietnam War. How can we when our Nam brothers are still dying prematurely all around us?

I tried looking up a Nam vet who I met back in the 1990s and exchanged many conversations with. Somehow, we lost touch. Then when I did a search for him, I found out that he committed suicide just a few years ago. Wow, that news stuck with me for a long time—I still think about him and the conversations we used to share together.

It's only natural to grieve. We sure had enough of that over there, enough to last several lifetimes. We cannot prevent ourselves from grieving—we need to grieve. We need to pay close attention to ourselves, especially when we are grieving, as we Nam vets are most vulnerable then.

I am learning now at the latter stage in my life to prevent my grieving from pulling me away from happiness. The single most difficult thing I have trouble doing when stress is getting to me is relaxing.

We've all heard this cliché … **ENJOY THIS DAY!** How simple and profound. My fellow Nam brother, regardless of what happened to us over there, or last year or last week or yesterday—**NOW** is what we need to focus on in order to have a chance for a happy rest of *this* day.

Earlier this morning, I felt a bit stressed but it passed. Then I took my big, frisky Newfoundland, Bella, for a long walk in the forest and I feel MUCH better right NOW!

Letter of Complaint About VA

It is April 23, 2013 and I am still in a dogfight with the Veterans Administration over illnesses that we combat veterans know are military service connected, yet the VA chooses to deny or ignore in spite of medical evidence that exists not in the VA's favor. My vet brothers know the drill.

One of my illnesses/diseases denied by the VA for compensation was **hypertension connected to PTSD.** VA examiners stated:

Your service records do not show any complaints, findings, diagnosis, or treatment for hypertension during service.

You are obese, you have a history of hyperlipidemia (high cholesterol), you are sixty-eight years old, and have sleep apnea. These issues can all impact hypertension. Your hypertension is not caused by or the result of service-connected PTSD.

Letter of Complaint … yes, you can write and I have sent a Letter of Complaint about this decision, their ridiculous reasoning, and other topics as well. Mine was sent to and copied to the following VA officials:

1. Supervisor of Compensation & Pensions Department
2. Patient Advocate Office
3. Disabled American Veterans
4. VA Primary Care Physician
5. VA Mental Health Psychologist
6. Veteran Services Director

My complaints about the VA examiners' Rating Decision on this one condition were as follows:

Of course, my service records do not show any complaints, diagnosis, or treatment for the hypertension that I and others suffered from our job responsibilities in Vietnam such as these:

A. Participation in more than 200 search-and-destroy missions by day
B. Participation in more than 100 air combat assaults into hot areas
C. Participation in more than 100 ambushes at night
D. Crossing into Cambodia on search-and-destroy missions
E. Suffering from malnutrition, losing fifty pounds the first three months
F. Spending eighty-eight consecutive days in the jungle conducting operations day and night, no hot meals, no cold beverages, no fresh uniforms, no dry socks, wearing rotted boots for weeks
G. Waking up with a cobra in a bush next to me
H. Crawling during a firefight and facing off with a bamboo pit viper
I. Waking up one morning with a black scorpion on my neck
J. Going sleepless for several days and nights in a row … often
K. Watching your buddies getting blown to bits, shot to pieces
L. Being grazed in the head by enemy bullet
M. Being overrun by several suicide-type human wave attacks
N. Witnessing innocent civilians, including children being mutilated as entire villages were destroyed

No, I was never treated or diagnosed for hypertension or high blood pressure over there, and no, there are no records of my complaints about those things! **I just did my job** and the medics never checked us for high blood pressure or hypertension. It was a given—we all suffered from it terribly.

Since or during my official diabetic time, my BP has risen and my cholesterol has risen, the reason I included increased hypertension in my claim.

Whether the elevated BP is related to PTSD or diabetes type 2 or both should be a no-brainer here. Several times my BP has read in the highly dangerous level of 160s/100s at different VA facilities, and it should be on record … I know it is.

In regard to the examiners' statements *"you are obese,"* etc., presently, I am 203 pounds and 5'11" tall. Before the probable diabetic condition, my weight always hovered within 192 to 195 pounds. Then, pretty much all of a sudden, from 2009 to 2011 it shot up to 217 pounds. Clearly, something was wrong. Since then, under medication and with limited diet and renewed exercising, I am back down to 203 pounds—not where I want, but winter weather is a hindrance to getting more exercise. Obese at 5'11", 203 pounds. Really? Again, the sudden weight gains were caused by diabetes.

Diabetes is a lethal disease, especially if left untreated for extended periods. The VA lab tests show that I had diabetic blood glucose readings for several years before officially receiving a VA physician's diagnosis that I was diabetic in 2010. Therefore, most or all of my present diabetes-related conditions went untreated for many years, causing internal damage along the way.

There is misinformation in the examiners' reports, almost to the point of negligence. And they are obvious. All of my medications for BP and PTSD have been *increased* to maximum levels in the last year or two, all during the rise of my diabetes, an Agent Orange-caused condition in service. Maybe if some of the examiners' erroneous statements were more accurate, the denied Ratings Decisions would have had a different result.

I feel that these oversights or omissions of pertinent information are clear examples of my situations or issues not being treated with the dignity, compassion, and respect I deserve as a combat infantryman who put his life on the line for the country I love. That is my opinion.

I could have sent a Letter of Reconsideration or a Letter of Disagreement, but I chose a Letter of Complaint. Dear readers, to follow this letter, depending on VA's response, I plan to send a Letter of Appeal if necessary.

*THEY Won't Believe This!

"Deny, delay until I die" is not my creation. It goes way back. If you go to the Internet and search for that exact phrase, you will find page after page of disgusting but factual examples of the horrors our veteran brothers and sisters have had to face because of delayed claims for disability, other benefits, and pensions. It would be impossible to list them all, and the list keeps getting longer. **Where are the so-called "do gooders" who protest wars? Why**

aren't they protesting the shameful treatment of veterans by our government?

If I had to use one or two words to dish out the proper credit this whole disgusting scenario deserves, here are a few appropriate words: vile, loathsome, nauseating, hideous, gross, contemptible, despicable, heinous, abhorrent, odious, repugnant, etc. I could go on forever. It just **STINKS!**

Chapter 14

DYING TOO SOON ... DURING AND
AFTER NAM!

We Vietnam combat vets quit feeling sorry for ourselves a long time ago. However, the rage and resentment are still inside many of us as we continue to die at a faster rate than our eighty-five- to ninety-year-old fathers and uncles. Our type of military training to fight, hate, and kill Viet Cong was intense and never addressed properly after we came home ... not for decades.

Anger? Hypertension? Why now? We Vietnam vets were ignored for decades. Even our GI Bill was gutted when we came back.

Most combat vets from Vietnam suffered from malnutrition on a massive scale. When I left for Vietnam, I weighed 177 pounds. Only four months later, I weighed 127 pounds. Dizzy spells were common on a daily basis. There were no hot meals, no fresh health foods, no fruit except spider-infested bananas, no vegetables (rice doesn't count), no milk. So many of us returned in a very deteriorated condition health-wise.

It's no wonder I have been faced with major bone deterioration in my mouth, jaw, and neck to lumbar and fingers, hands as well ... thank you, Agent Orange.

This has been mentioned elsewhere in the book, but it deserves repetition. Back in the 1980s a study was conducted by the State Department of Public Health and the Office of Veterans Services, which came to the following conclusions:

- Their research found more deaths among Vietnam veterans than non-Vietnam veterans due to auto accidents, suicides, strokes, kidney failure, tissue cancers, etc. Since that study, several other killers of Vietnam vets have made the list, such as diabetes, ischemic heart disease, and other cancers.

- The study proved that Vietnam veterans have had a much greater incidence of traumatic death, especially with Vietnam veterans who were in heavy combat.

When Colonel David Hackworth, one of the champions of combat infantry grunts, died in May 2005, it was very disappointing to most Nam vets, although not much of a surprise. I had the distinction of meeting "The Patton of Vietnam" at a Vietnam veterans rally in Kokomo, Indiana. The cause of his death was a form of cancer which has stricken many of our brothers who served over there. Agents Orange and Blue killed him.

Col. Hackworth's battlefield exploits puts him next to Sergeants Alvin York and Audie Murphy. The novelist Ward Just, who knew him for forty years, described him as "the genuine article, a soldier's soldier, and a connoisseur of combat."

At age fourteen, as World War II was sputtering out, he lied about his age to join the Merchant Marines, and at fifteen, he enlisted in the U.S. Army. Over the next twenty-six years, he spent seven years in combat. **He was recommended for the Medal of Honor three times.** I think the last application was still under review at the Pentagon. He was twice awarded the Army's second highest honor for valor, the Distinguished Service Cross, along with ten Silver Stars and eight Bronze Stars. He always said that he was proudest of his eight Purple Hearts and his Combat Infantryman's Badge.

A reputation won on the battlefield made it impossible to dismiss him when he went on the attack later as a critic of careerism and incompetence in the military high command. In 1971 he appeared in the field on ABC's *Issues and Answers* to say Vietnam "is a bad war … it can't be won. We need to get out." He also predicted that Saigon would fall to the North Vietnamese within four years, a prediction that turned out to be far more accurate than anything the Joint Chiefs of Staff were telling President Nixon or that the President was telling the American people.

With almost five years in country, Col. Hackworth was the only senior officer to sound off about the Vietnam War. After the interview he retired from the Army and moved to Australia.

"He was perhaps the finest soldier of his generation," observed the novelist and war correspondent Nicholas Profit, who described Col. Hackworth's combat autobiography, *About Face*, a national best-seller, as "a passionate cry from the heart of a man who never stopped loving the Army, even when it stopped loving him back."

Jack & Marty Gainey

On September 10, 2006, Jack "Bud" Gainey died at age fifty-nine from complications of multiple sclerosis, diabetes, and PTSD. Just years before Bud's death, his gallant wife Marty died from an aneurysm. Cause of death to both Gaineys? Vietnam!

Afterglow

*I'd like the
memory of me
to be
a happy one,
I'd like to leave
an afterglow
of smiles
when life is done.
I'd like to leave
an echo whispering softly
down the ways, of happy times
and laughing times and bright
and sunny days.
I'd like the tears
of those who grieve,
to dry before the sun
Of happy memories that I leave
When life is done.*

Martha Gainey

Marty exhausted herself trying to take care of Bud after he was confined to a wheelchair. She worked endlessly trying to keep Bud motivated, not to mention over twenty years of frustration with Veterans Affairs trying to get adequate and deserved disability compensation for her dear Bud.

My first visit to The Wall in Washington was with Bud and Marty. That was a memorable weekend in many ways. I remember it well. We acted like kids that weekend, pushing Bud all over town in his wheelchair, racing around, up and down giant escalators, laughing and teasing.

Unfortunately, that weekend in Washington was one of the last highlights in the life of Bud and Marty Gainey. Although we continued to see each other as often as possible, Bud's health was not good, and it would get worse. So would Marty's.

Jack (Bud) Gainey; Massillon, Ohio
B Co. 3rd 22nd 25th Infantry Division
U.S. Army – Vietnam
October 14, 1947 – September 10, 2006 (59 years)

Bud and I met in June 1968 in Hoc Mon Province. Bravo Co. had just survived a major ambush by an unknown Viet Cong force, and Bud was one of the replacements for our losses—which were many.

Although we were in different squads, we had ample opportunities to fight side by side together for the next several months. Bud and I enjoyed bragging about Ohio high school football, especially his own Massillon Washington High School.

Bud and Ski on Nui Bau Den – October 1968

Although we made a vow to remain in touch after we came home from Nam, I didn't see Bud again until 1987 when I visited his home. It was there that I discovered he was in a wheelchair as a result of multiple sclerosis. He also had diabetes, which would be classified later by the VA as an Agent Orange-caused disease. But his MS was not classified—even though it is now accepted that MS and diabetes are very closely related.

Bud and Marty and my wife, Ginny, and I saw each other many times while they were both still living. We visited The Wall together (our first visit) in 1988 with three other Vietnam veteran brothers and their wives. One of them was Robert "Smokey" Ryan, who fought with us in Vietnam. Smokey suffered multiple wounds in Vietnam and was also pretty messed up psychologically from his experiences over there.

We lived the battles with Bud and Marty as they suffered in trying to get Bud his just due for disability compensation. Marty worked long hours trying to provide for and take care of Bud while Bud tried his best to remain positive. He tried working from home in his wheelchair for a few years.

Marty never quit working hard for Bud and herself. Plus, they had two loving children to be cared for, Jennifer and Mike Gainey.

I don't know if Bud Gainey ever received the full disability compensation that he should have received, and for which he and his lovely wife fought so tirelessly. I think not.

Charlie Daniels, Bud, and Smokey, Cleveland, Ohio – 1988

Unfortunately, the long, tiring workload and the stressful battles with the VA took its toll on the Gaineys. Bud's health was going bad when a major disaster hit them like a human wave attack ... Marty Gainey died suddenly from an aneurysm on April 25, 2002. I visited Bud as much as possible, but he was no longer comfortable with public appearances. We enjoyed the Ohio State victory over the Miami Hurricanes in January 2003 together as we were both BIG Buckeye fans. Shortly after that game, Bud was sent to a nursing home in his hometown of Massillon. I visited with him two more times before I received the news ... Bud had passed away on September 10, 2006.

I was impressed by the fact that he fought on for four and a half years after his lovely wife had departed. They were so dedicated to each other and their children. In my mind, Vietnam caused both Marty's and Bud's deaths. Bud and I talked about it—he would have shared my beliefs.

Researchers Determine that MS And Diabetes Are Closely Linked Diseases

Science Daily (March 22, 2001) – *Toronto, March 20, 2001 – A team of researchers led by Hospital for Sick Children (HSC) senior scientist Michael Dosch has determined that multiple sclerosis and type I (juvenile) diabetes mellitus are far more closely linked than previously thought, including the role cow milk protein plays as a risk factor in the development of both diseases for people who are genetically susceptible. This research is published in recent issues of The Journal of Immunology (April 1 and February 15, 2001).*

Multiple sclerosis (MS) and type I diabetes mellitus are autoimmune disorders, where the body's immune system attacks its own tissue. The diseases are entirely different clinically, but have nearly identical ethnic and geographic distribution, genetic similarities, and as is now known, shared environmental risk factors.

In collaboration between The Hospital For Sick Children, St. Michael's Hospital and the Pittsburgh Children's Hospital, Dr. Dosch's laboratory discovered a high degree of similarity in the autoimmunity of MS and diabetes patients and that a widely used mouse model for diabetes could also develop an MS-like disease.

"Much to our surprise, we found that immunologically, type I diabetes and multiple sclerosis are almost the same – in a test tube you can barely tell the two diseases apart," said Dr. Dosch ,the study's principal investigator, a senior scientist in the HSC Research Institute, and a professor of Paediatrics and Immunology at the University of Toronto (U of T). "We found that the autoimmunity was not specific to the organ system affected by the disease. Previously it was thought that in MS autoimmunity would develop in the central nervous system, and in diabetes it would only be found in the pancreas. We found that both tissues are targeted in the disease."

Johnny Viktoryn, Jr., Cleveland Ohio

101st Airborne Division
U.S. Army
April 27, 1947 – May 8, 1968 (21 years)

Johnny and I hooked up in October of 1967 as trainees at Fort Knox basic training camp. It was like we had always known each other. We both loved sports. We were both pretty good at basketball (as far as white boys went back then), and we both grew up in racially mixed neighborhoods for most of our lives. So we were both pretty tough too, and we really liked most of the brothers—most of them.

Johnny was a star basketball player at Cleveland's Cathedral Latin High School. In fact, I still remember him talking about their BIG-time upset of a highly rated Cleveland East Tech team. He and his good buddy Kevin McNearny were only 6'1" and 6'3" tall, but they outplayed a much taller and much more talented squad because of their teamwork.

At Fort Knox we had a lot of time on our hands in the evenings and on weekends. We bowled a lot and played a lot of basketball. Johnny and I were almost unbeatable in the Fort Knox two-man tournament … again because of teamwork. John at 6'1" and I at 5'10" went against two brothers from Saginaw, Michigan, who were 6'6" and 6'4" … Man, did we get our clocks cleaned.

We were both strong prospects for officers candidate school (OCS), but we decided not to go that route. Hindsight says we probably should have.

We breezed through basic training together. I believe we both made perfect test scores on everything. So the Army wanted to hold us over for security clearances for something special, we guessed. Anyway, we were sent out without the clearances and got our advanced combat infantry training under way so that we could become better prepared for KILLING!

The Vietnam War was heating up. We were taking unexpected casualties, and there was pressure to get "fresh meat" over there with combat MOSs. So we were sent home for a thirty-day leave with our new orders in hand … ADVANCED INFANTRY TRAINING at Fort Polk, Louisiana—also called "Little Vietnam."

Johnny and I kept in touch during our leave back home and hoped that we would be together again at Fort Polk. Sure enough, our wish was granted! When I arrived at the barracks in North Fort Polk, also called "Tiger Land," there was Johnny, facedown on the ground doing push-ups and yelling at the top of his voice, "THANK YOU, SERGEANT, MAY I PLEASE DO TWENTY MORE?!"

There was no time for basketball at Tiger Land. We were always too tired, and the mindset there was much more serious than it was in basic training at Knox. In basic training, many of us just went through the motions like we were playing Army. Tiger Land was no playground. This was seriously tense stuff. They even used live ammo most of the time, and once in a while someone got seriously hurt.

Johnny and I did manage to get out of Tiger Land on a couple of weekends. We went over to Lake Charles and Baton Rouge too. We were free spirits. We never looked for trouble, but what do you expect a couple of cocky white boys to find in southern Louisiana? We found it.

Advanced infantry training at Tiger Land went way too fast. As expected, our next stop would be Vietnam. Johnny decided to take things to another level, going gung-ho to airborne school. I thought about it, and that maybe the war would be over by the time we finished airborne school. Not a chance, as the Tet Offensive was in full bloom at the time. I decided to get it on ASAP. Johnny and I flew home together and again we stayed in touch, mostly on the phone. We said our good-byes as I was heading for Fort Lewis and he was off to Fort Benning.

I was already a hardened combat veteran of nearly two months when the news reached me from my high school sweetheart, Madge. She told me Johnny was killed in ground combat in Binh Thuan Province just a few days after he had graduated from airborne school.

Every time I listen to a song that was the favorite of John's, "Baby I'm Yours" by Barbara Lewis, I break down and cry my eyes out, thinking about the good times Johnny and I had. It is so ironic that well after I married my lovely Ginny, I found out how she had a crush on this guy named Johnny when she was only thirteen years old. It was the same … Johnny Viktoryn.

Eldon D. "Babyson" Coldren; Rockford, Illinois
1st Platoon 3rd 22nd Infantry
25th Infantry Division
U.S. Army – Vietnam
September 11, 1968 (20 years)

Dean (Babyson) and I were introduced to each other sometime in mid-April 1968. He was just nineteen then, and I was an old man at that time—already at twenty-three.

Babyson kept us smiling when all we wanted to do was moan and complain. Whether we were filling sandbags, fighting off a red ant attack, or licking our wounds after a firefight, he always seemed to carry that devilish smile which made us chuckle.

Our relationship was short-lived as he was shot and killed by a wounded NVA after an all-night battle in northern war Zone C … on the morning of his 20th birthday. Actually, the commie who killed him was yelling "Chieu Hoi" (I give up) and holding his AK-47 over his head—the ultimate sign of giving up. Babyson never had a chance. As I went out to accept the NVA's surrender, the low-life gook lowered his AK-47 and emptied most of his magazine into our guy—on his birthday morning.

The 1st Platoon took their vengeance out on that enemy soldier that morning, as there weren't enough body parts left to bury. We greeted several would-be prisoners the same way for a while. I don't think anyone has any regrets about doing that to this day. After Nam, several of us talked to and visited with the Coldren family in Rockford, Illinois, for many years. They were very emotional get-togethers.

ROCKFORD MORNING STAR
Wed., Jan. 8, 1969

Thanks Sent by Buddies of Slain GI

Vietnam Mail Call, published in the Rockford Morning Star and Register-Republic, brought an "unreal" Christmas "a lost closer" to reality for 11 buddies of Eldon Dean Coldren Jr., who died Sept. 11 in Vietnam.

Persons in the Rockford area sent letters, packages and cards to these friends of Dean's, many of whom lived far from Illinois. Their names were submitted to Mail Call by Coldren's grandmother, Mrs. Richard Coldren.

"From the deepest reaches of our hearts, we thank all of you," wrote the men Dean knew as Bud, Shorty, Ski, Smokey, Farmer, Boo, Boone, Dusty, Slick, Dad and Curtis.

All are in the 1st platoon of B company in the Army's 3-22 Infantry.

During their time together Dean had written home about the men. The family "thought they knew them," his grandmother, Mrs. Coldren said.

So she and his family at 4806 Wisteria Court, continued to write the men.

To Dean's family the men of the 1st platoon sent a "special thanks."

Gary L. (Tets) Tetting; Shawano, Wisconsin
Bravo Co. 3rd 22nd 25th Infantry Division
U.S. Army – Vietnam 1968 – 1969
August 28, 1948 – November 22, 2009 (61 years)

Tets and I served together out of Dau Tieng with the 2nd 12th 25th ID, formerly of the 4th Infantry Division. I believe we joined up with the 3rd 22nd together right after the Battle of Good Friday. Gary was a multiple Bronze Star recipient for Valor as one of our M-60 machine gunners. He served his country far beyond what was expected of him.

I've seen Gary three times since we served together, once in his hometown of Shawano, once in Ohio, and once in Boston, Massachusetts, where the 1st Platoon staged its first ever reunion in 1988. Gary Tetting died from a cancer caused by Agent Orange at the age of sixty-one.

The helmet
Gary Tetting, my wife, Ginny, and me – 1988

Marvin Rex Young
Staff Sergeant
5th Infantry Regiment, 25th Infantry Division
U.S. Army – Vietnam 1968
Medal of Honor, Purple Heart
May 11, 1947 – August 21, 1968 (21 years)

I have mentioned Marvin elsewhere in this book. Although I did not know Marvin personally, we all heard of his heroic actions at one of the Battles of Dau Tieng (there were three or four). Some of our 3rd 22nd Regulars were at the July 4th Battle of Dau Tieng, so we took a very personal interest in our old base camp. His official Medal of Honor citation reads:

The President of the United States
in the name of the Congress of the United States
takes pride in presenting the
MEDAL OF HONOR
posthumously to
MARVIN REX YOUNG

Staff Sergeant
United States Army
for service as set forth in the following

CITATION:

For conspicuous gallantry and intrepidity in action at the risk of his life above and beyond the call of duty. S/Sgt Young distinguished himself at the cost of his life while serving as a squad leader with Company C. While conducting a reconnaissance mission in the vicinity of Ben Cui, Company C was suddenly engaged by an estimated regimental-size force of the North Vietnamese Army. During the initial volley of fire the point element of the 1st Platoon was pinned down, sustaining several casualties, and the acting platoon leader was killed. S/Sgt Young unhesitatingly assumed command of the platoon and immediately began to organize and deploy his men into a defensive position in order to repel the attacking force. As a human wave attack advanced on S/Sgt Young's platoon, he moved from position to position, encouraging and directing fire on the hostile insurgents while exposing himself to the hail of enemy bullets. After receiving orders to withdraw to a better defensive position, he remained behind to provide covering fire for the withdrawal. Observing that a small element of the point squad was unable to extract itself from its position, and completely disregarding his personal safety, S/Sgt Young began moving toward their position, firing as he maneuvered. When halfway to their position he sustained a critical head injury, yet he continued his mission and ordered the element to withdraw. Remaining with the squad as it fought its way to the rear, he was twice seriously wounded in the arm and leg. Although his leg was badly shattered, S/Sgt Young refused assistance that would have slowed the retreat of his comrades, and he ordered them to continue their withdrawal while he provided protective covering fire. With indomitable courage and heroic self-sacrifice, he continued his self-assigned mission until the enemy force engulfed his position. By his gallantry at the cost of his life and in the highest traditions of the military service, S/Sgt Young has reflected great credit upon himself, his unit and the U.S. Army.

(Source: www.virtualwall.org/dy/YoungMR02a.htm)

George S. Patton IV

Major General
11th Armored Cavalry Regiment
U.S. Army – Vietnam, April 1962 – April 1969

Another famous Vietnam veteran, the son of the General George S. Patton of World War II fame, Patton IV served three tours in Vietnam after serving in the Korean War. He claimed that his most intense tour was during 1968–1969 in Vietnam, where he was shot down three times while using helicopters as his mobile command station.

In the years after his retirement, Patton IV turned an estate owned by his father located near Boston into the 250-acre Green Meadows Farm, where he named the fields after Vietnam soldiers who died under his command. In 1997, Patton worked alongside author Brian Sobel and wrote *The Fighting Pattons*, a book which served as an official family biography of his father as well as a comparison between the military of his father's generation and that of his son, a time which covered five conflicts and almost seventy years of combined service. He died from a form of Parkinson's disease at the age of eighty in 2004.

N E W S F L A S H (October 13, 2009): VA extended Agent Orange benefits to more Vietnam veterans for three additional illnesses based on the latest evidence of an association with the herbicides referred to Agent Orange. These illnesses are:

- B cell leukemia
- Ischemic heart disease
- Parkinson's disease

Therefore, Major General George S. Patton IV died from a Vietnam War-related illness thirty-five years after he left Vietnam ... five years before Parkinson's disease was added to the Agent Orange list!

Billy Walkabout, Oklahoma
101st Airborne Division
U.S. Army Rangers – Vietnam
March 31, 1949 – March 7, 2007 (57 years)

I had the opportunity to march with this Native American hero of the Vietnam War at Cleveland, Ohio's Welcome Home Parade, which was put on mostly by Nam vets. Billy Walkabout is believed to be the most decorated Native American soldier of the Vietnam War. Some of the awards he earned are as follows:

- 1 Distinguished Service Cross
- 4 Silver Stars
- 10 Bronze Stars
- 6 Purple Hearts
- 1 Army Commendation Model (1 Valor and 2 Oak leaf clusters)

Billy was married in 2000 to Juanita Medbury-Walkabout, a Mohegan Indian. Billy, himself, was a full-blood Cherokee of the Blue Holly Clan, Anisahoni.

He suffered from complications arising from exposure to Agent Orange used in Vietnam. He was waiting for a kidney transplant and took dialysis three times a week before dying from pneumonia and renal failure. His heroic actions were extraordinary. He was known for these quotes:

War is not hell … it's worse.

I'm at peace with myself. I've got my dignity and I've got my pride … I never lost in Vietnam, I never lost a day of it. Even when I was wounded, I didn't lose. When I fought, I won … I won my wars—
                                        - Billy Walkabout
                                        3/31/49 – 3/07/07

David H. (Hack) Hackworth
Colonel
U.S. Army – Vietnam
1930 – 2005 (74 years)

Colonel Hackworth survived over fifty years on battlefields where the action was hot and heavy. "Hack," as he was called by those close to him, was the **champion of us grunts!** Even General Hal Moore, co-author of *We Were Soldiers Once and Young*, referred to Hack as "The Patton of Vietnam." If I had served under him, I know that I would have re-upped and re-upped again and again.

Colonel Hackworth was the real deal, which is why he was never promoted to general. He just rubbed the Army bureaucrats the wrong way. **And he did it often.** Hack was just fourteen years old when he lied about his age to join the Merchant Marines … fourteen years old, can you believe it? I was still playing PONY League baseball against Bob Feller's sons at the age of fourteen. Sergeants Audie Murphy and Alvin York had nothing on Hack when it came to the long list of battlefield exploits. His superiors found it impossible to eliminate him. However, he was denied the Medal of Honor three times—possibly because of his critique of the military's higher command. And he was quite candid with his opinions about the Vietnam War … "It can't be won," he said on ABC's *Issues and Answers*.

Hack learned early how to perform in battle. He once said, "The worst thing in battle is paralysis." In Vietnam, Hack took on an infantry battalion that was called worthless and hopeless. At first, the troops resented him, calling him a crazy "lifer," and they even put a price on him for anyone willing to frag him. It wasn't long before Hack had managed to turn this sad unit into a crack fighting force. His men grew to admire and respect him.

Hack died of bladder cancer because of his exposure to Agent Blue. To my knowledge, the U.S. Army did not approve any of the three Medal of Honor recommendations despite the urgings of every officer who ever served under Hack. He was buried in Arlington National Cemetery with full military honors.

Gary D. Gullickson; Minnesota
HMM 364 Purple Fox
U.S. Marine Corps – Vietnam
August 5, 1944 – January 2005 (60 years)
This is a brief excerpt of a story Gary shared with me back in 1992:

Looking back, I was just what the military was looking for. A little rough around the edges, but with a little training I would do whatever they asked, go anywhere they wanted and not ask many questions. A mistake I will never let happen again. Always question! I was the guy that would try anything once, twice if I liked it.

I suppose it natural I ended up in the military. My father served, as did his brothers. In 1966, I watched my brother, Larry go into the Army. I saw how proud he was and how proud people were at that time of all the guys going in. The attitude and outlook of rural America was quite different than folks from the big city. Pride was everywhere and in everything we did. A handshake was still the best promise a man could make. Back when "American made" meant something.

In December of 1968, I lost a good friend in Vietnam. I put this on his grave in Pine Island, Minnesota. It took many years for me just to visit his grave.

Buck,
Much too soon, much too young you left us. Just one more talk on main street, one more party together. You are always with me, Buck. I can see us riding cycle on the highway. Me on my Jawa, you on your Honda dream. The wind in your hair, the free look on your face. I miss you. DAMN THAT WAR! May you rest in peace my friend.

March 1970. Da Nang, South Vietnam.
I can remember when the door opened. The heat, the smell, those faces waiting to leave. To this day I can see those faces. I saw every emotion conceivable getting off that plane. As I got off, I heard remarks like, "You'll be sorry, Boot", "You're in deep shit", "This place sucks", "We're on our way back to the world", "Good luck."

Well, the stage was set. I was put on a truck with some others. It was really different from what I thought. It was pretty in a way, but the smell was terrible. A short ride and there I was, 1st Marine Air Wing, Mag 16, Marble Mountain, South Vietnam.

My first medevac was a high fever. Very scary going down onto the trail to get people. Charlie knew the 50-cal. went back and forth, but not up and down far enough. You had to lay out the window and watch up the hill for him. I hated that feeling. Some minor wounds and high fever medevacs and the day was over.

On the way back to the base we got a call for a "permanent" medevac. The pilot said he would be glad to help out. We changed direction. When we got to the area, it was tall grass with jungle terrain around it. As I looked down, I saw two Marines standing there. One had his t-shirt torn and put around his head; the other was standing with his M-16 at the ready position. I was on the chopper going in to get the body. As we landed, I was watching the area, but from the corner of my eye, I saw one Marine reach into the grass, pick up this body, walk into the chopper and throw the body forward. It rolled up next to me. As we lifted off and were clear, I looked down. I could see right into the back of this lifeless person. The Doc on board came over and turned the body over. He said, "Been dead awhile, rigor mortis has really set in." I looked into the face of the dead person. My first look at death on any level. My thought was, "How can we do this to these people?" He was the enemy, but so young. I went numb inside.

The unit I flew with was HMM 364, The Purple Fox. I think it was one of the best chopper units in Vietnam. We even gave out business cards.

I remember one mission specifically. We had to take a unit of Marines into Arizona Territory, a bad place to go. The morning we were getting ready to go was great. The sun was coming up; all these Marines were waiting by the flight line. They were getting their gear ready, loading ammo, shaking hands … hugging each other. As I got my gun ready and several Big Shells, I watched them. The flight line was full of choppers, CH 46's, Huey Gunships and Cobras. It was some sight and your feelings were intense. As I look back at it, I can hear the song, "Sky Pilot." The Chaplain came out and said a prayer before we lifted off. The sound of all those choppers starting up at one time was remarkable. I find myself at times missing it. Off we went.

When the word came we were going in, in five minutes, I gave the sign to the men. What I saw next will be with me forever. These guys were sitting across from each other with their rifles across their legs, just staring at each other. When they got the sign, they started pounding their feet on the floor. It was their way of pumping each other up for what they were about to do. It was like they were off to the big football game for the championship. I got so excited watching them, I could not wait to cover them while they got out of the chopper.

One of the last missions I had haunts me to this day. We had to take a load of wounded from the hospital to the ship. We put the seats up on the side of the chopper to make room for the stretchers. We got them on board and lifted off. On the way out, one of the guys pulled at my flight suit and pointed towards the back of the chopper. One of the seats had come loose and fallen down over the guy in the rear. I headed back, stepping over the wounded on the way. That was some task. I hated that feeling, having to walk over wounded. When I got there, I reached down and lifted the seat. I looked right into the face of one of the most horrific head wounds I had ever seen. As I stood there and looked at him, he just smiled at me. I thought, "You poor soul, you are hurt so bad and you can still smile at me." I felt so bad for him. I hope he is okay now. It is sights like these that wake me to this day. **His face never goes away.**

As the end of my tour got closer, I started to think about leaving the friends I had made and West behind. A hard thing to do. The day I got on the Freedom Bird was great, but so scary. You thought maybe Charlie was saving one more shot to pick you off as you left.

It seems like yesterday. I have many views about Vietnam then and now.

Not all can be said, but saying what I have feels good. I came home emotionally dead and filled with anger. A state that is still a large part of me and the anger can surface very quickly. They turned it on but never turned it off.

I got out of the Marines in December 1970, divorced in April 1971. It was like I wanted nothing to do with my past or anyone in it. Even now, I let people get as close to me as I feel they should. In so many ways, I miss being able to get close to family and friends.

I feel as if I'm walking a fine line each day. I feel the line is between here and nowhere. I think what keeps me here is not knowing what is on the other side, and how to get back, if I cross. I think we all have this in our own way. There are more than physical wounds from war.

When I think of Vietnam, I feel used. It is like I was not supposed to come home from that place. No one has really been able to truly tell me why we were there.

I care for other Vietnam Veterans because I know the price they had to pay. It bothers me when I think of Homeless Veterans, Disabled Veterans, Vets that have taken their own lives after Vietnam, our POW-MIA's, and any Vet that suffers from war. It seems as if it did not happen to you or close to us, it just does not matter. How wrong you are. Each day you should thank Veterans for the freedom you have. Your basic rights had a very high price and it was paid for by the Veteran. ALL VETERANS!!

I do not trust our government. They are so far out of touch with us; their reality is something else. Soon, very soon, there will be no middle class. Rich and poor, that will be the order. The middle class will be taxed right out of the picture.

Our next battlegrounds are prepared and the lines drawn. Your own street is the place. Watch your nightly news and you will see.

Each Memorial Day, don't just think of a day off, think of the Veteran. Visit the grave of a true American hero.

FREEDOM, do you know what it means? Do you care?

Robert (Smokey) Ryan; South Amboy, New Jersey
1st Platoon 3rd 22nd Infantry
25th Infantry Division
U.S. Army – Vietnam
April 24, 1947 – June 13, 2012 (65 years)

Smokey Ryan and I saw our first combat together with the 2nd 12th 4th Infantry, but it may have transferred over to the 25th around that time. Anyway, we were both reassigned to the Bravo Company, 3rd 22nd 25th Infantry in early April.

Smokey died prematurely, caused by PTSD and Vietnam's horrors. I will touch on Smokey more in this book—I had hoped to talk with Smokey and secure a story from him for this book, but his unexpected death came first.

Smokey Ryan was the ultimate combat warrior of the Vietnam War during its bloodiest era. Wounded three times, he would not allow himself to be removed from the field and returned to do battle with the 1st Platoon after each hospital stay.

I had the pleasure of fighting next to Smokey in battle, and we fought side by side with others who were less than respectful to combat grunts when we came from the bush entering a secure base camp. I guess they thought we were related to Sasquatch or something. We sure looked like it.

Smokey was one of the true icons of the 1st Platoon and the 3rd 22nd Infantry. One of his Bronze Stars for Valor could/should have easily been a much higher award.

It was an honor to know Smokey. And it was one of my greatest moments when I was there and able to help get him out safely when he was wounded the first time during a Viet Cong ambush on June 15, 1968.

Smokey, like many of us who fought over there, remained a loyal soldier to his last day. Ironically, he passed away in the same month he was wounded for the first time in Vietnam … almost on the same date.

Smokey, his wife Betty, John "Babyson" Martino, and his wife worked miracles coordinating a twenty-year reunion, locating and rounding up over a dozen survivors of the 1st and 2nd Platoons. Also attending that 1988 reunion was Major General Flynt, who was Colonel Flynt, our brigade commander, when we fought together in 1968–1969.

Smokey traveled around the country for different Coming Home Parades or to where the Traveling Wall was. He attended our coming home parade in Cleveland, Ohio, marching side by side with me.

Smokey was a true American patriot who went to a war few others were willing to participate in. If given the opportunity to serve his country again, he would have been at the front of the line—volunteering for combat duty all the way. Eventually, our country took care of Smokey by granting him 100 percent disability. However, his battles to win that status went on for many years and it exhausted him.

Smokey Ryan's name will not appear on The Wall. However, his death was caused by the Vietnam War in which he so proudly fought. Smokey Ryan was a great American, and America will miss him. Smokey was also **CON-DEMNED PROPERTY ... A Soldier of the Vietnam War!**

Robert "Smokey" Ryan – New Jersey
United States Army - Vietnam
Vietnam Service Dates: 03/1968 – 04/1969
100% disabled (PTSD), retired from USPS in 2004, past Commander of American Legion (3x), life member of DAV.

Married to Elizabeth Ryan, have two daughters: (Krista and Lisa) and four grandkids: Kelli, Arianna, Connor and Courtney.

Spent 13 months in Vietnam in infantry (25th Div.) All in the field. Have 13 Medals (including three Purple Hearts, two Bronze Stars, two Army Commendations Medals, Air Medal, V.N. Cross of Gallantry & 2 Unit citations. Came home as Sgt. (E-5) (also was POW MIA Chairman State of NJ) & Life Member of VVA-Kokomo-Ind.

This Time Custer Won!

George Armstrong Custer III
2nd 27th 25th Infantry Division
U.S. Army – WWII, Korea, Vietnam
Colonel
1923–1991 (67 years)

Colonel George Armstrong Custer III died at the age of sixty-seven in Toledo, Ohio, from a heart attack ... possibly caused by PTSD.

I remember the Wolfhounds of the 25th Infantry as they received as much press in *The Tropic Lightning News* as our 3rd 22nd Regulars did during the Tet Offensives of 1968. Lieutenant Colonel George Armstrong Custer III tromped in many of the same jungles, swamps, and rice paddies as we did. Two years later in 1970, he led the 2nd Battalion, 27th Infantry Wolfhounds of the 25th Infantry Division. They were also supported by our own Regulars of the mechanized 2nd Battalion, 22nd Infantry—a sister unit of my own 3rd Battalion, 22nd Infantry Regulars.

This ferocious battle as described in *The Tropic Lightning News* and *Vietnam* magazine was fought in the Tay Ninh Province, which was a densely wooded, double-canopy jungle close to the Cambodian border where tens of thousands of North Vietnamese were assembling for a major attack. This time Custer would not be surrounded and slaughtered to the last man. This time Custer would again be outnumbered, but his firepower would offset the numbers of the NVA/VC. The Renegade Woods of Tay Ninh battle in April 1970 included two battalions of the 271st Regiment NVA and 9th VC/NVA forces.

An article in the June 2012 issue of *Vietnam* magazine said:

Colonel Custer had some of the same propensity for taking risks as his namesake, but his luck and timing were better. What he did for his men on the ground was to put the lethality of air power where they needed it, when they needed it. He let them fight the battle on the ground, which is every combat infantryman's dream.

The Renegade Woods battle in early April 1970 was the largest and most important engagement of that year for the entire 25th Infantry Division. Lt. Colonel Custer never expected to be promoted to a general, so he never played the games that other officers did—he always told the truth and he was a fearless soldier. Custer was also a realist. Similar to Colonel Hackworth, Custer always believed that America would pull out of Vietnam, and North Vietnam would move in and take over South Vietnam.

Custer was reported to have put his life in harm's way often for his men. He also believed that every American life lost in Vietnam was a waste!

Custer's forces lost twelve—killed in the Renegade Woods Battle. The combined NVA/VC forces left over one hundred dead on the battlefield, but the multiple blood trails indicated a much greater body count was inflicted onto the enemy. **In this battle Custer was the winner. In the end, he lost the bigger battle in life, and Vietnam ended his life quite prematurely.**

Richard "Rambo" Loska
4th Infantry Division
U.S. Army, Vietnam
November 1, 1946 – January 31, 2007 (61 years)

Rambo and I befriended each other after we had both served our time in Vietnam. We were both working at a factory in Solon, Ohio, in the early 1970s called Jerpback-Bayless Company. While I moved on after series of major auto accidents, Rambo finished his career at JB Co. and we remained friends until his unfortunate death in 2007. I believe Rambo's Nam experience included the famous battle of Dak To in 1967, where American casualties were nearly 350. I believe he earned a Bronze Star for Valor at Dak To.

Rambo's family took me into their home for a full summer when I was really down and out and confused after returning from Vietnam. We went to our last Cleveland Browns game together against the Oakland Raiders when Brian Sipe threw the heart-breaking interception, ending an almost certain trip to the Super Bowl. Neither of us had seen a Browns game in person since, although I might take the plunge someday.

We golfed together, bowled together, drank together, and cried together about Vietnam and life's strange events in general. His civic work around the Chagrin Falls, Ohio, area is legendary, as he donated his time generously and tirelessly. He founded the Chagrin Falls American Legion Post, which exists today mainly because of Rambo's memory and the continued dedication of other veterans who knew and loved him.

Rambo also served his country after Vietnam as a member of Ohio's National Guard. I will remember him as a patriotic soldier for the country he loved until his final days with us in 2007.

Ed W. "Too Tall" Freeman
U.S. Navy, U.S. Army
November 20, 1927 – August 20, 2008

"Too Tall" was extremely unique. One war wasn't enough for him. After two years in the Navy in WWII, his next stop was with the Army in the Korean War, where he earned the rank of a "Top" or First Sergeant. He was a participant at the well-known Battle of Pork Chop Hill. He was one of fourteen survivors out of 257 men who made it through the earliest moments of this battle and earned a battlefield commission.

When Too Tall, who was 6'4", went to Vietnam, he was a captain in charge of a 1st Cavalry Division Assault Helicopter Company. At one of the Ia Drang Valley battles (probably the first), he earned the Medal of Honor for making at least a dozen trips in his UH-1 Huey in support of the surrounded Americans. Obviously, Too Tall was one of the exceptions as far as field officers were concerned. His character was portrayed in the 2002 movie (geez, over ten years already?) *We Were Soldiers*, which depicted Colonel Hal Moore (Mel Gibson) and the Battle of Ia Drang. Major Too Tall's long list of medals would fill this page.

Col. Robert L. Howard
Special Forces – Five Tours
U.S. Army, Vietnam
Deceased December 23, 2009 (70 years)

Colonel Howard was one of the Vietnam War's most decorated veterans at the time of his death. He spent fifty-four months in Vietnam. He was wounded fourteen times and received a Medal of Honor.

Capt. Joe Hooper
101st Airborne
U.S. Army, Vietnam
Deceased May 1979 (40 years)

Captain Hooper received thirty-five medals during his seventeen years of service, including a Medal of Honor and eight Purple Hearts—also one our war's most decorated heroes. He was credited with 115 confirmed enemy kills. He found his specialty in the Army … killing enemy soldiers. One of the more famous accounts of Hooper's amazing career happened during the 1968 Tet Offensive, when his small recon squad was ambushed by a company of North Vietnamese outside the city of Hue. There were six Americans under attack for six and a half hours. When reinforcements arrived, they found eighty-five dead NVA … All six Americans were wounded multiple times, but survived.

There are more stories about Hooper, just not as impressive. Life after Vietnam was not as exciting for Hooper. Going from guerrilla fighting to civilian life was a problem. As he said before he died, "In Vietnam you lived on, almost thrived on fear. Now, I'm a little flat." His boredom and memories led to trouble, and his drinking became excessive. Hooper died one night when a blood vessel burst in his head. The media mentioned his death briefly … **ONE FULL YEAR LATER!**

Special Salute – Bull Hemphill

He was just leaving by the time I arrived in Nam, but his reputation remained with Bravo Company 3rd 22nd of the 25th Infantry Division.

Captain Robert (Bull) Hemphill, mentioned earlier in this book, deserves a special salute for his exceptional leadership of Bravo Company 3rd 22nd Regulars from October 1967 – February 1968 in South Vietnam. He retired as a lieutenant colonel and was awarded a Purple Heart, a Silver Star for Gallantry, four Bronze Stars for Valor, of course, the highly prestigious Combat Infantryman Badge (CIB) and numerous other decorations. He authored one of the books entitled *Platoon*. Oliver Stone, who served with him, wrote the other one, including the movie.

As one chapter after another on Vietnam comes to close, the ongoing saga just won't seem to let up on us … but we who remain continue to fight on. I do regret not being able to dedicate more coverage in this book to the dozens of other Nam vets I knew personally who have died prematurely since coming home from that war.

Vietnam and Small Town USA … Twinsburg, Ohio!

Twinsburg is definitely a small town that is "on the map," so to speak. This August 2-4, 2013, the world's largest gathering of people, twins, and other multiples will congregate in Twinsburg, Ohio, for the 35th Annual Twins Day Festival.

I am the proud brother of a pair of twins who were born in Twinsburg, Ohio … Janie and Jimmy. Twins Days has been covered on most major media outlets, from the Discovery Chanel to the *National Geographic* magazine.

As I have already mentioned in this book, growing up in and being from Twinsburg has been a lot of fun. Most of the "Twinsburg family" remains in touch with each other, including golf outings, sports, class reunions, or just a lunch here or there. Twinsburg has been an integrated town for almost a century.

Small towns USA are everywhere from Kansas, Oregon, Alabama, South Carolina, and Maine to Ohio. They seem to be disappearing—becoming memories of rural America's nostalgic past. Twinsburg in the 1950s and 1960s was a small-town soap opera in live action with racial integration and brotherly love sandwiched in between all-white, upscale, neighboring towns like Hudson, Aurora, and Solon. Twinsburg was anything but upscale back then. Today it is often mentioned as one of America's best small cities to live in. In many ways, it was like "us against them" when we competed in sports against each other. Even today, although all of those towns (cities now) are also integrated, rivalries still exist because of the battles we had in the old days.

This environment in Twinsburg bonded us together, white and black, and solidified friendships that grew stronger over the decades to follow. It could be said that in Twinsburg, racially brotherly love was born here. **I will always call Twinsburg, Ohio, my home.** However, December 2012 was not kind to Vietnam veterans from Twinsburg, as we lost two of our Nam brothers who served over there. Billy Maxwell and Fred Brandon were the latest casualties of Vietnam's War from this little hometown of mine.

I believe statistics like these are typical of small towns around the United States back in the 1960s:

Vietnam War & Twinsburg, Ohio

1960 – 1969 Population:	2,200 – 6,098
2000 – 2012 Population:	17,000 – 20,000
Twinsburg residents sent to Vietnam 1962–1972:	110*
Twinsburg natives killed in Vietnam:	3
Twinsburg Nam vets who died after Vietnam:	13

*Estimated

Since exiting Uncle Sam's Army from Fort Hood, Texas, in 1970, I have watched way too many buddies die prematurely after coming home. My hometown has not been spared.

Twinsburg's participation in the Vietnam War was far from small townish. Here is the list of Twinsburg's warriors who fought for our great country in the Vietnam War and are no longer with us:

Alfred Brandon	Don Malicek
Fred Brandon	Ed Morgan
Darrell Burge	Pat Mortus
John Dunkins	Alvin Robertson
Jack Furka	Roger Short
Joseph Krapinski	Frank Slack
Bill Maxwell	Joe Stumpf
Danny McDonald	Walter Upshaw

I knew, played with, competed with, and laughed with nearly all of them, and I could probably write a short book about each one. Take Danny "Mac" McDonald, for instance. We also called him "Jock" because he was a successful jockey on thoroughbred horses … all 115 pounds of him.

Everyone who lived in Twinsburg in the 1950s on, knew, heard of, or remembers the McDonald farm on Liberty Road. Mr. and Mrs. McDonald had eleven kids. I knew them all and we all played on or worked on their other farms as well, which were in three counties. We used to drive tractors and trucks well before the legal driving age. This large Irish family offered safe places in their Aurora and Twinsburg homes for many kids who were experiencing problems in their own homes.

Long before I wrecked my first auto in 1972, I had the experience of being in (and surviving) two car wrecks with Danny Mac's older brother, Billy Mac McDonald. Both cars belonged to his dad. Sometimes, Billy drove his cars right off the road into a field just to see how far he could go.

Ed "Pork Chop" Morgan and Frank "Hurricane" Slack were Vietnam veterans from Twinsburg who also left us quite prematurely. Ed and Frank were good friends. I believe they even enlisted together—going in different directions after that. I grew up knowing both quite well. I attended both funerals.

Ed's family owned a food market in Twinsburg, where he and his siblings worked. Ed loved pork chops and usually brought one to school for his lunch … thus, his nickname. Ed and Frank had cute sisters, a couple of Homecoming queens I think. The one Morgan who stood out in many of our minds was Sheridan Morgan, Ed's dad. After the food market closed, Mr. Morgan had a series of businesses at which we all frequented or hung out. There was Morgan's Custard Stand, with a pool table and gigantic hamburgers that were at least a foot in diameter and an inch thick. Next, Sheridan owned a couple of "watering holes" or saloons, which also had pool tables, and we congregated there often. Ed and a couple of Morgan sisters worked there, too.

Sheridan was no one to mess with—really. Once a couple of very dumb would-be robbers attempted to hold up Sheridan at his Brass Horn Bar. The tale goes that Sheridan chased them both, tracking them down, and single-handedly apprehended them in Crown Hill Cemetery across the street from his Brass Horn.

Ed Morgan died from an auto accident as many Vietnam veterans have. Frank Slack died from a heart attack (age fifty-three?) and quite possibly, his demise was assisted by some PTSD, memories from his service overseas during the Vietnam War. Sheridan is still living and still pretty feisty. I saw him last at Ed's funeral.

The Twinsburg McDonald Farm (which is now a recreational park) was our favorite place to play. We hunted, explored, built things, caught snapping turtles, rode their horses, and had BB gun shooting contests with crows and chipmunks as our targets. We created lasting positive memories with the McDonalds—Margie, Eddy, Terry, Billy, Susie, Kathy, Danny, Marie, Mike, Mary Ann, and Johnny. I can remember something about each one of them. It seemed like they always had a smile on their faces, even though it was usually some mischievous thought they had on their minds that day.

The memories with the McDonalds are endless for many of us. An entire series of books could be written about them—from Mr. & Mrs. McDonald down to the youngest. Danny Mac, Bill Mac, and Susie Mac were closest to my age, so I knew them the best. Bill Mac is still a best friend to most of us who grew up with his family. Danny Mac and Bill Mac both went to Vietnam in the mid-1960s, spending most of their time in I Core, where the dangers were most severe at that time. Danny was Army; Billy was Navy Seabee. Susie had three sons who became Navy SEALs, and they were good ones, too. Danny and Billy were exposed to Agent Orange. Billy is fighting Agent Orange-caused illnesses to this day. We lost Danny to cancer on February 27, 2010. Agent Orange exposure was a probable contributor to his death at the young age of sixty-three.

Three of our Twinsburg heroes died over there. They were as follows:

Alvin W. Robertson; Twinsburg, Ohio
9th Infantry Division
U.S. Army – Vietnam
June 7, 1948 – December 28, 1968 (20 years)

At this time, Alvin was the second hometown brother from Twinsburg to die in Vietnam, serving his country.
The Robertson family of Twinsburg, Ohio—my real hometown—has produced a long chain of exceptional athletes who were really good people as well. Alvin was a younger brother of one of my best and longest running friends, Freddy Willis Robertson. Freddy and I became instant friends when

I moved to Twinsburg in the sixth grade from Cleveland, Ohio. We used to play dodge ball and basketball together in junior high. Freddy and I ran on Twinsburg's mile-relay team, and I also ran with Freddy's older brother, Walter, on the 880-relay team. All of our track and field teams were state powers back in the 1960s. Freddy, Walter, and their younger brother, Herman, and I remain good friends today. We golf and attend sports events together, including Ohio State football games and Twinsburg High School sports events.

Alvin Robertson died for his country three days after Christmas in 1968. I did not learn of his death until after I returned home in February 1969. He had been in country for only six weeks in Kien Hoa Province.

Patrick C. Mortus; Twinsburg, Ohio
B Co., 2nd BN, 1st Infantry Division
U.S. Army – Vietnam
August 11, 1947 – January 14, 1968 (20 years)

Pat Mortus was the first of three hometown brothers from Twinsburg to die in Vietnam. I didn't know Pat very well when we were at Twinsburg High (R.B. Chamberlin), but our town has a monument on the town square in his honor.

Donald J. Malicek; Twinsburg, Ohio
101st Airborne Division
U.S. Army – Vietnam
November 9, 1948 – May 18, 1969 (20 years)

Don and I did not know each other, but we could have very easily crossed paths during the latter part of 1968. Don died in action at the Battle for Hamburger Hill while I was finishing up my active duty at Fort Hood, Texas. Don was the third of three from our hometown to die serving his country in Vietnam.

No End to This Story?

As I mentioned earlier in the book, there is no foreseeable end to this story. When the last Vietnam veterans leave this planet, their offspring and all who were touched by the families and friends of Vietnam veterans will continue to keep the memories of our war living into future generations.

Before I could finish *Condemned Property?* two more of my home bro's from Twinsburg died prematurely. Both were Vietnam veterans and both suffered from Vietnam War-caused issues. I knew them both extremely well, and they were both great Americans. These two great guys will be terribly missed ... Fred "Bird" Brandon and Billy "Frog" Maxwell.

My friend Jim Ludwiczak, a U.S. Army Korean DMZ Conflict veteran, emphatically suggested that I try to get this book out ASAP because Vietnam War veterans were dying at such an alarming rate after the war ... he was right on.

Since I started *Condemned Property?*, two of my high school classmates—Vietnam veterans—have died! Therefore, I am sadly adding these two names to the book. Both passed away in December 2012.

Curtis "Tony" Daniels
B Company, 3rd 22nd Infantry
U.S. Army – Veteran
August 6, 1944 – April 8, 2013 (68 years)

"Tex" Daniels, mentioned earlier in this book, lost his battle with Vietnam-caused illnesses before I could finish this book. He was the third member of Bravo Company, 3rd 22nd Infantry to pass while I was writing *Condemned Property?* I made the trip to Dayton, Texas, to say my good-byes and be with his family. More comments later.

And the coffins came home to every city, town, and village ... but the media wouldn't allow Americans to separate this war from the innocent young warriors sent to fight it! It is okay to hate war, despise it if you must, but NOT THE WARRIOR!

Chapter 15

THE REAL SILENT KILLER ... PTSD!

After Vietnam, many combat veterans seemed to live ordinary lives with a bump in the road here and there. Yet there were also those who did not live ordinary lives, many have died prematurely, and now many of us have begun experiencing the traumatic memories of the experiences that we lived over forty years ago. How on earth does this happen after so many years?

Post-traumatic stress disorder (PTSD) is much more than a wound of our minds. It affects our inner soul, and **the cure could take up to the rest of a combat veteran's entire life** ... IF he/she lives that long.

I have been able to overcome every one of life's obstacles since the Vietnam War, but the Vietnam factor always appeared and reappeared. Over *there*, in the worst of battle conditions, I fought as well as any soldier did, better than most, and NO ONE can challenge me on that statement. But over *here*, I was beginning to doubt myself.

Over *there*, I fought to stay living and for others to stay living, for that glorious day of returning to "the world"—to our families and friends. Over *here*, I had been pushing the envelope with regularity, seemingly on a certain path of self-destruction (with suicidal thoughts never far away). Until I found one individual at Veterans Administration's Mental Health Department in 2007 or 2008, I wondered from day to day if I might take the plunge I had been dreaming about at night. And I mean literally "take the plunge." Just like the seventies, eighties, and nineties, during the 2000s the same nightmare kept visiting me. It had me driving off an old mountain road, crashing to the bottom. Over and over, I dreamed this for decades. WHY?!

What kind of illness erupts in a combat soldier's mind and soul thirty or forty years after the combat horrors took place? Is the combat horror itself causing the illness, or is it the trauma we faced after the war? Go figure!

Vets Under Siege
Vietnam generation fading as death rate rises for vets

Researchers found more deaths among Vietnam veterans were due to auto accidents, suicides, strokes, kidney and connective tissue cancer.

"Elevated risk of death due to motor vehicle accidents and suicide lends support to the hypothesis that Vietnam veterans have had a greater incidence of traumatic death since the end of the conflict than other non-veteran males," the study said.

This was the conclusion of a study done by the state's Department of Public Health and the Office of Veterans Services.

Before entering the U.S. Army, I had no political agenda. I always thought that if someone was truly patriotic and loved his or her country, it did not matter which political party he or she was aligned with. I did not consider myself a Democrat or a Republican in the 1960s. Since coming home from Vietnam, I have learned the difference between a liberal and a conservative. I have learned that the liberal "intellectuals" were not as much concerned with the truth about the Vietnam War as they were their personal agendas.

Ho Chi Minh used people like Hanoi Jane Fonda and Hanoi John Kerry and other liberals to convince people that it took more courage to protest the Vietnam War and desecrate the American flag than it did to fight a fierce enemy under nightmarish conditions in a foreign land. BULLS—-!

The majority of Vietnam veterans served America well. The majority of us live with more comfort in our decision then the draft dodgers and deserters. **I have yet to meet anyone who owns up to being a draft dodger— EVER!**

We Vietnam vets weren't pro-war. **We just put our country before ourselves.** When Ho Chi Minh himself made this infamous statement, most Americans paid little attention to his words, but they should have: *WE WILL DEFEAT THE AMERICANS FROM WITHIN, AND THEIR LIBERAL INTELLECTUALS WILL BE OUR TOOLS.*

My opinion is that one year of combat in Vietnam plus the forty-some years of alienation by our government and America in general is a joint effort in creating the Vietnam veterans' badly messed-up minds today. Whose responsibility was it to make sure the returning warriors from Vietnam received at least as good treatment as the draft dodgers and deserters received from America? Who should be accountable to make sure that the returning warriors of the Vietnam War were prepared to re-enter civilian life?

Since those violent years of protests, riots, LSD, and an unpopular war in Southeast Asia, most Americans no longer look at a Vietnam veteran with hate or shame. We weren't the alcoholic, crazed homeless misfits that the liberal media portrayed us to be. Most of us went on to successful careers, against stiff odds, not in our favor.

We Vietnam vets are fighting that war still. Many of us still living who care fight a daily war with diseases that one way or another were caused by our service in the Vietnam War ... either from in-country service or post-Nam problems at home.

It was just over three years ago, still over four decades after my in-country service in Nam, that I really bottomed out emotionally. I had gained a lot of weight, despite my usually rigorous exercise routine. I was not feeling well—on a daily basis. I was afraid to find out what my problems were.

Oh sure, I was well aware that I was a PTSD patient and I was seeking private counseling at my own expense—which I had done numerous times before. It never seemed to help. Then one day I almost lost it when I lashed out at an executive with the company I've been working for since 1980, although several different owners passed the baton since 1980. I mean, my blood pressure shot up, and I got dizzy—I was so crazed with anger at the company executive. He had belittled me for something in front of several others. I felt AMBUSHED! This occurred at a national sales meeting on the East Coast. Many others were present. Although others in that meeting consoled me by saying I was justified in getting angry that day, they had no idea just how angry I was and the severity of the thoughts I was entertaining.

It was just a couple months earlier when I challenged a carload of guys, waving my machete at them after they ran my car off the road. They pulled over to the side of the highway and so did I. When they saw me waving the machete and yelling at them, fortunately they retreated and drove off very quickly. Those two incidents, the sales meeting blow-up and the road rage confrontation, told me for sure that I was on a **MISSION OF SELF-DESTRUCTION!**

On the very next day after returning from the sales meeting, I checked myself into the Psychological ER Department at Cleveland, Ohio's Veterans Administration Hospital. That day at the VA-ER Department was a life-changing moment for me. Quite possibly a lifesaver. VA put me through an array of tests over the next several months. Not only did I begin with regular psychological therapy, **but this time it began to help me.**

Eventually, I agreed to begin taking medication (happy pills) to help curb my PTSD and very high blood pressure. After several experiments and different medications over a couple of years, things finally started to gel. To say that I slowly became "happier" and more at ease with life's challenges would be an understatement, to which my lovely wife would surely attest.

How do I know that my psychological therapy at VA has helped me? Here is a living example to answer that question. It is eerie in a way, but quite impressive, I think.

Lake Tahoe was hosting a fairly important trade show, so I decided to attend and have my wife accompany me. Neither of us had ever been to that part of the country. It was on our second day there that we took a sightseeing drive through the Sierra-Nevada Mountains when this really eerie feeling hit me like I had been on this mountain road before. It all looked too familiar to me, and I started to get cold chills and really clammy. This was the mountain road that I kept driving my car over the side of in so many previous night-mares. It was really was! It was all-too familiar It was like I knew what was around the next turn. Man, I slowed down in a hurry and looked for an area to pull over and get hold of myself. Ginny kept asking me if I was all right because my facial color wasn't normal. I reassured her that everything was okay, that I just felt dizzy from the thin air.

Geez, I was scared. Was I supposed to drive off this mountain road and take my lovely Ginny with me? I couldn't do it, I loved her too much. I thought this out quickly, remembering what Dr. Marcus kept telling me at my therapy sessions at the VA. "Mr. Trimmer, you Vietnam veterans are pretty darn good people. You are a very good person as well."

Oh, Dr. Marcus has told me a lot more than that and in more detail, of course. But on that day, at that moment, at that place **(where I had been before in my nightmares)** I just remembered that brief message from him. That impacted me because it was obvious to me that Dr. Marcus genuinely cared about us Vietnam veterans. He respected what we had been through, and he had sincere compassion for our suffering after coming home.

I snapped out of the twilight zone and drove safely back to our hotel. Ginny never knew the danger she was in, and I did not tell her until the summer of 2012.

Mission Possible!

Nam veterans who have struggled to find a renewed sense of purpose that might still be missing since leaving the battle scene should find a band of brothers again and bond. It has been priceless for my own inner peace. Sure, we shed more tears. Who else could be more qualified to shed them with—your non-Vietnam veteran neighbor or your brother-in-law who never served and doesn't care about your pain? But "real" Vietnam veterans can be a pain too, because of what they have been through. And finding a "real" item isn't so easy either. But it can be worth the hunt if you are lucky enough to find that next lifelong friend. Then again, YOU might end up helping another Vietnam veteran who may have been searching for someone like you ... so it is worth the search.

Having a healthy conversation among your peers is a good therapy session. Get involved with something again if you've been hiding in a closet somewhere. I volunteered to be a Color Guard for a ceremony on Veterans Day on November 11, 2012 ... wearing full dress greens. It helps me feel like I have a sense of purpose, of self-worth, sort of like I'm serving my country again, and it feels good to put that uniform on a couple times per year now.

Do you salute the flag when the National Anthem is played at a social event? We as veterans are authorized to do so—I've been doing it for a couple years now as do my veteran brothers.

Back in the post Vietnam years we weren't allowed to be proud of our uniforms—oh no—because we were those who fought in that despicable war—the one we lost—remember? Now people applaud us when they figure out who/what we are, and that would be **PROUD VIETNAM COMBAT VETERANS!**

Suicide ... Game Over!

There is no running score on how many Vietnam veterans have been lost since the war ended for us in 1973 due to suicide. Either the government can't figure that out or they won't! Regardless, suicide has been a topic of concern with Vietnam veterans and those close to them from the day the vet arrived home. Here are some figures I was able to uncover:

- Quote from the *Chicago Tribune* (March 18, 2010): *"According to data from the Veterans Administration, Vietnam-era veterans who died from just the years of 2000 – 2007 was 490,135."* (Most were under sixty.)

- Posted October 3, 2007 on Permalink: *Over the past few years, three out of four veterans seeking mental health treatment for the very first time were Vietnam veterans in the 55-64 age group.*

- A VA memo dated June 30, 1982 stated/identified a total of approximately 300,000 deaths occurred among Vietnam-era veterans from 1965 – 1981.

- On January 28, 1985, the Massachusetts Agent Orange Program of the State Office released results of a study which stated, "Mortality among Vietnam veterans in Massachusetts, 1972 – 1983 revealed that deaths due to suicides, motor vehicle accidents, kidney cancer, were significantly elevated" among Vietnam veterans.

- The March 6, 1986 issue of *New England Journal of Medicine* stated that Vietnam veterans were 86 percent more likely than non-vets to die of suicide in the years after the Vietnam War.

- On November 26, 2007, CBS News reported that at least 6,256 veterans committed suicide in 2007.

- On August 7, 2000, Media Release Minister of Veterans Affairs, Australia claimed that the children of Vietnam veterans have **three times** the suicide rate of the general community.

- In March 1990, Chuck Dean, Director of Point Man International, a non-profit support group for Vietnam veterans, once interviewed a retired VA doctor, and in that telephone interview, the doctor related that his estimate of Vietnam veteran suicides up to that time (1990) was 200,000 men. The reason the official suicide statistics were so much lower was that in many cases, the suicides were documented as "accidents" due to single-car accidents influenced by alcohol and/or self-inflicted gunshot wounds without a suicide note or statement.

Had enough of this already? I have. And to me, it is obvious that we have lost more of our Nam brothers since the war ended than our government will ever admit to.

My dear brothers, I have been there, but managed to pull out of it several times. In closing this story, I would like to end it with this advice:

- **There are NO mulligans for suicide!**
- **There are no instant replays with suicide!**
- **There are no second chances; there is no coming back from suicide—the game ends there!**

The Spartan or Warfighter Pledge

I will not take my own life by my own hand until I talk to my battle buddy first. My mission is to find a mission to help my warfighter family.

- Boone Cutler, Sergeant
U.S. Army Veteran (Retired)
Author, Radio Talk Show Personality, Advisory Board of Gallant Few

PTSD ... Real or Imagined?

THE OFFICIAL DIAGNOSTIC CRITERIA FOR PTSD
OF THE AMERICAN PSYCHIATRIC ASSOCIATION

Of the five official criteria that make the diagnosis of PTSD, all but the first are straight-forward clinical descriptions, broadly stated to apply to all PTSD, not only to combat PTSD.

The person has experienced an event that is outside the range of usual human experience and that would be markedly distressing to almost anyone, e.g., serious threat to one's life or physical integrity; serious threat or harm to one's children, spouse, or other close relatives and friends; sudden destruction of one's home or community; or seeing another person who has recently been or is being, seriously injured or killed as the result of an accident or physical violence.

A. The traumatic event is persistently re-experienced in at least one of the following ways:
   (1) recurrent and intrusive distressing recollections of the event (in young children, repetitive play in which themes or aspects of the trauma are expressed.)
   (2) recurrent distressing dreams of the event
   (3) sudden acting or feeling as if the traumatic event were recurring (includes a sense of reliving the experience, illusions, hallucinations, and dissociative [flashback] episodes, even those that occur upon awakening or when intoxicated.)
   (4) intense psychological distress at exposure to events that symbolize or resemble an aspect of the traumatic event, including anniversaries of the trauma
B. Persistence avoidance of stimuli associated with the trauma or numbing of general responsiveness (not present before the trauma), as indicated by at least three of the following:
   (1) Efforts to avoid thoughts or feelings associated with the trauma
   (2) Efforts to avoid activities or situations that arouse recollections of the trauma
   (3) Inability to recall an important aspect of the trauma (psychogenic amnesia)
   (4) Markedly diminished interest in significant activities (in young children, loss of recently acquired developmental skills such as toilet training or language skills.)
   (5) Feeling of detachment or estrangement from others
   (6) Restricted range of affect, e.g., unable to have loving feelings
   (7) Sense of a foreshortened future, e.g., does not expect to have a career, marriage or children, or a long life

C. Persistent symptoms of increased arousal (not present before the trauma) as indicated by at least two of the following:

    (1) Difficulty falling or staying asleep

    (2) Irritability or outbursts of anger

    (3) Difficulty concentrating

    (4) Hypervigilance

    (5) Exaggerated startle response

    (6) Physiologic reactivity upon exposure to events that symbolize or resemble an aspect of the traumatic event (e.g., a woman who was raped in an elevator breaks out in a sweat when entering any elevator)

D. Duration of the disturbance (symptoms in B, C, and D) of at least one month.

The official definition almost totally fails to convey how easy PTSD can be confused with other mental disorders. For example, the numbness, mistrust, hallucinated voices of the dead and social withdrawal of combat PTSD are easily confused with schizophrenia. Some combat veterans remain in an emotionally deadened, socially withdrawn state for prolonged periods, and many have been misdiagnosed as schizophrenic.

I first attempted to seek psychological consultation back in the mid-1970s when my mother suggested it, as I had her very worried with my reckless tendencies since coming home from Vietnam. Back then, I did not even know there was help available at the Veterans Administration. No one ever mentioned it back then, nor did I know anyone else who was receiving medical help from the VA.

The psychiatrist saw me for three sessions. It cost me $50.00 an hour—a lot of money to me back in 1974 or 1975. Plus I was still in a state of recovery from a serious one-car accident where I wrecked my Pantera at an estimated speed of 127 miles per hour. I had been in and out of hospitals for two years after that accident and was certain bankruptcy wasn't too far off.

The shrink had never heard of post-traumatic stress disorder from combat, and since Vietnam was never even referred to as a "real" war, whatever my imaginary problems may have been, he felt a couple more sessions would take care of me. Agent Orange? Wasn't even a discussion in the mid-1970s. He never heard of that either. End of therapy.

A few more single-car accidents later, including a boating accident, almost all alcohol-related, and bankruptcy became my only way out in December 1980.

Hallucinations! These were the years of the most vivid nightmares of my life. Vietnam was right there with me some nights, in living, animated color. So I went out more and drank more. There were a couple more single-car accidents later—I think my revised total had reached seven or eight by

1982—but I wasn't done yet. That was an average of one car accident every fourteen or fifteen months!

Court Rules Vets' Rights Are Violated by Delays in Treatment of PTSD

ON MAY 10 A FEDERAL appeals court ordered a major overhaul of the Department of Veterans Affairs in a blockbuster ruling that blasted the VA for failing to care for veterans suffering from PTSD and other combat-related mental illnesses. The 9th Circuit Court of appeals called the failures a violation of veterans' constitutional rights that contributes to the reported 6,500 suicides among veterans each year.

The appeals court took nearly two years to issue its decision in the suit, which was brought by Veterans for
Common sense and Veterans United for Truth against the VA, alleging systemic failures in the government's processing of disability claims and appeals of denied coverage. The 2-1 decision referred to a 2008 Rand Study that estimated 300,000 returning war veterans are suffering from PTSD or major depression.

The Vietnam War changed men like few other wars have. We were stripped of our dignity and our character. The war itself and the treatment dished out to us after we came home weren't our fault; we did not deserve it.

Combat trauma and post-traumatic stress disorder have destroyed and tortured many of us. We were tortured by the way the Viet Cong fought us. They got into our heads with their style of concealment, deception, and night ambushes.

Our contact with an invisible enemy was prolonged very comparably to what our fathers and grandfathers were exposed to in the two World Wars. Prolonged contact with an enemy in war begins to play on the mind. Mental functionality manifests and tortures us.

Then, after surviving all that, the warrior returns from Vietnam to face rejection from his fellow Americans, which our fathers and grandfathers did not face upon their return. The torture continues to this day for many Vietnam veterans, as we have had to watch many of our brothers from that war die prematurely back home. The torture just goes on and on!

That war was over forty years ago for me ... I should be over it by now, shouldn't I? Of course I realize that when a real Nam veteran commits suicide, the media jumps on it and promotes it as another Nam vet loses it from PTSD ... even if the particular suicide had seemingly no connection to Vietnam. But clearly, many of the problems that drive a Vietnam veteran to take his own life had their beginnings from combat trauma in Vietnam and/or PTSD afterwards. Some will disagree with me here, but I know of certain situations that ended with tragic results.

It was not until October 1980 when the VA recognized PTSD as a genuine service- connected disorder … seven to ten years after the first and last Vietnam veterans left Vietnam.

Can Combat PTSD Be Prevented?

Can the devastating character changes associated with combat PTSD or any PTSD be prevented? In the language of the public health sector, they say the main prevention of combat PTSD or any PTSD requires the complete elimination of the source. In this book, I am sticking with what the real culprit is … combat.

Therefore, when our global society eliminates wars completely, then the source of combat PTSD goes away. Simple formula, except man has been at war with other men since the first Neanderthals and the Cro-Magnons appeared on this earth.

I think we Vietnam veterans received adequate training. At least we were made to be in top shape physically. But Vietnam demanded more mental stamina than physical. Most Vietnam veterans I know felt deeply that their training for Vietnam's style of warfare was almost irrelevant to the actual conditions, situations, and for the style of enemy we had to face.

Then there are the well-documented deficiencies of the M-16 rifle versus what the enemy had … the AK-47. How could our country—with its technological superiority over any other country in the world—send its military into such horrible combat with a deficient weapon in hand? WHY? Probably because the bureaucrats simply DID NOT GIVE A DAMN!

In Colonel Hackworth's book *About Face*, he does not hold back his anger about the negligent training of soldiers for the Vietnam War. How could our training be much better than adequate when the weapon we would have to sleep with—and in many cases die with—was inadequate!?

As I already mentioned in Chapter 3 on brainwashing, I remember our training from basic in Fort Knox to advanced infantry in Fort Polk, they were trying to program us into believing that our enemy was not human—that they should be viewed as less than human. The enemy was a "gook" and nothing better. The Viet Cong was portrayed to us in training as a loathsome, devilish freak, a gook that deserved to be killed—before they killed us. After all, they weren't even human, were they? So why would they even care if they died? Someone had to kill the Viet Cong; might as well be us.

Sometimes I wonder if combat PTSD was always a part of their entire program to brainwash us … and keep us brainwashed!

PTSD from combat trauma in the Vietnam War was unavoidable. The longer you lived, the longer you were in the heat of battle and the worse your PTSD would likely be—that's my opinion as a pure combat infantry "grunt."

If you were one of the really lucky combat Vietnam veterans, you would live with your PTSD for your entire lifetime. Unfortunately, many have already died prematurely … too many.

Hallucinations?

I understand, from what I have researched and from what several psychologists and psychiatrists have told me, that hallucinating can involve sight, smells, hearing, and possibly tasting things that are not real!

Most people I know who are in my general age group of sixty to seventy years old experience "drifting" or "mental wandering," and the word "hallucination" itself comes from Latin words that mean "to wander mentally."

I don't see pink elephants in my awake state, but what I have seen several times from the 1970s to this year of 2012 are perceptions in my wakeful state that seem so real, they have caused me to take physical defensive or offensive actions to try and eliminate the perception or hallucination I thought I saw and believed to be real.

Hallucinations are not dreams or delusions, so say the psychiatric professionals. The shrinks also say this about hallucinating:

- Hallucinations are associated with psychiatric disorders or medical conditions—we all kind of figured that out on our own.

- Medical conditions causing hallucinations could include bipolar disorder, epilepsy, schizophrenia, brain tumors, delirium, dementia, stroke, and other seizure disorders.

- Medications abuse or overdose can cause hallucinations. Too much alcohol with certain medications will do it as well.

- Severe fatigue or sleep disorders can be causes.

My personal experiences with hallucinations have always been related to Vietnam, and I could not distinguish what I know I saw from reality. I was advised to seek medical/psychiatric care back in the 1970s, which I did in order to appease people who were concerned about me. I went through several psychiatric sessions but did not feel satisfied with the therapy or the results, so I stopped. The doctors have also told me that these distorted sensory experiences are generated by the mind and that they can be seen, heard, felt, smelled, or tasted. **I have felt the objects in my hallucinations touch me and my bed!** Obviously, stress enters into the equation here—or PTSD.

Nightmares?

- I was thrown into a bowling alley; the doors were locked after that. Everyone in there was a Viet Cong or North Vietnamese. I was told that in order to walk out of there alive, I had to beat their best bowler in a one-game match. They gave me a small rubber ball to use, the size of what they use to play handball. I didn't think I could knock one pin over with it. Fortunately … **I awakened before the match began.**

- One night I was separated from the rest of my platoon on a night ambush. All at once, a long line of North Vietnamese soldiers were trotting down a trail a few yards away from me, so I reached for my M-16 to lock and load, and all of a sudden it was a plastic toy gun. **I woke up right away.**

- One night, a new 2nd lieutenant arrived as our new platoon leader. We had been ambushed during the day by an unknown VC/NVA force, and half of our brothers had been killed or wounded, including our previous platoon leader. The FNG (Fricking New Guy) came to make a name for himself right away. His first orders to us were as follows: "Men, I know you've had a tough day, lost some of your brothers, but you have to suck it up and get right into the enemy's faces ASAP. We leave in fifteen minutes for a full platoon ambush. We will travel light and quickly. So there are no worries about your M-16s jamming … we are pulling this ambush with BAYONETS!" **I woke up immediately.**

Hallucination or nightmare … earlier in the summer of 2012 when I was just starting to really heat things up with the writing of *Condemned Property?* I was having a nightmare where I spotted several Viet Cong ahead, hiding in the bushes as I was walking point. **I woke up immediately and, oh my gosh, there they were—three of them with AK-47s, grinning at me. The next thing I remember from that night was my lovely wife, Ginny (GBT) yelling at me, "Dusty, what are you doing—are you all right?" I was walking around the bedroom with machete in hand, looking behind things, under things. I did not go back to sleep that night!**

I guess these few examples of the many nightmares a Vietnam War combat vet can suffer from gives the impression that over there we were constantly faced with a hopeless and unwinnable situation and that our ending was inevitable ... **CONDEMNED PROPERTY?** I pray not.

A major concern for anyone who has or is experiencing hallucinations is possible brain damage or brain illness. Lesions or injuries to the brain, like head injuries or concussions from explosions in the Vietnam War, can alter brain function and cause hallucinations.

Even people with good mental health will experience hallucinations. In most cases, medication is quite helpful in dealing with hallucinations. A recent increase in medication by a VA psychiatrist seems to have curtailed the hallucinations I was experiencing in the earlier months of 2012.

Hypnopompic hallucination is the term used to describe a hallucination that occurs as we are waking from our sleep—this has been my most common experience. In the 1970s and 1980s, my hallucinations were more chronic. However, my alcohol intake during those years was beyond what most people could comprehend or keep living with. In the 1990s, my alcohol consumption decreased a bit as I had a responsibility to my wife—not just myself—but the same problems did continue.

Each and every hallucination was the image of a Viet Cong or North Vietnamese soldier in an attack mode. These were so lifelike that I often took swings at them or threw my pillow at them. Most recently, in April 2012, I reached for the machete that I keep close by on my bedpost, swung at the hallucinated object (an NVA in this case), and hit the lamp on the nightstand next to our bed!

WHOA ... now this was getting a bit hairy. What if I had accidentally struck my wife? So I told the VA psychologist and VA psychiatrist and was given an increase in some medication for PTSD. Fortunately, I have had just a couple of minor hallucinations since, and I have not reached for the machete—which still hangs on the bedpost next to my bed.

Like I keep saying ... WE WHO FOUGHT IN HEAVY COMBAT IN VIETNAM WILL PROBABLY NEVER GET IT COMPLETELY OUT OF OUR MINDS!

Killing another human being in combat can cause the undoing of a man's character. When a country's government sends its men over to a foreign and hostile land to fight in vicious combat, that government should be prepared for and aware of what the consequences of the combatants' actions might be. That government should have a moral obligation to help those who killed in war adjust to society again and help them understand that what they did was right and necessary. This would be especially so in a controversial war like Vietnam.

I received no such readjustment consultation when I was dropped back into society, nor have I ever met another Vietnam veteran who was helped when they needed it most, which was upon their initial arrival back home.

So here we are in the 2010s and the VA is being flooded with Vietnam veterans who have sobered up, stopped doing drugs, gone through multiple disasters with families, and lo and behold, they are facing health issues, physical and psychological, and are seeking help. How dare we old veterans—who haven't died prematurely like many of our comrades have—now put a burden on the government that neglected to take care of us when they should have done so? HOW DARE WE OLD VIETNAM VETERANS DO THIS NOW?

I guess it can be too much to ask of our society to address what it did to 2.7 million men and women in the Vietnam War … thirty to forty years later. Why can't we who killed other men in battle just forget about it—GET OVER IT?!

Combat trauma, PTSD, or whatever one chooses to label it is magnified when the warrior comes home and finds that many around him, especially the government that sent him into combat to kill someone, is deceiving and dishonoring him and what they sent him to do. As a result, we end up having to confront another enemy … the enemy this time is those who sent us to serve them in combat.

One of my high school teachers and coaches, Mr. Powell, was one of a handful of mentors who would listen to my story about my life before and after Vietnam. I would not be here if it weren't for people like him, as suicide was never far from my thoughts, especially for the first thirty years after I left Vietnam. Revenge was also lurking in the back of my mind.

Walking point! No one wanted to. Usually, those who did were not of the politically correct group, and certain people never did it. SURPRISE … I wanted it, demanded it, and kept it. That eliminated a lot of arguing and stress and saved some lives for sure.

I don't know which is worse … being a POW or subjected to prolonged combat with the enemy. At least in combat we had the opportunity to fight back. Either way, both are conditions of enslavement with seemingly no foreseeable means of escape in the near future. I guess that is why it seems like my one year in Vietnam lasted for decades. **It did not go fast. Each day was like a week—each night like ten nights.**

We did not ask to be sent into combat with a weapon (M-16) that jammed constantly or just flat-out broke down … more betrayal and sabotage.

In a few of those short but very dragged-out months, many of us went from weeping miserably when we lost a guy to saying, "Oh f—- it; he's dead too. Move on—I might be next, and it ain't no big deal." But it really was a big deal.

We never had time to grieve over our lost comrades over there. They were gone the instant they died, and in came a replacement the next day … so we started all over with them. So, now we grieve every day for those guys … for the rest of our lives. Our anger continues, and the feeling of betrayal could go with us to our graves. That's just the way it is, I guess, and all of the medications in the world will never change this.

We used to try to deal with things by saying to each other, *"It don't mean nothin',"* a phrase used in Nam to help us get through each day. There were things that went on that were beyond what the average man's mind could cope with. "It don't mean nothin'!" was a way to forget one bad day, and maybe the next day would be better … not likely.

Sometimes your worst fears do come true when you least expect them to, and you are not prepared for the sudden occurrence.

Viet Cong (VC) were not "minutemen" types, supposedly fighting to depose an illegitimate and universally detested puppet government, as the American media portrayed them. VC were brutal terrorists who targeted defenseless civilians, village chiefs, schoolteachers, older men, government employees, women, and children, especially young males who refused to join their ranks.

Assassinations, abductions, and village bombings were daily events of the VC. They slaughtered tens of thousands of South Vietnamese civilians; they often did this publicly and in a horribly torturous manner of slow death in order to drive terror into the minds of the masses.

In Vietnam, Americans were looked upon as saviors—not as the conquerors like back home in America itself—due to media bias. Clearly, most South Vietnamese did not support North Vietnam or their VC mercenaries, and they did not have a burning desire to come under communist rule.

The 1970s … Blurrrrrr!

A complete decade out of my life was pretty much wasted after Nam. I can remember more specific details from my Nam tour in 1968–1969 than I can of all the years from 1970–1980. Alcohol was the reason … five to six days every week for years, just like a whole lot of other combat Nam vets. But I stayed away from the drugs. THANK GOD!

With high-risk auto insurance due to one speeding ticket after another and a ridiculous number of single-car accidents (like fourteen), I can't believe to this day that I never lost my driver's license—but I came close. De Tomaso Pantera (1972), Oldsmobile Cutlass 442 (1975), Ford Thunderbird (1977), Buick Riviera (1979), Buick Riviera (1982), Chevy pickup (1990), Hyundai Sonata (2007)—**ALL TOTALED—DESTROYED!** Not to mention the other dozen or more auto accidents I was involved with where I kept the car in a repairable state and was able to drive it again. Throw a boat and golf cart onto the list of single-vehicle accidents—those weren't fun either.

It is NOT a good thing when a soldier is transformed from an almost innocent kid into a battle-hardened killer who is no longer fazed by seeing people's arms and legs flying in different directions in war or seeing a man he has shared several months of twenty-four/seven brothership get killed right in front of him.

Violence of this magnitude profoundly affects the course of your life, which changes your personality and affects you for **the rest of your life!**

In the early months over there I would write home often, describing the atrocities, endless missions, unbearable living conditions, threat of death—constantly ... never knowing if I could continue on, doubting that I was ever coming home and NEVER imagining the impact I was having on everyone back home. I guess writing those letters, which took weeks to reach their destination back home, was some sort of release for us—I wish that I had not dumped that on everyone.

Pretty much everyone else was writing letters like mine. What else was there to say and describe? It SUCKED! As time went on, our letter writing began to drop in frequency from a daily routine to weekly and then hardly ever at all.

I guess that bullet through my helmet in Vietnam gave me a false impression that I was indestructible or something like that, but I was surely headed for a bigger crash. From 1970–2007, I had nothing but reckless abandon tendencies. Hey, I became a married man with the loveliest wife possible, and now I'm on Social Security, not thirty or forty years old anymore. WAKE UP, DUSTY!

Okay, so I have an extremely hard head and how, literally and physically. Now what as I get closer to seventy years of living?

It is quite conceivable that I have incurred several concussions, which prohibits me from taking certain medications that the VA doctors would like to prescribe for me. These multiple head bumps put a heavy strain on my ability to concentrate on what I am doing, with dizzy spells, blurred vision, bumping into things while walking, and worst of all, blacking out while driving on long trips.

From the first time I passed my driver's test in 1962 until I entered the military, I did not know what a speeding ticket was, let alone a "fender bender." My first car was a 1955 Chevy that I bought from Sonny Piazza, who I went to school with in Twinsburg, Ohio. Sonny also went to Nam. He came home in one piece physically, but he wasn't the same and is still affected by his experiences in Nam.

Just five years later after I entered the military to get prepped and brainwashed for the Vietnam War, by the end of the 1970s, I had already received many speeding violations. By the end of 1972, my auto insurance rates skyrocketed to well over $1,000 yearly. I was considered a "high risk" insured, and I was just one more citation away from losing my driver's license. No DUI's EVER ... thank you, dear God, because he knows I came close dozens of times—yes, dozens!

I can't say much about 1970–1980 because it was such a quick *blurrrrrr*. Even today, it seems like I was transported from my 1968–1969 tour in Southeast Asia straight to the 1980s by passing an entire decade in between. That is so weird to me today.

Most of my regrets about any part of my life are about wasting those years from 1970–1980. I did almost nothing during those years; I was just barely getting by from year to year ... drinking and more drinking, avoiding life's commitments and its rules. Living with a total reckless abandon mentality during those years, I put a lot of other people's lives in danger and, of course, my own.

Many Vietnam combat vets I knew lived like I did during those early years after Nam. I just lived them a lot longer than most, but quite a few of my Nam brothers died within the first ten years back in the USA. Many more combat Nam vets died in their forties and fifties and are dying in their sixties today at a much higher rate than non-Vietnam combat veterans. WHEN WILL THE VIETNAM WAR END FOR WE WHO FOUGHT OVER THERE?!

Will those of us who survived the horrors and unspeakable events over there and the torture of being forgotten since coming home ever find our way home?

I truly believe that we did not lose that war over there. I know we did not lose it—not on the battlefield. So why are so many of us losing that war today? No way is the Vietnam War over yet, not for many or most of the combat vets who are still fighting it over here ... STILL!

Americans, we are still dying from that war, so maybe the only way it will end is when the last combat war veteran is six feet underground. We thought we were the good guys! Don't we deserve better than this? We thought we were the good guys! We did what we were told to do. We thought we were the good guys!

I have met other Vietnam combat veterans who claim that they have never discussed the war with their children. Some have told me that their children don't even know that their father is a combat Vietnam veteran. THIS IS JUST NOT RIGHT!

This year, I met with a master sergeant named Will Craven, a sixteen-year U.S. Army veteran who has served in several hostile areas. Master Sergeant Will Craven told me how people stop to thank him and welcome him home on a regular basis ... which is really wonderful. Master Sergeant Will Craven also told me that from time to time his reply back to a fellow American who is thanking him for his service is this:

Thank you. But if you know a Vietnam War veteran or anyone else who knows a Vietnam War veteran, please say thank you to him.

I will always hold my head high as a combat Vietnam veteran, knowing that we served our country—giving it our all. I have nothing against those who did not go over there. It was their choice. My Nam brothers and sisters fought to keep that freedom of choice for Americans. But please don't continue to betray us. We deserve better. We earned the right for better treatment. Although most of us continue the battle to survive, many of us are still heading toward being *CONDEMNED PROPERTY?* I am trying to reach some of those troubled Nam vets.

Trading the Machete for a Five-Wood

Since I came home (physically) from Nam, I have always had a machete close by. I have never been far away from one. It was an extra special tool and weapon for combat infantry point men in Vietnam. This two- to three-inch-long, cleaver-like knife was critically necessary in the tropical jungles of Vietnam. I was never without one, so I still carry affection for them today. At home, I have three machetes, fifteen inches long, twenty-three inches long, and thirty inches long. The twenty-three-inch model can cut a small tree in half in a couple of swipes. I have cleared several paths through the woods at home and in Florida's Everglades with my machetes. One machete hangs on my bedpost. Another machete always traveled with me in my vehicle—either in the back or in the trunk if there was one. Sometimes I packed a machete into my golf bag ... never know what may be lurking in areas where I hit my golf balls. My machete went with me on the Amazon trip, and of course, I always had it with me on rattlesnake hunts in Texas or Pennsylvania and on the Everglades trips as well.

About five years ago, I pulled the machete out of my golf bag when the group behind us hit their balls into us and they had no apologies to offer.

Fortunately, they came forth with a Jane Fonda-type "I'm sorry," so I put the machete back into the bag … after displaying its functionality on a few healthy tree branches. When I got home, I removed the machete from the golf bag forever. That was five years ago.

It was only three and a half years ago when I was viciously cut off while driving on the highway. The other car, which had four guys in it, was clearly the aggressor. My rage came forth, giving them a gesture of my dissatisfaction about their amateurish driving. They waved at me, offering to meet me on the side of the road, and I obliged them quite enthusiastically. I'm not sure if I waited for my car to come to a complete stop before I was out of it—charging at all four of them with my machete waving in the air. No matter what they had, I was not backing off. God was with me again, just as he was when that Viet Cong bullet removed my helmet from my head … as he was when I rolled the Pantera several times at 127 miles per hour. All four aggressors quickly retreated to their car and drove off rather abruptly, and they never looked back.

My feelings after the golf course and the highway incidents weren't what I expected them to be. I felt no exhilaration and very little satisfaction like I would have felt in a combat situation in Vietnam or like I would have in the 1970s or even the 1980s. I felt badly about both acts.

Again, what had I almost done? The same question I asked myself when I pulled the trigger on my M-16 when a base camp warrior heckled a couple of my platoon brothers who had just come home from the bush for a breather. **What had I almost done … again?**

Oh, I've been cut off on the highway since that incident with the machete. But I no longer carry the machete in my vehicle. After forty years, I removed it. I take a much more defensive posture on the highway these days. However, a man has to have some type of protection when he does as much driving as I do. So I traded in the machete for a five-wood golf club. My VA psychologist says I've progressed nicely … but it has taken me a long, long time.

Survivor syndrome or **survivor guilt** is a mental condition that results from a self-generated appraisal that a person has done a bad thing because he/she survived a combat experience when others did not. Survivor guilt probably dates back to the beginning of mankind's existence on this great planet. As I understand, it was not actually diagnosed as such until the 1960s, or during the Vietnam War years.

During the revision of the *Diagnostic and Statistical Manual of Mental Disorders IV* (DSM-IV), survivor guilt/survivor syndrome was removed as a specific diagnosis. Instead, it was replaced as a significant symptom of PTSD.

My personal survival guilt stems from the time I was offered and accepted the option to leave the field and take on a base camp job at the 25th Infantry

Division's headquarters known as Cu Chi. Sure, Cu Chi was still in the middle of a heavy combat zone and it was mortared by the Viet Cong almost every day in 1968 and 1969. And several of those mortar rounds came close to hitting me.

There was risk when I would drive the adjutant general's jeep outside of Cu Chi, but this duty was pale in comparison to what I was doing out in the bush, where I had left the rest of my platoon. Every time our unit was hit and there was another casualty, I was a nervous wreck. Oh, don't get me wrong, some of us aren't really that close today, as we have all pretty much gone our own way since we fought side by side in Nam. Some of my platoon don't even want to be bothered, having almost disappeared from open communication. This is normal for many combat veterans.

Still ... it does bother me that I did not finish out my last days in country, out in the field with my fellow combat brothers. For a long time I denied suffering from anything like survivor guilt. After all, I held my own out there. I am very proud of that. And I helped save lives by risking my own life in order to do that. So WHY do I suffer from survivor guilt?

The answer is ... I DON'T KNOW. That is one reason I am presently accepting therapy for PTSD at the VA. It has been a lifesaver for me during the last few years, and I mean literally. If only they had been there for me during the earliest years when I came back from Vietnam ...

The therapists tell me that someone can develop PTSD and/or survivor guilt from non-combat situations. A car accident is one example. The Holocaust survivors are another example. People with survivor guilt can help each other in coping, so I am told! Why did I make it? Why not me? Could I have done something more to help save someone's life in Nam? These are examples of how PTSD can trouble someone.

Science News

PTSD Causes Early Death from Heart Disease, Study Suggests

ScienceDaily (July 7, 2008) – Vietnam veterans who experienced post traumatic stress disorder (PTSD) were twice as likely to die from heart disease as veterans without PTSD, a new Geisinger study finds.

Science News

Post-Traumatic Stress Disorder Linked to Death, Atherosclerosis in Veterans, Research Finds

Science Daily (Nov. 17, 2012) – Post traumatic stress disorder (PTSD) more than doubles a veteran's risk of death from any cause and is an independent risk factor for cardiovascular disease, according to research presented at the American Heart Association's Scientific Sessions 2012.

So … think Vietnam's combat vets don't have a humorous side? Absolutely, they do. Some of the funniest moments in my life have occurred during the last dozen years or so, just sitting around talking Nam-talk with some of my brothers who "really" served there.

We're not human time bombs twenty-four/seven, but then again, when some of my brothers wear t-shirts or hats with these statements, not too many people are likely to bother us—or bother with us …

VIETNAM COMBAT VETERAN—KEEP YOUR DISTANCE!

DYSFUNCTIONAL VIETNAM COMBAT VET … LEAVE ME ALONE!

OUR GOVERNMENT HAS ME ON MEDICATION TO PROTECT Y-O-U!

The backlog at VA for disability claims is at an all-time record high. WWII vets and Korean War vets have been checking in more recently because PTSD has become recognized as such a terrible illness. It can hit at any age.

Vietnam Combat Veterans' Rage!

Our military training for combat in Vietnam was meant to prepare us to **kill other humans**. Our military training at that time was unlike any war training Americans had ever received before. We were going to search for and force a confrontation with our enemies, and **someone's death was inevitable**.

The military training for Vietnam for the combat-skilled soldier was meant to create a feeling—a macho feeling—of rage. It was mandatory for the job ahead of us. When the unavoidable happened—a face-to-face battle with our enemy—**and death resulted**, wild, violent emotions were felt, and there was no way to tone them down. The jungle warfare of ambushes and booby traps turned us into human time bombs.

Again, as I have mentioned in other places in this book … there was no program in place for the returning Vietnam War combat veteran to tone down the anger and rage that had built up inside him. With many of us, it became a fixed part of our personalities.

A combat veteran's rage can be extremely dangerous, especially for those veterans who don't think they have a problem, and there are plenty of those.

I have been one of those so I monitor my situation closely and attend timely therapy sessions at the VA. Personally, I prefer one-to-one therapy in favor of the group sessions—to each his own.

Rage caused by PTSD is not an illness that I can afford to take lightly. I love my wife very much, so going to therapy and accepting the VA doctors' advice has become easy for me.

Like many other Vietnam War combat veterans, I have suffered from thoughts of revenge or retaliation on those who forced us to Vietnam and those who shunned us when we came home. Those dangerous thoughts seem to have subsided considerably for me in recent years. Again, I have to credit the VA's therapy and their prescribed medication for making me a more comfortable citizen in the country that I love so dearly.

I am also very fortunate that GBT, my loving wife and friend, has joined me in a couple therapy sessions at VA. I am grateful to her for caring.

As a Vietnam veteran who visits VA hospitals regularly, I know how the wounds of that war have damaged our bodies and minds. I also know and accept the important role that the VA has in our healing process.

The healing process! While many Vietnam veterans still living today have adjusted well to life at home, many did not adjust and became a casualty of that war, **after that war.** And a very large number of Vietnam veterans are still trying to find their way **ALL THE WAY HOME!** Non-Vietnam veterans who care about this country who read *CONDEMNED PROPERTY?* can help some of these brave and mostly forgotten warriors make it all the way home.

I am extremely hopeful that this book will find its way into your hands, but more important, into the hands of those troubled Vietnam veterans who have been trying so valiantly to come home ALL THE WAY!

Blind loyalty is what a soldier gives to our country. The Vietnam War veteran was no different than those who fought bravely in previous wars. We, too, gave allegiance to our country and its people with pure, unwavering, blind loyalty. The damage done to us by the mega-betrayals will haunt many of us till the day they bury us. This is why so many of us are battling to avoid becoming CONDEMNED PROPERTY of the Vietnam War.

Aussie Vietnam Veterans Suffered Too ...

On March 9, 1999, an Australian media source stated that the average life expectancy for their country's Vietnam War veterans was a mere fifty-six years! This statement came just thirty years after Australia's participation in the Vietnam War was over. *7.30 Lateline* has broadcast several statements from Aussie Vietnam War veterans, such as:

When I came back, I had no real release, so I never got Vietnam out of my system.

I couldn't talk to anybody, not even my family.

People told us Vietnam's war was a waste of time, had no real purpose. But I refused to believe that because if you did, then all those guys who died, died in vain.

I got off a Qantas jet to Sydney, coming home from Vietnam and as I was walking down the concourse, I was hit on the back of my head and knocked unconscious to the floor ... that's what coming home from Vietnam was like for a lot of Aussie veterans.
- Peter Forbes
Vietnam Vet, Australia
(Source: www.abc.net.au/7.30/archive.htm)

My point here is that anyone who had the opportunity to work with the Australians in Vietnam or visit their country while on R&R (which I did) knew that they weren't whiners or crybabies or baby killers. Neither were we. They, too, remain in a critical battle to avoid becoming *Condemned Property?* of that war.

The Vietnam War spared no one. Everyone who participated was touched emotionally, regardless of where they were or what their jobs were over there. Some of my dreams after coming home from hell were about how we used to be before Vietnam took us. I dream about playing with some of my battle buddies, walking through the woods together, riding around in hot cars together. I don't know if this is good or bad—I can't help it.

Sometimes the memories end with a blur. I remember them, but what actually did happen and what seemed to happen gets disorganized and leaves me confused. At this exact minute, I am seeing the cheerful face of a platoon buddy, Dean Coldren. We are teasing each other in our usual manner, jostling back and forth—then his face fades off and the daydream ends with a more frightful image of Dean. **His eyes are black and he is no longer smiling. He is no longer moving.**

*THEY Won't Believe This!

On February 21-22, 2013—forty-five years after I was introduced to Vietnam—a vivid nightmare became a lifelike form.

I was soundly sleeping when I dreamed that we were on a routine ambush patrol one night after conducting an all-day search-and-destroy recon mission. Everyone was flat-out exhausted. Whoever was pulling guard fell asleep, and the Viet Cong grabbed the opportunity; the ambush was on! They were on top of us in our bunkers. Then one of my brothers yelled at me, "**TRIM-MER, HE'S BEHIND YOU!**" I woke up. Nightmare over, right? WRONG! There he was, glaring at me with a nasty scowl on his face just a few feet away from my bed, where I was now sitting up completely awake, staring back at him. I screamed a couple of times. He raised his large knife or machete, and I kicked at him repeatedly and landed on the floor. His image faded away as hallucinations do, but it scared my wife and our dog. I was in a sweat, shaking, and could not get back to sleep. I had to take a couple of naps during the day.

The following night, I took sleeping aids and went to bed a little earlier, but I stayed awake into the early hours of the next morning listening, waiting … for what? Just another benefit of PTSD from a war too real forty-five years later.

I conducted some amateur research on this experience, and it seems this type of hallucination is called **peduncular hallucinosis** by the medical profession. It is described as a rare neurological disorder which causes vivid visual images in dark environments, lasting for several minutes. They are all too realistic, often involving people, familiar environments, including animation and full color, making it difficult to distinguish whether they are real or not.

Chapter 16

AGENT ORANGE & DIABETES II

Agent Orange is the code name for one of the herbicides and defoliants used by the U.S. military as part of its herbicidal warfare program called Operation Ranch Hand, during the Vietnam War from 1962–1970. It was given its name from the color of the orange-striped 55 US gallon (208 liters) barrels in which it was shipped, and was by far the most widely used of the so-called "rainbow herbicides." A 50:50 mixture of 2,4,5-T and 2,4-D, it was manufactured for the U.S. Department of Defense primarily by Monsanto Corporation and Dow Chemical. The 2,4,5-T used to produce Agent Orange was later discovered to be contaminated with 2,3,7,8-tetrachlorodibenzodioxin, an extremely toxic dioxin compound. Vietnam estimates 400,000 people were killed or maimed and 500,000 children born with birth defects.

During the Vietnam War, between 1962 and 1970, the United States military sprayed nearly 20,000,000 US gallons of chemical herbicides and defoliants in Vietnam, eastern Laos, and parts of Cambodia, as part of Operation Ranch Hand. The program's goal was to defoliate forested and rural land, depriving guerrillas of cover; another goal was to induce forced draft urbanization, destroying the ability of peasants to support themselves in the countryside, and forcing them to flee to the U.S. dominated cities, thus depriving the guerrillas of their rural support base and food supply.

The use of Agent Orange was a failed attempt by the American government to impose control over another nation, its people, and more so, its landscape. The fact remains, and it is mind-boggling to this day, that our government actually believed that they were spraying the same stuff on South Vietnam that was being used on weeds back in America! Agent Orange wiped out entire forests of trees. You can't do that kind of damage with Roundup!

Effects on U.S. Veterans

Studies show that veterans who served in the southern areas of South Vietnam during the war have increased rates of cancer, along with nerve, digestive, skin, and respiratory disorders. Veterans from the south had higher rates of throat cancer, acute/chronic leukemia, Hodgkin's lymphoma and non-Hodgkin's lymphoma, prostate cancer, lung cancer, colon cancer, soft tissue sarcoma, and liver cancer. Other than liver cancer, these are the same conditions the U.S. Veterans Administration has found to be associated with exposure to Agent Orange/dioxin, and are on the list of conditions eligible for compensation and treatment.

Military personnel who loaded airplanes and helicopters used in Ranch Hand probably sustained some of the heaviest exposures. Members of the Army Chemical Corps, who stored and mixed herbicides and defoliated the perimeters of military bases, and mechanics who worked on the helicopters and planes, are also thought to have had some of the heaviest exposures. Others with potentially heavy exposures include members of U.S. Army Special Forces units who defoliated remote campsites, and members of U.S. Navy river units who cleared base perimeters. Military members who served on Okinawa also claim to have been exposed to the chemical.

While in Vietnam, the veterans were told not to worry and were persuaded the chemical was harmless. After returning home, Vietnam veterans began to suspect their ill health or their wives' miscarriages or children born with birth defects might be related to Agent Orange and the other toxic herbicides to which they were exposed in Vietnam. Veterans began to file claims in 1977 to the Department of Veterans Affairs for disability payments for health care for conditions they believed were associated with exposure to Agent Orange, or more specifically dioxin, but their claims were denied unless they could prove the condition began when they were in the service or within one year of their discharge.

By April 1993, the Department of Veterans Affairs had only compensated 486 victims, although it had received disability claims from 39,419 soldiers who had been exposed to Agent Orange while serving in Vietnam.

Effects on Vietnamese People

The Vietnam Red Cross reported as many as three million Vietnamese people have been affected by Agent Orange, including at least 150,000 children born with birth defects. According to the Vietnamese Ministry of Foreign Affairs, 4.8 million Vietnamese people were exposed to Agent Orange, resulting in 400,000 people being killed or maimed and 500,000 children born with birth defects. Women had higher rates of miscarriage and stillbirths, as did livestock such as cattle, water buffalo, **and pigs.**

Children in the areas where Agent Orange was used have been affected and have multiple health problems, including cleft palate, mental disabilities, hernias, and extra fingers and toes. In the 1970s, high levels of dioxin were found in the breast milk of South Vietnamese women and in the blood of U.S. soldiers who had served in Vietnam. The most affected zones are the mountainous area along Truong Son (Long Mountains) and the border between

Vietnam and Cambodia. The affected residents are living in substandard conditions with many genetic diseases.
(Source: http://wikipedia.org/wiki/Agent_Orange)

My Agent Orange Physical

The first ad I recall in *VFW* or *VVA* magazine read like this:

Attention Vietnam Veterans!!
22 Million + Gallons of
Agent Orange Dioxins Sprayed
That Have Caused More Than
43 Approved
Cancers and Sicknesses
Including Diabetes II
Is that Reason Enough
For You to Get a
Full Physical with CAT Scans
Every Year?
This Could Save Your Life ...

I think it was in the fall of 2004 when I saw this ad. I responded by contacting the Veterans Administration in Cleveland, Ohio, in early 2005. The VA doctor who reviewed my test results that day was pleasant enough and took the time to go over everything with me. She gave me a thorough passing grade on everything that day in 2005. However, one thing she explained to me alarms me today even though I sloughed it off at the time.

She told me that Agent Orange was nothing more than a basic weed killer and that she thought the alarms being reported were highly exaggerated. HIGHLY EXAGGERATED?! Then why did President Bush do this back on February 7, 1991:

Bush Signs Agent Orange Bill
To Compensate Ill Veterans

AP

President Bush ended a two-decade dispute today by signing a bill to compensate Vietnam War veterans exposed to herbicide Agent Orange. The measure permanently extends disability benefits to Vietnam veterans suffering from two types of cancer presumed to be caused by Agent Orange: non-Hodgkins lymphoma and soft-tissue sarcoma. Agent Orange was sprayed by American troops in Vietnam to defoliate jungle cover. For years, the Government said there was no proven link between the herbicide and the two types of cancer.
February 7, 1991

REPORT: Agent Orange Risks Were Known by Maker

A DECEMBER CHICAGO TRIBUNE investigation revealed that in 1965, Dow Chemical Co. referred to dioxin, a contaminant in Agent Orange as "one of the most toxic materials known, causing not only skin lesions, but also liver damage." The Tribune also reported that documents it reviewed showed that techniques were available to drastically cut the amount of dioxin in the defoliant during manufacture. After examining court documents and government records in the National Archives, the newspaper concluded soldiers were exposed to Agent Orange without being informed of its risks, making exposure more dangerous. Chemical companies that produced the defoliant have been sued by veterans and Vietnamese who were exposed to dioxin.
(Source: *VIETNAM*, April 2010)

Soldiers of the Vietnam War were told this as they were fighting to survive firefights, ambushes, human waves, booby traps, wounds, death, and destruction:

- Our skin rashes were "jungle rot," our headaches, dizziness, and stomachaches were simply symptoms of "combat stress." All combat troops share these problems, so deal with it!

In December 2012 as I was putting the finishing touches on this book, I could still see my jungle rot from the Vietnam War in 1968–1969. It has subsided considerably, thanks to the VA doctors, but it has not gone away just yet. I know Vietnam vets who are still bothered by severe jungle rot conditions. It itches so badly, it hurts. The colors are awful-looking ... forty-plus years later!

Please keep in mind that the total body count of the Vietnam War will never be accurately reported ... never! Over 58,000 Americans and millions of Vietnamese from the south and north had died when the war ended officially in 1973 for the U.S. and its allies and 1975 for South Vietnam. BUT ... those who drank water and ate food sprayed with Agent Orange, slept on the wet ground soaked with Agent Orange, and sometimes got sprayed directly—**how many of them have perished prematurely since coming home?**

We are so grateful to those who challenged the government and the chemical companies back in the 1970s and 1980s over the damages being caused by the defoliants, herbicides, or whatever because we did not volunteer to defend America and accept the risk of being poisoned by our own war materials.

My jungle rot was so uncomfortable for many years after Vietnam that I spent more time at various dermatologists' offices than I did at pharmacy stores for cold and other minor ailment remedies.

Agent Orange spraying peaked in 1968 and 1969. The order was given to stop the sprayings in 1970.

Although the dermatology treatments offered me some relief, the rashes never went away, especially during the summer months or when I ventured to tropical climates—then the rashes would explode all over my body! Fortunately, it was finally discovered that treating the skin's rashes did not deal with the problem. The problem was more down under, not topical. It has been discovered by extensive, credible research that the Agent Orange dioxins sprayed in South Vietnam can be stored in the human body for many years. And the standard laboratory tests used by the VA in its Agent Orange examinations failed to detect the traces of dioxin in blood, urine, or spinal fluid. Then the VA doctors would determine that we were clean!

Agent Orange is stored in the fatty tissues of our bodies for many, many years, doing untold damage. Dear readers, it is quite possible for humans to be exposed to dioxins without suffering from noticeable side effects. But Vietnam veterans and, more specifically, those who spent extended periods in the bush were more likely to suffer because they were exposed to Agent Orange's toxic herbicides over a twelve-month period (or longer), and our exposure involved multiple routes. For instance:

- We ate contaminated food.
- We drank contaminated water.
- We were sprayed directly.
- We swam and walked in polluted water.
- We walked through sprayed bushes.
- We wore clothes for weeks that had been contaminated.
- We inhaled the air and fumes as it rose from the sprayed areas.

When we were over there, we often wondered why we rarely saw common wildlife like birds and rabbits. Even the domestic animals like dogs and cats in villages looked sickly ... remember, my brothers?

Well, I finally took the Agent Orange physical and I was given an A-OK on my health ... except for the jungle rot. Unfortunately, there was something else brewing, and it was not mentioned to me by the VA doctor who reviewed the physical's results with me ... **I was pre-diabetic at that time and should have begun treating the early symptoms then—back in 2005!**

Enemy Sanctuary Exists No Longer

1ST BDE – The dense jungles of the Hobo Woods, 54 kms northwest of Saigon no longer exist. A 56-day combined land-clearing and search and destroy operation conducted by the 25th Div's 1st Brigade has leveled 90 percent of the 13,000 acre former Viet Cong sanctuary. Specially equipped helicopters are presently making daily flights over the woods spraying the secondary growth with defoliating chemicals of Agent Orange.
(Source: 25th Infantry Archives)

Agent Orange Update

At the recent Vietnam Veterans Association Leadership Conference in August 2012, which Alan Oates chaired, his following statements were published in the September edition of *The VVA Veteran* magazine:

I reviewed Agent Orange research recommendations made since 2006 by the Institute of Medicine—all of which the VA has failed to act upon. I also discussed studies that supported preconception paternal toxic exposures resulting in adverse birth outcomes. There has been a large number of these studies since the last IOM Agent Orange Review in 2010. VVA will ensure that these studies are presented to the sci-

entists on the IOM 2012 Agent Orange Review Update.

Rick Weidman, VVA's executive director for government affairs, discussed the issues of Agent Orange use and storage outside of Vietnam, including in Guam, Thailand, Laos, Cambodia, Okinawa, Korea, Panama, Puerto Rico, and many places in the continental United States. He discussed blue-water veterans and the post-Vietnam use of contaminated C123 airplanes. Weidman also reviewed VVA's ongoing legislative efforts.

We now know that when we expose troops to toxins during their military service, we subject their children and future generations to the effects of those same toxins. Let us not forget that long after "Taps" has echoed over the grave of the last Vietnam veteran the Agent Orange legacy will live on in our offspring. That is why it is important for us to get answers and action before we leave this world.

Soon we will call on the VVA membership to do its part in contacting legislators to address the need for legislation on Agent Orange and our children. We ask that each of you answer that call.

Agent Orange Strikes … Diabetes II!

My primary care doctors at the VA were rarely the same person twice during my visits for physicals, blood tests, etc. from 2005–2010. Still, I put my trust in them as they usually seemed genuinely concerned about my health.

It was in the summer of 2008 that I began to feel a lot different about my health. A sudden and explainable weight gain, which I could not turn around, worried me, but I was more concerned about my decrease in energy on a daily basis. In fact, I could not prevent myself from wanting to fall asleep during the day. Worse yet, this happened while I was driving long distances for my sales career. These new health issues had me very concerned, and nobody had answers for me.

In the fall of 2009, I literally fell asleep more times than I could count while driving, nearly crashing my car numerous times. I had no idea what was coming over me. This was so sudden!

Several times, I blacked out all of a sudden, snapping out of it each time just before encountering concrete barriers or driving off the highways. Once, I pulled off the road to rest up as I had been swerving all over the road. A couple of guys pulled up behind me to see if I was okay. They said to me, "Sir, we've been watching you for several miles. We thought you may have been drinking and almost called the police." It was midday on a Sunday and I was driving from Cleveland to Minneapolis-St. Paul, a drive I had been doing for over twenty-five years.

Then my luck ran out! In late November 2009, after a long drive to central Pennsylvania and back, just twenty miles from home, I blacked

out again. This time, however, my 2004 Hyundai Sonata crashed into a concrete barrier and bounced into it a couple more times for good measure. The car was almost totaled out, with nearly $6,000 worth of damage. I had no visible injuries except a sore shoulder, sore neck, a very bad headache, and an obvious concussion. I did not seek medical attention other than chiropractic therapy. Dizzy spells lasted for months. My VA psychologist pleaded with me to check in with the VA-ER, but I just moved on—my fault on that.

Single-car auto accidents were nothing new to me, but blacking out while I was driving while seemingly wide awake was a new and very frightening experience. Thank God no one else had been hurt, not in this mishap or in any of the previous single-car accidents. There was one casualty ... my car insurance doubled!

Two months later in January 2010, things got horribly worse. My weight soared to a new high in my life at 212 pounds. A good number for me to be at consistently was around 190. On a return drive from Michigan one day I blacked out again on the Ohio State Turnpike. I was not going very fast then, as it was raining and I was in careful mode. I even made a few extra stops at service plazas to get coffee and rest up. It did not matter. Just sixty miles from home it happened ... I blacked out again, just for an instant, but that's all it took. My car hydroplaned, sliding into steel guardrails on the right, then spun around clear over to the other side of the three-lane Ohio turnpike, crashing into the concrete wall over and over again! Windows were broken, airbags opened, the car stopped on its own—on three wheels—and I'm not sure to this day how I was able to call 911, but I did.

Again, I did not seek medical attention, although I clearly had another concussion and my neck, back, and hip were hurting. This time the car was totaled out, the same car I had just wrecked a couple of months earlier.

I had not recovered fully from the previous accident, and the dizzy spills lingered on. Now I added more insult to injury ... just how much could my body take, and why had God spared me again and again?! I thanked God one more time that no one else was hurt—just me and my auto insurance rates.

Needless to say, these incidents were scaring the crap out of someone else besides me ... my lovely wife, Ginny. She was no stranger to my single car-accidents, and she had heard the stories from my buddies about my earlier mishaps before we married in August 1984. But these last two crashes were different. They happened for different and mysterious reasons. I was not driving with reckless abandon as I was in the earlier years. What was going on with my body ... my brain?

My car insurance company cancelled me, so I was back on high-risk insurance as I was in the 1970s when I was crashing cars and getting speeding tickets at light speed. Nor did I care because surely, I wasn't long for this world anyway—this was the mentality I carried back then.

Again, my VA psychologist pleaded with me to check into ER because of the dizzy spells, but I did not. However, because of my blackouts he insisted that I get another doctor at VA as my primary provider, so I did.

A new primary care doctor examined me in the fall of 2010 and it was then relayed to me for the very first time that **I was diabetic**. My initial reaction was shock. *Not me. How could this happen? When did it happen? Why did it happen and how long have I had this condition?!* I kept asking these questions. Why was this sprung on me so unexpectedly?

One must understand something. I had been in the care of other VA doctors for six years, taking regular physicals, and no one—I mean NO ONE—ever alerted me to a sugar problem to be concerned with.

- NO WONDER I was falling asleep in midday!
- NO WONDER my energy level had digressed markedly in recent years!
- NO WONDER I was experiencing blackouts on long drives and tiring much more easily than I ever had!
- NO WONDER I had gained over thirty pounds (I was now up to another all-time high of 217 pounds) and still climbing!
- NO WONDER I had two serious car accidents within a couple of months of each other!

How could the previous VA doctors not have caught this? They all missed it! As it turned out, my medical records showed that I was pre-diabetic when I took my first physical ever with the VA back in 2005. Agent Orange had been working on me back then—and how! No one on either side of my family has ever had a history with diabetes. On my mother's side, cancer was the biggest killer. On my biological father's side, the major life terminator for the Trimmers was old age. Living well into the upper nineties was common for a Trimmer. My father passed away at ninety-eight, and two of his sisters (my aunts) were closing in on age ninety-five in 2012.

Okay, enter lifestyle changes—OR DIE EARLIER THAN PLANNED!

New Problems – Early 2012

Because it went undetected for several years, diabetes had already caused seemingly irreversible health problems of major concern, such as:

1) <u>Spinal Decay</u> – disc deterioration
2) <u>Jawbone Decay</u> – gum infections/need for bone grafts
3) <u>Vision Problems</u> –eye retinopathy and retinal hemorrhaging; blurriness common now; vision worsening constantly
4) <u>Sleep Disorders</u> – still sluggish, falling asleep in midday
5) <u>Blood Pressure</u> – was already on meds for PTSD; recently an increase was required to control elevated BP
6) <u>Joint Problems</u> – fingers, wrists, knees with numbness and tingling.
7) <u>Carpal Tunnel Syndrome</u> – in both hands. Had one surgery done already—commonly seen in people with diabetes.

On August 13, 2012, I had an MRI performed on just one hand. This was not done through the VA. I consulted a private care facility called Advanced Diagnostics in Beachwood, Ohio. Their findings verified what I had been suspecting for the past year or so … neuropathy in the left hand.

Just over one month later, I was examined by a VA podiatrist on September 6, 2012, and the findings at that examination were positive for some neuropathy in both feet.

If someone has diabetes, he/she is at increased risk of various bone and joint disorders. Factors such as nerve damage (diabetic neuropathy) may contribute to these problems.

Diabetes can cause changes in the musculoskeletal system, which includes muscles, bones, joints, ligaments, and tendons. These changes can cause numerous conditions that may affect fingers, wrists, shoulders, neck, spine, and/or feet.

Osteoarthritis is a joint disorder characterized by the breakdown of joint cartilage. People with type II diabetes are said to have an increased risk of osteoarthritis.

Dupuytren contracture is the deformity in which one or more fingers become bent toward the palm. They may lock or stick and pop. This condition is due to metabolic changes related to diabetes.

Carpal tunnel syndrome is frequently seen in people with diabetes, as is trigger finger (locking of fingers).

Those are just some of the conditions that were/are in place, so going forward I am trying to prevent increased damage with these vital functions. Just taking it day by day. Okay, so now it appears time to implement some lifestyle changes OR DIE EARLIER!

At the time of this writing, my claim with Veterans Administration for Agent Orange-caused type II diabetes had not been approved. It was filed in

October 2010 after I was officially diagnosed with diabetes II by a VA doctor.

Vietnam veterans continue to struggle mightily with a long list of ailments caused by our exposure to Agent Orange. And it sure doesn't make us feel any better knowing that our country's government dealt the deadly act of spraying these toxic herbicides on us.

Heck, in 2009, French scientists researched and proved that one common brand of Roundup's ingredients—polyethothoxylated tallowamine (POEA)—was capable of killing embryonic, placental, and umbilical cord cells in humans. **Roundup is far less potent than Agent Orange!**

Yes, indeed, many Vietnam veterans and their families' frustrations were soothed over by the Agent Orange Act of 1991, which did establish presumed connections between exposure to Agent Orange and a growing list of illness and deadly diseases. However, the Agent Orange Act of 1991 cannot give us our health back, nor can it bring back the unknown thousands of Vietnam veterans who have died over the last forty-plus years from these diseases now.

Many of us are being compensated and taken care of by VA medical professionals. However, there are still many tens of thousands of Vietnam veterans who have not received any treatment or compensation … **IT IS FOR THEM AND THEIR FAMILIES THAT I WROTE THIS BOOK!**

VA to Adjust List of Agent Orange Disorders

By Patricia Kime
Staff Writer
Posted: Friday, August 17, 2012

Veterans suffering peripheral neuropathy from exposure to the toxic herbicide Agent Orange could be eligible for compensation from the Veterans Affairs Department. Early onset peripheral neuropathy is initially characterized by numbness, tingling or pins-and-needles in the extremities, progressing to symptoms of pain in hands and feet, loss of balance and weakness.

Waiting, Hoping for an Army to Die?

How would you like to be told this by your doctor … ?

Because of your exposure to those toxic chemicals in the Agent Orange that our government sprayed so generously in the Vietnam War, I am advising you and your spouse … under no circumstances should you ever consider having children!

In Fred A. Wilcox's first and second edition of *Waiting for an Army to Die*, he tells many factual accounts of such horrible experiences of Vietnam War veterans in America and Australia.

During the earliest years of the Vietnam War and afterward, if any of us went to the VA with health concerns, we were usually told, "You just have a mild case of war neurosis; take a couple of aspirin and you'll be fine."

Our government will never be able to compensate our brothers who died prematurely in the prime of their lives from Agent Orange's **toxic poisoning** of their minds and bodies.

If my claim into VA for my Agent Orange-caused diabetes is settled during or after this book is published, that would be nice as it was filed in October 2010 … over two years ago. Should I succumb from any or all of the ailments that PTSD and/or Agent Orange exposure can deliver, my obituary should read … **HE DIED IN COMBAT WHILE SERVING HIS COUNTRY.**

If there was an extension of the Vietnam War Memorial (The Wall) in Washington D.C. to include names of veterans who died prematurely after Vietnam from Vietnam War causes, it would probably stretch out to California—the left coast. This is not humorous. It is extremely sad.

Make no mistake; this angry Vietnam War veteran isn't making any plans to go underground just yet. I kind of like my life in this great country. And I will fight whoever or whatever confronts my path to living for as long as our great God wills it. **Preserving the life of a Vietnam War combat veteran is a lifelong commitment … I'M ALL IN!**

Diabetes Mellitus Type II and Agent Orange

The website www.publichealth.va.gov states this about Vietnam veterans with type II diabetes mellitus:

> *Vietnam veterans who develop type II diabetes mellitus and were exposed to Agent Orange or other herbicides during their military service **do not have to prove a connection** between their disease and military service to be eligible to receive VA disability compensation.*

Again, fellow Nam brothers/sisters … **we do not have to prove a connection between our type II diabetes and military service if we were exposed to Agent Orange** during our little vacation in the Nam.

The years of 1967, 1968, and 1969 saw nearly 15,000,000 of the total 19,000,000 gallons of Agent Orange that were sprayed from 1961–1971.

- III Corps received 4,086,229 gallons.

- I Corps received 2,355,322 gallons.
- II Corps received 1,054,406 gallons.
- IV Corps received 669,534 gallons.

The specific areas hit hardest with Agent Orange spraying were as follows:

- Phouc Vinh   643,769 gallons   III Corps
- Katum   558,815 gallons   III Corps
- Firebase Jewell   372,860 gallons   III Corps
- Cu Chi – Dau Tieng 300,690 gallons   III Corps

N E W S F L A S H ... our units of the 25th Infantry Division fought in 1967–1969, fought in III Corps, and we fought in those areas of III Corps that were most heavily drenched with Agent Orange herbicides.

Special Salute—Agent Orange Fighter!

In the September/October 2012 Issue of *The VVA Veteran* magazine, Dale Sprusansky wrote a brief and powerful article about George Claxton.

Claxton served as chair of the Vietnam Veteran Association's Agent Orange Committee for over a decade. He also started the Michigan Agent Orange Commission and continues to work tirelessly to bring awareness of the damages Agent Orange has caused to so many people who served or lived in Vietnam.

Claxton has taken five return trips to Vietnam since the war ended. Each trip re-motivates him to continue his long fight to prove Agent Orange is every bit as lethally toxic as the countless scientific studies suggest. He also said how saddening it is to see the many deformed children living in the most heavily sprayed areas surrounding Saigon. He believes we Vietnam veterans were shafted by our government and the chemical companies, and he plans to continue his work to prove the truth. **Thank you, George!**

*THEY Won't Believe This!

Most readers of *Condemned Property?* will already be aware of the Vietnam War veterans' fight with our own U.S. government. But most Americans, especially those who were war babies of our war, have probably just skimmed past our chapter in the history books, and they could not be aware of the battles being waged by Vietnam veterans on behalf of ALL VETERANS of today's wars and future wars. We simply cannot allow the U.S. government to continue getting away with the inhumane treatment of our brave soldiers.

Chapter 17

THE ITALIAN PRINCESS SAVES A LOST WARRIOR

Every one of us who survived the Vietnam War and is alive today is dying. Some of us will die sooner than others, and the cowards who sent us to Vietnam while they hid in their posh offices in Washington D.C. have left a legacy for Vietnam combat vets that will ensure a faster death for us than God had planned for us.

Because of my PTSD and diabetes (both from Nam), today I have one of the most difficult tasks before me that I have ever had to do in my life: maintain an entirely different lifestyle. I seem to be past the suicidal thoughts, conscious or subconscious. And really, other than Nam's nightmares haunting me more than ever during the last decade or so, my life has been on a very positive path ever since I met and married Ginny Brancato on August 29, 1984 on my fortieth birthday. But oh, the baggage Ginny took on when she met me. Those earliest years were exceptionally tough on her—on both of us. Regardless, Ginny has hung in there and stood by my side every step of the way. Ginny has become my best friend!

Ginny Brancato Trimmer (GBT) invaded my bachelorhood and made a domestic makeover like Grant took Richmond, and all I wanted to do was make her my wife! Little did I know that this spunky, very cute little Sicilian doll was sent to rescue me. Oh, I haven't stopped my life of adventure seeking, just toned it down a wee bit. This has proven to be a healthy move for my own well-being and those around me. And this makes GBT a happy puppy.

Ginny Brancato Trimmer was on the bad end of a very unhappy time in her life when we met. A bad divorce. She was pretty much disowned by every close family member except her loving children. But they were separated from their mother and terribly confused, and GBT was broken-hearted. I doubt that any of GBT's children know the truth to this day about what she went through. GBT would never tell them—I know that for sure. She has forgiven everyone. That's how wonderful GBT is.

Hey, maybe God meant for me to survive Vietnam to bring GBT and her kids back together, and our marriage was meant to do just that. If so, that was an extremely meaningful assignment for me, one that I was trained for by the U.S. Army, one that I gained precious experience for on the battlefields of Vietnam … in a strange way, I guess.

I doubt that GBT's children feel as though anyone saved them because I met their mother, fell in love with her, married her, and reunited them. I think one of them might—maybe even two of them … maybe. That's okay. I'm glad to have entered their lives. GBT knows that, and she reassures me from time to time with a warm hug and "thank you, honey." That tides me over.

Prior to GBT, I had already wrecked and totaled five cars, so at least she did not have to face that part of my life with me. Well … yes, she did. In 1990 or so, while driving at a very reasonable speed, I was driving Joe's pickup truck (one of GBT's sons) and I lost control of the vehicle on a wet, backcountry road. Joe's pickup hydroplaned, spun around a couple times, and landed in someone's front yard—with a large tree branch protruding through the driver's side of the windshield. Yes, the driver's side! I survived that one too, with bruises, scratches, and a concussion. Joey's pickup was a goner, **totaled out!**

Twenty years later, GBT had to endure two more of my auto crashes within a three-month period. These were Nam-related as I was diabetic now, but did not know it. I blacked out both times while driving—again no one was with me, which was most fortunate. The second of the two almost back-to-back accidents **totaled out the car.** Again … bruises, scratches, and a concussion were my only damages. Oh yes, there was one other damage. GBT was becoming stressed out again over my haphazard tendencies. Neither of us was aware that I had diabetes and that it was working against me now without my knowing it.

Laughter with GBT is common. We make each other laugh. Her cute humor and my seriously dry humor make for an interesting and challenging relationship.

Growing up has never been one of my dream things to do too quickly. Lots of males live the Peter Pan syndrome well into their thirties or forties. But hey … I am closing in on the big 7-0 in a couple of years—time to stop breaking my toys, one would think.

Maybe it is also time to stop hating those who sent us to Vietnam and those who showed their disrespect toward us when we came home? NAH … I'll think about that next year at this time if I'm still here.

On August 29, 2012, GBT and I celebrated our 28th wedding anniversary from the date we were married on my fortieth birthday. Nothing fancy, just a night out with a couple of neat friends, sharing the moment and reminiscing about our twenty-eight years of marriage plus one year before that.

GBT is not the adventurous type, even though she found me in a magazine classified ad—and kept me! GBT has been willing, though not exactly eager, to follow me just about anywhere. We have traveled together to places like Bangor, Maine; Boston; Lake Placid; Toronto; Gettysburg; Miami;

Naples; New Orleans; Minneapolis; Dubuque; Dallas; San Antonio/Austin; Montego Bay; Lake Tahoe; San Diego; San Francisco; Tijuana; Kansas City; Bahamas; Cancun; Carolinas; and Washington D.C. Not bad for a little lady who had never been anywhere else but Ohio to New York and back. She also gave in one time and accompanied me on a rattlesnake hunt. Even though she remained back at the camp, she did venture with me to the area we would be hunting the little reptiles … Understandably, she never went again. Nor have I tried to persuade her.

GBT has accompanied me to three of my Vietnam platoon brothers' reunions. She loved the very first reunion in 1988 when most of us saw each other for the first time since coming home from Vietnam. She would rather accompany me on one-to-one visits with the guys. I understand her preference and in some ways agree with her. GBT has even accompanied me to visits to the VA for PTSD therapy. I am proud of her for doing that—never thought I would ever think of going along with that—but things change. I think she wants to go with me again soon, especially after experiencing my recent hallucinations at night when I reached for my machete to behead the NVA that I illusioned a few times.

I might put out fish and rice for that NVA some night and maybe we'll become friends. On second thought … he might tell his colleagues and bring them some night. I'll put that one on hold for now and keep the machete close by.

Every Nam vet I have ever known has a hearing problem. Most have had it since their tour(s) in Nam, me included. Hearing aids seem to be the only solution, and I have yet to see another Vietnam vet wearing one—including me. The ringing is constant, sort of like a large conch seashell when it is put up to your ear. You just get used to it. GBT continues to believe that I have "selective hearing problems," especially when she is dishing out one of her to-do lists.

GBT has forgiven her family for accepting someone else's lies about her, but she has not forgotten what happened and I won't allow her to—I was trained or brainwashed not to forget an ambush, and GBT was ambushed. I can't change that. It's programmed into my makeup. In fact, I have a difficult time repressing my thoughts of counter-ambushing those who hurt her. They have no idea what I am capable of doing. So I pray for strength from God to restrain those thoughts.

Sometimes when I spend lengthy hours with other combat Vietnam vets, we talk about getting even. Getting back at anyone whoever wronged us—not just those lowlifes who sent us to Nam and then buried their heads in the sand while our brothers came home in body bags by the thousands every month in

1968. There goes my anger again—can you feel it? Can't help it—NO APOLOGIES!

The month of August 2012 will be remembered as one of the most pleasant in many years for me. The back-to-back visits with Curtis Daniels and his family in Dayton, Texas, was a special weekend, indeed, even though I did not like how he looked because of his Agent Orange-caused type II diabetes. He and I did share many old stories about Nam—nothing too heavy, just enough to choke us up a bit—and we laughed a bit too. I did not go down there all that way to have us both in tears. My goal was to enjoy each other's company and provide comfort to each other. Both our wives said we did that ... mission accomplished—GREAT!

Curtis Daniels will never be far from my thoughts, and I will visit him again whenever possible. He is my brother.

The month of August also brought a new friend into my life, compliments of my wife, GBT, because of a quilt she made for him. That new friend is Master Sergeant Will Craven. Master Sergeant Craven is a twenty-year active duty soldier in the U.S. Army. We hit it right off on our first meeting. He has baggage—I have baggage—we can share.

Then there is Sergeant Gary Cipa, a Vietnam veteran of the U.S. Marine Corp. Gary and I have been friends since 1980. We also hit it right off upon our first meeting thirty-two years ago. I visited Gary and his lovely wife, Sue, along with their husky son, Zac, at their home in Blandon, Pennsylvania on August 19th. Gary and I are Nam brothers too—will be for life.

I am finding that when I surround myself with people like GBT, Curtis Daniels, Will Craven, and Gary Cipa, my anger toward those who violated us becomes more manageable—barely.

Because they also have anger in a more controlled state, and I am willing to learn how to control my anger, I want to be around them and more people like them. One BIG problem is that there are fewer of us Vietnam veterans left these days and even fewer (much fewer) combat veterans, and I still have a difficult time putting much trust into a non-veteran for which I offer no apologies; that's the way it is.

Thinking about the above statement, I think that had GBT been a Vietnam combat veteran, we would have strangled each other by now.

Every day with GBT begins with a smile and a greeting of "Hi honey." Of course, her appearance to the new day comes about three hours after Bella (our 172-pound Landseer Newfoundland) has already jumped into bed, licked my entire face, and literally pushed me out of the bed. She taught herself how to do that—positioning her back against GBT and pushing me with her BIG paws.

God sent Bella to us—I know it. We lost our last BIG guy, Boo Bear, who was a mere 160-pound male (but looked like 220 pounds), an all-black Newfy who caused dozens of "black bear sighting" calls to the police in our area of northeastern Ohio. We rescued Bella from a breeder who took her back from the owners she was sold to because they abused her badly. Bella still has issues, but has come along very nicely, especially with children and me—since I am still a kid in some ways and I think she knows it.

Our dogs have always been wonderful therapy for GBT and me, and I wouldn't want to think of being without one—at least one. Since Bella is the size of two and half German shepherds, we'll stick with just one for now.

In Nam, we had scout dogs assigned to us when we were searching Vietnamese villages. They were wonderful to watch. I still remember one German shepherd scout dog in Cu Chi named Duke. Funny what you remember sometimes. Then again, there was also this pet monkey someone had—his name was Whiskey. Whiskey and Duke had issues from time to time, but the monkey rarely backed off. That always impressed us and even inspired us.

Decades after the war ended, many of us who survived the war still carry the rage that had been trapped inside us from the style of combat we were faced with on a daily basis in Vietnam. Guerilla warfare's tactics frustrated us. Booby traps, land mines, surprise ambushes followed by quick retreats back into their tunnels left us feeling like human time bombs. We wanted to retaliate instantly, but so often, we shot back at an enemy that had disappeared.

Then all of a sudden you're home, and that inner rage is still caught inside you, unfulfilled. Many of my Vietnam War buddies and I have had numerous conversations about getting our REVENGE. Yes, I am serious. Our fantasies of retaliating against those who sent us over there to die, those who were anti-war protesters, etc., would be our targets. Yes, even today these thoughts are still active in some Vietnam combat veterans' minds.

I can recall back in the late 1970s and early 1980s, several of us had met to discuss putting a plan together, where we would make our "last stand" and "take out" several local politicians who were known to be very unsympathetic toward Vietnam veterans. We had the means, the technology, the materials, and the attitude to carry out this operation, knowing it would be our last. It didn't matter to me. It was this or the mercenaries … either way I was game.

Then something unexpected happened. GBT entered my life! If she had not, I would probably be maggot food in the South American jungles or, worse yet, have died in an extremely inglorious attempt to assassinate some of those politicians we had resented so viciously. If GBT had not entered my life exactly when she did, on June 1, 1983 at Squires Restaurant in Solon, Ohio, I just would *not* be here today.

If I had not been given the business opportunity by John Pfuelb (mentioned earlier), I would not be here today. If Mr. Powell, a high school teacher, coach, and mentor, had not befriended me (we remained close friends until his death), I would not be here today.

If Pastor Schenck had not taken such a personal interest in me, I would not be here today. I have been blessed by many others who stepped into my world and cared enough to stay there with me ... and I have never been an easy one to build a close relationship with.

GBT has made my life worthwhile and she IS my world. She accepted me as me with all the baggage I carried—some of it continues to tag along. Still, GBT hangs with me.

The Italian Princess Saves the Warrior is no fairy tale. It is a true story of a lady who came into my life and rescued me from a certain path of self-destruction. Although she became my wife, in the beginning I had her at the bottom of the totem pole of my buddies. Because of my selfish ego, she had to work her way up that totem pole to become my present-day best friend. She had to work her way up to that? How self-centered and egotistical was I to put her through that ordeal. What a mess I was.

Today I feel lucky and blessed to have *earned* the privilege of having GBT by my side. I do thank God each and every day for her love, her complete forgiveness of my ways, and for helping to forge me into a better man. Even though I am still a soldier, I am a better husband, step-father, and step-grandfather than I could have ever been without GBT, my real-life princess. **THANK YOU, DEAR GOD!**

GBT – 1984

GBT in the Everglades with me – 1985

Marty Gainey (deceased), Ginny Trimmer, Bud Gainey (deceased), Smokey Ryan (deceased) – 1988

Chapter 18

CONTRIBUTIONS FROM OTHER VETERANS I HAVE KNOWN

When I mentioned the idea of this book to other Vietnam veterans whom I knew personally and/or served with in the Vietnam War, their reactions were mixed and somewhat guarded. Many said they would not be able to or did not want to talk about it. But a good portion of others were willing to participate. And when I mentioned this book to other U.S. military veterans of any war to share their feelings and opinions about Vietnam and its combatants, over-whelmingly they were sympathetic and eager to participate with comments to be published in **CONDEMNED PROPERTY? ... *Soldiers of the Vietnam War.***

What I failed to take into consideration for this project was that most Vietnam veterans (like 80 to 90 percent) did not serve in combat, so their responses to me were like this:

Dusty, I drove a truck ... I was an accountant ... I was a supply clerk ... I was a mechanic ... I served on a ship ... I was a cook ... Get the picture?

One very credible Nam vet told me that he didn't think he was qualified to sit down at the same table as the Vietnam combat vets, let alone write a story for my book. I was saddened by these types of responses and worried that maybe I had blown my horn a bit too loudly on behalf of the Nam combat vets. This made me very sorry and I have altered my attitude on the subject. I truly believe and know that without the dedicated backing of our support troops back at the base camps that many more thousands of us out in the bush **would not have come home alive. My sincerest kudos to ALL veterans of any military occupation of a hostile or non-hostile environment—THANK YOU!**

Fortunately, several non-Vietnam and non-combat veterans eventually agreed to participate in this section. And I believe the book will be much bet-ter for it.

This chapter might be the most important one for those interested in reading this book. I'll begin with the comments shared with me by a Korean DMZ Conflict veteran. When I mentioned that I was working on this book over the recent Memorial Day weekend, he made this profound statement to me:

Dusty, that's terrific. However I think you had better publish that book as soon as possible because ... I have read that Nam vets are dying at a faster rate than World War II vets and some of those guys are pushing 90 years old!

- Jim Ludwiczak
Captain – Recon Platoon Leader
U.S. Army – Korean DMZ Conflict
1968-1969

Jim lives in Owensboro, Kentucky, now where he owns a highly successful consulting firm that specializes in complicated blast designs and plans, blaster training, and many other demolition projects. Jim is a certified professional geologist.

John (Babyson) Martino
Sergeant
11 Bravo, 1st Platoon
Bravo Company
3rd 22nd 25th Infantry Division
U.S. Army – Vietnam, 1968-1969
Bronze Star – Valor, 2 Purple Hearts

Letter From A Platoon Brother

Dusty,

I was surprised but pleased to hear from you. Since life seems to work that way, you won't be surprised that I received your letter/package on the same day I arrived home after attending a group counseling session at the Veterans Center. Yes, I too, have been going through many of the feelings and dealing with the PTSD symptoms that you and so many others are currently dealing with. How strange is it that we should be facing this "enemy" forty plus years later?

*I have had a great deal of trouble maintaining contact with any of the platoon since the early reunions ... particularly the first one. That one was the most powerful experience I had felt in more than 20 years. **Something in me can't deal with that situation again**. I guess that I should have seen a hint about inner problems back then in 1988 ... but I missed it.*

It is strange that so many images are still so sharply embedded in our memory, yet I find that I cannot always put the images in the proper context. For instance ... I clearly remember your helmet being shot off your head but not where and when it happened? It's coming back to me now.

By the way, I have never had the courage to attend a "Welcome Home" event. Maybe someday I will. Take care and be well.
*   - Your Nam Brother*

Some General Thoughts

I was a child of the 50s and 60s, as were virtually all who served in Vietnam. We grew up knowing that the United States had saved the world twice in the preceding forty years (World Wars I & II) and that it was the only power in the world capable of holding the Soviet Union at bay. We were very aware of the cold war and had climbed under our desks during drills at school to protect ourselves from atomic bombs. We also grew up on John Wayne & Robert Mitchum starring in dozens of WWII movies, realizing only now that the movies never showed companies full of nineteen and twenty year olds. But then again, everything I have read indicates the average age for a serviceman in WWII was twenty-six. In any event, it was U.S.A. all the way and my country right or wrong (although wrong could not be imagined).

I was nineteen and naive when I enlisted in the Army. I was a well trained, nervous, probably somewhat gung-ho but still naïve nineteen year old infantryman when I arrived in Vietnam. I was certainly patriotic then and remain so now (although my current feelings of patriotism are tinged with confusion). I remember what it looked like outside the airplane window as we landed and how the air/heat felt once we deplaned but I cannot remember what I was feeling at the time. One of the things about the tour of duty in Vietnam that I believe worked against us from the very beginning was that, although we arrived (and departed) by the plane load, we arrived (and departed) alone. There was no unit cohesion, there were no relationships to fall back on, and there was no one you knew to guide you through the transition process. You reported to a Replacement Depot, received an assignment, received a few days of "in-country training" and were sent to your unit. You arrived at the unit either alone or with two to three other "newbies" whom you met while en-route (each of whom was also alone).

In my case, I "arrived" at Bravo Company, 3rd BN, 22nd Infantry, 25th Division at Dau Tieng with two other brand new soldiers, Billy W. Loftis and Dale Nowakowski. We were assigned weapons and sent to the range to fire and zero them. Due to our very mutual status, we quickly became friends. We were welcomed to the unit by Sergeant Manes, who was back at base due to a foot injury. He advised us that we would be assigned to 2nd (his) platoon, it was a good company/unit, we would be joining the unit in the field on Friday (Good Friday, April 12, 1968) and things had been fairly quiet. On Friday morning, Sgt. Manes advised us that the unit had been hit overnight, **there were many casualties and that we would be going to 1st platoon as the platoon had been pretty much wiped out.** *We had a couple of hours before we were to be flown out so we each took the time to write an "in the event* *of my death" letter to leave with our personal belongings. Shortly thereafter, we hit the field.*

Arriving at the LZ after the Battle of Good Friday was an experience that I will never be able to explain. It was literally life changing. That evening I was a scared, lost nineteen year old who knew he was involved in something way over his head (and missed his Mommy). After a night of turmoil, prayer, and very limited sleep, a very different person greeted the new day. Although I was still as green as can be, I was ready. Bring on the game. The frightened nineteen year old had been banished from my awareness and replaced by a gung-ho, immortal (or so I believed) infantryman, ready and eager for battle. I had totally shut down the feelings/emotions that related to my previous existence and internalized a new set of standards, standards that I had recently been trained to meet and that explained and justified the situation and environment I found myself in. Yeah, I was a whack job, but I didn't know it at the time. I didn't know it for forty years ... I thought I was normal?

We were on patrol the next day and took intermittent fire throughout. We were assigned to an ambush patrol the next night, life in the bush had started.

*The platoon and company slowly grew over the next few weeks as replacements came in but for a goodly period of time (several months at least), the platoon consisted of eight to ten people and the company totaled about forty (the expected size of a platoon). Our limited size did not limit our effectiveness however, and may have contributed to it because in the long run, we were not fighting for patriotism, we were not fighting for or against a political agenda, **we were fighting for each other.** And no closer bond exists than one developed under those conditions, in any war. We had not come as a "unit" but we had become one.*

*There was the daily challenge of patrolling in 100+ degree weather, carrying sixty or more pounds of gear through jungle or rice paddies or elephant grass (that would cut like a razor) and then digging in for the night, often in a three man position so that you could never sleep more than four hours at a time and usually less, and doing the same thing the next day and the day after for sixty to seventy days in a row, **exhaustion becoming the norm;** filling the ten sandbags you carried in your pack every night and then emptying them the next day so you could place them back in your pack, each day a little thicker and heavier; rejoicing when it rained as you could take off your fatigues and take a "shower". Until the Monsoon season that is, when you found yourself patrolling, eating and lying in the rain for days or weeks at a time. Then we prayed for a short hot spell to dry us out. And always, rain or dry, there were the mosquitoes ...*

There were many "lighter" moments also, although others may not consider them as such. There was the night we were on a forced march to join up with a sister unit experiencing heavy combat. Don "Bug" Jenner was walking point and as we traversed through a village, he turned a corner and came face to face with the point man for an NVA patrol that was coming towards us. The surprise reactions of each of the "point" men somehow resolved in such a way that no firefight developed. There was also the trip into Cambodia where we found ourselves in the middle of a huge bunker complex and supply depot, knowing if the "owners" came home, we were screwed. As we waited to be evacuated from the area, mortar rounds started to fall on the LZ. Billy W. Loftis found himself on the side of a termite mound, wanting to get down to ground level to avoid the shrapnel flying through the air but unable to as there was a pair of snakes fighting at the base of the mound. He kept trying to move up away from the snakes and down away from the mortars at the same time. Humor is where you find it.

*The platoon and company continued to expand as what would have been "the fall" at home approached, but somehow I do not remember most of the people that joined the platoon post-Buell. They would never be part of the **core unit**. As time went on, the number of "originals" remaining in the field dwindled to a precious few, as people who weren't wounded or killed were assigned much deserved rear echelon jobs. Due to my very" normal" mental state, it never occurred to me that I could/should get an assignment to the rear so I spent my tour in the field. At some point, it was suddenly mid-March of 1969 and I received orders to go home. I think it was three days from being in the field on patrol to arriving home in Boston, but it may have been four, I can't remember.*

As I noted earlier, people arrived alone and left alone. One day someone was in the field with you, the next they were gone, injured, killed, assigned to a job in the rear or rotated home and you never saw them again. There were no good-byes. *I think that is why I don't remember many of those who joined the platoon during the period of November 1968 through February 1969. I did not have the capacity to allow them "in" not knowing when they would be gone. And they would never achieve the status of the core group, they couldn't! [This is also what made the reunion of 1988 so powerful. We were able to reunite but we were also able, for the first time, to say good-bye to each other. I don't know how that was for others, but it really impacted me. When the last people left for home, I felt empty, completely drained, but I also felt like something long unfinished had finally been corrected.]*

In any event, three or four days after being in the field I found myself in dress uniform walking around in an airport in California (maybe LA?) trying to stay awake so I wouldn't miss my flight home. During that period, a group of three or four youngish people with long hair and beaded clothing (hippies, I guess) came up to me and called me a baby-killer. I was too tired to really take it in and too stunned to react so they soon left (probably in search of someone else in uniform more able to react). I continued walking until I boarded the plane for home and promptly went to sleep.

Did we (those who served) lose the war? Absolutely not. *But we could not have won it either. How can you win a war when you are not trying to capture and* *hold ground to advance into enemy territory and disrupt his supplies and ability to fight? What good is a body count if you fight for the same ground over and over again but still allow the enemy to take it back after each engagement? Did the government fail us? Yes, from the very start, but not with intention. It failed us because they believed the U.S.A. was far superior to this country of peasants and farmers and that we would quickly overwhelm them. When that did not happen, it never figured out what the new outcome was supposed to be or how we were to get there. Did our country fail us? Well, certainly a significant portion of the population lost faith in the "war" and then applied political pressure to end it, but that was their right as citizens of this great country. Unfortunately, during the process these same citizens confused the soldiers, those who served in the war we were sent to fight as the enemy, or at least let it be known that we weren't welcome" home." I guess that was their right also, but it was wrong, particularly since it was that kind of "right" we believed we were defending in Vietnam, which only led to more confusion on our part. What was worse, the year in-country or finally getting back to "the world" only to find a country that didn't want to acknowledge us?*

Anyway I had another eighteen months to serve so my final transition to civilian life in October 1970 may have been easier (or perhaps harder?) than those who were discharged when they got home.

Did the Vietnam experience have an effect on those who served? Absolutely. We were all changed by our experience, but I do not believe all of the impact was negative. No, we would never be the person we might have become had Vietnam not happened, but I believe in some ways we became "more" than we might have been without the experience.

We have seen and endured hardship when others don't even know what it is. We have traversed through the fire and emerged victorious on the other side. But there is always a price to be paid for that and many of us are still paying. We had served our country proudly and in our hearts, we knew it. Most of all, we fought and bled for each other, creating a bond that those who did not serve (or were not in combat units) will probably never understand. The real shame is that there are 58+ thousand names on a wall, names of those that "gave all" for a cause that was not worth the price, not worth one-tenth ᵇ of the price. We can't change that. I only wish we weren't still sending our young people to fight and die in foreign lands to accomplish questionable objectives. We are not the world's police force nor should we be dictating what type of government other people/nations must have. Will we never learn?

Sergeant Curtis "Tony" Daniels

Shortly after my lovely wife, Ginny, and I visited with Curtis Daniels and most of his family in August of 2012, I received his comments to be shared with the readers of my book. One clarification about Curtis; he carried four nicknames: "Tex" by his own self, "Sarge" by some he led, "Sergeant Tex" by

Curtis Daniels – in 1968

others he led, and "Tony" because he had curly hair in school. Sergeant Tex's comments are as follows, brief but profound:

I grew up in Louisiana and Texas. Born in Texas, I moved to the bayous of Louisiana till the seventh grade. We moved back to Texas, where I have lived the rest of my life except for my one-year vacation in that southeast Asian country we called Nam.

I grew up with white kids and Mexican kids. I was never preju-diced, so when I got into the Army, I always treated everyone the same no matter what race they were.

Fort Polk, Louisiana is where I was sent for Basic Training and Advanced Infantry Training (AIT) and then Fort Benning, Georgia for Combat Non-Com-missioned Officer School. The training at both places was real good. Since I grew up in the woods of Louisiana and Texas, I felt at home in most areas of Vietnam. And I felt like I had already been to Nam when I got there.

Fort Benning taught us "Mission First" but I always believed the men were first and then the mission, which is what I chose to practice in Nam.

My first night in Vietnam was in a hooch in base camp. We got mortared by Viet Cong that night, which was common, I was told, but we all jumped out of our bunks and crawled under them real quick as this wasn't a war game anymore. **WEL-COME TO THE NAM,** *everyone told us that night.*

When I got there as a buck sergeant, they made me a squad leader which included ten to twelve men usually. I remember that first squad I had real well. They were very good from the start and we worked well together. After just two months, as we suffered casualties, I became platoon sergeant and now I had twenty to as many as forty men under me, but we rarely kept it at forty for very long. One of my jobs was to go to meetings and get out mission's details for the day, then let the men know what was going on and then … get it done.

The First Platoon was my responsibility for my first several months, and some of the men I remember well were Trimmer, Nowakowski, Jenner, Ryan, Best, Par-ris, Karakas, Loftis, Martino, Davenport, Taylor, Tetting, Sheldon. There were many others that came and went.

Later in my year when the Second Platoon lost its leaders, I took over the Second Platoon and Sergeant Broussard took over the First Platoon. They became very good, too.

Our main areas of operation had names like Dau Tieng, Cu Chi, Tay Ninh, Nui Bau Dinh. Most of our time was spent on recon missions in the daytime and then we conducted ambush patrols at nighttime. I don't know which we like the worst.

We believed in never leaving a man's body behind, dead, wounded, alive; no one was left behind EVER! If anyone was trapped by enemy ambush, we went after them with a vengeance with as much fire power that we could dish out, for as long as it took
*... **UNTIL EVERY MAN WAS SAFE!***

Pretty much everywhere we went, Agent Orange was sprayed. It was in every stream, swamp, bomb crater—everywhere. Not only did we have to breathe that defoliant, maybe eat it too, but it affected the Vietnamese people too, including women and children.

I have diabetes type II, kidney failure and consequently, other problems related to my diabetes, which was caused by Agent Orange.

On our way over to Nam we were told not to get real close to anyone. I guess 'cause they wouldn't be around long. But I felt as if every G.I. near me, whether under me or not, was family to me. I treated them all equal, but made sure they knew that I was "Boss" at all times.

Curtis and Patsy Daniels – 2012

The Vietnamese kids were something else. They were rarely scared of us and were always trying to sell us a cold Pepsi or beer—which we rarely had out in the bush. They mostly liked us and we treated them pretty well, too, although we had to remain extremely vigilant at all times— never letting our guard down. The older Viets were more cautious towards us, possibly because the VC were always watching them or maybe some of them were VC. We could tell that some of the older adults really hated the Americans.

When we came home, we seemed to be treated many different ways. The west coast showed us some pretty unfriendly receptions. In the south, we were treated much better than G.I.s were in the northern states.

I know a lot of the guys have had many problems after they got home. They couldn't sleep or talk much to people and many of them still have those problems. Other than my diabetes, which is enough to deal with, I never experienced any other problems.

About twenty years after we had been back from Nam, members of the First Platoon assembled in Boston for a twenty-year reunion in 1988. It was hosted by John Martino and his family. There were about fifteen of us; that was all that could be found. Our families also came and we all got along very well. We had a couple more after that one and they were very good too.

*I had married Patsy Manning in 1972, just a few years after returning from Nam. We are both practicing Christians and still married for forty years. We have four children and six grandchildren—I love them all. **We have been very blessed.***

(Note: Curtis Daniels was hospitalized at the time this book was completed. His condition was critical and he passed away on April 3, 2013.)

Curtis "Tex" "Tony" Daniels had his share of demons when he came home from Vietnam, and they almost destroyed him before he met his true love, Patsy, and the beautiful family they had together. Curtis' love for his Lord, Patsy, and family allowed him no more room for anger.

Curtis' short story of his own life for *Condemned Property?* doesn't tell the whole story about this fine American hero. So, what kind of a man was our fallen platoon sergeant? Here is a brief description about him by his loving brother, John P. Daniels, written just three days before Curtis lost his final battle—or, as Curtis would have said, before his final *victory*, as he would soon meet his Lord.

Excerpts from John P. Daniels – Received April 8, 2013

MY BROTHER
Curtis (Tony) Daniels Jr.

I have had the opportunity to meet so many influential people throughout my life. Those of great wealth, famous athletes, politicians and religious leaders; but in my mind Tony Daniels is the greatest man that I have ever known. No, they will not have a television documentary heralding the fetes of his life, nor will we ever read about him in the history books; but those that knew him best will never forget him. The local newspaper will dedicate a couple column inches to his history in the form of his obituary, and that will be the end of his recorded history. Well, I think that he deserves more than that.

One day, Tony, with his twisted sense of humor, took great pleasure in mounting Ole Red, [our Tennessee walker horse], hitching a rope to the tongue of our Red Flyer wagon and pulling his not-so-brilliant younger brothers for what seemed to be a hundred mile ride. He then dropped the rope and went galloping off. You could hear him laughing all the way back to the house.

As kids we had our own shotguns, hatchets and knives; and lived like little pioneers. We built our own log cabin, made our own fishing poles, rode in goat-carts (not go-carts), caught a ton of crawfish, learned to farm, skinned squirrels and rabbits, butchered hogs; and on, and on, and on. I have just decided to write a book about this period of our lives, and I would bet that it will put Mark Twain's Tom Sawyer to shame. This period in Tony's life would probably best explain his love for the simpler things in life.

Our father was a well-loved and respected man, but he was plagued with an awful temper and abusive nature which led our mother to leave him in the winter of '56 and we moved to Houston to be near her family. We stayed with her brother for a few months, but Mother was very proud and independent and had to be on her own. She rented a very small one-bedroom house for the four of us in Golden Acres and worked two jobs to support her precious three little angels. (Mother never saw us as we really were.) As you might imagine, this placed Tony in the position of man-of-the-house. Now I can tell you with no reservations, he relished his position of authority. On the other hand, our brother, Dan was not so pleased with this arrangement, which probably explained their getting into fights on a daily basis. Do not get the wrong idea. Even though we would fight each other at the drop of the hat when we were youngsters, there has never been any brothers that were closer than us."

When Tony came home from the war he began drinking heavily; and I am not talking Pepsis. Within a year, he had racked up three DWIs and was faced with the likelihood of going to prison. That is when things started looking up!!! Up until that time, Tony had not much use for church or anything to do with it. Our extended family (aunts, uncles, cousins) made up about half of the congregation of the Second Baptist Church of Deer Park, and our pastor, Rev. Jack Wright volunteered to go to court with him when the time came. I am not sure if anyone knows exactly what was said and done that day, but Tony came home a free man and his life was changed forever. BTW, he accepted Jesus that day.

Well, we had a lot of match-maker ladies in that church and they could not stand that Tony was in his twenties, good-looking and single. There was a cute, slim, freckle-faced redhead named Patsy Manning that had been going to that church for most of her life and they decided that she was the one for him. I am not sure that Tony or Patsy had any say in the matter, but they were married in less than a year. I guess those little ladies were right. They say that there is a strong lady behind every great man. My brother could have searched the world over and never found anyone more perfectly suited for him. Patsy, I thank you for being so faithful and good to him. You are the one that deserves a medal!

Now after reading this mundane story you might ask me why I think of him as the greatest man I have ever known. Well, he is the only truly successful man I have ever known. The simplest things made him happy. He worried not about riches, fame, esteem, rank or all of the things of this world that most of us aspire to. All that concerned him was that his family and friends were doing well. He was totally selfless. I will never forget our last telephone conversation. He was so very ill, but his major concern was the drain that he was putting on Patsy.

When one brother would introduce another brother to a friend, the one that was being introduced would always say, "Yeah, I am the good-looking brother." This would always be followed by bantering back and forth. Well, Tony, if you are reading this too, (and I am sure that you are), I herewith concede that you were the most beautiful of us all because your HEART could be seen in your every act and deed. Until we meet again, via con Dios.

- John Daniels, Brother of Curtis Daniels

Bill White
Sergeant
United States Marine Corps; 1967 – 1971
South Vietnam, 1970

Everyone needs his memories. They keep the wolf of insignificance from the door.
-Saul Bellow

Once a Marine – From Campus to Dogpatch

Sometimes I'm sorry Vietnam wasn't the hell hole for me as it was for others. It was another world in 1970, the last and best year of my greatest adventure—the United States Marine Corps. Even today, when someone asks me to recite my greatest accomplishment I simply tell them that I kept my name off of The Wall.

Four years earlier, I knew college was not for me, at least in 1967. I enlisted. I became a Hollywood Marine. The recruiter said I had a choice and San Diego looked better than Parris Island. One reason Vietnam was less of a hellhole than I expected was that boot camp and infantry training at Camp Pendleton had already taken the cake. My California dreaming knocked the abstraction of endless TV news and body counts clear out of my head. My drill instructors—all Vietnam vets—planted a new reality squarely on my chest. There was nothing politically correct about Marine Corps boot camp in February, 1967. March or die, maggot.

The Marines value teamwork above all else. Our first lesson beyond the yellow footprints and shaving of the head was the command to "fall in". It was a quick lesson. We drilled incessantly. Those who did well were assumed smarter, leaders. I was a musician in high school and college. I traded my clarinet for an M-14. That magnificent hellish grinder in San Diego, home to Gomer Pyle, was band camp with teeth, a perfect equalizer for me, a non-athlete. We ran incessantly. For this one-twenty pound (wet) recruit, running was easy. Marching was easy. Music was my ticket.

When we got to the obstacle course, however, my gig was up. No upper body strength. Underweight. How in the hell did you get into my Marine Corps you maggot? They stuck me in the fat farm, a special platoon reserved for the large and out of shape. They doubled my rations, forced me to scarf up high protein shakes and calories four times a day, all with adult supervision under a Smokey Bear hat as my fellow recruits looked on, hating my guts.

In April, out of the fat farm, back in a mainstream platoon and now approaching my fourth month in boot camp I finally climbed the rope (the Marine Corps version – no knots); I aced the peg board and obstacle course, and joined my drill instructor by running the last half mile of our three-mile test with him—backwards. I now had the attitude.

I graduated second in my platoon. R.L. Jones, PFC beat me by a point. He was my first black friend, one of many blacks, Asians, Hispanics, Native Americans and Pacific Islanders that underscored the blessed reality that the only color in the Marine Corps is green. My platoon kicked ass in marksmanship, physical conditioning and academics. Graduation day on the grinder in May, 1967, with R.L. Jones carrying the guidon above our first place streamers was the proudest day of my life. Looking on was my commanding officer, Captain Charles C. Krulak, son of the Commandant, a tough officer who would himself become the Commandant of the Marine Corps. We were tight, we were blessed, we were bad, we were trained killers and we would die for one another. Some of us did.

Following an intense ITR (Infantry Training Regiment) at Camp Pendleton, I was designated an MOS 3071, Aviation Supply. What a crock. I wanted avionics. All Marines, me included, were automatically classified as infantry, MOS 0311. Now I was destined to be an office pogue. In June of 1967 I arrived at Naval Supply School, Millington (Memphis), where I spent the hot Tennessee summer learning the Naval Supply System. The upside—there were BAMS in our school. Broad-ass-Marines. Women. They were as tough as nails and we gave them no quarter. I respect them to this day.

In October I was bound for a place I'd never heard of—MCAF, New River, North Carolina. I was soon attached to Wing Headquarters Group Supply. We supported the helicopter squadrons as new pilots trained on strafing runs and ferrying grunts from Camp Lejeune. I learned all about the Huey, CH-46, CH-53 and later the Huey Cobra. I could recite part numbers for rotor blades, TACANS, actuators and engine parts. I often flew with the squadrons as they lifted off for MedCruise gigs on amphibious assault carriers out of Morehead City, only to return to my routine back at the base where I bartended after hours and eventually formed a band, The Prophets of Doom, with some Marines from Cherry Point. That's another story.

We never got close to our pilots; they were passing through, training with us for only a few months. The helicopter squadrons staged at New River before deploying to our home-away from-home, Da Nang. The squadron folks were tight and kept to themselves. Pilots and crew chiefs were vulnerable. The scuttlebutt connection between

New River and Marble Mountain a half a world away was a low-grade buzz feed. We knew about the losses, when and where, birds and people, tail numbers and faces, when and why they happened. Hydraulics, avionics, airframe and weapons dudes doubled as door gunners manning the M-60s port and starboard in the CH-46s and, when there was room, the Hueys and CH-53s. Later they would dip into the supply squadrons and we pogues would have our day.

In December, 1969, I was promoted E-5, the highest rank I could attain without reenlisting. My after-hours gig with the band, now a coastal Carolina chicken-wire babe magnet with a following in frat houses, dives and oyster bars along the Crystal Coast from Atlantic City to Wilmington, was replaced with orders for WestPac. This is what the Marine Corps called anything in the Western Pacific which, at the time, included Hawaii, Japan and Okinawa, the Philippines and the big show – Vietnam, where the Marines were based largely in I-Corps, the northernmost province of South Vietnam. My music was over.

When I left stateside, I did not know where I would end up until I passed through Camp Butler, the staging battalion on Okinawa, home to the famous thick and gooey gamma globulin shots for the plague. Since the Marines were active in and around Da Nang, Hue, Phu Bai, Chu Lai and numerous firebases in the north, I assumed I might be reunited with some of my buds from New River, plus other airdales from Santa Ana, California, the West Coast helicopter group.

Ironically, my greatest fear on Okinawa was that I would not make it to the show. Being an office pogue was bad enough; sitting out the war at a backwater base was not an option. I pleaded for Vietnam and I got it.

My flight from Kadena Air Force base to Da Nang was on a brightly colored Braniff International civilian charter jet painted by some Italian branding guru who thought sailing a popsicle into a combat zone was a good idea. This flight was the first of many outrageous experiences that confirmed the tales of Joseph Heller (Catch-22), M*A*S*H (Korea) and Good Morning Vietnam. By coincidence, a hometown friend, Mick McBride, sat next to me on the way over.

After a chilling reception on Hill 327, I took a jeep to the Headquarters Group compound adjacent to LZ-11. We were on the crap side of the Da Nang airbase, a place they called Dogpatch. At check-in I made my required visit to the Chaplain's office, walked in through the Memorial Chapel and saw a Hammond C-3 organ in the sanctuary. I'd just left my B-3 in North Carolina, certain I'd not see a keyboard again, ever. The Hammond is the signature keyboard for bands of the 60s, 70s and 80s, from Tommy James and the Shondells to Blood Sweat & Tears, Chicago, Chase, Crosby Stills & Nash and almost every wanna be group around the world.

Who plays the organ, I asked. He just shipped out, back to the world, said Jeff, the Ph.D. draftee from Minnesota, now a Chaplain's assistant who quoted Saul Bellow constantly. Why do you ask? I play keyboards, I said. He turned and said I'll be back and he left.

Chaplain Carnes walked into the office. What's your duty, son, he asked. Wing Supply, sir. Who is your commanding officer? Captain Kayloh, sir, but I've not seen him yet. The next thing I knew I was in front of the Headquarters Group commanding officer with the Chaplain, barely three hours in country, and already pissing off a superior officer I'd never met.

Here's the drill Sgt. White, said the Group Commander. We need an organist. There's no MOS for that. So I'm issuing an order that no matter what you do or where you go in this God-forsaken country, you'll have your ass back on this compound no later than 0730 Sunday morning, every Sunday, and provide uplifting music for the Lutheran service at 9AM, the Protestants at 10:30AM and those Catholics at noon. You will not be wounded, you will not be KIA, MIA or otherwise injured in any way, and you will learn The Navy Hymn (Eternal Father). Are there any questions, he asked. Sir, I responded, when should I practice? Son, make that Saturday, he said. I want you back on the compound in time for chow Saturday evening.

LZ-11 was my new home. It was spooky; across the road was the exit visa. I didn't know the official name; we called it First Morgue, a metal building located at the north end of the runway at the Da Nang airbase. Coffins were brought in by ship, off-loaded at the deep water pier and trucked to a staging area between the morgue and the dump where the sappers would hide, ready to fire a tracer round up the tailpipe of an F-4 doing a hot fuel on the runway. The coffins were stacked like rotor blade containers. Every week I watched the pile dwindle as fresh pallets were brought in to restock. I thought about the logistics. What is the lead time on coffins, stock number, minimum order quantity, price, account to debit, specifications, nomenclature. Let's see, Coffin, Military, Silver, Unfinished, Unit of Issue: Each. Order Quantity: Dozen. Does not include body bag.

A combat zone can be remarkably boring. I went about my business as an E-5 leading a platoon of sixty guys, mostly office pogues like me. We weren't grunts but we followed orders. Sometimes the war came to us—out on the wire, a grenade over the fence, rockets fired from the other side of Hill 327 scoring a random hit somewhere, anywhere. We grew to ignore the sirens. But we lost two office pogues, Robby Hanvey and Billy McTaggart. Their names are on The Wall, June, 1970. It was a bad month.

The grunts took the brunt of the war, of course; they always do. They were easy to spot, the Marines, Army, the Australians and South Koreans who were over to lend a hand and got an occasional in-country R&R up the road at China Beach. They had no time for rear echelon chicken shit or people like us. Who could blame them. Their world was different than ours, yet we occasionally entered theirs and they ours. The grunts clearly resented office pogues, as if it was our choice to sit on our asses ordering rotor blades instead of slogging through the razor grass and mud. I was not in the mood to apologize for following orders then, nor do I apologize now. The rockets that sailed over Hill 327, the sappers that sniped from the dump, the turds who threw grenades over the fence, none of them discriminated. Shrapnel was shrapnel. And the last time I checked, the hostile fire pay was the same.

One Saturday night I was in the Chapel playing Eric Satie's Variations on a Theme, which you'll remember from the Blood Sweat & Tears album Child is Father to the Man. Someone in a recently arrived detachment of the Marine Corps Band stashed in a hooch nearby heard the music. It turned out these dudes had been deployed to Quang Nam province for ceremonial events associated with command transfers to the South Vietnamese Army. When not on duty or on perimeter guard smoking weed, they worked out charts for some emerging rock bands taking the USA by storm. Being musicians, they started a pick-up band on the compound, The Mash Sinners, which was heavy on brass, reeds and percussion but they were without a keyboard player. The next day they jumped rank and requested me for some temporary duty through a most unlikely command channel: the US Navy Chaplains' Corps. For several months, the band was booked into enlisted, NCO and officers' clubs throughout the province, whenever we could be spared. Grunts were dying and the band played on.

But, buoyed by my mother's constant admonishment to practice, practice, practice, I was able to leverage my mediocre keyboard proficiency into a counterpoint experience to helicopter gunships, endless supply missions to firebases throughout the country, and in grunt-speak, sitting on my ass.

Music – and a little luck – kept my name off The Wall. Music had given me a head start into boot camp where close order drill was an extension of band camp but without the girls. Music kept me occupied during my years at Camp Lejeune and gave me an unofficial and unexpected purpose in Vietnam, playing keys for endless memorial services for the pilots and crew members we lost in I Corps throughout 1970.

My days and nights were interrupted by an occasional and terrifying gig on a CH-46, usually manning the port M-60, in and out of a firebase, on a medivac mission or ferrying a USO group to God knows where. We flew often, fetched people and animals from monsoon floods in the mountains, transported a pregnant mamasan and her family's water buffalo on the same flight. We spent Christmas, 1970 at the China Beach Orphanage, me playing music on a beat-up piano while the nuns sang timeless carols in French and Vietnamese and the locals served exotic dishes. Later, we celebrated TET with an impromptu festival on the compound, complete with music and food. I thought why can't we work this out with a fucking potluck dinner, North and South, exchange recipes, and just go home.

January 1971, I was short enough to sit on a dime and dangle my feet. Suddenly, it was over, fifty-one weeks and four days, just like that. I turned in my M-16 and .45, checked out, made it up to Hill 327 and over to the runway to board a Pan AM jet where babes and beer were the signature dish. After wheels up and a quick turn out east over the South China Sea we were done. Sitting next to me, once again, my hometown buddy Mick.

Homecoming? There was none, and none expected. My parents met me in Columbus and that was enough for me. I was a Vietnam Veteran, proud then and more so now. I take a strange comfort when I hear my baby boomer friends express remorse over sitting it out on exemptions, medical deferments, whatever. Today they know that they missed the greatest adventure of our generation and they often ask me what it was like. You had to be there, I say.

I was with a client in Singapore a few years ago and I had a young technical writer working next to me in the office. One Friday I asked her what she was doing for the weekend. Going home, she said. Where is home, I asked. Vietnam, she replied; have you ever been there? Yes, I smiled, nodded and watched her face as she slowly did the math and put me at a time and place that was well before hers.

She laughed. Would you like to go back, she asked. Yes, I said. Why, she asked. To eat, I said. She smiled and said come with me and my boyfriend tonight. My family would love to meet you. I would love to meet them.

I had neither the time nor the visa to make the trip, but on that Friday in Singapore, tucked away in an office on Changi Road, with a sweet, smart and articulate young woman at my side, born of parents who may have been North or South – it didn't matter – the Vietnam War was finally over for me and once again I longed to leave a beautiful Asian country and go home to Ohio.

Today, married for forty years with two children and two grandchildren, I believe joining the United States Marine Corps as a teenager and committing myself to my country for four years was the best decision I ever made. I would do it all over again.

Since then, nothing in business or otherwise has presented a challenge that I have not confronted with a kick-ass attitude and a response: What can they do, cut off my hair and send me to the 'Nam?

There are 58,185 names on The Wall. There are thousands more hurt, sick, wounded in spirit, yet survivors, me among them. I am one lucky son of a bitch.

Semper Fi.
Bill White, SGT, USMC, 1967-1971
CEO, Offenberger & White Inc.

Eternal Father

Eternal Father, grant, we pray,
To all Marines, both night and day,
The courage, honor, strength, and skill
Their land to serve, thy law fulfill;
Be thou the shield forevermore
From every peril to the Corps.

Robert (Bobby) Best
Sergeant
11 Bravo, 1st & 2nd Platoon
Bravo Company
3rd 22nd 25th Infantry Division
U.S. Army, Vietnam 1968 – 1970
U.S. National Guard 1970 – 1975
2 Purple Hearts
Army Commendation – Valor

We had dug down about two feet when I hit gravel. This was going to be a small foxhole because I could dig no deeper. Neither could anyone else.

Hey Best, came the call and I looked up to see Beckwith standing there with a big grin on his face. My orders came in and I'm going home. I can't remember if it was because he had a hardship discharge or he was an only son. Either way, he was going home. If you got orders, what are you doing here, I asked him. Oh, I just thought I'd stay out here one more night and say good-bye to all my buddies. I'm going up to see Strupp next. See you at chow.

Bob Best and Viet kid pal

About midnight, all hell broke loose. The NVA rained mortars and rockets on us for what seemed like an eternity. There were four of us at my foxhole. I can't remember his name, but my squad leader lost his leg from the knee down. DePhilip took him back to the C.P. That left me and Beck. To make a long story short, we fought from that foxhole all night. When it was all over with at daylight, I looked over the battlefield. I had killed three NVA who had tried to sneak up on my left flank. They were almost on top of me. There was a fourth NVA soldier there that I hadn't seen. But he was dead too.

My company, Bravo Co. had seventeen killed and forty-seven wounded. I was one of the wounded. Beckwith was one of the seventeen killed!! So was Strupp. They called it "The Battle of Good Friday". We had killed close to 150 as their bodies were scattered all over the battlefield. It was April 12, 1968. I had been in Vietnam exactly one month. This was my first battle. Unfortunately, it wasn't my last. I still had another eleven months to go.

In 1979, I found myself on the tenth floor of the VA in Durham, North Carolina. All the doors were locked so that the mental patients could not escape. I had a nervous condition, is what I told them and I couldn't understand why things weren't working for me. I just had this strong feeling that I needed to blow something up. Well, they put me through these tests where they'd ask questions like: Do you ever hear voices? Yes, I do. How often? Every time someone speaks to me, I said. You got out of the army in 1970. What have you been doing? I went to a community college for a couple of years. There were a lot of draft dodgers so I didn't do too well. They talked me into joining the National Guard and <u>all</u> of them were draft dodgers. How's your love life? Well, I got problems there, too. My girlfriend is nice enough, but she's got three kids. I get along with the kids o.k. But her husband doesn't care for me a whole lot. You see, they were separated when I met her, but then he found out how much the divorce was going to cost him, so he just moved back home. His kids told me not to worry, that he would be gone pretty soon, but he didn't.

After two weeks, they gave me a personality disorder and sent me home.

May of 1981 found me right back at VA in Durham, N.C. again. I can't remember his name, but my doctor was pretty good. I was obsessed with the loss of the war. Back in April of 1975, I watched as President Ford went before Congress and asked them to help the South Vietnamese. Every Democrat voted no. The Senate was the same. The Democrats controlled both. All I could see with the fall of Saigon was the loss of 58,000 men for nothing. To this day, I have never voted for a Democrat for President, for Congress or the Senate.

I had some problems with the law too. I got drunk the night Saigon fell. Got to where I couldn't even to go sleep without a few drinks. Bourbon and coke was my main drink. If I was sick with a cold or something, the doctor always said to drink plenty of orange juice. So I would switch over to screw drivers. Bottom line, I ended up with a driving record about seven pages long. It used to be eight computer print-out pages long, but they condensed it down to seven.

This time they sent me home with a general anxiety disorder. I applied for disability. Before I left, the doctor had asked me to stay on and do a twelve-week program. I said I would, but that I needed a few days to take care of some things. He said no, you need to do it now. I said look, I've got an appointment tomorrow and I promised I would make it. He said that I needed to make some sacrifices. I told him that I had two Purple Hearts and that was enough of a sacrifice. Then I left.

The next day I went to Little Washington, North Carolina. It was May 20, 1981. I kept my appointment with Kay Currie and filmed about fifteen minutes on her program. One of the questions she asked me was, what did I think about Israel's ultimatum to Syria. I said that Israel had given them thirty days to remove the missiles they had set up, so within the next thirty days those missiles will be gone. You can take that to the bank. Then she asked me if any other country was going to have any problems. I said that I believed that Bolivia was due to have another coup attempt. The reason she was asking me these questions is because the year before I had told her that El Salvador would be next since the Sandinistas had taken over Nicaragua and that the attack would come after the first of the year, which had happened this past February.

Anyway, the show aired on May 24, 1981. Two days later, some Colonel in Bolivia took over a whole city. The next day, Israel bombed the missile sites and that was that. Next thing I knew, I was in Washington D.C. at the Salvadorian Embassy. Eventually, I went on vacation to El Salvador. I'd have to check my passport for the dates, but I did visit during the 1980s – 1992.

After my visit to D.C., I went back home and back to the VA. I told them that I was willing to go through their twelve-week program. They told me that they didn't have a bed for me and that it would be quite a while before they did. I refused to leave. They called security on me and I was escorted off the property. Thank God they wrote it down in files. This was at the end of May 1981.

In the meantime, my lawyer called me on a traffic ticket and told me that he thought that the judge was going to give jail time this time. I said, don't worry about it, I'll take care of it. Then I packed my bags and left North Carolina.

I went to Virginia Beach, got a job at a hotel. Then I got a job pouring cement. I slept on the beach using a black garbage bag to cover me, to keep sand off of me. Then I spent the winter at a homeless center. The summer of 1982, I was back at the beach working as a bus boy at Sambos. Then I got a job that took me to Houston, Texas. I traveled all over until 1985. I ended up in Lawton, Oklahoma selling life insurance. Occasionally, I took a vacation to El Salvador. Then in 1989, around January, I got sick with bronchitis. The motor in my car blew up. I lost my business. I was homeless once again. One day at the hospital, this guy asked if I would come into his office. He said he had gotten my records in from the VA in Durham, North Carolina. He asked me if I was getting any disability. I said no. He asked, didn't you ever apply? I said yes, but they turned me down. So I just forgot about it. They didn't want to help me anyway. Then he asked if I had ever heard of PTSD. I said no. He ways, well, here is a list of symptoms. I said, which ones do you think I got? Sitting at his desk, he looked up at me and said, **I THINK YOU HAVE GOT THEM ALL.**

He sent me to the VA in Oklahoma City. I was in the hospital for eight days. Then they recommended that I go to a special hospital in Topeka, Kansas. However, I had to wait until July 16, 1989 to go. That was four months I had to wait. In the meantime, Disabled American Veterans took my case and filed for disability for me. About two months later, I went before a psychologist to determine how much disability I should get. Then I got a letter telling me they had turned me down again. So I went to the Oklahoma City VA and signed a release form to get a copy of all of my records. When they came in the mail, I started reading everything. While in the hos-

pital, my psychologist (who was also a lawyer) had asked me to write three pages on any combat I had seen in Vietnam. I started writing and before I knew it, I had written six pages. She wrote that I had written this as if it were yesterday and recommended that I receive compensation. The doctor that decided that I should not receive any compensation wrote that he admitted that I had stressors (as he put it) if I was telling him the truth. This guy was calling me a liar! It was ninety miles to Oklahoma City, VA from Lawton, Oklahoma. I got there about three o'clock in the afternoon and I was as mad as I have ever been. When I hit those doors to the Mental Ward and walked in, nobody even said a word to me. I went from office to office looking for Dr. Baker. I wanted to pound him into the floor! Naturally, security was called again and the DAV guy came down and assured me that he'd take care of everything. Bottom line, I was never allowed in there again.

In July, I went to the PTSD ward in Topeka, Kansas. It was supposed to be a ninety-day program. They kicked me out after sixty days. But while I was there, I learned a lot. I had a really good doctor by the name of Dr. Horne. He had been in artillery in World War II. Then he became a psychologist. After I had been there thirty days, my DAV guy called me to let me know that I had been awarded 30 percent disability and I would be back-paid to February. After I got out, I received 50 percent. Also, they agreed to allow me to come back and try again in July of 1990.

I got kicked out again after thirty days. They said that I needed to do this on an outpatient schedule because I could not conform to their structure. However, I ended up with 100 percent disability.

In 1991, I applied for back pay. The struggle lasted for thirteen years. Finally, in April of 2004 I received my back pay all the way back to 1979.

-Robert (Bob) Best

Robert Izo
Aviations Weapons Petty Officer
U.S. Navy – Vietnam, 1964 – 1967
USS Enterprise (CVAN-65)

Dear Dusty,
I read your manuscript twice with great interest ... the reading was familiar in some ways and different in other ways, but unique in a way you and only you can "tell your story." The manuscript is good.
I guess I managed to "untangle" my baggage many years ago and focused myself on education, family and church ... this formula has been successful for me so far. I am proud of my four years of service in Vietnam ... two twelve-month tours ('64-'65/'66-'67) and truthfully I will never forget that part of my life.
When we arrived in Alameda, California after our first tour ... people threw "dog crap" at us over the base fence when we went into the city ... name calling ... "Baby

Killers," etc. ... I know you experienced the same treatment. Did we want to "kick-ass" ... you bet ... but we didn't.

We were not treated well, ignored and in many cases still are ... as a Christian ... I forgive those people ... as a Vietnam Veteran ... I will never forget the treatment.

In my opinion, this "welcome home" stuff is nonsense ... I've been home since 1967 ... I know who I was and who I am and what I did ... I, myself don't need the recognition miles past the event.

It took my unit approximately forty) years to have our first reunion two years ago ... a few missing ... didn't show or dead ... we talked about the Nam, but mostly what we've done and are doing since then ... I doubt we will have another.

I "pulled" my weight as an 18-22 year old with pride and commitment ... met guys that during that period of time became and still remain my "Brothers" for eternity.
Your Friend,
Bob

I would like to add this about Bob Izo's service for our country:

The USS Enterprise CVN-65, formerly CVA (N)-65 is the world's first nuclear powered aircraft carrier. Like her predecessor of World War II fame, she was nicknamed the "Big E." She could have a crew of 4,000-5,000.

On December 2, 1965, the Big E became the first nuclear-powered ship to engage in combat when she launched aircraft against the Viet Cong near Bien Hoa. Enterprise launched 125 sorties on the first day, unleashing 167 short tons of bombs and rockets on the enemy's supply lines. On 3 December, she set a record of 165 strike sorties in a single day.

When Enterprise departed the Gulf of Tonkin on 20 June 1967, her pilots had flown more than 13,400 battle missions during 132 combat days of operations. (Enterprise Command History 1967, 29). As Vice Admiral Hyland stated in his congratulatory statement, "the entire Air Wing Nine has earned a resounding 'Well Done'." The carrier had steamed 67,630 miles in operations with the Seventh Fleet.
(Source: Wikipedia.org/wiki/USS Enterprise (CVN-65)

No wonder Bob Izo is one very proud Vietnam combat veteran. Without the support of the Big E, many more Americans would not have come home.

Doug Dobransky
Specialist 4
U.S. Army – Vietnam
11B10 to 71H20
Vietnam, January 1967 – January 1968

January 1967

The very first time I ever saw my father cry was January 1967. He tried valiantly to keep it a secret but failed. I was nineteen then.

We were all standing in the boarding area of our small local airport and I was surrounded by a lot of family members, saying goodbye and about to board a plane for Vietnam.

It has taken a lot of years to really think on this, but it must be a terrible dilemma for a father to see his only son go off to war. There must be sense of manly pride, in spite of having to imagine him returning in a long box, draped with a flag. There must also be a terrible sense of anxiety knowing your son is going to a dangerous place. Some men accept these things often without words.

As I hugged all the women and shook hands with the men, I slowly moved down the line to my dad and looked at his face to notice his chin quivering and his eyes a little wet from tears welling up. I had never seen that before so I didn't know what to say. He hugged me and whispered something in private in my ear.

"Be careful". I said, "I will". He wanted to say more. He wanted to say he loved me, that he was proud of me, and that he was sorry for all the things that happened during the course of life in our family, as in any family. His tears and not his voice told me all of that. I had never heard that before that night. As I walked out the door on to the runway, the snow flurries hit me in the face, and then I turned around for one last look. I saw all of them, especially my little sister Cheryl, standing huddled up looking at me and waving with tears flowing. I thought quite possibly I would never see them again, but it was an accepted thing. I have always thought about how brave all those people were standing cold in their coats and watching their young kid go off to war. I knew where I was going and what possibly it would be like, but they knew nothing. They would have to remain in their homes at night to battle their agonizing imaginations, as the long months of war would go by. They would picture their young son in a jungle far away with explosions and guns going off, with no one to take care of him.

The things a father must feel seeing his son fly away to war, I imagine, are gut wrenching. I never respected my father for that, simply because it never occurred to me, not being a father myself. It's a generation order in reverse. A father expects to take his turn in line, to die in progression. A son has his father to do that as an example and as a shield of protection against the oblivion of death.

To see a son go off to face death out of order must truly be a nightly terror, as the slow progress of war grinds on. Each night that my dad went to sleep, I'm sure he cried within himself wondering...wondering how I was every minute. Was I safe, was I scared, was I alone, so far away and so young. Men seem to expect that war is something we just do, and to see a son go off must be heartbreaking, but often they suffer in secret. The older men in my town looked at dying in battle as better than not doing your duty. For some reason that idea has always prevailed. At least until Vietnam came along. I guess when you put a war on television it's easier to second guess. Maybe this war thing isn't such a good idea. Good people can get killed and for no good reason. I myself have to stick with doing my duty as a proud and honorable thing, and something I'd be proud for my son to do, but I'm stuck with that opinion. To do otherwise would invalidate the bravery and sacrifice a lot of young men offered up, no matter the politics.

My dad never said much about how he worried, or missed me, or even loved me. He just did. Dads sometimes don't tell you those things, and maybe it's their natural instinct not to. Their reserve stands as a little bit of strength to make their sons walk a little taller. Sons crave approval from their fathers. All of the unspoken love that goes on between fathers and sons somehow might be by design. Trying to impress your father has always given a kid the power to try hitting one out of the infield in Little League, or keeping your eyes open during a polio shot. A little more bravery just comes up from somewhere when you know your dad is looking on. I don't believe that ever goes away. The night my father teared up saying goodbye to me at our airport told me that I was doing good, and that I was his son. If I died in Vietnam he would miss me, but he would have been proud that I went when my country called. That aspect is still sacred, and no matter the competence of who in Washington is calling the shots, Duty, Honor, Country still has meaning. As I looked in my father's eyes, I now know that he knew that, and a lot of love changed hands that night in January 1967 without a word being spoken.

After many years of reliving that night, it means a lot to me that he had tears in his eyes. Even to this day. The further out in to the world I go, and the more I look back on that little scene at the Youngstown Airport, with the family all huddled up watching a son going to war......it makes me think that as big as the world is, and as wide a gap as may exist in families, one thing is certain. Blood is sticky.

The Long Question

When I finally got there and that mechanical door opened, the heat slammed me in my young innocent face like a saloon door in a hurricane. Next was a particularly foul smell in the air, a thick strange air that my nasal passages had never before known. And that sun. Man, that sun was a hammer. Intense and punishing, even though the strange little people were going about their normal business, mostly on foot, without any visible damage from it. That first surreal minute and those shocking smells and sounds there will never leave me.

Vietnam was on the other side of the world, and although I had left all that sweat and blood in training for those last 17 weeks, I never did know where Vietnam was. I had to look on a map just before going there to see where I was going to spend one valuable year of my life. At least I was damned hoping it would be a year. Anything less would be bad news. I was a trained killer. Infantry. Fort Lewis, Washington Shooting Champion of my entire basic training company of 210 men, then Tigerland at Fort Polk, Louisiana. Nine weeks in the Everglades, so they told me I was a killer. Made certain that I knew it. I didn't look like any killer I had ever seen, and if anyone saw me carrying my M16 rifle they might better ask me if any grownups or authorities knew I was playing with that gun. I looked more like some kid delivering the Sunday Paper, not a killer sent to war in my unstained soul.

The 199th Light Infantry Brigade was a specialized unit. Recon and Search & Destroy Missions were the specialty, and I was now part of it. My uniform was still new green. Green as Irish grass, and my hair was clean. I had shiny boots and must have looked pathetic to anyone there with "bush experience" under their belts. I was the FNG and no one pays any mind or respect to one of those.

During my first days there in base camp, the adjustments were quick. I did not know anyone in Vietnam; it is often the case that replacements just get assigned individually and you then get transported to the unit you will be with, so being a total stranger was common. Seems odd. You are going to a war zone and in the line of fire, yet you don't even know anyone who might take a bullet for you. Rapid adaptations became your friends.

Eight days in, terror came cruising. Under a pale dead moon, the mortars rained in on us and mortifying explosions cracked our sleep as we all dove for the sandbags. Our tents were lined with them and at 2am, the darkness hurts. I remember thinking those first few minutes, and my first time in real combat ... "this is the night of my death". I actually saw how my body would be, lying scattered in shredded chunks, my blood cells and hair seeping in to the mud and decomposing banana leaves. How on earth would my family ever know it was me? I felt sorry for them because they would have to stack my bones, teeth, and pieces in a pile then close the casket. Even worse, what if they never did find my body. That is what I thought those first moments under fire. But after a few dozen explosions, I couldn't believe it. Jesus Christ, I was still alive. Maybe they would stop and this night would end. That was the longest night of my life. Then I remember counting in my head the number of days I still had left. About 340. How was I ever going to last that long if this one night was like this. That is what you think when you're an FNG.

The dawns ran and hid. Night after long night, like roaches in corners that you just couldn't find. But as the dawns came and nights passed, the friendships grew like the thin green sprouts of newly planted bamboo. Kinda weak at first, then stronger with the days. Similarities and hometowns helped. Mail eventually came. That helped the most. Someone back home had an address and it brought those written words. They knew where I was on some map and when they put the war on TV, the letters would tell us how bad it looked. I think it was worse on TV. Daily we crossed a big X through one more calendar date, and that was a big thing. One more day off the short-timers calendar. Everyone had a calendar, and it felt like an accomplishment crossing off even one date. I saved up. I did not cross days off one day at a time. I waited for a week or more and it felt like whacking off after a long save up, so I could cross off six or seven days all at once. I saved letters that way too. I would get mail and the ones from special girls I stuck up in my helmet to carry around for a few days. Didn't want to blow my wad too quickly. Didn't want to open and read those valuable connections to "the world" too fast, so I savored them for days until some quiet time blew in ad I could sniff and look at the writing.

I was not sure of my destiny there in the 199th, and my assignments to one of the companies out in the boonies were occasional ambushes. I was often in base camp at Long Binh and nightly guard duty was still a chore. Shit burning detail too. That's when you pull out all the outhouse barrels full, pour in the kerosene and Zippo the can, burning and stirring the excrement each day. Shit-burning detail was sweet. We lived our days out on the bunkers, smoking cigarettes and listening to Armed Forces Radio. Motown and the British Invasion were out on the airways, but no protesting political music permitted. Not Dylan, not folk singers, and no drug related tunes. MACV (Military Assistance Command, Vietnam), in Saigon saw to it that they kept the troops clear of any morale beating lyrics. Some pirate radio showed up, but mostly we heard the Temptations, Beach Boys and The Stones.

A month had passed and things had changed. A month is not much time in country and no one gives a shit about any guy with only a month, but it was my first small victory. Victory, because every once in a while, some newer FNG (Fricking New Guy) would show up looking pathetic in his very new fatigues and shined boots, not knowing anything about his fate. That new guy was even more pathetic then me because I had a month. Only eleven months left. But when a guy had only weeks to go, he was golden and even had this visible glow over his head. He was revered and worshiped. His life was valuable. On their last day, seeing a short-timer leave the company with all their gear in a jeep, on their way to Tan Sun Nhut Airbase was enviously ravaging. Your dreams of being in that same position were so far off that hope and fantasy were dangerous things. Hope during those early months was your own slice of hell and could drive some guys crazy, so the best thing was to forget about your incomprehensible remaining time and concentrate on just marking off those little early dates on your calendar. Forget about going home and just accept being dead. Made it easier just to be dead.

My second month came and went. Routine became the thing. Rumors were always flying around, and in a war zone, rumors were wishful thinking. We wanted to believe them because they were usually hopeful. Like this one time … someone had heard the greatest rumor of all. It was going around that J. Paul Getty bought Vietnam and he wanted everyone out in 30 days. No shit. That was an actual rumor and we really wanted to believe it. So we all started to imagine going home in the next four weeks, but during the next few days, as the rumor lost its glow, we all knew it was bullshit. J. Paul Getty never did buy Vietnam and why would he? There was not one horse in the whole damned country and everyone knew that if there were no horses, there would be no oil. Like in Texas. So why would Getty or anyone else want to buy Vietnam?

My days were numbered. I had been on a few operations in the Mekong Delta and I knew I was going out on patrol, setting up ambushes and recons soon, and we always got the word on casualties. KIAs and WIAs were those killed or wounded in action. There were also MIAs which we all now know are still missing and unaccounted for. During a steaming afternoon along the perimeter, I was taking a break, smoking a cigarette with my helmet off and my rifle against an ammo box. It was the usual day ... 104 degrees and 100 percent humidity. The smell in the air was still that rotten stench and the mosquitoes were lining up for their daily buffet of Caucasian, Hispanic and Black blood. Occasionally some Indian and Asian blood might have made their day, but they never did miss a meal. As I sat there, another guy came over and sat down. He lit up and started to talk. We talked about hometowns, women, cars, and the field. Going out into the field with all those patrols. I guess we laughed about how insane it was to think we were in this place, all the way on the other side of the planet, in some jungle area with rifles. A half year earlier, we were hangin around the bowling alleys or cruising Market Street or any hometown drag street lookin for chicks. But here we were in Vietnam. He told me his buddy, Paul, was leaving in one week and they were looking for someone to take his job. He told me that they needed someone to learn the job quickly and take over for him since his DEROS was up. Duty Estimated Rotation of Service, or at least something like that. What we all kept very focused on ... rotation back to the world.

Paul Ninomiya was an ultra short-timer and leaving in a week. What they needed was a guy who could learn the job and someone who could type. I looked over and said ... "I can type." I could actually type on a typewriter. I took it in high school and Mr. Brahny at Chaney High School in Youngstown Ohio taught me to type. So this guy next to me says"No shit! Hold on a minute." He went over to this captain's tent, about 100 yards back and returned to tell me that I was to report to that captain the morning. And so I did.

The dawn finally decided to show itself that next morning and there I went, over to see the captain. I had no idea what was in store, but when I walked in and saluted this thirty year old OCS 90 Day Wonder, he began running me through the paces. His eyes and brows were scrutinizing my personnel fire, naturally noticing that I had turned down OCS (Officer Candidate School) and he wondered why. My basic training marks were superior, I was the shooting champion and awarded the Expert Medal on the range, and my IQ was noticeably higher than some of those boys, dumb enough to get drafted, just like I did. I just said that I was not interested in being on recall to the military for the rest of my life, which officers are. Right then I figured that would have slammed the door on any opportunity for me, but no. He just looked up and eyeballed me up and down, then got back to the job at hand. After giving him the basics on an Underwood Typewriter he had sitting on the ammo boxes, and proving that I could actually type, he informed me that effective immediately, I was to report to Paul Ninomiya in the Casualty Unit and would be taking over those duties in one week.

A week later when Paul jumped into that jeep and waved goodbye, I was the new Casualty Unit Specialist for the 199th Light Infantry Brigade. My duties were to take in all the killed, wounded, and missing information on all operations for the Brigade, including the writing of letters home to the families of our young killed soldiers and the circumstances under which they died. I radioed in to MACV in Saigon, twice daily the numbers and statistics on all casualties in the field and on base, hostile or non-hostile.

My duties from then on were to work the Casualty Unit and keep all those names in my head, months after month, writing home the letters to the mothers and fathers on how and where their sons were killed, mentioning in all how they distinguished themselves in battle and how grateful the country was for their supreme sacrifice. I always pictured and wondered how it was for them to read the words that I wrote, explaining all of that about their young son. How do you explain that to parents who know their son was blown up or shot, just the same way I thought of it during my first months.

Larry Stanfield, from somewhere in the US, just happened over to me on that one hot steamy afternoon and had a smoke, casually mentioning to me that they were looking for a guy who could type. That is how I survived Vietnam without so much as a scratch. After all, they told me I was a killer. I did get injured badly during my 4th month in a football game, and did also spend a week in the hospital on my twentieth birthday with some FUO … (fever of unknown origin), but my adult lifelong sometimes disturbing question has always been … how did the planets line up in such a change of fate for me in the Republic of Vietnam at nineteen years old in 1967? How did I manage to be sitting in that heat, having a cigarette at that exact time and with that exact crossing of paths with some relative stranger who knew they were looking for a guy who could type? I would have normally and most certainly been on nine more months of recons or ambush patrols, probably taking shrapnel or bullet wounds, getting killed or wounded, or for sure, living with the mental terrors many of the guys lived or live with. My long question has been … Why Me? What was it about a light over my head and just that one delicate minute in two lives passing that resulted in my sanity and safety? That has been my One Long Question. Anyone know the answer to that? I would like to know. I would also like to thank Larry Stanfield, wherever he might be.

Jack Bellemy
Sergeant First Class
554th Combat Engineers 25th Infantry
U.S. Army
Cu Chi, South Vietnam; Class of 1967–68
1966 – 1992 Retired
U.S. Army National Guard

Jack Bellemy's first rattlesnake - 1980

Jack Bellemy - 2012

When Dusty first asked me if I could write an article for this book about my experience in Vietnam in 1967-68, I said, "Sure, I can do that." But the more I thought of it, and the more I read of his experience and those of the valiant troops that fought alongside him, I began to wonder, "What the hell can I really say that will make a difference?"

As a Combat Engineer, my job required a close working relationship with the infantry—ground troops and mechanized units. Blowing up enemy bunkers and tunnels as well as doing mine sweeps for road mines was pretty risky business and we counted on the infantry to cover our backs.

The Vietnam War was much worse than we thought it could possibly be. Dusty Trimmer's hard-core unit, the 3rd 22nd Infantry of the 25th had an outstanding combat record in 1967-1968. I had the honor of fighting beside them at places like Soui Tre, Trang Bang, Hoc Mon, Nui Ba Dinh, Go Da Hau. The horrible memories are embedded in our minds for the rest of our lives— Dusty and I talk about them often.

Well, men and women had died, been maimed both in body and soul and came back to a country that was indifferent to their efforts or their bereaved love ones. A mass media that thought nothing of embarrassing and belittling them when they returned and rewriting history to justify their indifference as to make the left in this country more comfortable. Sounds like a bitter man; don't think so! Soldiers have been doing their duty to ungrateful citizens for centuries. The only problem is that the citizens have to put up with those whom they created. They see us on the streets with broken bodies and bro-ken minds and try to continue to turn their backs, but they can't anymore. **Why? Because they now have sons and daughters who have joined the service and are going through the same nightmares their parents and grandparents have gone through. When will you folks learn?**

Respect is one of the things we asked for. But we also need for you to understand that you can't put a sane person under duress for a long period of time and not expect them to crack. Soldiers are not robots, they break. So think about that when you ask your sons and daughters to continue to be called up tour after tour in combat without regard to their wellbeing. **The press tried to portray Vietnam vets as crazy, you better start talking to your sons and daughters now.**

Peter Sparks
Fire Control Technician – PO3
U.S. Navy – July 1954 to Sept 1957

In my 75 years I have had the privilege of knowing combat veterans from many wars. Combat veterans have seen and experienced things that most others have not. This is something they all have in common and it gives them a common bond with each other unlike the bonds that folks have who have not seen the pointy end of the stick. Then there are differences depending on changes in battle conditions, rules of engagement and the public's attitude toward them when they returned from service.

The first combat veteran I met was my father. As a teenager growing up in Ger-many, he fought in the trenches in WWI for the Kaiser. He was thirty-six when I was born and my observations of him were during my first thirty-four years of life. He was a quiet man who never talked about the war. When asked, he would change the subject. Even as a youngster I could see that he carried bad memories that he did not want to think about. He was a proud American citizen and always had a special rela-tionship with the blue and gold star families who patronized his grocery store during WWII, extending them credit and giving them extra rationed items. If my mother had not told me, I believe I never would have found out that he served.

My father-in-law was a WWII Marine Combat veteran of Guadalcanal and Okinawa after volunteering as a high school dropout at seventeen. After the war, he suffered from depression, nightmares, malaria and jungle rot. He did not like to talk about his combat experiences, although he did tell me he lost many friends and always thought about them. I only heard him mention his specific war experiences twice. Once I took him with me to visit with my buddy, a four combat tour Vietnam vet-eran. We had a few drinks. I just sat there in the corner listening to them talk. I don't think they were conscious that I was there. On the way home, he asked me to take him to see Private Ryan. He was deeply affected by the realism and was silent for at least an hour after we left the theatre. All of a sudden he told me of an experience from Okinawa that he said he dreamed about every night since it happened. He told me how he mistakenly killed a mother and two children in a cave he thought was occupied by the enemy. Shortly before he died at age eighty-three, he had open-heart surgery. The first words he uttered when coming out of the anesthetic were "F—— the Japs." These words from a guy I never heard say anything stronger than "damn" in the thirty-five years I knew him.

The Vietnam combat vets I am privileged to call friends, including the author, have suffered from battle wounds, PTSD and other maladies, including effects from Agent Orange. All have struggled with alcohol and depression, some with violent and aggressive behavior. To top it off, they all bear emotional scars from the poor treatment they received from the public when they returned home. A few are finally getting psychological treatment but most still reject help.

Let me expand about the one that I know the best. I have changed his name and some details and remain anonymous to protect his privacy.

Sam served four combat tours in Vietnam as a Navy Corpsman in support of Recon Marines always in forward positions. At times his units suffered so many casualties that they had to be disbanded. He was then transferred into new units and sent back into action with little break.

Sam was wounded several times and spent over a year in hospitals overseas and back in the states. His knee joints are mainly pins and plates and his stomach still spits up shrapnel fragments to this day. Sam suffers from the remnants of jungle rot, which resist treatment and are a constant irritant. He uses a large pharmacopeia of medications to help deal with the constant pain and digestive problems that continue to plague his daily existence. **Then there is the depression, nightmares and other effects that don't respond to medication and still plague him more than forty years after his discharge.**

I learned that he has a deadly fear of snakes while playing golf with him. Sam hit his ball and it landed about twenty feet from a small pond. As we approached his ball, Sam suddenly turned white as a ghost and froze when he saw a few small harmless snakes near the water. He flat out refused to move until I retrieved his ball and gave him a free drop about fifteen yards from the pond. It took him about three more holes before he stopped shaking. After the round, we adjourned to the clubhouse for our customary scotch refreshments. After downing three doubles he calmed down and told me that seeing the snakes rekindled bad memories from his Vietnam experience.

Sam then recounted two of those experiences that sent chills down my spine in the telling. He mentioned being pinned down in his foxhole one night when a large cobra slithered slowly across his stomach. He said he did not breathe or move anything except his bowels until long after the snake was gone. The even more traumatic experience happened while they were walking single file through the jungle. His best friend was just a few feet in front of him. All of a sudden a small tree viper dropped from the branches above and wrapped itself around his buddy's neck He saw the snake strike his friend in the carotid artery. His friend slumped to the ground and died at his feet. It happened so quickly that there was nothing he could do to help.

Other than that, Sam did not discuss his experiences as they invariably brought him back to re-experience the carnage and horrors of his service. After a few drinks with friends; all except me, Vietnam combat vets; Sam would sometimes recount frightening experiences that had a humorous side to them.

Like the time they were dug in for the night behind rows of Concertina wire hung with tin cans and Claymores to give them early warning of enemy incursions. Another of his buddies was holed up some distance from Sam barely visible in the dark night. All of a sudden, the silence was shattered by his friend's panicked scream; "Get the f— off me!" At the same time Sam heard a nasty non-human roar and thought he saw a large shadow leap from his friend's hole and bound off though the Concertina wire, Claymores and tin cans without making a sound. Apparently, a Tiger decided to share Sam's friend's hole with him and the experience scared the bejeezus out of both parties. The next day that was confirmed by the bloody claw marks on his buddy's chest.

Other than humorous anecdotes, Sam and our other combat vet friends generally avoid sharing their experiences with anyone. Sam does not want to attend events like the Rolling Thunder dinner I talked him into one night. When one of the speakers started talking about Vietnam experiences, he had to get up and leave. He definitely suffers from PTSD and according to our other friends in the know; most likely from the effects of Agent Orange exposure.

I learned from experience not to touch him or startle him while asleep. *One morning while sharing a room on a golf trip, I reached down to touch his shoulder, quietly uttering; "Sam. Time to get up." He screamed something I did not understand and came out of the bed like he was shot from a cannon.*

Like almost all the Vietnam combat vets I know, Sam drinks to excess, but somehow manages to fulfill his daily responsibilities. *He holds down a physically demanding 55 to 60 hour a week job and is seen as an ultra-reliable, honest employee with great people skills. Almost every evening he goes home, takes care of his daily maintenance requirements, walks his frisky fifty-pound dog and spends at least an hour soaking his swollen knees in Epson Salt solution before getting to sleep. The guy is amazing. He mows his elderly neighbors' lawns, rakes their leaves in the fall and plows their driveways in the winter.*

Sam seldom complains and I could not have a better friend. I know I am a better person for my friendship with him and the other vets who have accepted me into their friendship circle. These men despite their own difficulties always reach out to help other veterans from all eras.

In particular, they all have tried to encourage Sam to seek more assistance from the VA and claim the benefits, which his Country owes him, but he wants no part of it. Some of his attitude comes from past experiences, some relates to his independent loner situation and some is fear of the unknown. Even the encouragement from friends who have utilized VA resources and made obvious positive improvements in their lives do not change his resistance. I have learned the best thing I can do to help him is to be his friend and listen.

I know many of his contemporaries. Some few have made tremendous strides to overcome their physical, mental and emotional wounds. Others still rely on alcohol and drugs to dull their pains. I know at least one who just dropped out of society and lives like a hermit showing up once or twice every year or two; only to return again to his hiding place. I have seen a couple who show up from time to time, usually in a bar, with that thousand yard stare; barely able to deal with social interactions.

As for me, I served in peacetime. I respect and honor every serviceman I meet; with a special place reserved for those who experienced the hells of combat. I know enough to realize these are different people who gave their all when called upon. They see each other as brothers who risked their lives for each other and their country in that order. It is a crime that many did not get the thanks and services they deserved and were promised. My heart aches every time I see veterans still suffering from their combat experiences. And even more for the Vietnam vets who received the gross indignity of outrageous hateful receptions at the hands of many of the citizens they served so faithfully.

Thomas Gretchko
Staff Sergeant
23rd Inf. Div., Co G/2 (Ranger) 75th Inf.
United States Army – Vietnam
1966 – 1992 Retired

My earliest memory of anything related to Vietnam goes back to around 1961 or so when I saw the iconic Life magazine cover photograph of a Buddhist monk immolating himself in protest of the Diem regime's treatment of Buddhists. I was just starting the sixth or seventh grade. For the rest of my junior and high school years, Vietnam would be ever present in the news as our country escalated our involvement in that little country so far away. Somehow, I always knew I would end up going there.

My parents were hard working and underpaid, but nevertheless provided a good home for my sister and two brothers. As our school years progressed, several of my older brother's friends were either drafted or enlisted in the military, went and came back from Vietnam. By the time I was ready to graduate high school in 1968 I expected to be drafted also. The Tet offensive of earlier that year had convinced me I would be called. I was willing to serve and believed it would be an honor to do so. I grew up on the stories of our WWII military victories and was certain our country could and would be victorious in Vietnam.

I did get drafted along with my twin brother, Tim in June of 1970. I have no proof but I suspect the draft board gave us a break due to the fact that my father died when I was in the eleventh grade and were being benevolent towards us with respect to our mother being a widow. Maybe true and maybe no. My mother then also died in late 1969 and within months, we were drafted, just after the Kent State shootings.

We went together to Fort Campbell, Kentucky and took our basic training there. Tim got orders for communications training at Fort Hood, Texas and I got orders to report to Fort Polk, Louisiana for infantry training. Anyone who went to Fort Polk knew where the next stop would be, so when they asked us what our preferred choices of next duty station we wanted, I listed Vietnam, Vietnam, Vietnam. In December of 1970, I landed at Bien Hoa airbase and began my tour of duty with the 25th Infantry, patrolling the jungles of the Iron Triangle.

My first firefight came on my thirteenth day in the bush. This was when I saw my first person killed by gunfire. I still remember what he looked like, a young sixteen or seventeen year-old Viet Cong boy who was shot after his AK47 jammed. During the next four months, our unit had several contacts with the enemy, although nothing like our troops experienced in previous years. I recall one particular firefight that started at 8:00 and lasted till 16:00 hours. We walked straight into the middle of a bunker complex. This was when our medic earned a Silver Star for rescuing a man in the line of fire.

The mood of the average troop at this point in the war was to just survive and come home. President Nixon had initiated the Vietnamization program and everyone knew the U.S. was not going to stay in Vietnam for long. Drug abuse and alcoholism were prevalent and disregard for military discipline was very evident. I feared for my safety as line troops were compromising our positions in the field and becoming lackadaisical.

In April of 1971, the 25th Infantry stood down and I was sent north to Chu Lai to serve with the 23rd Inf. Div. It was there that the 75th Infantry Rangers were recruiting for volunteers to join them. Several of us signed up. These guys were the epitome of a professional soldier and that inspired us to join. Recondo School would be an intensive three-week Ranger school culminating in an actual mission in the boonies where each candidate would be evaluated. It was one of the hardest things I ever did, but I graduated to Co G/2 Ranger Co. in Da Nang. For the next five months, our unit performed recon and ambush missions in the various areas surrounding Da Nang. I was abruptly rotated back to the U.S. in September of 1971 when the Rangers stood down.

Returning to the U.S. was something we always dreamed about, yet I missed and thought about the guys still there. I was ashamed that our country let the South Vietnamese down by reneging on our promise to support them. I remember when Da Nang fell in 1975 and thought about what probably happened to the Vietnamese friends I knew. For several years all I could think about was Vietnam, Vietnam, Viet-

nam. I turned into regular stumblebum for a couple of years.

Over the next few years I slowly began to adjust to life as a civilian. My soul found healing as I came to accept Jesus Christ as my savior and Lord. I began to see the world and its system in a different light. I accepted the things I could, could not change, and began to rely on the God who is there for comfort and guidance. Stress from war experiences, though still remembered, can be relieved through prayer and the knowledge and I know and am known by God.

As a consequence of my war experience, I have developed a continual interest in the political direction of our country. I love and respect the founders and framers of this great republic and have concerns that the foundations of our nation are being destroyed. Corruption within our government, wars on many fronts, the U.S. as the world's policeman and the use of our youth as so much cannon fodder cannot continue without it having a detrimental effect on all of us. If we as a people allow our God given rights to be taken from us, then we will indeed be a nation in bondage again.

I was proud to serve my country as a soldier in Vietnam. I was proud to have served with men, many of which gave their all. I was proud to have in my small way, try to obtain peace for the good people of South Vietnam. We did our duty. May the God of peace comfort you my brothers and sisters who are burdened today with the effects of your time in Vietnam.

A Nam Vet's Different View ...

Richard M. Arceci
Specialist E-5
Finance Division – Long Binh
U.S. Army – Vietnam 1970

I wouldn't want you to believe that I spend much energy thinking about Vietnam or my time as a soldier during that war. Actually, I have to work hard to remember my time as a U.S. Army soldier, SP5, during that "conflict" (as some hard-core WWII Vets would call it). However, my friend, Dusty Trimmer, who was very much more into the thick of the day-to-day heavy combat action, asked me to contribute to a book he was writing. He is interested, I believe, in how it forever impacted the lives of many men and women who served during that war; and how it also impacted their families, many of whom are living the aftermath.

Dusty is also interested to tell the story of how he and many of his friends and other soldiers contributed much more of their lives (and health) during and after their time serving in Vietnam. Dusty is also trying to right some wrongs that have and still are being levied against the participants of that war.

So I pulled out a photo album of pictures (although not many) that I took during my time in Vietnam to see if it would help to refresh my memory and could tell you something that is important to tell. For the most part, I saved the pictures that my wife had sent to me of my one-year-old daughter as she was growing up back home. Many of the other pictures I saved were of my base camp in Long Binh and some of my fellow soldiers that I grew close to, but sadly didn't keep in contact with after coming home. I'm embarrassed to say I do not remember the names of some of those in the snap shots. But now I have their faces to look at and hope that they are enjoying life as we tend to do in this great country of America.

I feel it is important to tell you that my personal profile was and is different than most soldiers in Vietnam, many of whom were drafted to serve in the military right after high school. I was older than most of my fellow enlistees and draftees. In fact, I believe I was also older than the first commanding officer of my unit in Vietnam. I had graduated from a four-year college with a degree in Finance, but it took me five years of study while working part-time. While attending college, I married my high school sweetheart, and soon after, passed my CPA exam and began a job with a large certified public accounting firm. However, just when it seemed my wife and I were living a fairytale, my draft papers came.

Many things go through your mind when you get your draft notice. Remember, this was a time when there was revolting in the streets, and the nightly news was using the "War in Vietnam" as an opening blast to catch the viewer's attention. Some here at home didn't like that Americans were "over there" and included the U.S. soldiers, along with the "Establishment" as warmongers. That was not the truth, at least about the troops. The soldiers (at least those drafted by threat of charges of treason if they refused) were just men and women caught in a situation made by politicians, whose intentions were never really accepted—nor even understood—by the American public. **Moreover, each soldier didn't know; nor would he or she ever have guessed the price that would be paid to find out the fate ahead.**

It was a warm day for December when my father-in-law drove me to the Army Center in downtown Cleveland, Ohio. As I shook his hand before exiting the car, he gave me encouragement to help me think positive. He had been in the "big one" (WWII). So I used that knowledge and his positive attitude to believe I would be coming home, too. Not ever having lived with my own father who was sickly shortly after I was born, I "adopted" my father-in-law as my own father. That was to my extreme benefit, and it has played well in the long run, too.

After a couple of flights of stairs, being told to stand in line and getting a quick "butt check" (you draftees know what I mean), I was quickly transported via a private bus company to my basic training camp: Fort Campbell in Kentucky. THAT'S A RIDE! There I had to build back my childhood muscles, compete while being a little overweight with boys, sometimes five years younger than me. I felt soft, defeated and that I couldn't be in much a worse place than in the Army. However, it all ended well with me in better shape than ever.

Shortly before beginning my advanced training at Fort Hood, Texas, my wife gave me the most wonderful news that we were having a baby … a girl! Within the year of advanced training, I had the opportunity to have my wife live with me off base with my daughter. That's a whole story of its own that's … well, wonderful; but I can't tell it here.

It was then, during my time in advanced training that I received orders for Vietnam and was assigned to the Military Finance Unit in Long Binh, Vietnam. I guess that is when the story Dusty is telling, begins.

I thought it very unusual at the time that, while I was under the auspice of the "Finance" division in Long Binh, my Commanding Officer assigned me to work through the Mail Post. I scratched my head over this, but it didn't become clear until later.

It was a simple enough assignment, but it turned out to be an interesting experience that I will never forget.

Getting mail from home was extremely important to the troops. Obviously, it was one of the few privileges a trooper had left … a message from home … "They still remember me." None of us could wait for the mail even though we saw tons of it. Simply said, we at the postal unit were always eager to hear from our own wives and families. It would come off the plane or chopper and be driven to our mail building: a metal roof shelter that was a heat box, approximately forty feet by twenty feet. The building had loosely attached walls. It was just a short truck ride away from the chopper landing site and within driving distance of the airport.

The Postal building was basically a wooden hut or building with a corrugated metal roof and surrounding corrugated metal walls, which kept the heat in very nicely during the hot temperatures common to Vietnam. There, in our private sauna, sorters would sort the arriving mail by Post location or Firebase location. In trade, we would bag and hand over the sending mail (mail from troops being sent home or wherever) to the pilot or his crew. The sending mail had been collected from the troops in surrounding Fire Bases, as we would make our own trips for purposes that I describe below. Sometimes the mail came and went twice a day. On a sour note, some days it didn't come or go at all.

I filled in many times for my commanding officer in communicating Division information and making sure enough staff were available to handle the daily operations. I sorted mail, too, if our manpower was down on any day.

My Finance responsibilities included an occasional flight by helicopter (as a passenger) to various "fire bases" for the purpose of delivering the mail, retrieving mail to be sent by the troops, and also selling money orders ("MOs") to soldiers who were "in the field."

Since U.S. currency was not and could not be used in Vietnam, "Military Currency" was used by all military personnel to buy items from the "Canteen", et al. It was used for all transactions on the base, including items that would be used or consumed directly by the soldier. It was also used to exchange for Vietnamese money, which could be purchased at certain authorized Military Finance locations.

Money orders were used to send money home or to purchase items from vendors all over the world, by mail. Some of the items purchased would be sent (by virtue of the order form) directly home. Sometimes the items would be sent directly to the soldier at his camp. Purchasing a "boom box" was common; although, not so if you were in the field.

Because I carried a significant amount of blank money orders <u>and</u> the "Rolling Stamp" (my words to describe the mechanism that made the money order "negotiable") I had a bodyguard to accompany me on a trip to any firebase. He happened to be a little over five feet tall, carried an M-16 almost as tall as he stood, and had a "45" (Army Issue) Pistol, which just about covered half of his leg. He also became my hooch-mate (or roommate—top bunk) when in Long Binh Post.

I remember so well our first field helicopter delivery of the mail and sale of money orders. Unfortunately, I cannot remember the name of the firebase, or its location. Nor can I remember the name of my assistant. (I regret, too, that I never took his picture. After being in Vietnam for a couple of months, I stopped taking pictures …)

Both my assistant and I were rather clumsy, nervous and anxious. We just got off the chopper when we met the firebase first sergeant ("Top"). It was near lunchtime and for those still in the base camp, food was being readied to be delivered (plopped) into each base soldier's plate—those tin plates—without aim or finesse. Top told my assistant and me to "just get your lunch now" and … "You can set up after lunch to do your money business." Then, just about the time I was being served my helping, a 50MM Howitzer Tank Cannon was discharged, causing the earth to shake and rumble … my eardrums to implode, my body to rise off the ground … AND at the same time, my plate of food fly into the air and eventually land on the ground. Well, I was the talk of that town. I had a lot of guys pat me on the shoulder while they laughed a sentence or two … none of which I would hear … but I understood. I figured I did something positive that day.

But … back to our Long Binh Postal Unit. It was in walking distance to where "Long Binh Jail" stood (a prison for American soldiers which was also commonly referred to as "LBJ" (just as was for the then President of the U.S., Lyndon B. Johnson). It was a prison for American soldiers who committed serious offenses, as well as many who were serious drug offenders—a casualty of the Vietnam War, enhanced by the many factors of being in a country such as Vietnam.

In contrast, our postal unit was also not so far from where General Abrahams had his American styled mansion—I should say "mansion plus". His place was a bit different than our corrugated metal walled "hooches" where we slept in our camp. Yet, I did feel guilty that unlike the troops in the bush, we had been able to use electric fans to try to keep us cool at night. We could also play our boom boxes without concern about the enemy. They knew exactly where we were.

My regret of being in Vietnam is not about serving, or doing the things that sol-diers need to do when necessary. My regret, if any, is mostly losing precious time to my new family—actually my whole family. What I regret, too, is that while political games and warfare were being played out and mishandled, there were many youth-ful men and women who were unable to have a typical teenage life. Their lives were, and continue to be forever changed by a war important only by political cronies of large financial interests—those who would say "greed is good."

So much was overlooked, because of greed. For instance, there seemed to be little done about drugs being offered, mostly in powder form by locals right in our base. The powder would be packed (tapped) into the soldier's cigarette between the tobacco and the ingestion of the drug would go unnoticed by someone not paying much attention.

"Hooch-maids" and other Vietnamese workers were typically selling powdered forms of drugs to GIs. I always imagined when visiting a fire base that transactions were going on, although I didn't' ask or seek to draw attention to others as to what I was thinking. Sometimes it seemed in plain sight. While I regret not making noise, I did fear that repercussions could occur in doing so. I am not ashamed to say that I was afraid in Vietnam. I would be stupid not to have fear. But there were times when I suffered from fear from both sides ... the enemy and the other enemy.

It seemed that there were no "typical" days, as I was learning something new all the time.

I felt anguish for the true soldiers of the Vietnam War. In a time when Ameri-cans thought that men and women of our country were able to tackle any problem anywhere in the world ... many, many young men were picked out of a crowd by fate, bad luck, or being born at the wrong time and put in a system of political games, and money warfare, unrecognized by our U.S. population until America suffered through its own political revolution. I don't know which of us are better or worse off than the other because of it.

Fortunes were made by some at the expense of the young men and women of the Vietnam War. As the driver for my CO, I'll never forget dri-ving in the streets of Saigon and seeing Jeeps (Army Jeeps), in the color of "EARL SCHIEB BLUE". (You "fifty years and older" know what I am talk-ing about ... that real light cobalt color.) My guess is that they were sold right off the SUPPLY Ships—our supply ships. I couldn't believe seeing them. I'm even afraid to mention it. How could it be? I have no proof. I'm not even sure exactly what I saw. But sadly, it's the feeling that it could be true.

There was even a higher cost of the Vietnam War suffered by the American and Vietnamese men and women who served for their Country and who are ill for life from chemical usage by the American and Vietnam militaries. For instance, what we know now as "Agent Orange" is still taking its toll on our troops and their children. I can imagine that the Vietnamese suffer too. There are many who were maimed and still suffer.

Leaving Vietnam and flying towards home (the U.S.), I experienced great antic-ipation of seeing my family. I knew that I was blessed just to be able to come home. I left two cartons of cigarettes on the plane when it landed in Oakland, California. My wife, Josephine, told me that our daughter was afraid of people with facial hair, those who smoked.

I pray for all those men and women who have illnesses, suffered hard-ships, divorces, loss of jobs and such other casualties of war, Just as I do for all who did not come home. I thank the Heroes and those who gave their life so that we can all have opportunity to live in the best Country in the World.

Haywood "George" Taylor
Sergeant
1st Platoon, Bravo Company
3rd 22nd, 25th Infantry Division
U.S. Army – Vietnam, 1968 – 1969

The following is based on a conversation with "George of the Jungle" on Sep-tember 8, 2012. One Sunday afternoon, a call came to me—caller ID had no idea who it was. Neither did my wife or I. Ginny answered; the deep voice on the other end with a south-side Chicago accent was unquestionably Haywood "George of the Jungle" Taylor, our M-60 machine gunner from 1st Squad, 1st Platoon of Bravo Co., 3rd 22nd Regulars 25th Infantry Division—Vietnam, 1968–1969. Holy cow!

"Hey, man, how doin', man?" George said. I had come to believe that George had disappeared into the sunset, never to be seen again. We had not seen each other, not had any dialogue, in more than a dozen years, so I had sadly written him off.

The irony of George's call is that we had just lost one platoon brother a few weeks earlier (Smokey Ryan), and then George pops back into our lives—WOW!

Over there in Nam, I considered Smokey Ryan and Haywood "George" Taylor my two closest comrades. Although each of us had been in touch off and on since Nam, the last dozen years had been very quiet between the three of us. When Smokey died, I felt emptier, like I had just lost another reason to believe that I or any Vietnam combat veteran had much of a future on this planet.

This is what George said during our conversation. Keep in mind that he is from the south side of Chicago and still lives there.

Man, I miss you guys. I am not gonna let it be so long again, I promise you. I read part of your book. You are doing a real good job—can't believe how much shit you

remember—where did you get all that stuff about us? How you doin'—you doin' okay, man?

Man, I had prostate cancer from that Agent Orange shit they dumped on us over there—VA made me 100 percent disabled, which I was—so I took an early retirement from my job at the hospital. Then when I got better, VA wanted to take away my disability compensation—like it never happened—can you believe that? How you doin', man? How's Ginny doin'?

Hey man, I still have nightmares. Damn NVAs are chasing me in the bush. I wake up swingin' and kickin'. My wife makes me go into the other bedroom. How about you, man?

Geneva and I have over 100 acres down in Mississippi, not too far south of Memphis, but far enough away from too many people. Have a hard time dealin' with lots of people anymore; don't like large crowds and I can't talk to no one about Nam anymore—NO ONE—unless they had been there, too.

We gotta get together again, man. I still remember what you did at that ambush at Catholic Village; you were all something that day.

When I got off the line in Tay Ninh and was sent to Qui Nhon, it wasn't nothin' like what we went through near the Cambodian border, but it was still the Nam and I was glad to get out of there.

Man, we got to have another reunion, just one more. I still think about that first one in Boston at Martino's place—you up to that, man?

Haywood "George" Taylor and I talked for over an hour and got caught up really well too. Our brotherhood remains solid ... for as long as we both live. When Haywood and Geneva move to their farm in Mississippi, my lovely wife, Ginny, and I plan to visit them.

The Vietnam War experience was one year that changed people's lives forever!

In other parts of this book, I have mentioned how a large percentage of guys who went to Vietnam did not actually do any real fighting in combat because there was such a great need for support in so many categories back at the base camps, such as communications, ammunition, military police, transportation, records, finance, hospitals, cooks/mess halls, air strips, mechanics, road and bridge building, mail clerks, and dozens of other fields.

Every job in a war is important. I don't feel one is more important than another. Combat duty just carries a higher level of danger. The highest level of exposure to that danger causes the longest term of recovery. Many times a soldier never fully recovers from their combat experiences … EVER!

Some combat troops were fortunate in that they learned how to thrive on their battle experiences—provided they lived through them. Remember this … it wasn't our choice, *it was just our time*. Someone else made the decision to send us there.

There is no comparison to seeing real blood gush and fly into the air or smelling it as it comes out versus watching it happen in a movie theater or video game … NO COMPARISON! And when it begins to decay, the smell is nauseating for the most hard core of us.

Chew on this one … the support guys back in the base camps had to unload the body bags of our fallen brothers out in the bush. Wonder if any of those guys still have any stressful memories of that delightful duty? Indeed, they do.

Don't forget, there were support people on the other end who had to put our brothers into those body bags in the first place.

Excuse me for this bit of slippage, but I have a hard time toning down this message that I hear over and over in my mind … **WHAT THE HELL WERE WE DOING OVER THERE?**

*THEY Won't Believe This!

On March 20, 2013, I accidentally bumped into a retired U.S. Army brigadier general and several of his buddies at one of Philadelphia's more infamous pubs, Rotten Ralph's on Chestnut Street. This general served with the 25th Infantry, including a secret mission into Cambodia during the 1975 "killing fields" horror via Thailand. He said that Vietnam War combat veterans were thrown to the lions and that our lives were discounted for the benefit of good "body count" reports to the U.S. government. Essentially, we were put into one of the most difficult situations in the history of American military and left unprepared to overcome it. We were NOT SUPPOSED TO WIN THE VIETNAM WAR! The fact that we had won it before victory was pulled from our grasp speaks very highly of the combat soldiers who were "sacrificed lambs" in Southeast Asia.

And the coffins came home to every city, town, and village ... but the media wouldn't allow Americans to separate this war from the innocent young warriors sent to fight it! It is okay to hate war, despise it if you must, but ... NOT THE WARRIOR!

Chapter 19

WE WHO WENT THERE AND CAME BACK WILL NEVER FORGET

I would like to begin this chapter by borrowing the most recent *Bravo Regulars*, December 2012 newsletter, which followed a reunion of Bravo Company 3rd 22nd Regulars of the 25th Infantry:

[Chaplains Corner] *I'm not perfect. I'm not a Muslim. I'm not a Socialist. I'm not a Democrat. I'm not a Republican. I'm not for abortion. I'm not going to be controlled by a big union. I'm not going to be told what to do by anyone. This is not what freedom is all about. I am a Christian and an electrician. I am who I am, believer of Jesus Christ and what he gave to us, our fallen comrades and what they stood for. What they stood for is the most important thing—Freedom.*

- Ted Rowley, Chaplain
Bravo Regulars 3rd 22nd 25th Infantry

We are still and should remain soldiers always! They will never be forgotten—the brave combat soldiers we fought with and those who have died over here. We are still fighting to preserve the memories of their sacrifice for the United States of America, its people, and their FREEDOM!

Someone said that the "old soldiers just fade away." I never liked that phrase and I don't agree with it. Some soldiers are indeed warriors to the end of their lives. I hope that when they die, other soldiers will carry on the fight.

All too often someone has told me about a person they knew or were related to who served in Vietnam, but they never talked about it. I understand and appreciate how some of my brothers have remained silent about what happened over there. They probably do not want to burden others with their painful memories of Vietnam.

VIETNAM

TAKE A MAN THEN PUT HIM ALONE
PUT HIM 12,000 MILES FROM HOME
EMPTY HIS HEART OF ALL BUT BLOOD
MAKE HIM LIVE IN SWEAT & MUD

THIS IS THE LIFE I HAVE TO LIVE
AND WHY MY SOUL TO THE DEVIL I GIVE
YOU "PEACE BOYS" RANK FROM YOUR EASY CHAIR
BUT YOU DON'T KNOW WHAT IT'S LIKE OVER THERE

YOU HAVE A BALL WITHOUT EVEN TRYING
WHILE OVER HERE OUR MEN ARE DYING
YOU BURN YOUR DRAFT CARDS & MARCH AT DAWN
PLANT YOUR SIGNS ON THE WHITE HOUSE LAWN

YOU ALL WANT TO BAN THE BOMB
THERE'S NO REAL WAR IN VIETNAM
USE YOUR DAYS AND HAVE YOUR FUN
AND THEN REFUSE TO LIFT A GUN

THERE'S NOTHING ELSE FOR YOU TO DO
AND I'M SUPPOSED TO DIE FOR Y-O-U?
YOU MADE ME HEAR MY BUDDY CRY
YOU MADE ME WATCH MY BUDDIES DIE

I SAW HIS ARMS, A BLOODY SHRED
I HEARD THEM SAY "THIS ONE IS DEAD"
IT'S QUITE A PRICE HE HAD TO PAY
NOT TO LIVE ANOTHER DAY

HE HAD THE GUTS TO FIGHT AND DIE
HE PAID THE PRICE BUT WHAT DID HE BUY
HE BOUGHT YOUR LIFE WHILE LOSING HIS
BUT WHO GIVES A DAMN WHAT A SOLDIER GIVES

HIS WIFE DOES AND PROBABLY HIS SONS
BUT THEY'RE ABOUT THE ONLY ONES

A GI
VIETNAM 1968

Anyone who has served in Vietnam has a story to tell, even the "Saigon cowboys." If you think your story is not worth telling, I respectfully urge you to think again. I have told my story here as hundreds or thousands of other Vietnam veterans have already done so in one way or another.

If you are a Nam vet—one of those silent ones who has never opened up—it's never too late. If you are not a Nam vet but you know one or more, ask them about their story over there … It's not too late. Most people will listen to what a Nam vet has to say. Maybe that wasn't so twenty to forty years ago, but it is now … IT'S NEVER TOO LATE!

I want Vietnam veterans to be remembered and honored in a positive way. That's all. Why not? We served our country well, and the price many of us are still paying is way too high.

Bankruptcy hit me twice since coming back from Nam. I used to look down on myself for that, but not anymore, because both times I fought back and there were some seriously bad circumstances that occurred which I never saw coming. That's not supposed to happen to a former combat infantry point man. I was trained to see dangers ahead before they happened. But I did bounce back both times. I was trained to do that because this great country allowed me the opportunity. I remain grateful to America for that.

Everyone who served in the Vietnam War deserved much more than the American government, the American media, and the American people have been willing to give. Over four decades later, that war which has never left our daily thoughts still arouses us when the subject is brought up. And yet, most of us still love our country.

Vietnam has come back to haunt many of us forty to fifty years later— Agent Orange, diabetes, PTSD, cancers, jungle rot, mental horrors, nightmares/day mares, physical disabilities, etc. Nam brothers have been dying left and right before our very eyes over the past fifty years or so. It has been said that most Korean War vets will outlive us.

There are disability denials, backlogs with preference given to other/younger vets, in hope that we Nam vets will simply die … die … die. We cannot die so easily—not after the way we fought so hard in Nam.

Every month I read the *Vietnam Veterans* magazine's special section near the back. It is called "TAPS." This is our obituary section. It's too long for my liking, and I expect it will continue to be too long for a few more years at least.

Our Oath to Defend the USA Had No Expiration Date!

We were young soldiers once. Some of us are still soldiers … but not so young anymore. Like a lot of guys and gals did, I entered the U.S. Army in 1967 and swore an allegiance to defend the American way, our FREEDOM from all ENEMIES—foreign and domestic! That *Oath To Defend* began like this:

I, Roland E. Trimmer, do solemnly swear that I will support and defend the Constitution of the United States against all enemies, foreign and domestic; that I will bear true faith and allegiance to the same; that I take this obligation freely, without any mental reservation or purpose of evasion; and that I will obey the orders of the President of the United States and the orders of the officers appointed over me.

Let's see—we Vietnam veterans who fought for our country in the most controversial war in American history have remained loyal soldiers to our country to this day or till the end of our days, and yet …

- Our politicians, left and right, Democrats or Republicans, can lie, cheat, steal and even murder … but that's just politics?

- We are unable to close our border with Mexico and prevent millions of undesirables and illegal aliens (including terrorists) from infiltrating our homeland, but we can send our military to far-off lands to help them protect **their** borders?

I don't believe in anarchy, and the last thing that I ever want my grandchildren to experience here is another revolution within! The *Oath to Defend the USA* that I swore to way back in 1967 said that I would defend the United States and its Constitution from all enemies … foreign and DOMESTIC! **That Oath to Defend the USA also HAD NO EXPIRATION DATE!**

Whether you were a Navy SEAL, Army Green Beret, Army Ranger, Marine, Air Force, Seabee, combat engineer, armor, artillery support group, or combat infantry grunt, we all took that same *oath to defend the USA.* Say no more. You know what I am saying here. Anyone who violates the U.S. Constitution—ANYONE—is a criminal no matter what office or title he/she holds, at a corporate level or within our own government.

The "father of our country" once said this to the Continental Army before a major battle:

The fate of unborn millions will now depend, under God, on the courage and conduct of this army. Our cruel and unrelenting enemy leaves us only the choice of brave resistance or the most abject submission.

- General George Washington
August 17, 1776

Patriotism

My dear fellow "patriots," if you are standing pat in life—I am sure you have your own reasons. However, please make no mistake about this … **PATRIOTISM TO THE USA IS NOT BEING TAUGHT IN OUR SCHOOLS AND COLLEGES TODAY.** Patriotism may be mentioned in our history books—something that Americans used to believe in back in the 18th and 19th centuries. Think about this, dear fellow patriots; think about it long and hard! Please excuse me for repeating this, but we veterans, especially we Vietnam veterans who were persecuted during and after our service to our country, have an obligation to protect this great country from its enemies … foreign and DOMESTIC!

"Real" Vietnam veterans know that we **did not lose** the Vietnam War. The demise of South Vietnam began during the Tet year in 1968. When we were spilling our guts in battle, politicians back home were stabbing us in the back with the help of our media. The misguided protesters (including some Vietnam veterans) gave North Vietnam the shot in the arm it needed to continue on and eventually take over South Vietnam. Of course, it did not help our cause when our politicians forced South Vietnam into signing the Paris Peace Accords in 1973 and, as we know, North Vietnam did not sign them in good faith. The rest is history.

We all know that the South Vietnamese army did fight on—even without our help. They actually fought on bravely—like we taught them. The battle of Xuan Loc was evidence of their bravery and capability to defeat North Vietnam on the battlefield. South Vietnam's army of rangers and airborne soldiers were badly outnumbered at Xuan Loc, but they were winning what would have been a strategic victory for them.

Only after South Vietnam's president Duong Van Minh broadcasted his cowardly surrender of April 30, 1975 did the South Vietnamese lay down their weapons, following the order of their commander in chief.

My patriot brothers and sisters, **heroes die, but their heroic spirit must live on. It must!** Please, we need to maintain our *Oath to Defend the USA* for as long as our great country needs us—for as long as we are still breathing. The United States of America—our country—is not the enemy. The corrupt politicians who are raping America are the enemy.

The Green Berets, a 1968 movie, featured John Wayne and David Janssen. John Wayne was inspired to be a part of this movie because of the anti-war atmosphere in the U.S. He received complete cooperation and information from the military and President Johnson.

John Wayne actually visited South Vietnam in 1965, which prompted his decision to produce a film about the U.S. Army's special forces in Vietnam as a tribute in support of them. **How patriotic is that?!**

The Green Berets portrayed the Viet Cong and North Vietnamese Army as sadistic terrorists (which they were). It also gave them credit for being highly capable and willing to fight a good fight (which they did). This movie showed how sophisticated the VC and NVA spy ring was in infiltrating the government and military of South Vietnam. *The Green Berets* also showed how the war in Vietnam had no front line and that the enemy could show up, attack at any moment, and disappear just as quickly.

Much of the film was shot in the summer of 1967 at Fort Benning, Georgia. The United States Army provided several UH-1 Huey attack helicopters and a C-7 Caribou light transport, while the United States Air Force supplied two C-130 Hercules transports for use in the film. The Army also provided authentic uniforms for the actors to use, including the OG-107 green and "tiger stripe" tropical combat uniform (jungle fatigues), with correct Vietnam subdued insignia and name tapes. Some of the Vietnamese village sets were so realistic they were left intact, and were later used by the Army for training troops destined for Vietnam. The commander of the United States Army Airborne School at Fort Benning can be seen shooting trap with John Wayne.

The defensive battle that takes place during the movie is very loosely based on the Battle of Nam Dong, during which two Viet Cong battalions and the PAVN attacked the Nam Dong CIDG camp located in the valley near the Laotian border of the South Vietnam central highlands. The camp was defended by a mixed force of Americans, Australians, and South Vietnamese troops on July 6, 1964.

The movie was highly criticized for glorifying the Vietnam War. One Chicago newspaper critic gave the movie a zero-star rating and referred to it as a "cowboys and Indians," old-fashioned type movie. Despite many poor reviews, the movie went on to be a terrific success. John Wayne attributed the poor reviews to the negative bashings from the liberal press, which he believed were actually criticism of the war rather than the movie itself. **YA GOTTA LOVE JOHN WAYNE IF YOU LOVE THIS COUNTRY!**

Patriotism means to stand by the country. It does not mean to stand by the president or any other public official, save exactly to the degree in which he himself stands by the country. It is patriotic to support him insofar as he efficiently serves the country. It is unpatriotic not to oppose him to the exact extent that by inefficiency or otherwise he fails in his duty to stand by the country. In either event, it is unpatriotic not to tell the truth, whether about the president or anyone else ...

- President Theodore Roosevelt

So what if we Vietnam veterans suffer from a vast array of ailments caused by exposure to Agent Orange? So what if we were exposed to this toxic herbicide by our government? So what if some of us remain angry about the situation? BIG DEAL! Andso what if our brothers and sisters from the Middle East wars are dying from suicide at levels not seen in over a decade ... SO WHAT?!

Over the last forty years there has been one research study after another completed about Agent Orange and its effects on the health of Vietnam veterans and any other vet who was exposed to it. We have to presume that our worries were resolved for the most part by the Agent Orange Act of 1991, which did establish a connection between exposure to Agent Orange and a long list of diseases and illnesses.

PROBLEM: No one can give back us Vietnam veterans our good health as it existed prior to Vietnam. Okay, now many of us are finally receiving badly needed and long-past-due compensation and benefits for our seemingly unappreciated service in Vietnam.

There is no doubt that our country failed the Vietnam veterans. We were overlooked, and we are still trying to recover from that ignorant injustice dumped on us by our own country. Oh God, I hope we don't let history repeat itself again and again. However, I feel that America is not prepared to adequately care for the hordes of soldiers that returned from Iraq and Afghanistan who will be suffering from PTSD!

Every American who has been touched by any of our wars—from Korea to the most current one—should feel indebted to Vietnam veterans. Because of the Vietnam War, Americans know that PTSD can and will strike at anytime—sometimes right after the horror happened or several decades later. It is because of the Vietnam veterans' pain and sufferings that doctors and the VA have a much better understanding about what PTSD can do to a veteran's life and his or her family's lives.

These days most Americans who see military personnel coming and going from Afghanistan show them far greater respect and admiration than they did for Vietnam veterans when they came home. Think about this … isn't the reversed treatment of our soldiers today like making up for the way we Vietnam vets were treated?

It's okay. I also respect, admire, and offer encouragement to many soldiers in today's military. However, after they come home, many of their problems have not manifested yet. **PTSD lurks ahead.**

As I mentioned earlier in the book, one of the most recent reports from the VA was that returning veterans from the Middle East or Gulf wars are committing suicide at the highest rate in several decades.

The VA's website clearly states that serviced connection for exposure to Agent Orange is presumed for anyone who has "set foot in Vietnam, regardless of the length of visit." Great—then what is the level of danger for **those who were exposed to the Agent Orange family of herbicides on a daily basis for an entire year out in the field where it was physically sprayed?** Do you feel my anger and frustration? **HOPE SO!**

I *am* a patriot! I fought and risked my life for this country! And I still believe that the USA is by far the GREATEST COUNTRY IN THE WORLD. I would risk my life for fellow patriotic Americans again if I had to, regardless of my age.

This book may not be the last one ever written about Vietnam, as the story of our war over there and back home has not ended yet. However, this book about the Vietnam War could be one of the few that every true American absolutely needs to read.

Dear fellow patriot, consider this—and if you are not a Vietnam War veteran, at least try to put yourself into our position. Here's the scenario:

- World War II has always provided a sense of pride in abundance—for most Americans. The history books command it.
- Our sons and daughters (of Vietnam vets) would like to feel that same pride for us ... Do they?

THIS IS ANOTHER REASON I HAVE WRITTEN THIS BOOK! As for our war, the Vietnam War itself, history books placed in libraries and used in our school are pieces of toilet paper, and that should be their function.

It is NOT too late to extol or praise—YES, PRAISE and, most importantly, thank—a Vietnam War veteran. Military heroes in America have been on a decline for many years. TOO BAD! WHAT A DEPRESSING TREND!

Oh my ... if you read Senator John McCain's account of his very long captivity in North Vietnam, in his 1999 memoir, *Faith of my Fathers*, you will be moved—even if you are not a veteran of any war. Let's face it; Vietnam veterans remain an unacknowledged part of America's recognized heroes. But the Vietnam War stands out in the back of many Americans' minds as ANY other war our country was ever engaged in.

When it was all over—or "said and done,"—there was NO teamwork between American citizens and Vietnam War veterans ... and the distance between us widened as more of us came home ... often in disillusioned states. WWI and WWII mobilized the entire planet!

When the USA got involved in Vietnam after France "bailed out," get this: Great Britain (the great colonizer) offered us no support ... France, Vietnam's colonizer, showed no pride in accepting our financial and military support against the Viet Minh. And when the war escalated between North Vietnam and America, France became "neutral!" WHEN WILL WE WAKE UP? (They don't like us, but they will take our money!)

Most Americans, if given a choice today of which war to fight in, would not choose the Vietnam War. And yet, there is something very honorable about fighting in and surviving such a horrible, unpopular war, don't ya think?

I suspect some Vietnam veterans who read this book will feel threatened in that I have attempted to bring them and their buried memories out of the closet. In spite of that, I had to proceed, as our war story needs to be reopened to Americans.

Vietnam veterans deserve to be remembered as warriors who went forward when so many others refused, and we fought to save the concept of serving one's country ... How old-fashioned of us!

Those Americans who have attempted to push aside any remembrance of Vietnam's war experience have been a bit on the "unpatriotic" side, though few of them would ever acknowledge it. Our deceased Vietnam War veteran brothers should be remembered as part of a courageous and valorous heritage in which hundreds of thousands of Americans made the ultimate sacrifice … without ever being thanked. Yes, hundreds of thousands … 58,000+ during the war and one million+ since the war ended. **Bottom line: VIETNAM VETERANS OWE NO ONE ANY APOLOGIES!**

When Hope Hits A Detour

The September 2012 issue of *The American Legion* magazine published a heavy article, written by Andy Romey, titled "When Hope Seems Lost." Mr. Romey says:

An exact number for veteran suicides is difficult to pinpoint, but current estimates are alarming the military and veterans communities alike. New data from the Centers for Disease Control and Prevention (CDC)—the federal agency that tracks suicide rates—show that veterans could account for about 20 percent of suicide deaths annually. Put another way, that's eighteen or so veterans who take their lives each day.

There is great concern about these numbers, especially considering that one million men and women are expected to leave the U.S. military in the next five years.

Right now, only about one-third of veterans use VA facilities, and they're free to opt out of the military health system after they separate from the service. This makes it difficult to get reliable statistics on veterans' medical conditions, especially mental health. Lawmakers and officials from VA and CDC are working together to develop more concrete numbers on veteran suicides, and their findings are expected to be released this year.

Mr. Romey's article also states that even though the suicide rate among younger veterans who are returning from Afghanistan and Iraq is a problem, the group that the VA is most concerned about is Vietnam veterans!

Something that all of us Nam vets have known for years (and apparently the VA is only recently recognizing it) is that the suicide rate for Vietnam veterans is much higher compared to their non-Vietnam veteran civilian counterparts. Suicides by Vietnam veterans is actually still the largest group in the population of veterans, Mr. Romey's article also states.

My dear fellow Vietnam veterans … we all need to reach out to a troubled veteran and not just our Vietnam vet brothers—to ALL veterans from any war. Being a friend to someone can be a life-saving gesture, especially if his or her hope factor has detoured. Hope is something that belongs to you. No one can touch it or take it away from you, not if you choose to hang on to it.

Better Extremely Late Than Never?

Not really! Roughly forty-five years after the peak of Agent Orange spraying (1967–1969), our country has agreed to begin a very, VERY tardy effort of cleaning up one of the messes it created in Vietnam. Actually, the first day Agent Orange was "tested" in South Vietnam was on August 10, 1961 … over fifty-one years ago.

Unfortunately, the U.S. cannot possibly right the devastating wrongs done by its Agent Orange program, such as birth defects, never-ending skin diseases, heart diseases, type II diabetes, several types of cancer, and **deaths in the hundreds of thousands!** Hats off to former Cleveland *Plain Dealer* columnist and Pulitzer Prize winner Connie Schultz, who teamed up with Associated Press photographer Nick Ut, who also earned a Pulitzer Prize in 1972 for his war photography of the damage the Vietnam War has done to Vietnamese civilians by our napalm and Agent Orange spraying. Maybe her article helped get things going.

CONDEMNED PROPERTY? There is an ungodly amount of correcting to be done by our country for all of the destruction that was inflicted upon the lives of Americans and Vietnamese. The reported estimated cost of the clean-up program is less than $45 million at the time of this writing (8/25/12). SO WHAT? What is the value of just one life, never mind the hordes of casualties dealt by the mass Agent Orange spraying? Agent Orange defoliant is reported to be twenty to fifty times more powerful than normal defoliants used for agricultural use. **How could our leaders not expect the damage and destruction to be limited to plants, bushes, and palm trees?**

This section of my book was written on August 11, 2012, the same day I received the news of our so-called chemical clean-up of a couple dozen sites in Southern Vietnam. Today also makes it exactly one year and ten months since a Veterans Administration physician's official diagnosis of type II diabetes was recorded and when he advised me to file my disability claim for damage from Agent Orange.

Time to Fight Back—Get Mad!

When I received an early out from the Army in September 1969 to return to college full time, the U.S. government paid me about $175 a month. Granted, going to college in 1969 wasn't nearly as expensive as it is today. You don't want to know how much the current GI bill pays our veteran brothers and sisters … it would literally blow your mind.

Today, returning veterans receive excellent counseling and therapy. *We did not.* Today, returning veterans get rushed through the VA systems backlog for quick disability checks. *We did not*. In fact, we still get pushed to the back of the line for disability claims.

I understand why many Vietnam veterans have given up. We were ignored and disrespected by our country … even our so-called brothers from World War II. I wish I had a dollar for every time a WWII veteran told me that we Vietnam veterans did not fight in a real war—not like the BIG ONE. **Bull f— -ing shit!**

Let's get down to the real hard, cold truth. When we came home, we Vietnam veterans were not even welcomed at the various service organizations by our WWII brothers/ fathers/uncles because we fought in an "undeclared" war and they fought in the BIG ONE! I am so tired of hearing that crap.

Like most Vietnam veterans, I did not/could not finish college. Dealing with PTSD (although there was no treatment available then), working to try and pay for that education, dealing with family issues galore—when NO ONE knew what PTSD was—all of this pretty much kept my head screwed up.

Hey, Vietnam vet—you still with me? We aren't supposed to be around today. We were supposed to die already with the hundreds of thousands of other Nam vets who have bitten the dust.

Over there, real combat veterans were not fed well, not clothed well, and not treated well for diseases, ailments, and wounds. I dropped fifty pounds in less than three months over there. I passed out at least three times from dehydration or malnutrition—and no one ever diagnosed it or treated it.

Fresh C-rations weren't even available, so "eat/drink what you can" was the rule in order to make it to the next day and the next. We rarely saw hot meals, fruit (except native, insect-infested bananas or pineapples), no vegetables, milk (what was that?), no juices, no fresh foods, nothing that even resembled healthiness. When we came home, our health was terrible, but there were no programs to take care of us. **"Take two aspirin and get a good night's sleep"** were our instructions. GET A GOOD NIGHT'S SLEEP? How does one do that, going out on ambush patrol every other night?

Okay, We're Home—Who Will Take Care of Us?

Over there, many of us ate so poorly that we looked like we were starving. Little did we know that our health was in jeopardy for future years—those who would live beyond age thirty to fifty. Those of us who have made it to our sixties and seventies have a multitude of health issues that were not caused by the inevitable process of aging.

Agent Orange was eating away at us. We just didn't know it when we came home from hell. We fought with severe skin conditions called chloracne, which we referred to as "jungle rot." Then came the cancers, diabetes, heart problems, and a disease that resembles Parkinson's. Vietnam vets have been dying at an ungodly rate. How many of us have died back here from our Vietnam-related problems may never be known. Over two million in all is the estimate of many.

Our fellow Americans' reaction? Ignore the Vietnam veteran. Ignore their sacrifices. Downplay their combat experience. Deny their claims. Delay their claims. Wait for them to die.

Our WWII brothers not only kept us out of the service organizations, they were also instrumental in downgrading the GI bill that was there for them when they came home, as the WWII veterans were major influencers of VA policies.

Ignore Vietnam vets and that is just what Americans did during the early years after we came home from hell. If anyone tells America that "real" Vietnam combat veterans did not contribute their participation generously to the prisons and homeless community, they are lying! If anyone tells America that "real" Vietnam combat veterans did not engage heavily with alcohol, drugs, and suicide, they are lying! If anyone tells America that "real" Vietnam combat veterans had little difficulty with marriages and family life in general, they are lying!

"Real" Vietnam combat vets? The "real" ones came from hell, with Silver Stars, Bronze Stars, Commendation Medals, and Purple Hearts, not to exclude wounds that may never heal. The fact that we came home at all was a miracle. We were sent to Vietnam to be used up and thrown away. If we survived, it would be a pure bonus.

As I have mentioned elsewhere in this book, feeding us grunts out in the boonies was never a high priority. Feeding us well wasn't even considered. Same policy for getting ammunition, clothes, boots, etc. out to the remote areas where combat troops lived. I guess this was pretty darn good training after all, so we should have been able to mingle better when we came home from hell. We should have, but way too many never adjusted, and few Americans helped them.

Now that I have been home from hell for over forty years, it blows my mind that the abuse of Vietnam vets is still going on. Only those who continue the fight with the VA make any progress. The recent wars have hurt Vietnam vets by making us a lower priority—how could we be lowered from where we were before? There is nowhere to go after they put you at the bottom.

Some of our African-American brothers believe that America owes them reparations for what their ancestors went through years ago. We Vietnam combat veterans are still living the pain and horror we were put through in the war, and we are still living the aftermath each and every day. If each of us was handed a large sum of money as reparation, none of our losses, none of our sad memories could ever be reversed. We will live with these wounds until we breathe no more.

Forty-four years ago, I came home, leaving behind me the most hellish experience of my entire life. I did not expect that the battle would continue and that seemingly so many Americans would turn their backs on us. My anger changes nothing about where my allegiance to America rests. I am still a soldier. My heart is with my country and fellow patriotic Americans. I have doubts about who is a patriotic American these days.

Vietnam vets care about all of our brothers in combat from all wars. Even those WWII brothers who blackballed us when we came home from hell! Vietnam veterans were as brave, as loyal as any American military force before them or since. I expect that we will continue to be just that … till our day's end. Vietnam veterans have been decimated since coming home from hell. Some would go further to say that we were murdered by our own country-men. Well over forty years of disrespect, lies, deceit, disappointment, conflict, animosity, hostility, breaches, outrage, ridicule, and abuse, and still, we remain soldiers for our country.

Vietnam veterans and their families are some of the most deserving people in America to be allowed to live out the rest of their lives with honor. That's all we want … the **honor** that was stolen from us.

In the military, we were taught to do an abrupt about-face while standing at attention … never while on the move. However, I was going to learn a new marching step: an about-face while moving forward at a brisk pace. I had to learn it.

Most people have gone through some very hard times in their lives, but most often, they were not really expected to give up the things they loved to do. It can take awhile, especially in our later years, but **IT IS NEVER TOO LATE!**

Doing an about-face in life is not about taking a slight detour around something. It is about turning around 180 degrees and changing course in a completely opposite direction.

My about-face in life didn't happen in one minute, not in one day or one week or one month. In fact, I am still working on that move, and it is not simple.

Is it possible that the extremely difficult times I faced in the Vietnam War was my early but highly advanced training to cope with what my body and mind is going through now? I wonder. Some say that surviving difficult experiences can result in stronger convictions.

People like their habits and routines, and we will often keep doing them even though we know they are not good for us. Changing a bad habit takes time and determination.

When I saw that my glucose readings were running 100 points higher than a couple of years ago and my weight was staying in the 215-217 range, I started my about-face ASAP! I won't go into the details of my program, as there isn't room in the book, but believe it … I am on board and I plan to hang with it. On that note, I am going outside for a short but worthwhile bike ride, then a short walk in the woods with my Newf, Bella. This is all part of my struggle against becoming **Condemned Property of the Vietnam War!**

Praying for Hope …

One of my heroes and mentors in life was a man named Pastor Paul Schenck, who was an amazing man—in more ways than words can describe. He was like a second father to me as he was to many other lost kids.

My life without Pastor Schenck would have gone in another direction, one that I would not have written about to anyone. He was a tall man at 6'5" who was a star basketball player at Cleveland's Shaw High School and Cedarville Baptist College. He coached our makeshift baseball team of thirteen- and fourteen-year-olds. He taught us how to play basketball and how to pitch fast-pitch in softball (I pitched a no-hitter at fifteen years old against an adult team!). He helped us build our own baseball field, and most important, **he taught us how to pray.**

Pastor Schenck convinced us that we did not have to be ministers or devoutly religious to pray. That praying was **communicating with God**. We used to pray before every athletic event … not to be the winners, but to play well, safely, and with good sportsmanship.

All savvy soldiers should understand that they should keep an open line of communication with their leader. So then, praying to our supreme commander in heaven should be a soldier's highest priority before, during, and after the battle. That would be our God.

I've been told that Satan hates it when we pray. Satan is constantly firing thoughts of doubt at us that can be defeated with faith and trust. Whatever praying means to you, by all means, please include praying for "hope" in your program on a daily basis. Not every day is going to be a good day; most people's days are not completely good days. However, every day has at least a few seconds or minutes of good happenings. These moments of NOW should be utilized as much as you are able. There again, living in the present will pay off for you.

There are so many of our Vietnam War brothers who gave up since they came home from over there. There are oh so many of our Nam brothers who have reached a place of hopelessness and are in various stages of giving up. But we who are mentally and physically able to help them **should not let them give up**. We didn't do that over there in the Nam, did we?

The complaints about the Department of Veteran Affairs have been flooding in for many decades; many are justified. Good news, my brothers and sisters … our own American Legion is giving out high marks for several VA facilities they visited this past year. The Legion's report praised the high quality of care it witnessed.

I personally can testify that VA facilities have come a long, long way since those days during and after the Korean and Vietnam wars. So keep the faith and know that there are quality people at the VA, quality and caring enough—trust them.

Fellow Nam veterans and patriots of other conflicts in life: **KEEP YOUR FAITH, KEEP YOUR HOPE, AND KEEP PRAYING FOR EACH OTHER!**

No one knows more about PTSD and how to treat it than the VA. If you're looking for more information from the "official source," check out the Veteran Administration's National Center for PTSD website. If you have gone through trauma—war-related or otherwise—or know someone who has, check out the "Public" section of the site. What is PTSD? How is PTSD measured? What treatment options are available? You'll find all this and a lot more at these URLs: www.ptsd.va.gov and www.ncptsd.va.gov.

No Condemnation … the New You!

The first step is that we Vietnam veterans have to come out of hiding. We are worthy enough to do that. We are worthy enough to come home … FINALLY!

The odds were against us over there. Those of us who physically came back should have been better prepared to handle and deal with the unexpected back here. The odds were against us again, and many of us didn't handle it.

I am not going to get real religious on you here, even though I was raised by a Baptist missionary mother who had attempted to save the world during her short lifetime. You know what, my dear war buddies, we all have bad days, and we had mostly really bad days over *there* which have caused extended bad days for some of us over *here*. Bummer—I know it. Still, those of us who have survived do have a purpose for being here. Each and every day that we wake up, we enter a brand-new day with brand-new challenges and opportunities.

Since the Vietnam War was the only war for most of us, why not utilize what we learned from that experience to the max by helping others? Why not do it?

What's on your mind? What do you crave to do when you wake up initially in the morning? A great cup of coffee or tea? A soothing shower? Or a brisk exercise routine, then the shower and coffee or tea? How about just saying THANK YOU! Whether you wake up in a homeless shelter, in a tent, in the backwoods, or in a nice suburban house ... if you wake up, you are way ahead of the game, so why not say THANK YOU and then go and enjoy the day.

The Bible refers to how David saw the necessity of seeking God to direct his steps. He looked to God for guidance for his needs for the rest of the day, for each day. I guess that THANK YOU had better be directed to whom it belongs ... GOD. To follow that sincere and humble THANK YOU could be a heartfelt prayer. All of this will have taken seven to ten minutes of your busy day. Can you find the time to do that? One thing I pray for is **the gift of forgiving.**

Judge not, and you shall not be judged. Condemn not,and you shall not be condemned. Forgive and you will be forgiven.
- The Bible

We were treated far worse than any American soldier coming home from any war was ever treated—for decades this contempt toward us has continued. Funny thing, I can't recall very many newsflashes about crazy Vietnam veterans going on rampages of revenge since the war ended. I know a lot of suicides resulted—more than some are willing to admit—and I know that many of us either disappeared completely by finding that quiet hiding place in the wilderness or returned to Vietnam and stayed there.

Our friendly media used to jump on the opportunity to exploit a bank robber when he turned out to be—what else—a Vietnam veteran. Come on, of the crimes that are committed out there, clearly Vietnam veterans do not make up an abnormal representation.

Most of our war buddies just did not want to be bothered anymore. Very few of them continued to carry the ANGER with them that I still carry. I am still searching for **the gift of forgiving**. I make no bones about it. I want it. I no longer want to be a disgruntled, revenge-seeking old Vietnam combat veteran. Sure, I would like to slap the shit out of John Kerry (please God, allow me that opportunity). And I would also like to choke Jane Fonda (and have some fun with her first), but I'm an old Vietnam combat veteran who can't run as fast or as long as I used to. I can't react as quickly as I used to (although I think I can sometimes), but by golly, I am willing to conform, willing to listen, willing to learn again, and willing to try and forgive so that I can do something like this ... RENEW MY MIND!

In our minds, many of us sinned over there in the Nam. Just ask our "hero," John Kerry. Many of us still carry a guilt complex because we made it back from that disgusting war while so many of our war buddies did NOT! Plus, too many of us were forced to watch them die. Many of us condemn ourselves. Who are we to survive when our war buddies did not? Dumping tons of condemnation on our shoulders will not provide the remedy—never will.

I have no idea what I am writing about in this section. I'm just writing from my gut ... and shaking my head and rolling my eyes at the same time. I have no idea ...

Over there we were trained and brainwashed to win. What a unique concept ... winning over losing. I read an article recently entitled "Training to Win." I don't know anyone who ever intentionally trains to lose. I think training to win is preferred by most; however, few have a clue of how much pain, suffering, dedication, sacrifice, discipline, hard work, pressure, perseverance, persistence, resilience, tenacity, trust, healthy faith, and trust in God is required.

Back to square one ... **never give up!** We Vietnam veterans have never known what it feels like to outnumber our adversaries. We were deceived over there, **brainwashed** into thinking that we outnumbered the enemy ... BULL!

Do you remember what your life was like before you physically became a Vietnam veteran? Do you?

Suck It Up, Soldier ... Take the Pain!

Hey troops, remember hearing that in basic training, advanced training, and in the heat of or after the heat of a battle in Vietnam? That was part of the brainwashing plan, which is still working on many veterans long after coming home. It has worked for many of us as we have kept our mouths shut since coming home. Shame on us!

Since I have finally stumbled onto the capable TLC of a few VA medical/psychological professionals during the last few years, I have learned more about how we can heal ourselves of the worst traumatic memories imaginable by a human being. I've learned that those abusive, traumatic horror images that many of us have lived over and over in our afterlife of the Vietnam War will most likely never be completely erased from our memories. Never? Yup.

So, is the "suck it up—take the pain" order we were given time and time again the path to closure or healing? How long can a man be expected to lump it, push through it, take it like a man, and all that baloney?

How confusing is this scenario? The same U.S. government that spent untold millions on brainwashing 2.8 million American soldiers is now investing billions trying to erase the brainwashing. Confused? We Vietnam vets should be.

I'm tired of "sucking it up." I'm tired of thinking that if I let it be known that Vietnam screwed a lot of us up, it's a sign of weakness. That is BULLSHIT!

The U.S. government's brainwashing program will take time to turn around—a long time, with lots of talking through it with buddies and with therapy groups. There is no shortcut. I've learned that. But we all have to start somewhere or remain brainwashed for life.

Psychologists tell me there is no such thing as complete amnesia from our past horrors. Different levels of closure is the best that we will ever accomplish, and Y-O-U and I are the only people who can make that closure happen. Wow ... I wish someone had told me that ten, twenty, thirty years ago, but no one knew back then. Most of us have been trying to repress the ugly memories. It's the natural thing to do. We never knew of any other way to try to relieve ourselves. Trouble is, that doesn't work and no one ever told us.

Complete closure requires a whole new mindset, just like losing thirty pounds on a new diet. All the advice and therapy in the world won't make the plan succeed ... **WE have to make it work for ourselves, and IT'S NEVER TOO LATE TO DO THAT!**

I wish I could do it for all Vietnam vets right now, heal their hearts. Healing our hearts ... this might never, ever happen. But let's try anyway. All of a sudden, it seems that we jumped from the rice paddies of Southeast Asia to this ... satellites, lasers, laptops, smartphones, ATMs, etc., and some of us are still not able or won't learn how to turn on a computer ... I said "some of us."

Ask anyone these days this one question ... "Hi, how are you doing?" The most common answer is "Busy." Maybe the world and all its fast technology has left most of us behind, and there is no catching up. Maybe.

All I know about this is that the thought or challenge of ending well or focusing on the finish line has never been more important than now ... for Y-O-U and me.

Welcome Home Twenty Years Later?

As I briefly mentioned earlier in the book, Cleveland, Ohio, allegedly held a welcome home parade for its Vietnam War veterans in September 1988. This was held fifteen years after the Americans came home in 1973 and twenty years after 1968's Tet year, the peak year of the war.

"Firebase Cleveland," as it was called, was thought of, created by, and put on by Cleveland's Vietnam veterans themselves. Two of my former platoon brothers (both now deceased), some of my closest friends, and I marched in that parade.

People hugged and thanked us; we hugged them back, we hugged each other, we cried, we screamed for a couple of hours, and then it was all over.

The next day we read about the event, including such things as this:

- How corporate Cleveland did not contribute to supporting the parade; after all, this was still the time when it wasn't cool to be a Vietnam veteran, living or not.

- We read about the protestors at our coming home parade … yes, protestors.

I can still remember that day, which was twenty-five years ago. There were an estimated 20,000 people there, mostly spectators. It was appreciated, even though we Vietnam veterans put the thing together ourselves, so I guess **we welcomed ourselves home**. That's another example of what it has been like being a "real" Vietnam War veteran. A lot of "thank you" and "welcome home" back and forth to each other.

Here are a few pictures from our welcome home parade twenty-five years ago in Cleveland, Ohio, to end this chapter softly.

Coming Home Parade, Cleveland Ohio – 1988

Coming Home Parade, Cleveland Ohio – 1988

Bud Gainey, Bill McDonald, Smokey Ryan, Dusty Trimmer, Jack Bellemy – Welcome Home – 1988 (20 Years Later)

Chapter 20

VIETNAM & GULF WARS COMPARISONS

The last U.S. soldiers left Iraq in December 2011, which marked the close of a nearly nine-year war that began in March 2003 with missile strikes on Baghdad aimed at ousting President Saddam Hussein. The war cost some 4,500 American lives, and tens of thousands of Iraqis perished. It ended with Iraq still struggling to maintain a fragile democracy with internal violence.

Since the conflict started, scholars, historians, politicians, pundits, and the public have debated the similarities and differences between the Iraq and Vietnam wars.

Whatever the differences, both U.S. wars saw troops withdrawing and returning home quietly—and then the Iraq veterans were being redeployed to Afghanistan. And in both Iraq and Vietnam, unresolved conflicts and uncertainty on the ground remained in the wake of the withdrawals.

To mark the end of each war, Presidents Richard Nixon and Barack Obama addressed the nation. Nixon spoke from the White House on March 29, 1973: "Tonight, the day we have all worked and prayed for has finally come. For the first time in twelve years, no American military forces are in Vietnam."

Obama, in his speech given at Ft. Bragg on December 14, 2011, said: "Today, I've come to speak to you about the end of the war in Iraq. Over the last months, the final work of leaving Iraq has been done."

Both speeches by the two Presidents were quite similar in that they seemed "empty" considering the massive loss of American lives.

Richard Nixon: *On this day, let us honor those who made this achievement possible: those who sacrificed their lives, those who were disabled, those who made every one of us proud to be an American as they returned from years of Communist imprisonment, and every one of the 2 ½ million Americans who served honorably in our Nation's longest war. Never have men served with greater devotion abroad with less apparent support at home.*

Barack Obama: *For nearly nine years, our nation has been at war in Iraq. And you—the incredible men and women of Fort Bragg—have been there every step of the way, serving with honor, sacrificing greatly, from the first waves of the invasion to some of the last troops to come home.*

Nixon: *The 17 million people of South Vietnam have the right to choose their own government and because of our program of Vietnamization, they have the strength to defend that right.*

Obama: *We're leaving behind a stable and self-reliant Iraq, with representative government that was elected by its people. We're building a new partnership between our nations.*

TWO WARS BY THE NUMBERS

Duration	**Iraq:** 8 years, 9 months
	Vietnam: 11 years (1962–1973)
Cost	**Iraq:** $823.2 billion
	Vietnam: $200 billion (in 1970 dollars)
U.S. Killed	**Iraq:** 4,487 combat deaths
	Vietnam: 58,282 (total)
Wounded	**Iraq:** 31,921 (hostile)
	Vietnam: 303,635 (total)
Peak U.S. Troop Level	**Iraq:** 168,000
	Vietnam: 543,400
Total U.S. Troops	**Iraq:** 1,500,000
	Vietnam: 2,800,000

Vietnam veterans served our nation in a critical time in history. They stood up to the threat of communism while facing criticism at home but yet they never turned their back on our country or fellow veterans. Today they are the leading voice for veterans rights ... they are the giants upon which we all stand today.
> \- Rocky J. Chavez,
> Former Acting Secretary, California Veterans Affairs

(Source: *VIETNAM*, April 2012)

Our Iraq War brothers and sisters will discover (sooner or later or both) what we Vietnam War veterans had to learn the hard way. Time does NOT heal all wounds. There are still 500,000 or more Vietnam War veterans who, thirty to forty years later, still suffer from the nightmares, flashbacks, fear, and anger of PTSD plus Agent Orange-caused diseases and additional stress problems.

I still remember the heart-wrenching documentary about our psychologically damaged Vietnam War veterans, "CBS Reports: The Wall Within," several years ago. Dan Rather was the CBS correspondent for this program, and he said things like this:

Time does not heal PTSD—if time could heal it, I guess it would not be much of an illness to beat.

Remember, this program and Dan Rather's comments were many years ago. Rather also said this on that program:

"The Veterans Administration had to be forced to help the Vietnam veterans, and usually the response was to treat the men with drug problems and then be done with them.

It took a very long time to get the VA to go out and try to find these people. When they finally were forced to do it, they were so stunned by the numbers they discovered that a real effort was made to COVER IT UP!

One reason very little has been written about these Vietnam War veterans and even less shown on television is that their stories were so horrific."

I remember other parts of that documentary where it was said that nearly 200,000 Vietnam veterans had been hiding themselves away from society in the wilderness of Washington State. Many more were believed to be hidden in remote areas of other states as well. How horrific was that?

Remember ... after World War I it was called "shell shock." After World War II it was called "battle fatigue." Also remember this ... after those two wars our troops came marching home to open-armed embraces—a hero's welcome and a hero's life. NOBODY came back from Vietnam to those warm welcomes!

Our brothers from the Middle East wars are coming home to much better receptions, in large part because of the way America treated Vietnam veterans. I don't know of anyone, especially Vietnam veterans, who do not reach out to our troops in uniform today ... I am proud of that.

Even Robert McNamara, often referred to as the architect of Washington's failed Vietnam War policy in the 1960s, waited thirty years before conceding in his 1995 memoir, *In Retrospect: The Tragedy and Lessons of Vietnam*, that **he had waged the war in error**!

Thanks for the after-thought, Mr. McNamara, and may you rest in peace along with several hundred thousand of our Vietnam War vet brothers and sisters. No wonder so many of us have displayed such rage to others around us.

There are many reasons for our rage. Military training equated rage with masculine identity in the performance of military duty. Whether one was in combat or not, the military experience stirred up more resentment and rage than most of us had ever felt. Finally, when combat in Vietnam was experienced, the combatants were often left with wild, violent impulses and no one upon whom to level them. The nature of guerrilla warfare—with its use of such tactics as booby traps, land mines, and surprise ambushes with the enemy's quick retreat—left us combatants feeling like time bombs, wanting to fight back, but our antagonists had long since disappeared. Often we unleashed this rage at indiscriminate targets for want of more suitable targets.

When we returned from Vietnam, the rage that had been tapped in combat was displaced against those in authority. It was directed against those the veterans felt were responsible for getting us involved in the war in the first place—and against those who would not support the veterans while we were in Vietnam or when we returned home. Fantasies of retaliation against political leaders, the military services, the Veterans Administration, and antiwar protesters were present in the minds of many Vietnam combat veterans. These fantasies are still alive today and generalized to many in the present era … I know this for a fact.

When some Vietnam veterans feel the rage emerging, they will immediately leave the scene before somebody or something gets hurt; subsequently, they drive about aimlessly. Quite often, their behavior behind the wheel reflects their mood. A number of veterans have described to me the verbal catharsis they've achieved in explosions of expletives directed at any other drivers who may wrong them … I can personally relate to this from my own experiences and what I have witnessed from some of my Nam vet brothers.

I will go to my grave with the belief that those who fought in the heat of battle in the Vietnam War were second to none! We were often outnumbered in direct combat. We were often ambushed at any hour of the day or night, and WE WERE NOT SUPPORTED AT HOME BY THE MEDIA, OUR GOVERNMENT, OR THE AMERICAN PEOPLE WHO PROTESTED IN THE STREETS!

Are things better for us Vietnam veterans today? Yes, for many of us who have managed to hang around this long—which many Nam vets were not able to do.

All veterans deserve better and more prompt care and attention when they come home from a war … any war. Never in a billion years did any of us think that we would come home from Vietnam and HAVE TO KEEP FIGHTING WITH OUR OWN GOVERNMENT!

Yet another sign of the times

FORECLOSED!
3 TOURS IN IRAQ
BUT NO BAILOUT
FOR PEOPLE LIKE ME.

Abandonment Of Gulf War Veterans Must Stop!

Who will step up to Help 250,000 to 300,000 Veterans?
By Denise Nichols

The data that shows VA has not done well by the III Gulf War veterans of 90-91-Operation Desert Storm is piling up. These veterans are very ill and many have died in the intervening 21 years. The Gulf War veterans truly feel like the abandoned forgotten veterans. They are feeling like they were placed in the expectant Triage Category at the time of the War and true action to help them has not occurred. The only body that has stood up that is continuing to battle for them is the VA Research Advisory Committee on Gulf War Illness Research (Law enacted in 2000 and meetings began in 2002).

Sound familiar, my dear Vietnam vet brothers? This is why we ALL need to team up and speak out—NOT clam up. We have to help each other because they won't—those who send us into war to fight their battles.

Iraq War Replaces Vietnam?

The war that started with Operation Shock and Awe also ended without a decided victory, very similar to the Vietnam and Korean War endings—in a stalemate. We Vietnam vets still claim that we were never beaten on the battlefield. We are correct in saying that, but the media and historians tell it differently. Iraq War vets will tell you that they were never defeated on the battlefield and that they also won their war. Historians may not see it this way for either war.

American troops left Iraq without much fanfare. At least we Vietnam vets created attention when we came home … lots of boos and jeers with NO cheers. The Iraq War's cost was too high to be called a major victory. Here are some depressing facts:

- America's cost was approximately $3 trillion! (Yes, trillions, not just billions.)

- Since the war started, the U.S. economy went from nearly $200 billion surplus to nearly $17 trillion in debt … and growing at this writing!

- **We were still finishing up another expensive war in Afghanistan at this writing!**

- Iraq's War took the lives of 4,500 Americans with 32,500 being wounded. (Note that the Vietnam War's bloodiest year—the Tet year in 1968—suffered nearly four times as many casualties … IN ONE YEAR!)

- Civilian casualties in Iraq were far less tragic than Vietnam. Approximately 114,000 died in Iraq; one to two million died in Vietnam. (Most were killed by the Viet Cong and NVA!)

- We are claiming Iraq to be a free and sovereign country (South Vietnam was absorbed by North Vietnam), but the internal wars continue on between the Shiite and Sunni Muslims.

- After closing the Iraq War, America tried to forget it and expected those who fought there to just get over it and move on with their lives.

He Never Talks About the War … Really?

If I had a dime for every time someone told me, "I know a Vietnam veteran, and he never, ever talks about it!" **NO SHIT!** Please allow me the opportunity to clue Americans in on why that is! Ever heard of the term **VIETNAM SYNDROME?**

Some background on this is needed. One of my favorite people, President Reagan, once gave a speech to Veterans of Foreign Wars (VFW) where he used the term "Vietnam Syndrome" for the first time. He was referring to the time in which the Soviet Union was becoming more powerful than the United States because they were outspending the U.S. in the global arms race.

President Reagan knew that we could have defeated the Viet Cong and the North Vietnamese Army had the American public not turned against the war. He felt strongly that we soldiers were let down by Presidents Johnson and Nixon because they would not allow us to win that war.

The "Vietnam Syndrome" in President Reagan's mind meant feelings of guilt, feelings of doubt, and that those 58,000 young Americans who died over there were being dishonored as though they died for a shameful cause. President Reagan stated that the soldiers in the Vietnam War fought as bravely and as well as any Americans have ever fought in any war. He said that they deserved America's gratitude, respect, and continued respect.

Vietnam Syndrome is described in many ways, all of them negative. Here are a few that I uncovered from various sources:

- Refers to an "ailment" stemming from America's involvement in the Vietnam War ... An "ailment"?

- Refers to America's humiliating "loss" in Vietnam despite the U.S. wealth and military superiority!

- Refers to America's reluctance to use military force abroad because of the trauma caused by the Vietnam War!

- Refers to the guilt that soldiers experience for surviving when their buddies didn't and also guilt over the million or so Vietnamese civilians killed!

- Vietnam Syndrome is having lost faith and having a defeatist attitude.

- It is used to describe being lost in a quagmire of an unwinnable situation!

- How about this one ... a psychological term used for the consequences of participation in the Vietnam War!

- President Bush declared this after the Gulf War ... "America has kicked the Vietnam Syndrome once and for all."

- It also has been referred to this way … The strategies Vietnam veterans developed to survive with combat did not work once they were thrown back into civilian life … many became dysfunctional!

- Also refers to American public opinion that the U.S. soldiers fought a war abroad that was morally wrong!

- It even meant to some that treatment for veterans with Vietnam Syndrome symptoms included drug therapy!

Vietnam Syndrome often refers to a form of post-traumatic stress disorder found in approximately 40 percent of Vietnam War veterans. Our symptoms could include most or all of the classic PTSD symptoms, such as addictions, rage, depression, anxiety, intrusive combat-related thoughts, flashbacks, and nightmares.

No wonder we did not talk about it—not with non-Vietnam veterans. We chose carefully whom we opened up to.

Hold on, America! The Vietnam Syndrome has been replaced by the Gulf Wars Syndrome. Are you surprised? America, do you care?

YOU BETTER CARE. These veterans are the children of all of you who did not care about the Vietnam Syndrome. **You had better care, because many of those young men and women could also become CONDEMNED PROPERTY?**

We Vietnam vets had to combat the diseases and illnesses caused by Agent Orange. Our Gulf War comrades may have a long list of illnesses with which to contend. Here are a few:

- Asthma and bronchitis
- Sexual dysfunction
- Breathing difficulties
- Fatigue and sleep disorders
- Bacteria in the bloodstream
- Fibromyalgia
- Impaired neurological function
- Diminished ability to think or calculate
- Respiratory disorders
- Post-traumatic stress disorder

Many Vietnam War veterans have suffered from most of these problems in addition to other life-threatening diseases caused primarily by exposure to Agent Orange … **WAR IS HELL!**

Get over it? Move on with your lives? That has a familiar sound to it. We were told the same thing forty-plus years ago after Vietnam.

Iraq's war had its own My Lai-style massacre—at Haditha. Every war has had them. Iraq's war displaced over two million refugees. There were kidnappings, illegal interrogations at secret prisons, and there's Guantanamo.

Maybe, just maybe, they want everyone to get over the Iraq War quickly because there is another war brewing. (Source for some of the statistics above obtained from newamericamedia. org/Forgetting the Iraq War)

Iran's war threat and nuclear crisis looked pretty darn scary at the time I was writing this book. U.S. military presence was increasing in the area, not decreasing. A strike by Israel on Iran was looking more threatening every day. And just a reminder that Iran's goal is to eliminate Israel from the face of the earth—completely. I hope this doesn't happen before my book publishes.

American historians have been treating the entire Vietnam experience on a whole as a black eye. Vietnam caused unbelievable grief when it was happening, and it is still doing that today for those who fought there … who are still living. On the other hand, the Vietnam experience developed a lot of young people to their full potential, which they may have never reached without it.

I am extremely proud to be a Vietnam veteran. Those around me or those who read this book can consider me however they like, but know this … I will continue to give 110 percent for Vietnam vets who need help and will accept it. I know what they went through and understand and feel all of their pains.

When we were sent off to war, we were happy young boys. We returned wounded men who were no longer recognized by many who knew us before. When we came home, the Vietnam War was something no one wanted to talk about—and for the most part, we did not. Many of us were viewed as outcasts or misfits within our own families. So we gravitated to other Vietnam veterans who were going through the same discomfort.

I, too, am still on that unenviable journey … still trying to find my way home, still trying to find inner peace. It has not been easy, but I do believe that many of us are healing; many of our lives today are good. We will still stumble over a few bumps on our road of living, but nothing, absolutely nothing, can ever compare with what we went through over there … NOTHING!

Winning support of the masses of people in Vietnam and at home could have ended the Vietnam War in half the time that it lasted. America's leaders did neither; therefore, they contributed to losing the war even though we the soldiers earned the right to be hailed the victors on the battlefield!

Our Vietnam War and now the Gulf Wars have an all-too familiar ring to them … **AMERICAN ARROGANCE!** In Vietnam, American leaders always thought that "we" would win this war with or without the help of

South Vietnam's military or the support of their people. In Iraq, American leaders again failed (or refused) to accept that there was an insurgency there— as the Viet Cong were in Vietnam. Overconfidence, insensitivity, and arrogance have repeated themselves. And some critics kept saying that the Vietnam War would not repeat itself in Iraq or Afghanistan? Really!

In Vietnam, our supreme leaders held steadfast with their arrogant stand for too long—up to and including the Tet year of 1968. History has in fact repeated itself. America's leaders were just as disconnected with the Iraq situation as they were for far too long with the Vietnam experience. The Vietnam blunder has repeated itself in Iraq and Afghanistan with the winning (or losing) American public opinion. The confidence of the American people for the Iraq War was lost some time ago ... just like it was lost in Vietnam.

General Petraeus might have made a more positive difference in Iraq, had he arrived on the scene sooner. General Abrams likewise in Vietnam. Too little too late.

Guess what, folks? America's leaders have also displayed their unwillingness to correct their previous errors as they have continued to display the same level of arrogance in Afghanistan. Once again, they have attempted to force American-made solutions on someone else's country with total disregard for the state of mind of its peoples and their cultures. BE WORRIED, MY FELLOW PATRIOTS ... BE VERY WORRIED.

If I continue down this road in this section of my book, it will lead to another book by itself. Therefore, I must and I will end this section with these statements—my observations and opinions. Just like **Radical Communism** was our biggest and most dangerous threat in earlier decades—and during the Vietnam era—it continues to loom as a major threat via our "friends" over in China and even Russia, too. Those two combined would be an unbeatable adversary, and neither of them likes America. Fortunately, they have no special love for each other—too much bad history between them.

Add to this threat **Radical Islamic Extremism,** which has made its presence known and how! This enemy has publicly stated that their goal is to destroy America.

The United States of America is at war. It is well into World War III right now. If the American people continue to bury their heads in the sand and just hope all the bad guys will go away, then the good old USA will be defeated sooner rather than later.

World War II brought Americans together. They became more like real patriots once again, like they were after our war for independence. Patriotism today seems to apply to a lesser part of our population than it did during WWII ... This is obvious, not just one man's opinion.

If you are living in America, if you are an American, and if you want this country to survive, it will be necessary for its citizens to feel America, to love America, and to be prepared to defend America. One of our more controversial figures once said:

Your foreparents came to America in immigrant ships. My foreparents came to America in slave ships. But whatever the original ships ... we're all in the same boat today.

　　　　　　　　- Reverend Jesse Jackson

If only the Reverend Jackson would practice more today what he said then.

The United States of America has been and remains such today ... a model for mankind. Our virtues, our honor, our justices, our truth, and our sincerity are what molded this country. To me, this IS worth SAVING! **THIS LAND IS OUR LAND ... GOD BLESS AMERICA!**

Gulf War Illness, PTSD, Agent Orange

In January 2103, I read in several news media sources that 200,000 to 300,000 veterans of the three Gulf Wars are suffering from what has been labeled as Gulf War Illness. Another term used is chronic multi-symptom illness, formerly the Gulf War Syndrome. I wish they could decide on one name and stick with it. They all sound fine.

Initially, our brothers from the first Gulf War in 1991 were hit with this illness, but now our brothers and sisters who fought in Afghanistan and Iraq have developed symptoms, and they are in need of treatment and therapy. PLEASE, AMERICA ... take care of them better than you took care of us back in the 1970s, 1980s, and 1990s.

Unfortunately, treating these deserving warriors will most likely affect us Vietnam War veterans with lengthier delays as our claims are moved further down the list—something we should be used to.

This is extremely eye-opening. I discovered the facts I'll mention here from this website, www.diabetesselfmanagement.com in an April 21, 2010 article by David Spero. Agent Orange has been a generous contributor to type II diabetes for hundreds of thousands of Vietnam War veterans. Many more Vietnamese people were also victimized from that herbicide. However, as David Spero points out, **"Among ALL veterans of ALL wars receiving Veterans Affairs (VA) healthcare, the rate of diabetes is more than double the rate of the general population."**

Stress and pollution seem to be the common factor for military personnel, and certainly, combat service is stressful and traumatic because **feeling the**

constant threat of danger weakens one's immune system and creates insulin resistance.

Bottom line, serving in the military during wartime in a combat zone does nothing good for one's future health-wise. People who don't to go war live longer. Duh!

Afghanistan/Iraq Vets File Claims at Record Rate!

God bless our battle brothers/sisters from these wars. They deserve to be taken care of, and they are not being as bashful about it as we Vietnam veterans were when we came home with multiple ailments and illnesses. Then again, we were usually flat-out denied. Our appeals were delayed—denied—delayed—delayed—denied—and denied again. So many of us died during these battles with VA for justifiable compensation—so many.

With the cost of lives in Afghanistan at over 2,000 and Iraq over 4,000, the number of wounded could be ten times that. What will this do to the long overdue claims from Vietnam veterans? Well, as of January 30, 2013, my claim for disability compensation for Agent Orange-caused diabetes II and many complications from it was approaching two and a half years in pending status. WE NAM VETS DON'T DESERVE THIS!

Just like Vietnam veterans, many veterans from the Gulf, Iraq, and Afghanistan wars will be physically and/or psychologically disabled for life with some form of PTSD because of the killing experiences in their wars … killing of enemies and civilians.

Today's brainwashing tactics haven't changed much since my war. The military begins their dehumanizing process in Basic Training, where soldiers are taught to hate their future "rag head" adversaries … to prepare them to KILL, KILL, KILL!

As mentioned earlier, the techniques used to brainwash us are abusive, degrading, and cruel. They have to be, I guess, as the ultimate goal is to make killing a conditioned reflex, which is the ultimate purpose.

By the time we were sent to Vietnam, our military had programmed us to kill without hesitation. I have seen that conditioning put into a horrible rage after coming home by several Vietnam veterans, including myself. Today, they are using more realistic training techniques like video games. Yes, the same video games kids play.

Our war brothers and sisters in the Gulf Wars also fought wars without a front line, and they could not differentiate the enemy from innocents. Just like in Vietnam, women and children can be the enemy, and they have to be taken out. Then, just like Vietnam vets, the Gulf War vets had to come home after the long, painful dehumanization process and get back to normal just like that. GET OVER THAT WAR ... SURE!

*THEY Won't Believe This!

Just like Vietnam War veterans, Gulf War, Afghanistan, and Iraq War veterans feel out of place when returning home—civilian life and relationships are no longer easy to cultivate. So many of them re-enlist. Just like Vietnam veterans, the divorce rate is extremely high. Many of the Middle East wars' veterans have simply lost the joy for life they once had before their war experiences. Counseling and therapy are more readily available for them now, and it is critical that they receive it, as well as understanding and patience from family and friends. Unfortunately, this is all too late for most Vietnam War veterans ... **most have been gone well before their time!**

Just like Vietnam veterans, our warriors coming home from the Afghanistan and Iraq wars have been finding themselves in serious need of medical support and benefits, and they, too, are finding themselves betrayed, denied, disillusioned, and very upset as they face the process of **DENY, DELAY ... TILL THEY DIE!**

April 3, 2013: As of this date, the U.S. wars in Afghanistan and Iraq will have cost American taxpayers between $4-6 trillion according to a study by a Harvard professor. The cost of the Vietnam War is still mounting!

Chapter 21

REAL VIETNAM VETS ... STEP UP!

If you are a Vietnam-era American or post-Vietnam-era American, you have probably been associated in one way or another with a real Vietnam War veteran ... then again, maybe **NOT!**

It is completely mind-boggling to me and other "real" Nam veterans why anyone would want to pose as a Vietnam veteran and go to extreme measures of fraud throughout their lives till they die to help them fool so many people. It is little wonder why the VA stalls the "alleged" Vietnam veterans' disability claims as though we had the black plague. They have an almost impossible task in verifying who the real McCoy is and who is not.

On the opening page of *Stolen Valor*, the authors, B.G. Burkett and Glenda Whitely, speak of killers who have fooled the most astute prosecutors and gotten away with murder; phony heroes who have become the object of award-winning documentaries on national network television; and liars and fabricators who have flooded major publishing houses with false tales of heroism that have become best-selling biographies. Totally mind-boggling and disgraceful.

Tens of thousands of "real" Vietnam veterans have passed away while waiting for a pending disability claim, with partial blame going to the lowlife, phony "wannabes." And our court system gave the Stolen Valor Act so much trouble? **WHY?**

The false Vietnam War veterans have been filing phony disability claims, backing up the entire system at record levels, but this is old news, and it has been covered by others over and over. I'm not so sure very many people care anymore, but I do.

After I read *Stolen Valor* about twelve years ago, it found permanent residence on my bookshelves, and I refer back to it often. Again, after reading *Stolen Valor* and reading about the rampant phonyism going on, which I was not aware of at the time, I went to the Internet to try something. Although I have all my orders and original certificates for my medals, I wanted to see if I could custom order them without going through the U.S. Army's office in St. Louis, Missouri. Sure enough, at least two or three companies were able and willing to reproduce certificates for just about anything ... Silver Star, Purple Heart, Combat Infantry Award, etc. Their price was about $19.00 per certificate ... for a counterfeit piece of paper?

When I think of my Nam war brothers who were shot or mangled by shrapnel in multiple areas of their body, who lost arms, feet, legs and someone has the

425

lowest moral standard imaginable to counterfeit an award certificate for a Purple Heart? Makes ya want to puke. Trouble is … as the "real" Vietnam veteran continues to die prematurely from Nam-caused problems, an amazing phenomenon is still taking place … the "alleged" Vietnam veteran population now exceeds (by five times over) the total of all who did officially serve there in country. This is not new news to some who may read this book. To others, it will be confusing and SHOCKING!

How Many Vietnam Veterans Are Still Alive?

After going to every website that hinted at offering an answer to this question, without sourcing each website, I found dozens of different answers. I realize that these reports were completed at different times, and most of them do not differentiate between the Vietnam War and the Vietnam era. It is confusing, misleading, and very overwhelming information.

From what I can determine from the many reports (too many), here is a more realistic comparison between Vietnam-era veterans and Vietnam War veterans:

Estimated Vietnam Era Vets Served	11,544,000
(Includes Vietnam War Vets)	
Estimated Vietnam Era Vets Living	8,250,000
(Includes Vietnam War Vets)	
Estimated Vietnam Era Vets Served	7,391,000
(Excluding Vietnam War Vets)	
Estimated Vietnam War Vets Served	2,800,000
Estimated Vietnam War Vets Living	**850,000**
Estimated Americans Claiming to be Vietnam War Vets	**13,853,000**

N E W S F L A S H: Recent "unofficial" survey results from census figures and *VFW* magazine polls show that of the estimated total of 21,532,000 American veterans still living from all wars, **almost 60 percent claim to be Vietnam War veterans … 13,853,000!**

(Sources: www.infoplease.com; www.answers.yahoo.com; en.wikipedia.org; www.vfw.org; www.chacha.com; wiki.answers.com)

Now, before anyone gets their dander up over this, here is what an "official" U.S. Census Bureau reported in the 2000 census ... "Of the 2.8 million Vietnam veterans who served in country Vietnam, there were 1,027,000 alive."

On or about February 13, 1987, a comprehensive study was conducted pertaining to military veterans' health after their service had been completed. The parameters used were pretty basic. They were U.S. Army veterans who had entered the service between 1965–1971 and served just one term. The participants were randomly selected from a database of Vietnam War veterans and Vietnam War-era veterans.

This study, called the Vietnam Experience Study (VES), revealed that Vietnam War veterans experienced nearly 20 percent higher risk of post-service mortality than veterans who served in Germany, Korea, or at home in the United States. Since that study, Vietnam War veterans' mortality rate has worsened, but has gone unnoticed.

I have not come across any current research that can pinpoint how many of us have died specifically from suicide and other Nam-caused illnesses, PTSD, Agent Orange, or vehicle crashes. Maybe the government doesn't want Americans to know the answers. But according to the Veterans Administration, in March 2010, their research revealed the following statistics:

- Fifty-eight percent of 490,135 Vietnam veterans who died between 2000–2010 were younger than sixty.

- Over the past few years, three out of four veterans seeking mental health treatment for the first time were Vietnam veterans in the under-sixty-four-year age group.

- An April 9, 2010 study stated that the Vietnam veteran was dying between the ages of fifty-seven to sixty-eight years old.

Anyone interested in more details on the above, I strongly recommend reading *Waiting for an Army to Die: The Tragedy of Agent Orange* (1989) by Fred Wilcox.

Vietnam War's Damage During The War

Vietnamese civilians killed	2,000,000
Army of Republic of Vietnam killed	250,000
North Vietnamese Army killed	1,100,000
Viet Cong killed	250,000
Americans killed	58,282

South Koreans killed	5,099
Australians killed	500
Thai (Thailand) killed	351
New Zealanders killed	39
Philippinos killed	57
Cambodians killed	250,000
Laotians killed	100,000
Total Estimated Deaths (1955–1975)	**4,014,328**

Damage Done After The War

- 25,000 South Vietnamese civilians killed instantly
- 600,000 interned into government camps
- 3.5 million fled as refugees
- 500,000 refugees died
- 200,000 were executed
- 2.5 million died from political violence
- 3 million Cambodian civilians were killed by Khmer Rouge communists

(Source: en.wikipedia.org/Vietnam War casualties)

Ladies and gentlemen, the next time you veterans from WWII, Korea, Persian Gulf, Afghanistan, Iraq, and Vietnam are participating in your VA therapy session or a VFW, American Legion, Vietnam Veterans, Purple Heart, or Disabled Veterans meeting, think about what the chances are that everyone present claiming to be a Vietnam War battle-hardened veteran really isn't. About 850,000 to 875,000 of us are left, and almost 14,000,000 claim to be us!

Maybe we need the "millions" of phony Nam vets in order to continue telling our story. After all, these guys have studied us thoroughly, thanks to the Internet, dozens of Nam movies, and hundreds of Nam books even though most are fiction. A good phony Nam vet can fool or impress the average citizen—even family members. I've encountered three of them in the last dozen years, and they became really nervous when I started getting into their heads.

Well, whether there are one million of us left or less, or if we count the other thirteen million storytellers, at least our story is still being told. And they do have to rehearse a lot!

Seriously though, with most "real" Vietnam vets having passed away already and many of those remaining still taking the "I don't want to talk about it" routine, is it fair to just fade away and let historians say what they want about us after we have become **EXTINCT?**

When a species or breed dies away and there is no capacity to re-breed and replace, that species/breed will not ever reappear again. When the last Vietnam War veteran (real one) dies, our breed will become **EXTINCT**! Sure, the offspring of our breed can carry on the genetics, but what can they share with others after we are gone if **YOU WON'T TALK ABOUT IT?**

Every day another Vietnam veteran dies from a disease attributed to something related to the Vietnam War. Every week approximately 500 Vietnam War veterans die, usually from something related to his/her service in the Vietnam War. We do not require any help in speeding up our extinction process … Eventually, the last "real" Vietnam War veteran will die, and that will be the end of our presence on earth.

It is old news now—the 112th Congress failed to recognize Vietnam veterans. The House Bill H.R.3612 and Senate Bill 5.1629 to "restore" the Agent Orange Equity Act did not make it. As the 113th Congress convened in mid-January 2013, it appeared that the quality of life for Vietnam War veterans was not a high priority for Congress, so reported retired U.S. Navy Vietnam veteran John J. Bury on January 11, 2013. It's back to the trenches, my brothers, so what else is new?

Hopefully, by the time this book is published, many Vietnam War veterans will have resumed the fight. What choice is there other than to just GIVE UP?

Never, ever, ever, ever, ever, ever, ever, ever, ever, ever, ever give up! Never give up!
- Winston Churchill
October 29, 1941

"Real" Vietnam Veterans Who Impacted Others!

As I watched *We Were Soldiers Once and Young* for the 29th time last week, this idea came to me about mentioning all three of those true heroes in one brief story: Lieutenant General Harold G. Moore Jr., Command Sergeant Major Basil L. Plumley, and journalist Joseph L. Galloway.

Hal Moore served in Korea and Vietnam. Plumley served in WWII, Korea, and Vietnam. He passed away October 10, 2012. Joe covered the Persian Gulf War as well as Vietnam. The one thing all three of them had in common aside from being true heroes is the Battle of Ia Drang in 1965 against the North Vietnamese Army.

Most readers of *Condemned Property?* will have seen the movie or read the book (or both) in which three amigo brothers were the main characters, so I won't take any space up about that. I just wanted to make sure that these three gentlemen were mentioned and America was reminded that there were Vietnam veterans like these over there. (This was no comedy team.)

Hal loved his men. He would have put his life up countless times to serve any of them. Supposedly, he, too, suffers from the guilt complex that many of us carry with us to our graves because some of our guys died over there and we did not. He was a West Point grad with honors, and his post-military career was also fascinating. Of course, many of us remember his 7th Cavalry Regiment as the same one Custer fought with.

Career soldier Plumley was Hal Moore's battalion commander at Ia Drang ... better known by some as "Old Iron Jaw." Very fitting as he was a coal miner's son from West Virginia. It has been said that he prized his CIB (Combat Infantry Badge) as highly as any of his forty to fifty medals and awards.

Joe Galloway's part at Ia Drang was different but no less important than the other two of our three amigo brothers. Galloway was awarded a Bronze Star of Valor for his rescue efforts of wounded soldiers at Ia Drang ... the only civilian to be awarded for such a high award.

My sincerest thank you and way-to-go to these three who are real-life examples of Vietnam War veterans.

Rocky Bleier

Robert Patrick "Rocky" Bleier was from Wisconsin and starred at Notre Dame and the Pittsburgh Steelers in football. I had the pleasure of meeting Rocky, as he was a featured speaker at Cleveland, Ohio's, coming home parade, called Firebase Cleveland.

After his 1968 rookie season with the Pittsburgh Steelers, Rocky was drafted into the U.S. Army in December 1968. He volunteered for duty in the Vietnam War and shipped out in May 1969, serving with the 196th Light Infantry Brigade. On August 20, while on patrol in Heip Duc, he was wounded in the left thigh by a rifle bullet when his platoon was ambushed in a rice paddy. While down, an enemy grenade landed nearby after bouncing off a fellow soldier, sending shrapnel into his lower right leg.

While Rocky was recovering in a hospital in Tokyo, doctors told him that he would never play football again. Soon after, he received a postcard from Steelers owner Art Rooney, which just read "Rock – the team's not doing well. We need you. Art Rooney." Bleier later said, "When you have somebody take the time and interest to send you a postcard, something that they didn't have to do, you have a special place for those kind of people."

One year after being wounded, Bleier reported to Steelers training camp. Upon his return, he couldn't walk without being in pain, and weighed only 180 pounds. He spent two full years trying to regain a spot on the active roster, and was even waived on two occasions. Bleier never gave up, and said that he worked hard so that "some time in the future you didn't have to ask yourself 'what if?'"

An off-season training regimen brought him back to 212 pounds in the summer of 1974. From that point in time, he would be in the Steelers' starting lineup.

After his football career, Rocky wrote a book of his struggle to recover from his war wounds called *Fighting Back: The Rocky Bleier Story*, and it was made into a television movie in 1980, with Robert Urich starring as Bleier, Richard Herd as Steelers coach Chuck Noll, Art Carney as team owner Art Rooney, and many of Bleier's teammates (including Matt Bahr and "Mean Joe" Greene) as themselves. He also did some acting work, appearing on SCTV and in the film *Backstreet Justice* as himself. He also tours the United States as a motivational speaker.

John McCain

Sure, everyone knows who he is and that he is a Vietnam War veteran. And that he is a long-running United States senator who was also the presidential nominee for the Republicans in 2008. What many people are unaware of is that John McCain did not have to spend five and a half years in the Hanoi Hilton POW prison, where he was beaten and tortured. When the North Vietnamese learned that his father was a high-ranking officer, a four-star admiral (so was his grandfather), the North Vietnamese offered to release him. McCain REFUSED.

George E. Day

Retired U.S. Air Force colonel and command pilot, known as "Bud," he served in Vietnam, including five years and seven months as a POW in North Vietnam. He was also awarded the Medal of Honor, Air Force Cross, Distinguished Service Medal, Silver Star Distinguished Flying Cross, four Bronze Stars for Valor, four Purple Hearts, and more. Before his Vietnam War service, he also served in the Korean War and WWII.

He was considering retirement in 1968 as a major. Instead, he volunteered for the Vietnam War in April 1967. On August 26, 1967, in an airstrike north of the Demilitarized Zone (DMZ), Bud's F-100F-15-NA aircraft was hit and disabled by .33mm anti-aircraft fire and he had to eject.

Bud's full story is a very worthwhile read for any patriotic American; you will not be bored. Some of his noteworthy experiences were:

- Injuries from the 8/26/67 ejection … broken arm in three places, eye and back injuries; was captured immediately.

- Escaped from his North Vietnamese captors within a few days, despite his injuries.
- Recaptured by Viet Cong in South Vietnam, wounded again in the leg and hand.
- Returned to NVA camp and was beaten, tortured, and starved periodically. ARE YOU JANE FONDA LOVERS READING?
- Shared a cell with Navy Lieutenant Commander (Senator-to-be) John McCain, who was reported to have worse injuries, was undernourished, sickly, malformed, and gaunt. ARE YOU JANE FONDA LOVERS READING?
- Active member of Florida Republican Party; involved with the Swift-boat Veterans and POWs for Truth.
- Served in the U.S. Air Force, Army, and Marine Corps.

Bud Day was one of the leaders, if not *the* leader, of a group of Vietnam veterans who launched a non-profit organization called the Vietnam Veterans Legacy Foundation back in 2005. They were Vietnam veterans frustrated with the amount of misinformation that was spread so generously about Vietnam War veterans. Bud Day had referred to the Vietnam War veteran as "The Greatest Generation." Remember, Bud Day was a veteran of WWII and Korea as well as Vietnam.

Oliver Stone

Oliver Stone in Vietnam.
© Oliver Stone Collection

Already mentioned earlier in this book, Stone fought and survived some of the bloodiest battles of the Vietnam War (and never mentioned by the media).

On the night of January 1, 1968 into early January 2, a 2,500-man force of NVA and VC attacked elements of the 25th Infantry Division of which Stone was a member. Stone's final battle scene in his movie *Platoon* is a dramatization of the real battle, often called The Battle of Soui Cut. Stone was baffled that this major battle, which included a casualty total of 1,000-plus men on both sides, never received any media coverage. American casualties totaled 176.

Gary Sinise

Actor Gary Sinise, who played a Vietnam War amputee in the movie *Forest Gump,* has been a man of his word in that he has never forgotten about other Vietnam veterans or other veterans from any war. He has performed in and sponsored numerous fund-raising events. Sinise is a successful film director, musician, and actor, of course. He has won many top awards, including an Emmy and a Golden Globe award.

Karl Marlantes

A Marine Vietnam veteran, Yale University graduate, and Rhodes Scholar at Oxford University, he was awarded the Navy Cross, Bronze Star, two Navy Commendation Medals for Valor, two Purple Hearts, ten Air Medals, and other awards. He is a successful author, including a best-seller novel, *Matterhorn.*

Arthur E. Teele, Jr.

Although he left a legacy as being controversial in his Dade County, Florida, political career, he was a brilliant political figure serving in Ronald Reagan's U.S. Department of Transportation and two terms on the Dade County Commission in Florida. He ran but lost a run for Miami mayor but rebounded to become Miami city commissioner. Until his very end of life, he was very competitive, often giving credit to his military combat experience. He once said this about his military days in Vietnam during 1967–1968:

The wing of the military I came from was the most right-wing, bloodthirsty, highly decorated soldiers in the Army at that time. But if you performed, you made it, especially in combat. Merit mattered.

John Murtha

Representative John Murtha became the first Vietnam War veteran elected to Congress. He was an officer in the Marine Reserves when elected in 1974. Controversy shadowed his congressional service, but he always remained one of the most avid supporters of the military amongst Democrats. He had voted in 2002 to support President George W. Bush to use military force in Iraq, but he became frustrated with the handling of the war. Murtha volunteered to go to Vietnam and served as an intelligence officer in 1966–1967.

Oliver Laurence North

North is a retired twenty-two-year veteran of the United States Marine Corps. Lieutenant Colonel North served in Vietnam as a platoon commander, where he earned the Silver Star, Bronze Star, and two Purple Hearts. He is known as a commentator, television host, military historian, and author. His illustrious career did not escape scandal as he was the center of attention during the Iran-Contra affair in the 1980s.

Michael Hossack

Remember the drummer with the Doobie Brothers band? Hossack played with them from 1971–1973 and again in the late 1980s. He served in the U.S. Navy during the Vietnam War. He died of cancer at age sixty-five on March 12, 2012.

Vang Pao

Pao was the leader of the American CIA and backed Hmong guerrillas of Laos who waged their own war against the North Vietnamese during the Vietnam War. Pao immigrated to the United States in 1975 after the communists seized control of South Vietnam and Laos and was called "the biggest hero of the Vietnam War" by former CIA Chief William Colby.

In 2007, however, he was arrested and charged in a U.S. federal court with conspiracy in a plot to kill communist officials in his native country of Laos. Those charges were dropped in 2009, but his life continued with controversy, as he showed no warm and fuzzy feelings to the communists. He brought tens of thousands of his countrymen safely to America. The president of the Lao family community compared Vang Pao's heroic role to that of America's own George Washington.

Jan C. Scruggs
Founder & President, Vietnam Veterans Memorial Fund

Ten years after he was wounded in Vietnam, Jan Scruggs conceived the idea— and charged ahead with it—to build a Vietnam veterans war memorial in Washington D.C. As they say … the rest is history, but thank you, Jan. (If you wish to know more, please refer to https://donate.vvmf.org.)

Gulf War Heroes – Vietnam Veterans

Colin Powell and Norman Schwarzkopf, Jr.

Both of these U.S. Army heroes of the Gulf War received their on-the-job training in the Vietnam War.

Colin Powell was promoted to major while in Vietnam. He was injured twice, once by a Viet Cong booby trap, the other by a helicopter crash. His ultimate command duties included Chairman of the Joint Chiefs of Staff and Army Forces Command. He made four-star general and, of course, later became Secretary of State in the Bush administration.

Norman Schwarzkopf also became a four-star general and was appointed Commander-in-Chief of the U.S. Central Command during the Gulf War with Iraq. It was his initial plan that was used in the defense of Saudi Arabia or Operation Desert Shield. We have seen "Stormin' Norman" often since his retirement from the U.S. Army, mainly on Fox News.

After the Gulf War, Schwarzkopf was offered numerous positions, including that of Chief of Staff of the United States Army, but he refused the promotion. After he retired in 1991, he wrote an autobiography, *It Doesn't Take a Hero*, published in 1992. He died before I finished this book, spending many of his final days with charities and community activities.

A Few Other Well-Knowns ...

Roger Staubach - Notre Dame and Dallas Cowboy football star; participated in two Super Bowl wins

Al Bumbry – Major League Baseball All-Star

Dennis Franz – Actor

Pat Sajak – *Wheel of Fortune* Host

Tom Ridge - Governor of Pennsylvania

Gray Davis - Governor of California

Steve Kanaly – Actor, *Dallas*

Sean Flynn – Actor (Son of Errol Flynn)

Steve Croft – TV Correspondent, *60 Minutes*

Fred Smith – Founder of Federal Express

John Kerry – Congressman/Secretary of State

Al Gore – Vice President

Chuck Hagel – Senator

Tony Knowles - Governor of Arkansas

Joseph Galloway – War Correspondent, Author

Harold G. Moore – Retired Lt. General, Author

Then, of course, every Medal of Honor winner could be included in this list and the list of **Vietnam veterans who made an impact on others.** This is not a short list. **BE PROUD, VIETNAM VETS—YOU ARE ALL HEROES!**

Combat Doctor ... "Medic!"

When the 1st Platoon of Bravo held its first reunion ever in 1988 at John Martino's home in Boston, everyone present took on a stoic look—eyes bulged, jaws dropped, and total silence hit when one of the guys mentioned the word MEDIC! It gave us chills when the reality hit us that **none of our medics made it.**

In fact, I have never found a living medic from the Vietnam War since coming home in 1969 ... not even one. What does this tell you about the dangers they faced in Vietnam? Even though I've mentioned these guys earlier in the book, there cannot ever be enough said about them and what they did over there in that "in your face" war.

The Geneva Convention, Chapter IV, Article 25 states that "Members of the armed forces specially trained as hospital orderlies, nurses or stretcher-bearers, in the search for or the collection, transport or treatment of the wounded and sick shall likewise be respected and protected if they are carrying out these duties." Right! Unfortunately, our enemies in the Vietnam War did not honor this code. In fact, they went out of their way to kill or wound our medics. We can remember the VC yelling out the word as we often did during a battle, "Medic, medic, medic!"

Combat medics and corpsmen may have had the toughest and most important employment during a war. These guys were real Vietnam War combat veterans, and they saved thousands of lives in Vietnam, almost always risking their own to carry out their mission ... God bless the combat medics.

There have been several Nam books written by/about medics. A couple worth reading are *Vietnam Medic* and *Combat Medic-Vietnam*.

Those Unforgettable "Donut Dollies" ...

I could not write a book about the Vietnam War without mentioning the combat warriors' "cheerleaders," the American Red Cross Donut Dollies. They inherited their nickname from American Red Cross workers who made World War II more bearable with donuts and the activities they put together for the troops..

Their Vietnam program was revived in 1965 as a morale booster. And like most of us, their commitment was for one full year. Many of the Donut Dollies were college graduates, single women in their early to mid-twenties, and usually a bit older than the troops they entertained. They were like replacement mothers or sisters to us.

Just like many of us combat veterans, the Donut Dollies' lives would be changed forever because of their experiences in the Vietnam War. Many don't like to talk about it to this day. Maybe this book will reach a few of them. If so ... **THANKS TO OUR LOVELY DONUT DOLLIES ... "REAL" VIETNAM VETS!**

Their jobs were tough, entertaining thousands of guys every week who might have just come out of a battle where some of our buddies were killed or wounded. I saw them in places like Long Binh, Cu Chi, and Tay Ninh. They seemed to understand what we understood ... THAT COMBAT VETS WERE LIVING ON SACRED GROUND THAT ONLY PEOPLE WHO HAVE BEEN IN A WAR COULD POSSIBLY UNDERSTAND!

They always inspired us, telling us what a privilege it was to have the opportunity to meet and talk with us and to support us.

Today, during the ongoing Gulf Wars, a lot of people talk about supporting the troops. Well, the Donut Dollies walked their talk! **THANK YOU, DONUT DOLLIES. WE LOVED YOU THEN AND WE STILL DO!**

Remember Bobbie the Weather Girl?

We first saw Bobbie the Weather Girl while we were combat assaulted to the fighting in Saigon's Cholon district, I think. It might have been Bien Hoa or

Tan Son Nhut—I'm just not sure. It was inside an Enlisted Men's Club where we saw real live flushing toilets and running water, a television, and we had a hamburger with fries. Man, did that taste good!

Bobbie had a nightly broadcast from Armed Forces Vietnam TV Saigon, bringing weather reports from the DMZ to the Delta region. She bounced, she danced, she did kicks in a miniskirt, but most of all, she sent us warm and friendly wishes for safety.

Bobbie "served" in Vietnam from 1967 to 1969, the bloody years. Although she worked for the U.S. Agency for International Development as a secretary at her day job, Bobbie was an unpaid volunteer for her weather broadcasts. Bobbie also made countless trips to the bush to try and bring some cheer to us out in the boonies. She loved her Nam vets and was quoted once as follows:

The rewards were worth more than a million dollars and the experiences over-whelming enough to last a lifetime.

Just like another female hero, Chris Noel, Bobbie passed up R&R trips to visit the troops. She volunteered at hospitals for the Red Cross, and when the Tet Offensives hit Saigon in February and May 1968, she volunteered to serve chow, wash dishes, and deliver box lunches to troops fighting in the Cholon district.

Bobbie always ended her show with a sexy wink and wished us all a pleasant evening weather-wise and good wishes for otherwise. **Thanks, Bobbie ... you were one of us, a "real" Vietnam War veteran!**

Army's Last Vietnam War Draftee Retires

When CLYDE GREEN was drafted in 1970 at age 20, he had no idea he would end up serving for almost 40 years. "I didn't want to join the Army," said Chief Warrant Officer Green in October 2011. "When I got that letter," he said, "I thought my whole world was ending." That draft letter, from President Richard Nixon, came at the height of the Vietnam War's unpopularity, and it uprooted Green from his family's farm. He shipped off six months later. "I got over the draft thing quick," he said. "The Army matures you, develops character."

Green was retired as the Army's longest serving draftee in a September ceremony at Fort McPherson, GA. Speaking at the event, Lt. Gen. Richard P. Zahner praised Green's remarkable military career.

Green served as an "intelligence soldier" in Vietnam from June 1971 to May 1972. After applying for a warrant, he rose to the rank of chief warrant officer 5. He served in the Persian Gulf in 1990 and returned to Vietnam from 1995-2001 with the Joint Task Force - Full Accounting (MIA/POW). His team helped to discover the fate of three MIA's, including a soldier who had served in Green's unit 30 years before.

*THEY Won't Believe This!

As a Vietnam combat veteran who "walked the walk," I can and do "talk the talk." So can all of the people I have mentioned in this chapter. So can these veterans, cooks, accountants, instructors, mechanics, administrators, and all real, honorable veterans who served. They all deserve to hold their head high above the crowd. We learned to cover a buddy's back when we were facing our own personal Armageddon and our adrenaline rush had reached an unbelievable high.

We who have been there and walked the walk can talk the talk. On the other hand, those who did not do not know the score, and they would be more of an asset to our country to just get out of the way and let the veterans do their jobs.

Veterans fought for your home. Now, many thousands of them are homeless. The words "homeless" and "veteran" should NEVER be used together. If you know of a homeless veteran, please call the VA National Homeless Veterans Hotline at (877) 424-3838, twenty-four/seven, 365 days per year.

Please keep in mind that Vietnam veterans were robbed! Our history has been distorted and our heroes downplayed—almost completely shoved under the rug. This book reveals that—it proves that. This is a book every Vietnam veteran and every American who loves this country should keep on their bookshelf ... FOREVER!

And the coffins came home to every city, town and village ... but the media wouldn't allow Americans to separate this war from the innocent young warriors sent to fight it! It is okay to hate war, despise it if you must, but NOT THE WARRIOR!

EPILOGUE

What Were The Chances?

One out of every ten Americans who served in Vietnam became a casualty before leaving the war. Of those who were wounded in Vietnam, amputations or crippling wounds were 300 percent higher than they were for WWII veterans. The average age of combat infantrymen in Vietnam was twenty-three; I was twenty-three. The average WWII veteran was twenty-six. As a rule, people who lived in Southeast Asia during the Vietnam War will say to this day that the Vietnam War did prevent communism from overrunning the entire region. We who fought there **did have a purpose for being there.**

All "real" Vietnam War veterans still living today earned the right to be proud that they fought in that war. Take whichever estimate one chooses; only 30-32 percent of the 2.8 million of us who served there are living at the time I finished *Condemned Property?*

I would like to give credit to the Vietnam War experience for making me a better person. Unfortunately, that would not be completely true. Vietnam nearly destroyed me, not once or twice, but hundreds of times … but I made it! Vietnam did teach me the art of survival.

All of the events that happened to me from the earliest days in combat to now changed my life, such as dozens of close calls from enemy bullets, rockets, and mortar rounds, including a bullet that grazed my scalp, removing my helmet cleanly from my head. I almost killed a fellow American in Vietnam during a personal fight; had numerous concussions, with other nicks and bruises mentally and physically; drove home dozens of nights at 100 mph+ speeds for twenty years after Nam; completely destroyed my Pantera at 127 mph; totaled six more vehicles; had boating accidents; rolled golf carts; considered mercenary offers; survived the Amazon jungle and over 100 trips into Florida's Everglades; participated in dozens of rattlesnake hunts; experienced moments of violent RAGE; lived wildly with a total reckless abandon into my forties and fifties, when I married for the first time; inherited/accepted four step-kids; started my own business after trying and failing with nearly two dozen employers; and went through two bankruptcies during my post-Vietnam years. But I am still here … because of a "Higher Helper."

My lovely mother made it mandatory to attend Sunday school at a Christian church, and I was even a choirboy from the age of ten through twelve. Later, she used to send me to Camp Patmos, a Christian camp on Lake Erie's Kelleys Island in my earliest teen years. She was responsible for the foundation in my life and for the *never give up* attitude I still have today. She introduced me to my "Higher Helper," and I am thankful beyond words.

Camp Patmos Bible Camp is where I truly found God, where I was "saved" as they say. I found my "Higher Helper" also because of one of the many big brothers who adopted me throughout my life, Pastor Paul Schenck, whom I mentioned previously. Pastor Schenck also taught me to be a pretty good fast-pitch softball pitcher, and I threw two no-hitters and several one-hitters before I was sixteen years old. And of course, there was always our loving, God-fearing mom in the background—she always had our backs.

Yes, I managed to overcome a lot, and it's not over for me yet as I continue to create more challenges and roadblocks for myself that must be faced head-on almost daily. Oh, did I say "I" managed to overcome all those challenging events? Forgive me … that "Higher Helper" deserves the credit. All of those hundreds of second chances for me happened for one reason … GOD IS FULL OF SECOND CHANCES, and I am forever indebted to him.

When I came home from Vietnam, I was a different Dusty than the boy my mother used to send to Sunday school and Baptist camps in the summers in the early 1960s. Today, I am searching for that Dusty everyone remembered fifty years ago.

Every veteran is a sacred stamp who has walked on sacred ground … because he or she is that special. Believe it!

What are the chances? Very few combat infantry warriors walked as point man every day. Some of us (I did) would accept that responsibility every other day. If a soldier or Marine walked point just every third day, his odds of becoming a casualty were within six to ten missions or … about two months! We all need a "Higher Helper" in our lives.

When I think back on what my war buddies went through over there and back here, I think of them as super-soldiers. Accused of committing atrocities, generalized as "baby killers," when we lived and died believing in the same principles of our fathers, uncles, and grandfathers: "DUTY, HONOR, COUNTRY." Our children, grandchildren, mothers, sisters, brothers, and so on never got the opportunity to read or hear about the stories of heroism exhibited by their Vietnam veteran fathers, uncles, brothers, sisters, and those who never came home and those who never lived long enough after coming home.

This is the real purpose of *Condemned Property?*—trying to bring our story back to life. As one of our heroes of the Vietnam War once said:

When John Kerry decided to transform truth into fiction and honor into dishonor, we took action. We had no choice. It was our duty to protect and defend not just our honor, but the honor of every past, present and future member of the armed forces. Fellow POWs and I came forward to SPEAK THE TRUTH about our imprisonment and to explain the detrimental consequences of electing John Kerry, a man who defamed both our country and our warriors, to be our president.

- Col. George "Bud" Day
Retired U.S. Air Force
Vietnam War POW
Medal of Honor (Many other Honors)

As Bud Day said, it is essential that we document and recount the years of misinformation about Vietnam … to keep setting the record straight about those who fought in Vietnam. TRUTH will prevail, and their sacrifices must be remembered.

I guess this book has turned into a compilation of just about everything that I can remember about Vietnam while I was there, and everything that happened around me in connection with Vietnam since coming home. However, some things that happened over there were intentionally left out, addressed in one-on-one discussions only with other Vietnam veterans.

Forgiveness does not condone what has been done. It means abandoning your right to pay back a perpetrator in his own coin!

- Desmond Tutu
Archbishop of Johannesburg

While Desmond Tutu would not have been my first choice to end my book with a strong close, his statement is right on. Someone else, who many admire and some are envious of, said this—and I love it:

It's just a game, but if we have been a good role model we can make a difference in someone's life.

- Tim Tebow
Dinner Comments
Banquet for Rimrock Christian School

I would like to believe that this book will make a difference in someone's life, and that will be my "payback" to those who violated us during and after the Vietnam War. In fact, this book impacted some people before it was even published. I shared early versions with some family, friends, customers whom I consider friends, other veterans, and of course, some of my platoon brothers. The response has been overwhelmingly favorable. I know that not everyone will agree with some of the book's content, and I am prepared for that.

In many ways, which I have described in this book, our government can be our own worst enemy. But it's still the best damn place to live in the world ... the good old USA. And I am proud to have risked my life and shed some blood and tears so others can enjoy this great country.

When you see a soldier in uniform, regardless of his or her rank, and you look at the decorations on their uniforms (it's hard not to), go ahead and stare—go ahead! If you recognize decorations like these—Purple Heart, Combat Infantry Badge, Bronze Star for Valor, Silver Star for Gallantry, Commendation Medal for Valor, and for some higher awards—talk to that soldier. Let him or her know that you noticed.

If you see a soldier in uniform who does not have those medals of bravery, please keep in mind that they may be wearing them soon ... if they live long enough. So talk to those soldiers, too—they will appreciate it and they will remember the kind gesture.

Bottom line fact ... The Vietnam War was always about stopping communism. It was not a revolution by loyal patriots, as the Viet Cong were used and discarded by North Vietnam. The Ameri-Cong left-wing media and the left-wing protesters were also used **TO DEFEAT THEIR OWN FEL-LOW AMERICANS!** (Refer to Roger Canfield's www.americong.com.)

I just wish and pray that we Nam vets could forget how we were treated when we came home from our war. Unfortunately, many of us just cannot get over it. However, we Nam vets are NOT condemned property. Although the media would have Americans believe that, with generations of very inaccurate reporting—actually, they have been LYING! Many of us are still fighting to survive; many of us are winning again just as we as a generation have always been ... **winners!**

In my opinion, whoever survived their wars—Korea, Vietnam, the Gulf Wars—and leveraged or cross-referenced what they learned in their war, had or has an excellent chance of being a success in civilian life.

It doesn't matter what your field of endeavor in civilian life is—construction, cab driver, chef, nurse, veterinarian, carpet cleaner, machinist, sales, or whatever. Success is success, and surviving your war can benefit your road to a happier and more successful life.

"God does not guarantee tomorrow." I believe every day on this earth should be lived to the fullest. Waste no minute—except for needed relaxation or meditation to heal from pains and injuries, of course. Use your time on this earth wisely and productively, and your healing will be much more gratifying and thorough. **GOD WILL HELP THOSE WHO HELP THEM-SELVES!**

Dear Nam vets and other vets as well. Preserving the war veteran's future is a lifetime job. And if God is not done with you, he isn't done with you, so keep hanging in there. I hope *Condemned Property?* will find its way onto your bookshelf as a permanent keepsake.

Winston Churchill once wrote "The history of the English-speaking peoples will show that a civilian population and a government can behave in a very treacherous, discriminatory, and oppressive manner out of sheer malice for unjust political reasons and/or profit." Churchill described, on one occasion, returning war veterans from Europe, officers, and enlisted men were thrown out onto the streets or forced to become highwaymen and hunted down until all were killed.

I guess our lesson from Churchill's story should be that our very unjust and disgusting treatment has happened to veterans of other wars from other countries in the past. When a government demands you to sacrifice your future or your life for them through military service so that the majority of the citizens can enjoy their freedom, don't wait around for them to willingly compensate you for that sacrifice. If you do, be prepared to be sacrificed again … for their economic and social needs, if you allow them to.

Our Nam vet brothers who ignore or just remain unaware of what is happening and never speak up on behalf of our brothers, our family are guilty of allowing those bureaucrats who threw us under the bus off the hook they deserved to be hung from. I am still one *very* pissed-off Nam vet who will not sit back and wait to be abused again!

I do understand that we should quit blaming the world for everything bad that has happened to us in our lives for our present problems. But everything that happened DID HAPPEN! I personally believe it is our job, those of us who have survived Nam's aftermath, to continue spreading the word about what we went through over there and continue to go through since coming home … *to this very day*.

Our country showed us the way to Vietnam and we went. America has not shown many of us how to come back from Vietnam. So many of us feel like we are still CONDEMNED PROPERTY , BUILT IN THE VIETNAM WAR! At least there seems to be those who are still trying to keep us there—we can't allow that.

We are all products of our past, but we don't have to be prisoners of it. God specializes in giving everyone who is deserving and who seeks it a fresh start. It is never too late, my brothers.

*THEY Better Believe This!

Here is some worthy advice to all non-Vietnam War veterans who have read this book. Please do not ever tell a "real" Vietnam War veteran to GET OVER THAT WAR!

Final Words

I had made plans to close the book on April 4th and send it off to the publisher for the long editorial, proofing, and copy-checking process. I was! Then I received a call that another platoon brother had passed away on the evening before this writing. It was Patsy Daniels, letting me know that our beloved platoon Sergeant Curtis Daniels had lost his final battle (on this earth) with the Vietnam War! I had to go to Texas and say my final good-bye to our fallen war buddy, but we will meet again. The story of Vietnam veterans continues for many who may be **CONDEMNED PROPERTY?**

It seems like it was just yesterday when I was making travel arrangements in the summer of 2012 to visit Curtis and Patsy Daniels when the news came that Smokey Ryan had lost his final battle with Vietnam's horrors. Rushing off to New Jersey to say good-bye to Smokey wasn't easy, but I had to do it. After returning home, I caught my breath, grabbed my lovely Ginny, and we flew to Texas to see Curtis and his family. **Sure glad I did, as it would be the last time I would see him … alive.**

Our August 2012 visit with Curtis and his family was a wonderful experience. However, it was very obvious to me that the poisons from Vietnam were taking a heavy toll on his body's immune system, and I told Ginny on the way home that I needed to revisit with him ASAP. My expected return visit on April 8-9, 2013 would be my final salute to Curtis … in his coffin.

Patsy Daniels asked me to sit with the family during the service at First Baptist of Dayton, Texas, because he loved his Vietnam War buddies as though we were part of his family. The feelings were mutual. I was honored to sit with the family for the final tribute to our fallen platoon sergeant who was and will always be an American hero.

As I was flying home from Houston on April 9th I wrote this entry for *Condemned Property?* and the Vietnam War continues on and on for many of us!

If the United States was invaded tomorrow, I am very confident that most abled bodied Vietnam Veterans living today would be among the very first to take up arms to defend our country.

STATISTICAL FACTS
FOR NAM VETERANS

- Thirty percent of Vietnam veterans suffer from PTSD.

- Eighty percent of Vietnam combat veterans suffer from PTSD.

- Fifteen percent of veterans from the Iraq Wars suffer from PTSD.

- Ten percent of Desert Storm veterans suffer from PTSD.

- Twenty percent of the soldiers deployed in the last six years have PTSD.

- In 2012, the number of diagnosed cases for military personnel jumped by 50 percent, and that is just diagnosed cases through military institutions.

- Seventy-one percent of female military personnel develop PTSD.

Note: These figures do not include service members who have never sought treatment or may have sought treatment through private therapists, counselors, or doctors. All of these figures are subject to change.
(Source: Department of Veterans Affairs)

These shocking statistics prove how combat-related PTSD is now a pressing national health crisis.

- Total In-Country Vietnam Vets Served: 2,800,000
- Estimate of Vietnam Vets Still Living: 850,000 – 900,000
- Average age of the 58,000+ killed in Vietnam was 23.11 years, not nineteen years, which has often been reported.

(Source: http://winoverptsd.com/wp/tag/combat-veteran-ptsd-statistics)

STATISTICAL SUMMARY OF THE HERBICIDAL WARFARE IN VIETNAM
August 10, 1961 – October 31, 1971
(3,735 Days)

OPERATIONS TRAIL DUST & RANCH/HANDS			
YEAR	**TOTAL GALLONS USED**	**TOTAL ACRES AFFECTED**	**TOTAL SQ. MILES AFFECTED**
1962	17,171	5,724	27
1963	74,760	24,920	117
1964	281,607	93,869	440
1965	664,657	221,552	1,039
1966	2,535,788	845,263	3,962
1967	5,123,353	1,707,784	8,005
1968	5,089,010	1,696,337	7,952
1969	4,558,817	1,519,606	7,123
1970	758,966	252,989	1,186
1971	10,039	3,346	16
Year Unknown	281,201	93,734	439
TOTAL:	**19,395,369**	**6,465,123**	**30,305**

Fixed Wing Only
(Areas of Heaviest Spraying)

I Corp   **2,355,322 Gallons**
- Firebase Rakkassan   176,555 Gallons
- Firebase Jack   156,055 Gallons
- LZ Sandra   163,745 Gallons
- LZ Rock pile   133,140 Gallons
- Con Thien   108,685 Gallons
- Cam Lo   101,820 Gallons
- LZ June
- Firebase Barbara   101,600 Gallons

II Corp   **1,054,406 Gallons**
- Plei Jerang   151,255 Gallons

III Corp   **4,086,229 Gallons**
- Phouc Vinh   643,769 Gallons
- Katum   558,815 Gallons
- Firebase Jewell
  LZ Snuffy   372,860 Gallons
  Cu Chi-Dau Tieng/
  Trang Bang   300,690 Gallons
  Nha Be   247,650 Gallons
  Ben Cat   190,955 Gallons
  Nui Ba Den   188,620 Gallons
  Bien Hoa   163,520 Gallons
  Phu Loi   162,430 Gallons
  An Loc   156,830 Gallons
  Loc Ninh   152,170 Gallons
  Phu Cong   114,130 Gallons

IV Corps   **669,534 Gallons**
- Nam Can   214,640 Gallons
- Tan An   126,000 Gallons

(Source: www.landscaper.net/agent2.htm)

AMERICA'S LARGEST WARS: TOTAL KIA/WIA CASUALTIES		
World War II	1941 – 1945	1,076,245
Civil War (Union only)	1861 – 1865	646,392
Vietnam War (Includes non-hostile casualties)	1955 – 1975	362,924
World War I	1917 – 1918	320,518
Korean War	1950 – 1953	128,650
Revolutionary War (Estimated)	1775 – 1783	50,000
Iraq War	2003 – 2011	36,395
War of 1812 (Estimated)	1812 - 1815	25,000
Mexican-American War	1846 – 1848	17,435
Afghanistan War	2001 – Present	12,035
Philippine-American War	1898 – 1913	7,126
Spanish-American War	1898	4,068
Indian Wars (Black Hawk, Dakota, Modoc, Sioux, Ute, Chippewa)	1862 – 1898	2,665
Northwest Indian War	1785 – 1795	1,881
Seminole Indian Wars	1817 – 1818 1835 – 1842 1855 – 1858 (Total)	83 1,535 53 1,671
Gulf War	1990 – 1991	1,231

VIETNAM WAR KIA CASUALTIES BY YEAR	
Year of Death	**Number of Records**
1956–1959	4
1960	5
1961	16
1962	53
1963	122
1964	216
1965	1,928
1966	6,350
1967	11,363
1968*	**16,899**
1969	11,780
1970	6,173
1971	2,414
1972	759
1973	68
1974	1
1975	62
1976–1979	0
1980–1986	0
1987	1
1988–1989	0
1990	1
1991–1999	0
2000–2006	5
Total Records	**58,220**

*Tet Offensives & Counteroffensives – Bloodiest Year
Record counts provided for informational purposes only, not official statistics.
(Source: http://www.archives.gov/research/military/vietnam-war/casualty-statistics.html)

Country of Casualty	Number of Records
Laos	728
Cambodia	523
China	10
North Vietnam	1,120
South Vietnam	55,661
Thailand	178
Total Records	**58,220**

Record counts provided for informational purposes only, not official statistics.

Service Component	Number of Records
National Guard	97
Regular	34,508
Reserve	5,762
Selected Service	17,671
Not Reported	182
Total Records	**58,220**

Record counts provided for informational purposes only, not official statistics.

Service	Number of Records
Air Force	2,586
Army	38,224
Coast Guard	7
Marine Corps	14,844
Navy	2,559
Total Records	**58,220**

Record counts provided for informational purposes only, not official statistics.

Race	Number of Records
American Indian/Alaska Native	226
Asian	139
Black or African American	7,243
Hispanic One Race	349
Native Hawaiian or Other Pacific Islander	229
Non-Hispanic More Than One Race	204
White	49,830
Total Records	**58,220**

Record counts provided for informational purposes only, not official statistics.

VIETNAM WAR'S OTHER CASUALTIES (MILITARY) KIA/WIA	
South Vietnam (ARVN)	1,393,511
South Korea (ROK)	21,467
Australia	3,400
New Zealand	267
North Vietnam/Viet Cong	2,000,000

(Source: cybersarges.tripod.com)

MAJOR U.S. COMBAT UNIT TOTAL CASUALTIES IN VIETNAM		
U.S. MARINES (All Divisions)		101,715
25th Infantry – ARMY	ARMY	35,708
1st Cavalry – ARMY	ARMY	32,036
101st Airborne – ARMY	ARMY	22,270
9th Infantry – ARMY	ARMY	21,455
1st Infantry – ARMY	ARMY	21,165
4th Infantry	ARMY	17,760
7th Fleet	NAVY	12,032
173rd Airborne	ARMY	10,495
Americal Division	ARMY	9,045
1st Aviation	AIR FORCE	6,864
196th Light Infantry	ARMY	6,595
11th Armored Cavalry	ARMY	6,489
199th Light Infantry	ARMY	5,433
7th Air force	AIR FORCE	5,196
5th Mechanized Infantry	ARMY	4,651
5th Special Forces	ARMY	3,250
82nd Airborne	ARMY	1,193
Coast Guard Squadrons		64

Totals include all wounded and killed in action. Does not include non-hostile casualties.

(Source: Congressional Research Service)

CASUALTIES IN THE VIETNAM WAR

A little history most people will never know. Interesting. Veterans' Statistics off the Vietnam Memorial Wall:
There are 58,282 names now listed on that polished black wall, including those added in 2010.
The names are arranged in the order in which they were taken from us by date and within each date, the names are alphabetized.
The first known casualty was Richard B. Fitzgibbon, of North Weymouth, Mass. Listed by the U.S. Department of Defense of having been killed on June 8, 1956. His name is listed on the Wall with that of his son, Marine Corps Lance Cpl. Richard B. Fitzgibbon III, who was killed on Sept. 7, 1965.
There are three sets of fathers and sons on the Wall.
39,996 on the Wall were just 22 or younger.
8,283 were just 19 years old.
The largest age group, 33,103 were 18 years old (57%).
12 soldiers on the Wall were 17 years old.
5 soldiers on the Wall were 16 years old.
One soldier, PFC Dan Bullock was 15 years old.
997 soldiers were killed on their first day in Vietnam.
1,448 soldiers were killed on their last day in Vietnam.
31 sets of brothers are on the Wall.
31 sets of parents lost two of their sons.
8 women are on the wall. Nursing the wounded.
244 soldiers were awarded the Medal of Honor during the Vietnam War; 153 of them are on the Wall (91 Survived?)
The most casualty deaths for a single day was on January 31, 1968—245 deaths.
The most casualty deaths for a single month was May, 1968—2,415 deaths.
The most casualty deaths for one year was 1968—16,592 deaths.
To those of us who survived the war, and to the families of those who did not, we see the faces, we feel the pain that these numbers created. We are, until we too pass away, haunted with these numbers because they were our brothers, friends, fathers, husbands, wives, sons and daughters.

What if there was a wall for those who died prematurely after they came home? Suicide, PTSD, and Agent Orange have taken more Vietnam combat veterans before their time. How many names would be on it? How long would it be?

Please note that the most recent and correct number of names on The Wall is 58,282. I apologize for the varying figures in the book as some statistics were calculated from earlier sources. Ten new names were added in 2012 per a memo received by Jan Scruggs, founder of The Vietnam Memorial Fund.

Names Added
To The Vietnam Veterans Memorial

During the Vietnam War, there was no overriding reason to keep close track of names of the men and women who died as a result of military service in the war zone. A decade after the withdrawal of U.S. forces, the Vietnam Veterans Memorial was approved for construction. The service branches went back through their records to identify our dead by name.

Inevitably, some men who should have been named on the "Wall" were not. Over the years, additional names have been inscribed on the Wall—some were men who died after the war as a result of wounds received in the war, and others were men whose names were overlooked in earlier years. A different website, Touch The Wall, has details of years not listed here. All the men whose names have been added have personal memorial pages on The Virtual Wall ®. Click on a name to see that person's memorial page.

(Source: http://virtualwall.org/ipanels/NamesAdded.html)

NAMES ADDED - 2012	
Joseph W. Aubin	Panel 09E Line 012
Johnny O. Brooks	Panel 16W Line 106
David L. Deckard	Panel 28W Line 094
David M. Desilets	Panel 10E Line 077
ATR3 Richard C. Hunt	Panel 07E Line 112
SP4 Larry M. Kelly	Panel 19W Line 095
Albert K. Kuewa	Panel 02E Line 042
LT Walter A. Linzy	Panel 08E Line 017
CPL Frank A. Neary	Panel 15E Line 096
ATR3 Richard D. Stocker	Panel 15E Line 036

And the coffins came home to every city, town, and village ... but the media wouldn't allow Americans to separate this war from the innocent young warriors sent to fight it! It is okay to hate war, despise it if you must, but NOT THE WARRIOR!

NOTES ON SOURCES

The material for *CONDEMNED PROPERTY?* has been put together from several sources: my personal experiences and observations and my platoon brothers' experiences and observations, including members of the 1st Platoon of the 3rd 22nd 25th Infantry Division as well as other qualified Vietnam veterans I have interviewed personally, and the extensive body of information published on the subject of the Vietnam War by the 25th Infantry Division and the United States Armed Forces.

I have attempted to source anything that was not in my personal information from experiences in Vietnam. Whenever possible, I have credited people by name for their contribution.

If I had depended entirely on my dimming memory for the information put together here, the end result would have been inadequate.

I am grateful to the many pioneers and warriors before us who fought for acknowledgment of our endless and growing list of illnesses that we have incurred from the Vietnam War.

Here are most or all of the sources from which I may have extracted my research and statistics:

www.Records Base.com/Infantry-Divisions
www.25thida.org
www.legacy.com/memorial-sites/vietnam-war
www.yale.edu/glc/Stratford/vietnam.htm
www.pbs.org/battlefieldvietnam
www.virtualwall.org/linksvw.htm
www.besthistorysites.net
www.thefreedictionary.com/bourne
VetFriends.com
www.dailycomet.com
en.wikipedia.org/wiki/vietnam_war_veteran
www.army.mil
www.defense.gov

Most of the photographs in this book that were not mine personally have been sourced to the owner or where I found them. There were very few of those that were not mine or my Nam brothers'. Some photographs used can be found on numerous media, therefore impossible to source original.

Photo Credits

The following photographs/images, which were not mine, were obtained from the 25th Infantry website, the 25th Infantry yearbook, and vva.org: Pages 31, 43, 48, 51, 77, 158, 164, 166, 170, 172, 173, 185, 234, 432, 437.

As I mentioned earlier, I had been working on the book for one year, physically that is. Actually, it has been almost two years now! Mentally, I've been writing it since the day I came home from hell. Here are a few suggested readings, as these are some of the books I have enjoyed or could relate well to. They deserve credit for some of my ideas and for inspiring me in completing my own book:

Stolen Valor, Burkett & Whitley (1998)
The Aggressors, Catino (2010)
Vets Under Siege, Schram (2008)
Steel My Soldiers' Hearts, Hackworth (2003)
Unheralded Victory, Woodruff (1999)
Hard Men Humble, Stevenson (2002)
Achilles in Vietnam, Shay (1994)
Comrades in Arms: How the Ameri-Cong Won the War in Vietnam Against the Common Enemy—America, Canfield (2012)
Waiting for an Army to Die, Wilcox (1989, 2011)
War Stories, North (2003)

Interested readers should also look up an article in the February 2013 issue of *Reader's Digest* entitled "Building the Warrior Brain: How the Present Day U.S. Military Has Turned to Science To Discover Newer and Better Ways to Create More Resilient Fighters and Prevent or Reduce PTSD." Of course, my opinion on this is that they can STOP BRAINWASHING US, but how else can they turn us into killers?

'NAM TALK' GLOSSARY

ABN	Airborne
Agent Orange	Chemicals used as a defoliant in recent years found to cause medical problems in Vietnam Veterans
AK-47	A Russian assault rifle
AIT	Advanced Infantry Training
Alpha Bravo	Slang for ambush
Ameri-Cong	Term used in *Comrades in Arms* by author, Roger Canfield, PhD
APC	Armored Personnel Carrier used by mechanized infantry units, carries machine guns and an infantry squad
ARVN	Army Republic Vietnam
Ba muoi ba	33. Vietnamese beer, also called panther or "tiger piss"
Bee hive round	Artillery round that releases thousands of steel darts
Boat people	Immigrants for Vietnam, Cambodia, Laos
Body Bags	Plastic zipper bags for corpses
Boom Boom	Sex
Boonies	Out in the field, jungles, swamps, etc.
Bu-coo or Bucu	French slang for large or many
Bush, The	Hostile jungle
Cao Dai	Religious sect in Tay Ninh area
CAP	Combined Action Platoon
Charlie	Viet Cong
Chieu Hoi	Vietnamese government surrender program
Chinook	Army (CH46 Marine) A large, twin bladed helicopter used for transporting men, materials and used in Medevacs
Cholon	Chinese sector of Saigon
Choppers	Helicopters
Chu Hoi	I surrender
Claymores	Mine packed with plastique and rigged to spray hundreds of steel pellets
Click	One kilometer
Cobra	Helicopter gunships heavily armed with rocket launchers and machine guns
CIB	Combat Infantry Badge
CH-47	Helicopter (Chinook)
CP	Command Post
C-Rations	Combat food in cans
C-4	Plastique explosive
C-127	Transport Plane
C-130	Cargo plane used to transport men and supplies
Dinky Dau	To be crazy
Division HQ	Command Headquarters
DMZ	Demilitarized Zone
Dong	Vietnamese currency
Dung lai	Halt or stop
Dust Off	Evacuating wounded by helicopter
Egg beater	Helicopter
Electric Strawberry	25th ID patch with red/yellow taro legs
Fire Base	Reinforced bases established to provide artillery fire support for ground units operating in the bush.

Firefight	Gunfire
Fire mission	Artillery mission exchange with the enemy
FO	Forward Observer
Fragging	Killing an American officer by own troops
Freedom Bird	Jet aircraft taking you from Vietnam to the U.S.A.
Free Fire Zone	Area where everyone is deemed hostile
F-4's, F-100's	Jet fighter aircraft
Gooks	Slang for the enemy
Greased	Killed
Grunt	Slang for a combat infantry soldier fighting in Nam
Gung Ho	Military enthusiastic
Gunship	Armed helicopter
Hamlet	Cluster of homes; several make a village
Hanoi Hannah	Tokyo rose of Vietnam
Hoi Chanh	Returnees under Chieu Hoi program
Hooch/Hootch	Slang for any form of dwelling place (living quarters)
Hot LZ	Landing zone under fire
Howitzers	Large cannon
Huey	Helicopter used for transporting troops; Med-evacs
Humping	Slang for marching with a heavy load through the bush.
Incoming	Receiving enemy mortar or rocket fire
In-Country	In Vietnam
Iron Triangle	Viet Cong dominated area near Cu Chi
KIA	Killed in action
Klick, Click	One kilometer (0.62137 mile)
Koonza	Marijuana
Lai day	Come here
La Vay	Beer
LAW	Light Antitank Weapon
LBJ	Long Binh Jail
Lock & Load	Chambering a sound invasion
LP	Listening Post
LRRP	Long Range Reconnaissance Patrol
LZ	Landing Zone
MACV	Military assistance Command, Vietnam
Medi/Medivac	Medically evacuating the wounded by chopper or plane
MIA	Missing in action
Million Dollar Wound	Just bad enough to get out of the bush, but not serious
Mona	Rain
Monday pills	Anti-Malaria pills
MOS	Military occupational specialty
M-14	Rifle used before M-16
M-16	Standard automatic weapon used by American ground forces
M60	A machine gun used by American combat units
M-79	Grenade launcher used by infantry
NAM	Vietnam
Napalm	Jelly like substance in bombs – burns everything it contacts
NDP	Night Defensive Position
NVA	North Vietnamese Army
NVR	North Vietnamese
NLF	Regulars National Liberation Front – Communists
Num bah-one G.I.	Big spending soldier
Num bah-ten G.I.	Not a big spender
Num bah-ten thou G.I.	The worst spender

Ordinance	Bombs or rockets
Over the Fence	Crossing into Cambodia
P-38	Can opener worn with dog tag
Papa Sierra	Slang for platoon sergeant
Phantom	A jet fighter (F-4)
Pointman	The lead man on a patrol through the bush
Puff	A C-47 armed with mini machine guns; 'Puff the Magic Dragon'
Punji Stick	Booby trap with pointed bamboo stakes pointing up
REAL LIFE	Civilian life
Recon	Reconnaissance
Reconnaissance-In Force	Replaced the former term of Search and Destroy in the 1967-1968 timeframe
Red LZ	Landing zone under attack
Rock N' Roll	Full automatic on an M-16
ROK	Republic of Korea ground troops
RPG	Rocket propelled grenade
R&R	Rest and relaxation
RSVN	Republic of South Vietnam
RTO	Radio-telephone operator
Rucks	Backpacks
Ruff Puff	Regional/popular forces of South Vietnamese militia. Usually poorly trained and equipped, not effective in severe combat situations
Saddle Up	Load up, get ready to march
Saigon Cowboys	Officers and non coms working in base camps or large cities
Sampan	Vietnamese peasant boat
Sappers	Viet Cong infiltrators with explosive charges attached to their bodies
Satchel Charges	Explosive packs carried by VC sappers
Sgt.	Abbreviation for Sergeant
Short	You were close to the end of your tour in Vietnam
Sin loi minoi	Sorry about that, honey
Sitrep	Situation report by radio
SK's	A Russian carbine
Slick	Huey chopper
Spooky	Plane with electric mini-guns
Swift boat	Navy patrol boat used for coastal rivers
TET	Southeast Asia Lunar New Year
The World	Home – U.S.A.
Ti ti	Small, insignificant
TOC	Tactical Office Command Post
TOP	Company first sergeant
Tracer	A bullet with a phosphorus coating designed to burn and provide a visual indication of the bullet's trajectory
VC	Viet Cong
Viet Cong	The local militias fighting Americans in South Vietnam
WIA	Wounded in action
XO	Executive Officer
105mm	Howitzer cannon size
81mm	Mortar shell
50 Cal	50 caliber machine gun
51 Caliber	Bullet

CPSIA information can be obtained
at www.ICGtesting.com
Printed in the USA
BVHW011924270619
552146BV00006B/12/P

9 781457 525339